Gender and Religious Leadership

Gender and Religious Leadership

Women Rabbis, Pastors, and Ministers

Edited by
Hartmut Bomhoff,
Denise L. Eger,
Kathy Ehrensperger, and
Walter Homolka

LEXINGTON BOOKS
Lanham • Boulder • New York • London

Published by Lexington Books
An imprint of The Rowman & Littlefield Publishing Group, Inc.
4501 Forbes Boulevard, Suite 200, Lanham, Maryland 20706
www.rowman.com

6 Tinworth Street, London SE11 5AL

Copyright © 2019 by The Rowman & Littlefield Publishing Group, Inc.

Supported by the German Federal Cultural Foundation.

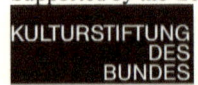

All rights reserved. No part of this book may be reproduced in any form or by any electronic or mechanical means, including information storage and retrieval systems, without written permission from the publisher, except by a reviewer who may quote passages in a review.

British Library Cataloguing in Publication Information Available

Library of Congress Cataloging-in-Publication Data Available

ISBN 9781793601575 (cloth)
ISBN 9781793601582 (electronic)

To Women of Reform Judaism—
Empowering Women Worldwide Since 1913

Contents

Preface: Honoring the Legacy of Rabbiner Regina Jonas: A Call to Let Religious Women Write Alternative Narratives of the Future   xi
Denise L. Eger

Acknowledgments   xxi

Introduction: Women as Religious Leaders   1
Hartmut Bomhoff, Denise L. Eger, Kathy Ehrensperger, Walter Homolka

Part I: New Roles for Jewish Women in Modernizing Germany and America

1 The Discourse of the Other: The Transformation of the Jewish Woman in Nineteenth-Century Germany   11
Yael Kupferberg

2 Patterns of Reform: Tracking Women's Changing Roles in Synagogues and Communal Life within Nineteenth-Century American and German Judaism   33
Karla Goldman

3 Women Students at the Berlin Hochschule für die Wissenschaft des Judentums   53
Esther Seidel

4 "The Woman in the House of God" (1926) Revisited   71
Hartmut Bomhoff

5	Paving the Road to Women Rabbis, 1889–2015 *Pamela S. Nadell*	89

Part II: Three Pioneers of Female Leadership

6	Henrietta Szold: A "Pretty Certain Miriam" *Gail Twersky Reimer*	113
7	The Religious as the Political in Margarete Susman *Elisa Klapheck*	127
8	Remembering Regina Jonas: On the Intersectionality of Women's, Jewish, German, and Holocaust History *Katharina von Kellenbach*	145
9	Memory and Identity: Female Leadership and the Legacy of Rabbi Regina Jonas *Stefanie Sinclair*	163

Part III: Personal Reflections

10	They Married What They Wanted to Be?: Rebbetzins and Their Unconventional Paths to Power *Shuly Rubin Schwartz*	183
11	Looking Back: Religion as Container for Memory and Tradition *Sandy Eisenberg Sasso*	203

Part IV: Comparing Notes

12	Women's Leadership in the Roman Catholic Church: A Survey of Half a Century's Development with Particular Reference to Germany *Marie-Theres Wacker*	225
13	The Impact of Women in Protestant Christian Ministry Today *Renate Jost*	245
14	Rereading Male Chauvinism: Muslim Women's Own Approach to Their Holy Text *Katajun Amirpur*	267
15	The Ordination of Women and the Question of Religious Authority *Judith Frishman*	289

Index	307

About the Editors 315

About the Contributors 319

Preface

Honoring the Legacy of Rabbiner Regina Jonas: A Call to Let Religious Women Write Alternative Narratives of the Future

Denise L. Eger

Celebrating[1] Rabbiner Regina Jonas and her ceiling-shattering achievement of being ordained as a rabbi in 1935 means acknowledging that she was a teacher of Torah and ministered to people in some of the darkest hours of the Jewish people and the world. She was a real person, not some figurehead, full of passion that let nothing get in the way. She brought hope where there was terror and fear. She lifted up faith when many had no faith left at all. From the wellspring of her spirit, Regina Jonas led by example even when others cruelly tried to destroy her voice and her calling. Her fate reminds us of the many women worldwide whose voices of inspiration and leadership have been stifled and muted by religious patriarchies—and still can be twenty-first-century agents of change. These women, like Rabbiner Regina Jonas, have created the opportunity for women's spiritual lives and religious experiences and scholarship to be part of the mainstream.

We know all too well that, beginning with the story of Eve and the Garden of Eden, it is often women who were blamed for humanity's downfall. And today, women's voices and questions continue to rattle the status quo. One of many examples is the Rabbinical Council of America's recently reaffirmed vehement opposition to Orthodox women clergy and to those who hire them. When religious women of the Catholic Church have challenged the Vatican Curia by offering sacraments, especially when there have been no priests available, they were told that people should not have Communion rather than be served by a woman. The leaders of a women's mosque teaching the empowerment of Islamic women have been condemned for stepping into the male realm. Religious women's scholarship and leadership have been twisted and attacked whether Jewish or not.

And yet in earlier millennia and around the world, women's spiritual leadership was and is, in some aboriginal religions, the norm. Goddess worship both in the Ancient Near East and among Native American tribes or the tribes of Central or South America continue to uplift holy women. The priestess is central to the spiritual expression of various African tribal religions. Today in Buddhism women can be abbots and monks serving their communities with deep reflection and honor. Every faith and tradition had a woman leader or two—from the Baha'i, to Islam, to Christianity, and Judaism—and yet, the patriarchal pendulum seemed to swing toward making it more difficult for women's voices and leadership and scholarship to be heard.

Whether the ancient prophet Deborah divining the future under her date palm tree; Mother Mary praying for miracles; the Lakota Goddess White Buffalo Calf Woman; Freyja, the Norse goddess of fertility, sexual liberty, abundance, and war; or Parvati, Hindu Divine Mother, the embodiment of the total energy in the universe, Goddess of Power and Might—women have led and shaped the religious and spiritual and cultural life all around the world.

Rabbiner Regina Jonas, too, shaped her world in the darkest of moments. Her ordination was a radical move, perhaps out of desperation, since her initial attempts at becoming a rabbi were rejected, even though she was an outstanding student in Berlin at the Hochschule für die Wissenschaft des Judentums. In 2014, I came to Germany as part of a delegation consisting of several female rabbis to learn more about Regina Jonas's life and to dedicate a memorial plaque to her at Terezin. In Berlin, we saw what was left of her letters and notes, a small stack. We read her ordination letter written by Rabbi Max Dienemann, who was the head of the Liberal Rabbinical Association, because she was denied ordination when her own teacher in charge of ordination at the *Hochschule*, Eduard Baneth, died and his successor Hanoch Albeck refused to ordain her. I was struck as we read the words conferring her *smicha*. She was an outstanding student, writing her thesis on the question, "Can a Woman Be a Rabbi According to Halakhic Sources?" But more than her academic credentials and teaching abilities, she was described as "having the heart of a rabbi." Historian Deborah Dash Moore wrote: "Jewish women rabbis, once thought to be an American innovation, products of a revolutionary Jewish feminist movement, now had an older, European history, tied to the central Jewish tragedy of the 20th century."[2]

This is a legacy to women religious leaders today, whether priests, pastors, scholars, rabbis, teachers, abbesses, or nuns, who are indeed agents of change. In my own work as a rabbi, I have noticed that when women organize or are part of a gathering, the dynamic is incredibly different. Women listen. They listen to all the voices in the room, often without regard to the size of the checkbook or power structure. Even those of us who have risen to leadership in the primarily male-dominated power cultures—when we get to the top, we tend to wield our power differently. And yet we are often still trying to navigate the world of male-dominated religious scholars and clerical leaders. It is a delicate and nuanced balance between how women have to operate and how we would prefer to operate. Religious and spiritual institutions in the Abrahamic traditions are still male-dominated. How often are churchwomen who speak out called "uppity women?" How often, when women rise to leadership positions in the temples, they are told, "This is such a wonderful example for the girls of our community?" Rather than saying it is an example for both girls and boys?

Often it is our presence, women leaders' and scholars' presence, that is the change itself. We don't even have to say anything. Just being at the table of conversation, being present in the room or sanctuary, transforms the entire enterprise.

But there is more. And the more is: when we share from our intellect, our hearts, our prayers and souls. When women religious leaders gather across faith and denominational lines, there is an opportunity to put the obstacles for dialogue aside. When women relate to each other as women first—rather than entrenched in our religious or spiritual or political frameworks that often define us, we women can set a common agenda for the future. I often think: what if women were left to negotiate the political crises around the world? What if women could be the agents in creating a world where children are protected from bombs and violence? This, I believe, is the opportunity religious women and scholars have as change agents.

When women lead, different things happen, change happens. In preparation for this contribution, I interviewed a good friend of more than thirty years, the Rev. Elder Dr. Nancy Wilson. Rev. Wilson was the head of the Universal Fellowship of Metropolitan Community Churches. A denomination in the Protestant tradition, it is known as the gay church. It was founded only in 1968 by a former Pentecostal male preacher who was a gay man. This denomination is now a worldwide church with over 60,000 adherents. Not big when you look at the size of the Catholic church or the number of adherents of Islam or Buddhism. But through the years, Rev. Wilson has sat at the interfaith and ecumenical councils with worldwide male religious leaders. Her interfaith credentials have taken her to be the denomination's head representative to the World Council of Churches, the Parliament of World Religions, and to various committees and hearings at the United Nations. She is a marvelous example of the spirit of Regina Jonas in that she changed the future, helping people visualize and understand the power of women as religious leaders. She also symbolically helps shatter the notion that gay and lesbian, bisexual and transgender people are wanton sinners. She has changed the conversation and the future in which we now live: the present. Rev. Elder Wilson says: "For many women, I was the first woman, the first lesbian, they saw in a clergy collar, heard preach, saw run a large, denominational meeting. It changed everything for them to see that and know that they too could offer leadership in a faith context."

I asked her: How are women as clergy—and in particular since you have been the head of the denomination—how are you changing the future? And what specifically do you think that women do as change agents that is different than men? These were her answers, which I believe hold true for the experiences of women in religious leadership positions:

- Women tend to be more relational and team-oriented in our leadership style, less top-down.
- Women in leadership pay attention to what women think, want, and need, the human rights of women, who are more than 50 percent of the population.
- Women in faith leadership make visible the moral agency of women; and empower women to become leaders in the future.
- When women are in leadership, when women thrive, children and families thrive.
- Women in leadership in faith organizations make real that we are all made "in the image of God," and that the Divine includes all genders.[3]

In Wilson's experience, our mere presence doing what religious women in leadership do, teaching, preaching, running meetings, researching, living, breathing, leading our communities, changes the future because we pay attention to different issues. We pay attention to families and their needs. We pay attention to the needs of the future because we pay attention to our children. For they are truly our future. Rev. Dr. Wilson reinforces anecdotally what we know from scholarship of women scholars, like Carol Gilligan, psychologist, ethicist, and author of *In a Different Voice*, who describes feminist, womanist, ways of organizing, listening, and leading, deciding ethical dilemmas: that is the relational. Gilligan has argued, against her teacher Lawrence Kohlberg, that much of established research on the moral development of individuals was male-oriented and thus could not be generalized to women. Gilligan thus proposed her theory of stages of female moral development based on her idea of moral voices. According to Gilligan, there are two kinds of moral voices: that of the masculine and the feminine. The masculine voice is "logical and individualistic," meaning that the emphasis in moral decisions is protecting the rights of people and making sure justice is upheld.[4] The feminine voice places more emphasis on protecting interpersonal relationships and taking care of other people. This voice focuses on the "care perspective," which means focusing on the needs of the individual in order to make an ethical decision.[5] For Gilligan, Kohlberg's stages of moral development were emphasizing the masculine voice, making it difficult to accurately gauge a woman's moral development because of this incongruity in voices. Gilligan argues that androgyny, or integrating the masculine and the feminine, is the best way to realize one's potential as a human. Gilligan's stages of female moral development have been shown in business settings as an explanation to the different ways men and women handle ethical issues in the workplace as well.[6]

I asked my friend and fellow activist, Rev. Cannon Susan Russell, an Episcopal priest who is the associate pastor at All Saint's Episcopal Church in Pasadena, the same questions as Rev. Dr. Wilson. And these were her answers:

> It is arguable that most—if not all—of the greatest challenges facing our human family in the twenty-first century result from domination systems that diminish the interconnectedness of all and privilege the power of a few. Far too often our religious systems have been used to prop up those domination systems, becoming vehicles of racism, classism, sexism, homophobia, and exploitation of the environment.
>
> One of the most influential roles women of faith can play is to be agents of change by working within their own traditions to challenge patriarchal values

of domination, exclusion and demonization of "the other." Mobilized and organized, women have the power to reframe the toxic theological narratives of judgment and condemnation by focusing instead on God's values of justice and compassion. And we have the opportunity to not only imagine but to create a future by building bridges across political, theological and cultural divides, seeking common ground on issues that unite us rather than inciting conflict over issues about which we differ. We can be the change we want to see.[7]

Rev. Russell argues that women must be the embodiment of the world we want to see; that we carry within our bodies and our presence a different message for the future. Women in religious leadership, although always having to break through the bonds of a male-dominated culture and story, can write a different narrative of the future by framing the narrative of the human family through examples of courage and uplift rather than by negative examples of judgments and harsh condemnation.

These two great religious women leaders (yes, they are western religious leaders but that is the world I inhabit) are change agents because they breathe and work in their churches and have risen to positions of power and authority by listening and being authentic to their calling. We learned this from the writing of Rabbi Regina Jonas. She didn't take no for an answer, and followed her calling, finding someone who would listen, and assist in helping. Rabbi Jonas wrote the following when asked to write a reflection on being a woman rabbi: "I hope a time will come for all of us in which there will be no more questions on the subject of 'woman:' for as long as there are questions, something is wrong."[8]

Women across religious boundaries must find more reason to come together in conferences like the one reflected in this volume. Women across national and ethnic lines must find more opportunities for dialogue and to address thorny issues together. When Palestinian and Israeli mothers dialogue together as they do, the future is different. Take, for example, the story of two such mothers featured in the *New York Times*: Robi Damelin and Bushra Awad are two mothers on opposite sides of a bitter conflict, bound together by grief. Both women have lost sons to the fighting between Israel and Palestine. And both are determined to channel their private tragedies into a force for change.[9] Together, through the Parents Circle Forum, they and men and women like them are tackling some of the most difficult issues of our times: through grassroots, relational means like the Parents Circle—

Families Forum (PCFF), an organization of bereaved Palestinians and Israelis that promotes reconciliation as an alternative to hatred and revenge.

It has become crystal clear to me and to Rabbiner Jonas: This isn't a woman-only project, but men and women and those in between can and must work together to create a different future narrative than the track our world is on. Women as change agents do so through relationship building, dialogue, organizing, listening, and seeing the humanity in the other. Both women and men are capable of this. But women's religious leadership in particular has brought this gift to the table, because we organize differently. Even as we have to blast through the hierarchical and academic institutions in which we all work and intersect, we can bring a measure of grace and compassion to these places to smash the idols of militarism, terror, and power. When we lift up the voices of other women and girls, when we as women religious leaders and academic leaders mentor younger women and men, we can shape new futures for ourselves and for future generations.

Sometimes I hear complaints from older European and North American feminists about younger women: "They don't get it. They take for granted their equality." And they do. Because they haven't faced what some older women faced trying to climb the ladder of success in chosen career paths. Younger women assume their total equality. They often have rude awakenings as they enter the workforce and find their voices silenced because it's still a man's world, in business as it is in academia, as it is in the business of religion. But this is all the more reason for us so-called "old-timers" not to give up. They will need mentors and older women's experiences even more in the years ahead to forge that future, so they can go deeper and higher than we even dare imagine.

We hold on to these hopes at a time of terror attacks and refugee crises. We are witnesses and participants in a world being transformed through technological innovations, medical breakthroughs, and more opportunities for women and girls. The future must include women along with men who will see the other as a reflection of the Divine. Only when we truly see the holiness and humanity in another can we touch our own humanity. Religious women along with men who live in this way can create a different path for the global future, by calling out injustices and pushing our governments and political leaders to account for their actions. But if we can together make a different future for our planet, we must do as Rabbi Regina Jonas taught:

"God has placed ability and callings in our hearts without regard for gender. Thus each of us has a duty, whether man or woman, to realize those gifts God has given. If you look at things this way, one takes woman and man for what they are: human beings."[10]

That is the challenge for women as agents of future change. Women, and in particular *religious* women leaders and scholars, can chart a course of a different narrative for our unfolding futures when we talk across cultural, national, religious, and ethnic boundaries. We must continue to work on both subtly and loudly, challenging the male-dominated systems that have kept women subjected and silenced. We must invite like-minded men and our brothers, fathers, lovers, husbands, friends, and co-workers to this very same journey. It is critical to tell the story of how we can see the future for, as we know only too well, when the histories are written unless they are written by and with women, women's contributions are omitted. This is exactly the story of Rabbiner Regina Jonas. Viktor Frankl, who worked side-by-side with her, erased her from his own story because of the terror and horrors of his experience. As our colleague and teacher Rabbi Laura Geller wrote in *Tablet Magazine*: "The reason in part may [be] found in the forward [sic] to Frankl's classic, *Man's Search for Meaning*. He wrote that he erased from his memory everything that happened before he entered Auschwitz. Part of what he erased was the legacy of Regina Jonas."[11]

Our challenge to change the future for the better, to heal the world, and to hear God's call, means a language of inclusion, and an opportunity for women and men to uplift the voices, learning, and leadership of women.

NOTES

1. This article is based on the inaugural Regina Jonas Lecture, delivered at the Potsdam conference on women in religious leadership roles on November 19, 2015.

2. Deborah Dash Moore, "Saving Regina Jones," *Frankely Speaking* (2014): 2. https://lsa.umich.edu/content/dam/judaic-assets/judaic-newsletters/December.Final.pdf.

3. Rev. Elder Dr. Nancy Wilson, in private email correspondence on November 11, 2015.

4. Rolf E. Muuss, "Carol Gilligan's theory of sex differences in the development of moral reasoning during adolescence," Adolescence 23 (1988): 229–43.

5. Richard Kyte, "Moral reasoning as perception: A reading of Carol Gilligan," Hypatia 11 (1996): 97–113.

6. Thomas White, "Business, ethics, and Carol Gilligan's 'Two Voices,'" *Business Ethics Quarterly* 2 (1992): 51–61.

7. Rev. Canon Susan Russell, in private email correspondence, November 14, 2015.

8. Rabbiner Regina Jonas, *Central-Verein-Zeitung. Allgemeine Zeitung des Judentums*, June 23, 1938.

9. Brigit Katz, "Israeli Robi Damelin and Palestinian Bushra Awad have a Plan for Peace," *New York Times*, April 7, 2015, http://nytlive.nytimes.com/womenintheworld/2015/04/07/israeli-robi-damelin-and-palestinian-bushra-awad-have-a-plan-for-peace/.

10. Jonas, *Central-Verein-Zeitung,* June 23, 1938.
11. Laura Geller, "Rediscovering the first woman rabbi," *Tablet Magazine,* October 15, 2014, http://www.tabletmag.com/scroll/186315/rediscovering-the-first-woman-rabbi .

BIBLIOGRAPHY

Geller, Laura, "Rediscovering the first woman rabbi," *Tablet Magazine,* October 15, 2014. http://www.tabletmag.com/scroll/186315/rediscovering-the-first-woman-rabbi .
Jonas, Regina, *Central-Verein-Zeitung. Allgemeine Zeitung des Judentums,* June 23, 1938.
Katz, Brigit, "Israeli Robi Damelin and Palestinian Bushra Awad have a plan for peace," *New York Times,* April 7, 2015. http://nytlive.nytimes.com/womenintheworld/2015/04/07/israeli-robi-damelin-and-palestinian-bushra-awad-have-a-plan-for-peace/ .
Kyte, Richard, "Moral reasoning as perception: A reading of Carol Gilligan," *Hypatia* 11 (1996): 97–113.
Muuss, Rolf E., "Carol Gilligan's theory of sex differences in the development of moral reasoning during adolescence," *Adolescence* 23 (1988): 229–43.
White, Thomas, "Business, ethics, and Carol Gilligan's 'Two Voices,'" *Business Ethics Quarterly* 2 (1992): 51–61.

Acknowledgments

This volume is the result of the international conference organized by the Abraham Geiger College and the School of Jewish Theology at the University of Potsdam on "The Role of Women's Leadership in Faith Communities" which marked the eightieth anniversary of Rabbi Regina Jonas's ordination in 1935. Over forty presenters from Europe, Israel, and the United States explored the impact of women in the rabbinate in particular and the ministry in general and discussed issues of leadership and authority, women's religious scholarship, and gender (in)equality today. More than 250 participants from all over the world engaged in lively discussions, which are reflected in the proceedings published here.

Many colleagues supported this project with their advice and guidance, and deserve to be mentioned here, but the editors would express their gratitude especially to Debra Hirsch Corman, and Dr. Juni Hoppe and Dr. Markus Krah, who were patiently dealing with all the detailed work required to get this book to the stage of publication.

Introduction

Women as Religious Leaders

Hartmut Bomhoff, Denise L. Eger, Kathy Ehrensperger, Walter Homolka

God has placed abilities and callings in our hearts, without regard to gender.

—*Rabbi Regina Jonas (1938)*

In 1837, Rabbi Abraham Geiger (1810–1874) addressed the position of women in the Judaism of his time. In this truly emancipatory article, he suggested that rabbinical scholars should grant the same religious obligations to men and women, allow women full participation in public worship, and reject the notion that they were spiritually incapable.[1] The question remains why it took even progressive Judaism nearly a century to acknowledge the spiritual and moral equality between both sexes.

Jewish activism and scholarship have been crucial in linking theology and gender issues since the early twentieth century. The ordination of Regina Jonas in 1935 in Offenbach, Germany, by Rabbi Max Dienemann represents the key event for Judaism in this process. Due to the disintegration and destruction of Jewish life in Germany and throughout Central Europe in the Shoah, the field subsequently progressed and grew particularly in the United States. The objective of this volume is to analyze historical and recent developments in female religious leadership within Judaism in the context of larger issues shaping the scholarly debate at the intersection of gender and religious studies/theology.

More than seventy years after the Shoah, leading scholars of the United States, the United Kingdom, and Israel are engaging with their counterparts in contemporary Germany to examine the neglected transnational dimensions of the field's development in the past and present. The renewed institutional presence of progressive Judaism in academic and vocational training in Germany provides an occasion and an intellectual venue for such a scholarly dialogue.

A first multivoiced and multilayered conversation took place in the course of the 2015 interdisciplinary conference entitled "The Role of Women's Leadership in Faith Communities," organized by the Abraham Geiger College and the School of Jewish Theology, University of Potsdam. The meeting brought together scholars and female leaders of different faith traditions from Europe, Israel, and the United States. The diversity of the participants brought into play in the debate the internal pluralism of modern Judaism. Moreover, the conference allowed for comparative analysis of female religious leadership in other religious traditions, including mutual perceptions and interactions.

The contributors to this volume, which grew from that conference, address not only questions related to changes at work within the various religious traditions, but also crucial questions of women's and gender studies: How do women exercise leadership in different historical, social, and religious constellations? Do female religious leaders replicate or change, deconstruct and reconstruct structures, texts, and practices, for example, by creating new practices and revising texts specifically for women? Do they affirm established religious images (e.g., of a male God) and narratives, or do they offer counter-narratives? Which fundamental approach within the overall gender discourse do female religious leaders take ideologically and practically: emphasizing and validating gender and role differences or questioning their validity?

Based on the conference discussions and results, this volume aims to consider the ordination of Rabbi Regina Jonas and developments in other liberal faith traditions in a larger context. Key among these are broader processes of transformation in societies moving toward greater gender equality in social participation and political representation, as they are reflected in reforms in religious and other social institutions to this day. The drive in faith communities for female access to clerical and other leadership positions on equal standing with their male colleagues is related to fundamental processes of change that are taking place in the religious sphere in general and in particular religious traditions.

The volume analyzes key aspects of these transnational developments from historical and comparative perspectives. Part I gathers historical accounts of larger developments, which became concrete in the experiences of individual women, past and present (parts II and III). From the nineteenth century onward, these changed the (self-)perception of Jewish women and thereby helped set in motion processes that brought women into formal and informal social, political, and religious leadership roles, including the rabbinate. The concluding part IV relates the developments within Judaism comparative to changes within other religious traditions, thereby highlighting parallels, mutual perceptions, differences, and interactions.

I. THE CONTRIBUTIONS

The volume opens in the preface with the inaugural Regina Jonas Lecture, in which Rabbi Denise L. Eger, then-president of the Central Conference of American Rabbis, issues a powerful call "to let religious women write alternative narratives of the future." Drawing on the biography of the first female rabbi, she points to the transformative power that female leadership has had in several religious traditions. These experiences should encourage both contemporary practitioners and scholars of religion to explore the untapped potential of female religious leadership.

The historical section draws our attention to the innovative roles Jewish women played in the modernization of Judaism in Germany and in the United States from the nineteenth century to the present. Yael Kupferberg analyzes the interplay of Jewish and non-Jewish gender relations in the transformation of these roles in the context of acculturation and emancipation in Germany.

Relations triggered by migration and the exchange of texts and ideas between German and American Jewries make for a complex set of parallels and differences between the respective experiences. Karla Goldman studies how nineteenth-century American and German Jewish women's public identities were shaped by organizational life in their respective contexts, specifically by synagogues and communal life.

The effects of the emancipation and acculturation processes became manifest in an institutional setting that was crucial to the (re-)formation of German Judaism in its changing social, religious, and political context: the Berlin Hochschule für die Wissenschaft des Judentums. Esther Seidel uses her findings on female students at the Hochschule as a prism to explore the divergent attitudes and aspirations of these women pioneers of Jewish learning in the 1920s and 1930s.

Hartmut Bomhoff focuses on a symposium that took place in Berlin in 1926. In response to the development in the German Protestant Church, in which women became candidates for preaching positions in 1925, progressive Jewish leaders discussed not only the role of women in community and synagogue governance but also in the rabbinate.

Pamela Nadell traces the historical development culminating in the ordination of the first female rabbi in the United States, in 1972, from its beginning in the late nineteenth century to the present. She points to the questions facing women ordained as rabbis today as they encounter the expectations, reservations, and opportunities posed by their seminaries, congregations, and male colleagues.

The role of women within Jewish life (religious, social, and in many other ways) is particularly complex and contested within the Orthodox stream, especially in the United States, where it has "shifted to the right" in the face of opposite developments in its larger societal environment.

These large historical developments become more concrete in the section on individual "trailblazers," who carved out leading roles for women in Jewish communities.

Gail Twersky Reimer complicates established views of Henrietta Szold (1860–1945) by pointing to her early struggles with the common view of women as unfit for religious leadership roles. While she set out on a path that led male students to the rabbinate, Szold exercised her transformative leadership role ultimately in a different sphere of Jewish life.

Elisa Klapheck recovers another female Jewish voice whose religious-political significance was ignored for a long time, philosopher Margaret Susman (1872–1966). She was a thinker long appreciated particularly in the context of Jewish-Christian dialogue; she is here reclaimed as an original and influential thinker linking the religious and political dimensions of exile, revelation, and Torah.

Two scholar-activists of female religious leadership engage the afterlife of Regina Jonas from their very different experiences. Katharina von Kellenbach relates her own efforts researching Jonas's ordination as a reflection of "factors that render women mute and the need for feminist solidarity to overcome silence and invisibility across religious boundaries." Stefanie Sinclair looks at the long disinterest of mainstream historiography in Jonas and her "rediscovery" by means of the categories of "memory" and "identity," as female leadership is "naturalized" in religious and other communities.

Female religious leadership can unfold its transformative power in the different settings that have constituted and shaped Judaism as a religion; the study and interpretation of texts is one such crucial sphere. While it would take until the second half of the twentieth century to see women ordained to be rabbis in the United States, the actual social and religious transformations that paved the way to this change began decades before. Drawing on her own experience, Shuly Rubin Schwartz explores the distinct leadership exercised by rebbetzins, who became important role models for female rabbis and other forms of female religious leadership.

Sandy Eisenberg Sasso describes how Jewish women engaged with texts as transmitters of male-dominated religious memory and how they revolutionized the way Jews read texts by reconstructing memory through the addition of female perspectives. She concludes her personal account of these processes by stating that this struggle both strengthened and renewed Judaism.

"Comparing Notes," the final section of the volume, broadens its perspective by looking at other religious traditions.

Marie-Theres Wacker surveys the developments in the Roman Catholic Church over the past fifty years, similarly looking at the intersection of gender, status, and power. She argues that the question of women's ordination as priests and other leadership roles must be solved on theological grounds, since humans, irrespective of gender, are created in God's image.

Renate Jost analyzes the historical development toward female ministers in Protestant churches and explores the theological and other impacts of the issue, as feminist theologians use deconstruction and intersectionality to place it in larger intellectual and political contexts.

In her article, "Rereading Male Chauvinism," Katajun Amirpur presents the struggle of Muslim women for religious leadership roles as a matter of authority in Qur'anic interpretation. She introduces readers to two female *engagé* scholars-activist, who ground their arguments for female leadership in such interpretations of sacred texts.

Judith Frishman studies the relationship between halakhic rulings on the topic and actual practice, with a special focus on the debate about women's ordination within the "Modern Orthodox" segment of Judaism.

II. SCHOLARLY AND RELIGIOUS CONTEXT

In 2010, Abraham Geiger College graduated Rabbi Alina Treiger, the first female rabbi to be ordained in Germany since Regina Jonas. Rabbi Treiger stated that for her, "women rabbis are the norm and no innovation," but nevertheless each of these women would have to carve her own path.[2]

The contributions in this volume discuss various ways of defining religious leadership. They critically engage existing scholarship and debates on female and gender roles in religion and faith at the intersection of several disciplines, such as religious and gender studies, theology, leadership studies, and sociology, and bring them into conversation with one another.

The question of what is "female" provides a particularly rich hermeneutical tool for the analysis of religion. The perception of the (female) "other" as defined by a male (self-)understanding, is but one of various aspects that are challenged and redefined in this volume. Given the claim of most religious traditions to provide authoritative statements about the nature of (wo)man, supposedly divinely revealed and enshrined in sacred texts and history (which marginalizes or even silences *her*-story), and due to the historically powerful ideologies and institutions built on such ontological claims, changes in religions' perspectives on gender can undermine their entire structure—and thereby lay open their deepest foundations for analysis. As scholars assert that gender is central in the emergence of "new religions," the emergence and development of "old" religions can fruitfully be interrogated by using gender as a hermeneutical tool.[3]

In gender studies, female religious leadership can be profitably seen as specific examples of female agency, a primary concept of gender studies. Therefore, categories established in scholarly literature can be applied to the study of such leadership roles and can, in turn, shed light on the contested conceptualization of female agency, a scholarly debate well beyond the field of religious studies. Such categories for the study of female religious leaders could be "resistance agency," "empowerment agency," instrumental approaches, and compliant approaches to female agency.[4] By testing these (and other) categories against concrete historical and contemporary cases, the volume aims to contribute to this ongoing debate.

Female religious leadership is furthermore a subject of the sociological analysis of the "feminization" of religion in general. In a particular historical constellation, the increasing role (or visibility) of women in American Jewish religious life has been critically discussed as turning male participants away.

The larger issue behind this phenomenon is the notion, empirically asserted, that women are more religious than men, which makes it all the more relevant to analyze in our volume why, for most of even modern times, the numerically largest and most influential monotheistic religions—Judaism, Christianity, Islam—have been led by men.[5] Whether male dominance has been justified (and challenged) by theological arguments or not, power interests lurk obviously behind official explanations, just as male dominance has for centuries been so embedded in theological ideas and ecclesiastical structures that it tends to replicate itself.

The recognition of gender as a sociocultural concept—a basic starting point of this volume—undermines the notion of a God-given (or "natural") order of the sexes and beyond, as it renders other fundamental assumptions about the nature of men and women contingent.[6] Depending on the political, social, and cultural context, this would question traditional understandings of religion more broadly and might affect the ways by which individuals and groups identify with specific religious traditions. If the (leadership) roles of women affect religious identities in this way, the topic at hand would tie into recent religious developments such as the gradual dissolution of clear demarcation lines of religious identities due to pluralism, hybridity, migration, and general decline of institutional affiliation.[7]

Related to the dissolution of clear religious identities, the different answers of various religions to women's quest for leadership roles could also change traditional taxonomies of religion. Distinguishing between "gender-traditional" and "gender-progressive" religions allows for a fresh perspective on the traditional taxonomy of religions according to theological beliefs and institutional boundaries.[8]

The volume demonstrates how developments at the intersection of gender and religious studies reflect the above-mentioned crucial changes that are going on beyond the sphere of religion. Both gender studies and religious studies tend to destabilize supposedly stable concepts, such as their very subjects: the notions of what is female and male turns out to be as contingent, at least over time and places, as what characterizes "religion."[9]

Irrespective of these questions, the interest in the intersection of gender and religion is based on the assumption—empirically verifiable for almost all societies past and present, with the notable exception of Western Europe—that religion and religions retain a powerful hold on societies and cultures, their norms and values, by bestowing ultimate meaning and legitimacy and by socializing individuals, not least in gender roles. In view of this, we hope therefore that this volume will make a distinct contribution to the emerging scholarly field of theological gender studies.

NOTES

1. Abraham Geiger, "Die Stellung des weiblichen Geschlechtes in dem Judenthume unserer Zeit," *Wissenschaftliche Zeitschrift für jüdische Theologie* 3 (1837): 1–14.
2. Hartmut Bomhoff, "Journey from the Margins to the Mainstream," *Jewish Voice from Germany* 14 (October 2014): 24.
3. Cf. Laura Vance, *Women in New Religions* (New York: New York University Press, 2015), 8.
4. Cf. Kelsy C. Burke, "Women's Agency in Gender-Traditional Religions: A Review of Four Approaches," *Sociology Compass* 6, no. 2 (2012): 122–33.
5. Marta Trzebiatowska and Steve Bruce, *Why Are Women More Religious Than Men?* (New York: New York University Press, 2012).
6. Cf. Uta Pohl-Patalong, "Gender—An- und Aufregungen in Theorie und Praxis," in *Unbeschreiblich weiblich? Neue Fragestellungen zur Geschlechterdifferenz in den Religionen*, ed. Christine Gerber, Silke Petersen, and Wolfram Weiße (Berlin: Lit Verlag, 2011), 14. As the perspective shifts from "being" male or female to "doing gender" as a performance, religion can be reconceptualized as a stage for such performances.
7. Manuela Kalsky and Katharina von Kellenbach, "Interreligious Dialogue and the Development of a Transreligious Identity: A Correspondence," in *Feminist Approaches to Interreligious Dialogue*, ed. Annette Esser et al. (Leuven: Peeters, 2009): 41–58.
8. Cf. Burke, "Women's Agency in Gender-Traditional Religions."
9. Cf. Riv-Ellen Prell, introduction to *Women Remaking American Judaism*, ed. Riv-Ellen Prell (Detroit: Wayne State University Press, 2007), 19.

BIBLIOGRAPHY

Bomhoff, Hartmut, "Journey from the Margins to the Mainstream," *Jewish Voice from Germany* 14 (October 2014): 24.

Burke, Kelsy C., "Women's Agency in Gender-Traditional Religions: A Review of Four Approaches," *Sociology Compass* 6, no. 2 (2012): 122–33.

Geiger, Abraham, "Die Stellung des weiblichen Geschlechtes in dem Judenthume unserer Zeit," *Wissenschaftliche Zeitschrift für jüdische Theologie* 3 (1837): 1–14.

Kalsky, Manuela, and von Kellenbach, Katharina, "Interreligious Dialogue and the Development of a Transreligious Identity: A Correspondence," in *Feminist Approaches to Interreligious Dialogue*, ed. Annette Esser et al. (Leuven: Peeters, 2009): 41–58.

Pohl-Patalong, Uta, "Gender—An- und Aufregungen in Theorie und Praxis," in *Unbeschreiblich weiblich? Neue Fragestellungen zur Geschlechterdifferenz in den Religionen*, ed. Christine Gerber, Silke Petersen, and Wolfram Weiße (Berlin: Lit Verlag, 2011), 11–30.

Prell, Riv-Ellen (ed.), *Women Remaking American Judaism* (Detroit: Wayne State University Press, 2007).

Trzebiatowska, Marta, and Bruce, Steve, *Why Are Women More Religious Than Men?* (New York: New York University Press, 2012).

Vance, Laura, *Women in New Religions* (New York: New York University Press, 2015).

Part I

New Roles for Jewish Women in Modernizing Germany and America

Chapter One

The Discourse of the Other

The Transformation of the Jewish Woman in Nineteenth-Century Germany

Yael Kupferberg

The Jewish Reform movement has been the core project of German Jewry since the dawn of the Enlightenment.[1] This Reform movement significantly promoted the *social* emancipation of German Jewry as a bourgeois community.[2] However, its habitual effects and the way in which it shaped the social and private fabric, particularly the role of Jewish women, is a topic for sociological studies, which has yet to be researched in more depth and breadth. For many years, the Jewish woman was invisible in historiography and also as author of any texts:[3] Up until the 1970s, we find scarcely any academic contributions on the history of Jewish women.[4]

Some light can be shed on the historical background of this untold history of Jewish women. By the third century at the latest, when emergent Christianity was becoming more significant, vast swathes of Jewish communities turned to Christianity. Those Jews who either had no wish to follow suit or were unable to do so went on to adopt the nascent Rabbinic Judaism in Palestine or Persia. This was a form of Judaism that, like Christianity, was established as a patriarchal religion.[5] The passages where we encounter exemplary, responsible women in rabbinic literature are therefore few and far between. The esteem in which individual women were held by rabbis does little to hide the fact that the dominant characteristic style was discriminatory. Here, there is little to distinguish the three monotheistic religions of late antiquity from one another: they are marked not just by their monotheism and high moral sensibility, but rather also by the fact that they were/are fundamentally patriarchal and, often enough, misogynistic.[6]

Rabbi Eliezer's tenet "Whoever teaches his daughter Torah is teaching her obscenity" draws a striking conclusion and paints a picture of a socialized inadequacy on the part of Jewish men when it came to dealing with the educated women of whose existence we know.[7] The historical outcome of this attitude was that the traditional yeshivot were to the greatest possible extent institutions that were, and indeed remain, dominated by men.[8] But historiography itself also reflects historical reality, insofar as we are able to grasp it, as a history of men. It was only in the last thirty years, as the historian Monika Richarz argues in an attempt also to explore the history of the woman from a female perspective,[9] that a new way of describing history established itself in the German research arena.

Simone de Beauvoir's famous 1949 remark *"On ne naît pas femme: on le devient"* is a reference to the fact that gender is attributed as a role only once it has become part of the discourse.[10] "Gender" is a social and ideological category. To see how precise this is, one has to consider the changing role patterns within German Jewry, which, as part of the processes of acculturation and emancipation,[11] also allowed itself to be guided by the non-Jewish gender relations found among the German bourgeoisie.[12] Here, one can witness the gender model being redefined and codified.

1. REFORM AS ACCULTURATION

The process of cultural transformation that German Jews have undergone since the second half of the eighteenth century has had a decisive impact on gender-specific orientation.[13]

Strong religious, social, and cultural change inevitably also ushered in change to gender roles. The scope of halakhah, which established a male dominance, had clearly been on the wane as norms regulating extensive parts of daily life of urban Jews since the end of the eighteenth century. Studying the Talmud became less important; Talmud schools gradually lost their significance and most of them were eventually closed by the 1830s. Jewish men received less and less religious education, and kashrut (Jewish dietary rules) and Sabbath observance was in decline. The transformation of halakhic Judaism into a bourgeois-liberal Judaism was accompanied, as historian Monika Richarz concedes, by a sustained and progressive process of secularization, particularly in the second generation after the close of the nineteenth century.

The strictly religious life and strict Jewish observance were now no longer coupled to prestige or social recognition.[14]

In this respect, religion now ceased to provide a durable basis for social identification. On the contrary, another model, the bourgeois model, became popular, a model that was connected to the promise of social integration; the adoption of a non-Jewish bourgeois set of values became an ideal and practical guide—with far-reaching consequences for the Jewish family model. The new, burgeoning set of values had a profound impact on relationships between the sexes and established a new male dominance based on both Protestant and secular notions. The great minds behind the development of the bourgeoisie, that is, from Immanuel Kant to Georg Wilhelm Friedrich Hegel and others, stood for a determined idea of two factually and idealistically separated gender spheres. This model wove its way through the theoretical projects designed by civil society:

> For varying reasons, the binding of the woman to the household and the family and the orientation of the man toward the public, the law, and the state was established as a fundamental, irreversible exemplar of the division of labor in society. All glorifications and idealizations of femininity, from the Romantics to Humboldt or Schiller, did nothing to change the basic principle of the functional differentiation of "humankind" into two genders, which was adopted as an elementary organizing principle of bourgeois society.[15]

These ideological parameters found their way into the Jewish communities, which—at least the protagonists of the Reform movement—were eager to adopt them in the form of the predominant bourgeois narrative and its acculturation. The formerly employed Jewish woman now gravitated further and further toward the role of caring mother and fully educated "priestess of the house." Ideally, she followed the fashions, picked up bourgeois habits, and took her cue from the aesthetics of the educated middle class. She also found herself in charge of the children's religious schooling. Pushing the Jewish woman into the bourgeois model had mixed results.

2. TRADITIONAL AND NEW ROLES

Acculturation was an integral component of the social and legal emancipation of the Jews; it was also demanded by the non-Jewish majority during the late eighteenth century. As one of the consequences of emancipation and the loss of the legal autonomy Jewish communities had possessed for centuries, Jewish law (*halakhah*) lost some value, although other factors were involved here as well. However, Judaism embarked on several paths, with varying outcomes for legal developments and women's position in society.[16] Reform Judaism was calling for religious equality between men and women as early as 1846, and significantly contributed to achieve this.[17] Halakhah stipulations, which had put women at a disadvantage, were altered or abandoned.[18] Jewish emancipation coincided with a process of "embourgeoisement" or "bourgeoisification"; this is—though unspecific—a finding of most recent research.[19]

"Bourgeoisification" does not just describe a socio-economic process. Rather, it obviously also involves sociocultural socialization processes, changes to the legal status and to political behavior. Above and beyond this, "bourgeoisification" stands for the appropriation of education, aesthetics and fashions, changes to family life and the world of experience, and to styles of living and habitus.[20] The core components of bourgeois existence—and Reform Judaism was a bourgeois movement—had a significant effect on the issue of gender.[21] The revitalization of the public sphere caused a growing distance between the former domain and the experiences lived out in the house and with the family, which provided a sanctuary from the acceleration so characteristic of the epoch.[22] "To the extent to which men, through their professions, through the expansion of community life for the bourgeoisie and a more active participation in political life, were more strongly connected to public life, itself growing in importance, they distanced themselves from home and family life, which, in turn, transformed into an exclusive space for women and children."[23]

The central determinants in the bourgeois project and the new everyday reality also included a new definition of gender-specific attributions. The lifeworlds were distributed between the public sphere (which was dominated by men) and the world of the family, which was predominantly shaped by women. Fulfilling one's duties, being in gainful employment, and enjoying a social life outside of the home were part of the masculine living world, while it was incumbent upon the woman to support and embellish the family's inner space.[24] It fell to the women to bring up the children in a loving environment, run the household, and maintain those social contacts that brought with them representational duties and could therefore even extend to public life.[25] Even though historical conditions, which had changed several times since the dawn of the eighteenth century, presupposed different forms of sociocultural concepts and notions of piety, religion played a prominent role in the way the ideal citizen and his wife set out their lives and modified themselves.[26] What applied to the vast majority of women in German society was dictated by the reformers: the Jewish woman was recognized as the guarantor of piety. Indeed, it was the intention of outspoken reformers to strengthen the role of women. The passive role needed to be overhauled. "Or should, perhaps," as the Bohemian *maskil* (Hebrew Enlightenment philosopher) Peter Beer asked provocatively in 1837, "this important half of the human kind forever remain physically and spiritually enslaved, as in ancient barbaric times, as it is now, even though it is emancipated and on an equal footing with the male gender in all educated nations of present time, and not just in bourgeois relationships but also religious ones?"[27]

Educator and preacher Eduard Israel Kley was already criticizing, in very clear terms, what he perceived to be the contempt in which women were held in the traditional religious service. Kley believed that the woman's status would be enhanced, in particular, through a process of harmonization. After all, the contempt for women was "what so shook the building of faith in Israel and made it so unstable, as the cornerstone had been discarded and not paid sufficient attention. This is what could, in the bleakest scenario, lead to a total collapse."[28]

Here, "educated nations" provided a benchmark. As Kley pointed out in 1818/1819, "The stone that our fathers did not heed in the building of their godliness becomes, in our times, the cornerstone, the firm pillar. . . . Hasn't the woman long been a cornerstone in the building of societal life, in the quiet temple of domestic bliss, in the cocoon of peace and contentedness?"[29]

3. THE BOURGEOIS "VALUE SYSTEM"

The spiritual roots of acculturation can be traced back to the time of the Enlightenment.[30] It was during this time that the concepts of acculturation and bourgeoisie habitus emerged, thus paving the way for the harmonious union of "heart" and "reason" as well as continual introspection. This also meant the introduction of moral and ethical self-improvement, or rather, the bourgeois internalization of moral order.[31] This process of internalization, which encouraged and supported a specific worldview, set of values, and, yes, a specific habitus, especially applied to the Protestant bourgeoisie.[32]

Within the Protestant bourgeoisie, religion developed first and foremost into an inventory of conscience and feeling, devotion and edification, and thus also—as Lässig argues—"into a phenomenon that was increasingly shaped by supposedly feminine elements and spheres."[33] The status of the woman in halakhic Judaism tells a different story. Here, the majority of significant religious rituals reside in the masculine domain. In the religious interpretation system, women were excluded from studying the Talmud and the Torah, that is, the central texts and forms of Jewish religious and social communitarization. They played only a passive role in religious services.[34]

This separation of women and men, which also translated into a spatial divide in the synagogue and the absence of an equivalent rite of passage such as the bar mitzvah for girls, is a symbolic and ritual reflection of a certain culture, which consisted of a both essential and functional imbalance between the sexes. Historian Simone Lässig draws the following conclusion:

> The extreme spatial separation of the sexes, as witnessed in the synagogue or also in the fact that rites of passage comparable to the bar mitzvah did not exist for girls, symbolized this functional lack of equality between the sexes, which had far-reaching consequences: since traditional Jewish day-to-day life was geared toward halakhah and Torah, including outside the places of worship, its heavily masculine approach provided the objective legitimization of a sociocultural marginalization of the Jewish women that extended beyond the synagogue.[35]

This assessment is, admittedly, arrived at with the benefit of hindsight and amounts to a stance that is strongly pejorative of traditional Judaism. However, communities and families, as historian Monika Richarz has already demonstrated, were essentially organized patriarchally. The role of the Jewish woman was traditionally a secondary one.[36] To assess the impact of these structures on women's self-perception and the representation of women in their surroundings, primary sources, that is, ego-documents or other sources should be consulted.

Against this backdrop, a fundamental paradigm shift coincided with the varied efforts of the German Jewish Reform movement.[37] One might posit that the extent to which the reformers endeavored to bring worship in line with bourgeois notions of religiosity and aesthetics was echoed in the extent to which men were also instructed to change their everyday religious lives and practices.

It is of historical note that changing gender roles also altered the role of the Jewish man.[38] In the view of the rabbis, wives could do meaningful religious work by making it possible for their husbands to pursue religious studies.[39] This gender-specific division of labor thus potentially translated into the allocation of all gainful employment to the woman, while the man could devote himself to undertake spiritual work, as Monika Richarz informs us.[40] Philosopher of religion Daniel Boyarin sees the exclusion of women from studying the Torah therefore as amounting to the functional equivalent of the gender-specific division of labor in other patriarchal societies.[41]

4. CHANGING JEWISH TRADITION

The redetermination of gender-specific tasks is invested in the process of reform within the religious system, as Lässig observes:

> To the extent to which the reformers endeavored to adjust the service to comply with bourgeois notions of piety and aesthetics, so they had to devalue the masculine elements found in the religious system—halakhah and Talmud-Torah studies, lectures, and disputes—and strengthen those elements that ascribed a feminine character to the contemporary discourse.[42]

This also involved, in particular, acculturation in the sacred field and the development of the "citizens' synagogue."[43] The bourgeois aestheticization of worship and the introduction of sermons delivered in German contributed considerably toward a new model for the Jewish woman, one that took its cue from non-Jewish paradigms. German-language sermons, introduced by the reformers, thus partially abolishing the Hebrew service, played just a small but significant part in the bourgeoisification of the Jewish woman.[44] As for what this meant: the transformation of traditionally female roles—and of Judaism as a whole—came about through the implementation of a new language practice. After all, moving toward a form of piety that responded to the need for edification, prayer, emotionality, aesthetics, and inwardness and also complied with "reason," that is, the fundamental imperative of the Enlightenment, made it necessary to overcome linguistic obstacles. In the communities, the reformers encountered uneducated Jews, young people, and, above all, women who could scarcely follow the readings held entirely in Hebrew at services. Given that religion had, until then, predominantly been shaped via the male privilege of Jewish learning, Hebrew had for centuries remained a language of men. This said, there were also many men for whom Hebrew posed a challenge. Many Jews could read and repeat Hebrew texts but had scarcely any cognitive grasp of them.[45]

This situation is relevant because the services could be used to popularize a new cultural orientation as embodied by the reforms. Now that texts were being understood, intellectually speaking, in terms of language and content, this could provide a foundation to change education and habitus—all the way to the patterns of the German bourgeoisie.

This also applied to the Jewish woman. Women, on whom the traditional service had mostly little influence because they were not included as active participants in the service and had just a little knowledge of Hebrew, were to be instructed in the emerging Reform synagogues as to their roles as custodians of the Jewish tradition. The reformers were concerned not just with a formulaic piety and established rituals, but rather, entirely in the spirit of the German, educated middle class, with the "aesthetic education of humankind," as Friedrich Schiller postulated.[46] Should the divine word fail to reach the woman's soul, observed rabbi, preacher, pedagogue, politician, and Bible translator Gotthold Salomon in 1822, then her visit to the synagogue could only end in "harmful sanctimony."[47] In the end, Jewish women had, as Rabbi Meyer Keyserling also posited, "memory and imitation, but no religion—they know the formulas but not the truths that should be expressed through these formulas."[48]

For Gotthold Salomon, language was the central medium of emancipation/self-emancipation. The inability of many to understand Hebrew would, in his view, lead to Judaism being eroded and Hebrew being seen by the majority of society—who, naturally, did not understand Hebrew—as suspicious, a secret language, concealing the absence of loyalty to the German fatherland.

Hebrew was viewed by the majority society as "sinister." It was incomprehensible and, at the same time (such was the feeling of resentment at that time), "dangerous."[49] As for Yiddish, it occupied an even lower rank in the eyes of society and was considered the language of the "ghetto Jew," from where the "enlightened Jew" was meant to escape through cultural change.[50]

The fact that language was associated with "culture" is obvious. In Germany in particular, the German language of art and literature had, since the Romantic period at the latest, amounted to a sacred code; German language skills operated as a social badge of honor. In this respect, the German language—alongside Christian religion—was an "entrance ticket" to German society. Therefore, keeping to Hebrew liturgy was considered to be an obstacle on the path toward German society; the language, which was already incomprehensible to many Jews, would lead—according to the reformers—to social separation.[51]

The linguistic change of course thus aimed to achieve two things: it guaranteed an emphatic relationship to Judaism and enabled people to gain entrance into the German bourgeoisie. To that extent, it made political sense that many reform efforts focused on language change. Initially, prayer books were printed for women and girls, which did "have ties to devotional literature (*techinot*), but were no longer written in Western Yiddish, but rather in High German."[52] The burgeoning sector of German-language Jewish journalism furthered the bourgeoisification of the Jewish woman. A female readership was very much desired—and also available: the ideal type of Jewish woman had been created.[53]

As noted, a milestone on the path toward language change was the introduction of the German sermon. Unlike the traditional lectures, which were given in Yiddish and sometimes also in Hebrew (*derashot*), sermons were, from the beginning of the religious reforms around 1820, held entirely in German.[54] Here, women were addressed directly; the sermon can thus be considered an instrument of female integration and education. This amounts to the enhancement of the role of the woman. With the Reform synagogue, a public space was created in which men and women were addressed as equals. These speeches conveyed a bourgeois content; these new sermons were thus already building a bridge to the spiritual discourses of the age, from the Enlightenment to the Romantic period. Reason-based ideology and the right to education promoted by the Enlightenment were also imparted, as were bourgeois notions of virtue and morality, all charged with emotion and feeling.[55] The sermons were, nevertheless, noticeably guided more by Enlightenment ideals than by Protestant sermons.[56] The biblical text may have served as a point of departure, but was not central. What was much more apparent was a new culture forcing its way to the surface: the enhancement of, or change in, the role of the woman within Judaism and the fact that women were considered the addressees of a new Judaism at all were happening at the same time that the study of Hebrew texts was losing its significance.[57]

To this process, a further sociocultural particularity was added. The very notion of exempting women from many of the men's religious obligations meant that the women's religious education was merely superficial; women could barely read or write Hebrew. Religious or edifying literature for women was written in Yiddish, the Western Yiddish of German Jews; there was, for example, a Torah commentary in Yiddish for a female audience, which was written in Hebrew letters until the eighteenth century.[58] These gender-specific educational differences also formed the prerequisite for an arguably faster process of acculturation on the part of Jewish women to German majority culture since the end of the eighteenth century. Women participated in the culture of the secular sphere. Their relationship to scripture was not a sacred or ritual relationship but rather, already, a secularized relationship.[59] The process of acculturation thus proceeded on a complementary basis to that of linguistic practice. As soon as Jewish women had learned to read Latin letters, they read German contemporary literature and at least participated in a non-Jewish culture. By the end of the eighteenth century, the reading of novels was already viewed in Berlin as a characteristic activity of Jewish women from the middle and upper classes.[60] The interest in languages and literature brought cultural and habitual acculturation in its wake.[61]

In this respect, paradigms were adopted within the Reform movement that derived from the non-Jewish bourgeoisie, and indeed from the bourgeois model of the woman as defined by the *Zeitgeist*. This bourgeois core discourse was based on the premise that women were highly skilled at absorbing and conveying emotion. Consequently, so the argument continues, women were called to make a specific contribution to religious education and the moral structure of their families and thus act as guarantors of a Judaism that could assert itself against anti-Judaism as well as against the entire surrender of Judaism.[62] The reform of sermons, in particular their emotionalization and aestheticization, was also a reaction to the bourgeois model of the woman. At the same time, the reform also involved the consistent implementation of a bourgeois concept of piety, which tended to include feminine features, as Simone Lässig points out.[63]

The assertion that the bourgeoisification of the religious system within German Judaism went hand-in-hand with a fundamental reevaluation of the gender model has yet to be verified.[64] However, it was in this very religious area that the gulf between Jewish tradition and bourgeois, Protestant existence regarding women's status and position needed to be tackled. Monika Richarz postulates for developments in the economic sphere, "What can be observed is that Jewish men clearly, as a matter of course and without a great deal of discussion, managed to make the move from the traditional form of the patriarchy to the bourgeois form of male hegemony."[65] In analogy, this could possibly also be argued for the religious realm.

The following should be stressed: not a great deal changed in the nineteenth century as far as the position of the woman within Jewish law was concerned. Emancipating women within the system governed by religious laws, that is, by accepting them as members of the minyan or admitting them to lead prayers and read from the Torah, failed.⁶⁶ The religious domain was dominated by men. Formally speaking, the man remained untouched in the halakhic system, and as historian Sharon Gillerman concludes, "The liberal religious reform movement, which has garnered so much attention in the historical literature, did not, however, fundamentally transform the role of women in Judaism."⁶⁷

However, one can assume that, with the religious and ideological reforms in Judaism, the emergence of another, new bourgeois Jewish culture had also been established. A process of secularization was thus underway within religious practice. One could say that quite a few ideas and ideals of German Enlightenment values were popularized inside the synagogue and the new conception of man was incorporated into Judaism. To this extent, the religious domain can therefore be deemed a central theater of bourgeoisification, not least because of the new role patterns that were rehearsed here. One could argue that the success in the modernization of German Judaism could therefore be measured by religion, which had, until then, acted as a guarantor against change.⁶⁸ The emancipation of the Jews and of the Jewish woman was also a project taking place within religious practice—which broadcast its message to society and changed the private, social, and societal role of the Jewish woman considerably.⁶⁹

5. THE PRIVATIZATION OF JUDAISM

Judaism also changed from an institutional point of view. The collapse of traditional community structures, which were aligned with political bodies, and the adaptation to bourgeois living environments set in motion a process of privatization of Judaism as well as of religion that fundamentally changed Jewish life in particular.⁷⁰ This transitional period of bourgeoisification was characterized by an erosion of the integral community defined in religious terms. The transition was what first spawned the notion of the individual, a concept with which anyone familiar with the German bourgeoisie will be acquainted.⁷¹ The bourgeois family emerged as a counter-model to a society shaped by economization. Only the man went out to work and represented the family to the outside world. At the same time, he commanded a strong authority within the family. Here, the woman's role was complementary. In the majority society, she was shut out of any involvement in sociopolitical affairs. She represented, at most, the well-run household, ran the day-to-day life of the family, and socialized the children; the Jewish wife also assumed important spiritual tasks in the home.[72]

One aspect that was symptomatic of the German bourgeois society was the separation of the public and the private spheres.[73] The developing of a modern, specifically German Reform Judaism also put this process into effect. It privatized itself, becoming a family religion; in this respect the woman found herself assigned an important role, given that she was the dominant force in the house. Private religion was insofar handed over to the care of women. The transformation of Judaism into a bourgeois religion within the family thus also strengthened the role of the Jewish woman, albeit within predefined parameters, more specifically, the predefined parameters of majority society. The transformation of Judaism into a "private" religion was a project in which both Reform Judaism and traditional Judaism, as well as neo-orthodoxy, could be contained, as historian Shulamit Volkov argues.[74]

6. NEW ROLES, SAME GENDER HIERARCHY?

The transformation outlined above did not mean, however, that the status of the Jewish woman within halakhah had also undergone a transformation. Rather, what one can concede is that here, alongside the traditional Jewish practice, a contemporary culture was being created in order to found a religious sense of belonging and a Jewish identity—adapted to the ideals of the enlightened narrative. Nevertheless, this specific kind of bourgeoisification had to assert itself on two fronts: on the one hand, there was a broadly perceived specific need to uphold Jewish tradition and practice, and on the other hand, the need to draw closer to the bourgeois, non-Jewish living environments, as historian Marion Kaplan has shown.[75]

In this respect, the reform of Judaism affected both genders. One can assume, as historian Simone Lässig asserts, that "the bourgeoisification of the religious system in German Judaism was accompanied by, or, if one wants to be provocative, was the price one had to pay for, a completely and utterly dramatic re-evaluation of the gender model."[76]

Lässig demonstrates that sermons in particular gave the woman's duties more scope than they did to those of the man by shifting the center of religious life from ritual obligations to other religious practices.[77] Nevertheless, certain expectations were also placed on the man's shoulders, albeit ones that transcended the sphere of religion: he was called upon to show strength, an entrepreneurial spirit and activity, a sense of responsibility, and self-discipline. Education and rationality were supposed to guide him in his actions; he was expected to take a leading role in his own self-improvement. This notion was once again in keeping with the spirit of the German, educated middle class; it was not just about "having," but rather also about "being." This said, being in gainful employment was his primary duty: he had, as Gotthold Salomon preached, "to become a guiding star: people look to you! Your house is an educational institution, in which people are trained to work for the state, for the country, for the world and for the heavens."[78]

The Jewish male model could be seen as a reflection of the educated middle-class male model found in non-Jewish leading discourse. Both partners, men and women alike, should enjoy a worldly education, and the marriage should be a place of learning in which both partners strive for self-improvement. Both genders had had their roles assigned to them. An astonishing number of preachers proclaimed an ideal of femininity as shaped by the bourgeois majority culture. The orientation and emphasis on virtue, feeling, and mind helped both with regard to the integration of Jews into the non-Jewish habitus and the privatization of Judaism, which was also driven by the new role of the woman. In the contemporary discourse, motherhood was talked up in a very sentimental fashion, and marriage and the family in general were rendered as sacrosanct.[79] In 1802, reformer and pedagogue Peter Beer called for an end to the "oriental barbarism" regarding the traditional gender models and urged that women finally be placed on an equal footing with men.[80] Within the increasingly bourgeois discourse, the man represented the "head" of the family, while the woman at his side represented the "heart." The woman was valorized within the family as the person who vouched for the viability of the family and that of the Jewish religion; after all, without a "beating heart, even the cleverest male head could not exist."[81] Against this ideological backdrop, many preachers were endeavoring to establish the new tasks for women, in using contemporary gender stereotypes, and in so doing to consolidate the new female and male bourgeois habitus.[82]

A remarkable number of sermons take as their theme marital and domestic cohabitation, which was increasingly meant to provide protection from the coldness of the competitive, performance-oriented society outside of the home.[83] "Warmth," "feeling," and "security" were now imparted by the woman, who was supposed to create the space of trust and coziness in which the man could relax.[84]

Even though both partners had a right to love and fulfillment, the primary concern of the woman was to support the man.[85] In a pious family, so many sermons purported, all jostled to offer their passionate support to the father. The woman was allocated a defined space; that of the home.[86] Here, according to the sermons, was where she could find her happiness and sphere of action. Activities outside the home undermined the requirement of caring solely for her husband and children. However, this she should do with a sense of passion. To cite Gotthold Salomon:

> Is that not to your liking? Are you trying to suggest that God excluded you from this world because he had assigned you another, your house? Did he not entrust you with the task of working particularly on the moral refinement and the veritable happiness of our sex? Wives and mothers, through you, life can be made more beautiful, and the earth can obtain a better form.[87]

Allocating responsibilities in this way also imparted a specific habitus: a woman's happiness and gratification were to be derived from making her husband and family happy. She herself should be modest, hard-working, and disciplined; these are all bourgeois virtues.

Of course, a specific education was a basic prerequisite. It behooved women, above all, to ensure that their children received a loving and up-to-date upbringing. This also included the shaping of character. While the mother was to be in charge of transmitting knowledge and taking responsibility for her child's or children's moral and religious conduct, for the man, bringing up children meant acting as a role model in his profession and in public life. Beyond all these tasks for men and women, and for the new Jewish family, which are only outlined here, it was imperative to further religious life within the family; the woman served as the priestess of the house.

The bourgeois model of the woman increased in value within the Jewish family through being assigned the religious task. Whether we could talk of "emancipation" in a sense of female self-determination here is questionable.

The obvious adoption of bourgeois values and standards promoted the acculturation of Judaism to a considerable degree. Simultaneously, the Jewish social order transformed, moving from a culture of male-dominated religious learning and observance to a contemporary religious system that was shaped by bourgeois values. In this respect, the Jewish woman moved to the center of a new Jewish culture of piety and family.

The reason this process is so remarkable could be explained by the fact that, within religion and via sermons and language change, shifting mentalities, and, yes, a kind of bourgeoisification of Judaism, a form of secularization had taken place. Nevertheless, the changing role of the Jewish woman was brought about to no small degree by a gender model defined by men which had been influenced by the standards of the majority of society.[88]

NOTES

1. Eberhard Wolff, "Ankunft in der Moderne: Aufklärung und Reformjudentum," in *Die Geschichte der Juden in Deutschland*, ed. Arno Herzig and Cay Rademacher (Bonn: Ellert & Richter Verlag, 2008), 114–22, here 114.
    Cf. Deborah Hertz, *Jewish High Society in Old Regime Berlin* (New Haven and London: Yale University Press, 1988); Michael A. Meyer, *Response to Modernity: A History of the Reform Movement in Judaism* (Detroit: Wayne State University Press, 1995).
2. David Sorkin, *The Transformation of the German Jewry, 1780–1840* (New York: Oxford University Press, 1987), 5; Benjamin Maria Baader, *Gender, Judaism and Bourgeois Culture in Germany 1800–1870* (Bloomington: Indiana University Press 2016), 75–76.
3. See Susannah Heschel, "The Impact of Feminist Theory on Jewish Studies," in *Modern Judaism and Historical Consciousness. Identities, Encounters, Perspectives*, ed. Andreas Gotzmann and Christian Wiese (Boston: Brill, 2007), 529–48, here 529: "While we know that Jewish women existed, we do not have any texts that they authored, and we can only surmise that their voices at times may have been recorded by attribution to men. The absence of texts known to have been written by women, preserving their points of view, interpretations, and sense of identity, does not simply leave a gap in women's history, it also destabilizes the category of Jewish history, rendering its claims uncertain as well as incomplete." Marion A. Kaplan, *The Making of the Jewish Middle Class: Women, Family, and Identity in Imperial Germany* (New York: Oxford University Press, 1991), 7.
4. Kaplan, *Making of the Jewish Middle Class*, vii–ix.
5. Kaplan, *Making of the Jewish Middle Class*, 64–65.
6. Micha Brumlik, "Gelehrte Frauen. Regina Jonas und ihre Vorgängerinnen," in *JMB Journal*, ed. Stiftung Jüdisches Museum Berlin (Berlin: Jüdisches Museum Berlin, 2014), 11–14, here 14. See also Birgit Heller, "Gender und Religion," in *Handbuch Religionswissenschaft*, ed. Johann Figl, (Göttingen: Vandenhoeck & Ruprecht, 2003), 758–69.
7. Babylonian Talmud, *Sotah* 20a; *The Babylonian Talmud*, trans. I. Epstein (London: Soncino, 1936).
8. Charlotte Elisheva Fonrobert, "Frauen im Judentum," in *Handbuch zur Geschichte der Juden in Europa*, vol. 2, *Religion, Kultur, Alltag*, ed. Elke-Vera Kotowski, Julius H. Schoeps, and Hiltrud Wallenborn (Darmstadt: Primus Verlag, 2001), 79–88, here 84.
9. See Monika Richarz, "Geschlechterhierarchie und Frauenarbeit in der jüdischen Geschichte," in *Deutsch-jüdische Geschichte als Geschlechtergeschichte. Studien zum 19. und 20. Jahrhundert*, ed. Kirsten Heinsohn and Stefanie Schüler-Springorum (Göttingen: Wallstein, 2006), 87–104. Monika Richarz nevertheless makes the following complaint: "The history of gender-specific work and the division of labor in Judaism has scarcely been paid any attention hitherto as a topic within gender history. This is all the more astonishing given the fact that every society is characterized to no small extent by the way in which it distributes work between men and women. No social history has as yet been conducted on women's and men's work within Judaism which considers how the division of labor will unfold in the long-term" (Richarz, "Geschlechterhierarchie und Frauenarbeit in der jüdischen Geschichte," 102).
10. Simone de Beauvoir, *Le deuxième sexe* (Paris: Gallimard, 1949), 285–86.

11. I will use the term "acculturation"—not "assimilation"—which refers to both a social and an individual process of transformation into society. See Verena Lenzen, "Judentum zwischen Emanzipation, Akkulturation, Assimilation und jüdischer Renaissance," in *Integration durch Religion? Geschichtliche Befunde, gesellschaftliche Analysen, rechtliche Perspektiven*, ed. Edmund Arens, Martin Baumann, Antonius Liedhegener, Wolfgang W. Müller, and Markus Ries (Zürich: Nomos Verlag, 2014), 103–16. Kaplan also argues, "The use of the term 'assimilation' provides an inaccurate picture of German Jews. It focuses exclusively on public conduct and conscious identity ('we were so German'), taking both at face value. It ignores unconscious identity and important emotional and behavioral factors, particularly in the private sphere. . . . Moreover, it slights what anthropologists call 'culture'—'the totally socially transmitted behavior patterns, arts beliefs, institutions, and all other products of work and thought characteristic of a community'" (Kaplan, *Making of the Jewish Middle Class*, 11).

12. Hereafter, the terms "citizen," "bourgeois," and "bourgeoisie" are applied in terms of a model that was also intended to be universal, but that was nevertheless always being colored and broken up into specific social, gendered, or denominational categories. Admittedly, it is an overwhelmingly masculine perspective that informs these terms, as gender history has mapped out; see Ute Frevert, "Bürgerliche Meisterdenker und das Geschlechterverhältnis. Konzepte, Erfahrungen, Visionen an der Wende vom 18. zum 19. Jahrhundert," in *Bürgerinnen und Bürger* (Göttingen: Vandenhoeck & Ruprecht, 1988), 17–48.

13. Shulamit Volkov, *Das jüdische Projekt der Moderne* (München: C.H. Beck, 2001), 65–66.

14. Cf. *Jewish Life in Germany. Memoirs from Three Centuries*, ed. Monika Richarz (Bloomington & Indianapolis: Indiana University Press, 1991), 17–38.

15. Frevert, "Bürgerliche Meisterdenker und das Geschlechterverhältnis," 30–31. (All translations by the author, unless indicated otherwise.)

16. Marianne Wallach-Faller, *Die Frau im Tallit. Judentum feministisch gelesen*, ed. Doris Brodbeck and Yvonne Domhardt (Zürich: Chronos, 2000), 74.

17. Historian Sharon Gillerman, however, doubts the social and religious improvement of women in Reform Judaism and argues, "Yet when it came to practice, the nineteenth-century Reform movement failed to eliminate many of the traditional religious restrictions that kept women in a subordinate status. In the synagogue, women could still neither be counted in a prayer quorum nor called to the Torah, and they often remained seated apart and comfortably out of view in the women's gallery. Despite pronouncements against the segregation of women, religious reformers ultimately made few substantial improvements in women's status." (Sharon Gillerman, "Germany: 1750–1945," in *Jewish Women: A Comprehensive Historical Encyclopedia*," March 1, 2009, Jewish Women's Archive, https://jwa.org/encyclopedia/article/germany-1750-1945).

18. Cf. Wallach-Faller, *Die Frau im Tallit*, 57.

19. Baader, *Gender, Judaism and Bourgeois Culture in Germany 1800–1870*, 14.

20. One could say that *Bildung* was the significant term of bourgeoisification: "*Bildung* appealed to the universal, encouraging the self-cultivation of the individual—a clear invitation to women. In addition, *Bildung* implied far more than an appropriate intellectual stance or an appreciation of high culture. It also meant manners and breeding and thus included women in a subtle but powerful way: they were to raise a family of *Bildung*" (Kaplan, *Making of the Jewish Middle Class*, 9).

21. "Gender" refers to the sociocultural sex.

22. Frevert, "Bürgerliche Meisterdenker und das Geschlechterverhältnis," 32–33.

23. Ibid., 32.

24. Simone Lässig, *Jüdische Wege ins Bürgertum. Kulturelles Kapital und sozialer Aufstieg* (Göttingen: Vandenhoeck & Ruprecht, 2004), 327.

25. Lässig, *Jüdische Wege ins Bürgertum*, 327. Regarding the woman's tasks, see also Monika Richarz: "However, in the patriarchal orthodoxy . . . women have specific religious duties. Their chief task is to fulfill the commandment of fertility through giving birth to and bringing up children. Moreover, their duty is also to run a kosher house in line with Jewish dietary rules and the lighting and blessing of the Sabbath candles at the start of the Sabbath. Both are, typically, rules which are adhered to at home and which thus attach a high sense of importance to the woman when it comes to religious practice in the home. In her dealings with her husband, the woman owes him love and respect—as he does to her—and is duty-bound to apply the commandments of the Torah, which regulate sexual life, to the letter. The marked separation of roles according to gender in religious and family life did not mean that the woman was subservient to her husband in every relationship. . . . The husband's job was not just to sire children, but rather also to satisfy his wife emotionally, which was associated with respecting her as a human being." Monika Richarz, "In Familie, Handel und Salon. Jüdische Frauen vor und nach der Emanzipation der deutschen Juden," in *Frauengeschichte–Geschlechtergeschichte*, ed. Karin Hause and Heide Wunder (Frankfurt am Main: Campus, 1992), 57–66, here 59.

26. Baader, *Gender, Judaism and Bourgeois Culture in Germany 1800–1870*, 23.

27. Peter Beer, *Reminiscencen* (1837), quoted in Lässig, *Jüdische Wege ins Bürgertum*, 329.

28. Eduard Israel Kley, *Predigten* (1819/1820), 1. Teil, 50, quoted in Lässig, *Jüdische Wege ins Bürgertum*, 329.

29. Ibid., 329.

30. Mordechai Eliav, *Jüdische Erziehung in Deutschland im Zeitalter der Aufklärung und Emanzipation* (Münster: Waxmann, 2001), 3–16.

31. Regarding the adoption of a bourgoise habitus, see Uffa Jensen, *Gebildete Doppelgänger, Bürgerliche Juden und Protestanten im 19. Jahrhundert* (Göttingen: Vandenhoeck & Ruprecht, 2005), 61, 102.

32. See Volkov, *Das jüdische Projekt der Moderne*, 121–22.

33. Lässig, *Jüdische Wege ins Bürgertum*, 327.

34. See Kaplan, *Making of the Jewish Middle Class*, 64–69.

35. Lässig, *Jüdische Wege ins Bürgertum*, 327.

36. For a comparison with the woman's religious task according to Orthodox standards, see Rachel Biale, *Women and Jewish Law* (New York: Schocken Books, 1984).

37. Lässig, *Jüdische Wege ins Bürgertum*, 327.

38. Gillerman points out, "If Emancipation affected Jewish men and women in distinct ways, the pace and extent to which Jews adapted themselves to the demands of German society also differed according to gender-specific patterns. Because social acceptance was made contingent upon the acquisition of the basic customs, behaviors and values of German society, Jewish men and women took different paths toward, and found different means for, becoming at once fully German and distinctly Jewish. Jewish men tended to adapt to the demands of middle-class society by abandoning public religious behaviors, including the observance of Jewish dietary laws and the prohibition of work on the Sabbath. They also concerned themselves less with Jewish learning and worship than with secular education, which they pursued with unparalleled enthusiasm" (Gillerman, "Germany: 1750–1945).

39. Richarz, "Geschlechterhierarchie und Frauenarbeit seit der Vormoderne," 88–89.

40. Ibid., 89.

41. Daniel Boyarin, *Unheroic Conduct: The Rise of Heterosexuality and the Invention of the Jewish Man* (Berkeley: University of California Press, 1997), 153.

42. Lässig, *Jüdische Wege ins Bürgertum*, 328.

43. This term is used by Lässig, *Jüdische Wege ins Bürgertum*, 326. Lässig refers to Gangolf Hübinger, "Kulturprotestantismus, Bürgerkirche und liberaler Revisionismus im wilhelminischen Deutschland," in *Religion und Gesellschaft im 19. Jahrhundert*, ed. Wolfgang Schieder (Stuttgart: Klett-Cotta, 1993), 272–99.

44. The history of the Jewish sermon is interwoven in the most complex history of the emancipating Jewry of this time; see Alexander Deeg, *Predigt und Derascha. Homiletische Textlektüre im Dialog mit dem Judentum* (Göttingen: Vandenhoeck & Ruprecht, 2006), 136–161.

45. Lässig, *Jüdische Wege ins Bürgertum*, 332.

46. See also Hans Otto Horch, "Friedrich Schiller, die Juden und das Judentum," in *Aschkenas. Zeitschrift für Geschichte und Kultur der Juden*, vol. 16, ed. Hans Otto Horch, Robert Jütte, Miriam Rürup, and Markus J. Wenninger (Berlin: De Gruyter, 2007), 17–36.

47. Gotthold Salomon, in *Kanzelredner*, ed. Meyer Kayserling (1870), 212, quoted in Lässig, *Jüdische Wege ins Bürgertum*, 333.

48. Meyer Keyserling, *Kanzelredner* (1870), quoted in Simone Lässig, *Jüdische Wege ins Bürgertum*, 333.

49. Cf. Sander Gilman, *Jewish Self-hatred: Anti-semitism and the Hidden Language of the Jews* (Baltimore: Johns Hopkins University Press, 1986).

50. Volkov, *Das jüdische Projekt der Moderne*, 86–96.

51. Lässig, *Jüdische Wege ins Bürgertum*, 333.

52. Ibid., 333.

53. Ibid., 334.

54. See Deeg, *Predigt und Derascha*, 127–29; Andreas Brämer, *Judentum und religiöse Reform. Der Hamburger Israelitische Tempel 1817–1938* (Hamburg: Dölling und Galitz, 2000).

55. Lässig, *Jüdische Wege ins Bürgertum*, 334.

56. Ibid., 334.

57. Ibid., 334.

58. Richarz, "In Familie, Handel und Salon," 59. See also Julia Haarman, *Hüter der Tradition. Erinnerung und Identität im Selbstzeugnis des Pinchas Katzenellenbogen (1691–1767)* (Göttingen: Vandenhoeck & Ruprecht, 2013), 253.

59. Richarz, "In Familie, Handel und Salon," 60.

60. Ibid. From the beginning of the eighteenth century, the Jewish family began to change. The Haskalah broke down the walls of the spiritual ghetto, and men and women started taking an interest in majority culture—of a gender-specific nature. See Jacob Katz, *Aus dem Ghetto in die bürgerliche Welt. Jüdische Emanzipation 1770–1870* (Frankfurt am Main: Jüdischer Verlag, 1986), 54–69.

61. Here, Rahel Varnhagen, Henriette Herz, and Deborah Mendelssohn stand out as representatives.

62. Lässig, *Jüdische Wege ins Bürgertum*, 328.

63. Ibid., 328.

64. Ibid., 326. See also the remarkable study of Kaplan, *Making of the Jewish Middle Class* .

65. Richarz, "Geschlechterhierarchie und Frauenarbeit seit der Vormoderne," 95.

66. Lässig, *Jüdische Wege ins Bürgertum*, 328.

67. Gillerman, "Germany: 1750–1945."

68. See Michael A. Meyer, *Response to Modernity*, 3–6.

69. Shulamit Volkov, "Die Erfindung einer Tradition. Zur Entstehung des modernen Judentums in Deutschland," in *Schriften des Historischen Kollegs*, ed. Stiftung des Historischen Kollegs (München, 1992), 1–30.

70. Regarding the transformation of Jewish communities, see Michael A. Meyer, "Jüdische Gemeinden im Übergang," in *Deutsch-jüdische Geschichte in der Neuzeit 1780–1871*, ed. Michael Brenner, Stefi Jersch-Wenzel, and Michael A. Meyer (München: C.H. Beck, 1996): 96–134, here 111–34; Olaf Blaschke, "Bürgertum und Bürgerlichkeit im Spannungsfeld des neuen Konfessionalismus von den 1830 bis zu den 1930iger Jahren," in *Juden, Bürger, Deutsche: zur Geschichte von Vielfalt und Differenz 1800–1933*, ed. Andreas Gotzmann, Rainer Liedcke, and Till van Rahden (Tübingen: Mohr Siebeck, 2001), 33–66, here 46–47; Walter Grab, *Der deutsche Weg der Judenemanzipation* (München: Piper 1991), 108–33.

71. Baader, *Gender, Judaism and Bourgeois Culture in Germany 1800–1870*, 8.

72. See Kaplan, *Making of the Jewish Middle Class*, 25–41.

73. Andreas Gotzmann, "Zwischen Nation und Religion: Die deutschen Juden auf der Suche nach einer bürgerlichen Konfessionalität," in *Juden, Bürger, Deutsche: zur Geschichte von Vielfalt und Differenz 1800–1933*, ed. Andreas Gotzmann, Rainer Liedcke, and Till van Rahden (Tübingen: Mohr Siebeck, 2001), 241–62, here 254.

74. Volkov, *Das jüdische Projekt der Moderne*, 121–22; Lässig, *Jüdische Wege ins Bürgertum*, 334.

75. Kaplan, *Making of the Jewish Middle Class*, 84.

76. Lässig, *Jüdische Wege ins Bürgertum*, 328.

77. Ibid., 328.

78. Quoted in Simone Lässig, *Jüdische Wege ins Bürgertum*, 347.

79. Julius Carlebach, "The Forgotten Connection: Women and Jews in the Conflict Between Enlightenment and Romanticism," quoted in Lässig, *Jüdische Wege ins Bürgertum*, 334.

80. Lässig, *Jüdische Wege ins Bürgertum*, 349.

81. Ibid., 349.

82. Paula E. Hyman, *Gender and Assimilation in Modern Jewish History: The Roles and Representations of Women* (Seattle: University of Washington Press, 1995), 8.

83. Jewish identity and bourgeois habitus fall together, which is illustrated here: "Every Friday evening, after she lit the candles, mother blessed us. She laid her hands on our heads and said words in Hebrew. . . . A warm kiss ended this small, solemn ceremony. . . . [Afterward] we had dinner. A beautifully set table, with the Sabbath candles burning. . . . [On Saturdays] our parents always had lots of company. . . . We . . . played . . . read, and if there were enough of us . . . we read from the classic, dividing the roles [for] *Don Carlos*, the *Maiden of Orleans*, *Iphigenia* or another" (quoted in Kaplan, *Making of the Jewish Middle Class*, 3).

84. Kaplan, *Making of the Jewish Middle Class*, 69–84.

85. Lässig, *Jüdische Wege ins Bürgertum*, 351.

86. Gillerman resumes: "While middle-class status for men was to be achieved through self-improvement and education (*Bildung*), the most important determinant of middle-class respectability for women and for their husbands was her status as full-time 'priestess of the home.' Paradoxically, an important measure of specifically Jewish and middle-class acculturation was a new form of family-centered Judaism that arose out of the strong emphasis placed on the family in bourgeois culture on the one hand, and the decline in traditional Jewish religious practice on the other. The nineteenth-century bourgeois ideal for the family was a prescriptive model based on a rigid gender-based division of labor that delimited women's activities to the domestic sphere and men's activity to the 'public' arena" (Gillerman, "Germany: 1750–1945").

87. Quoted in Lässig, *Jüdische Wege ins Bürgertum*, 351.

88. Gillerman exposes a significant point regarding Jewish emancipation in general: "Yet historians have generally treated the Emancipation of the Jews as an event of universal significance for German Jewry without paying significant attention to the gendered aspects of its unfolding. After a long and often painful process, Jewish men did finally achieve full political and civil rights with the unification of Germany in 1871. In principle, if not entirely in practice, this removed most remaining legal disabilities that had prevented the full integration of male Jews into German society. But at the time of Emancipation, Jewish women—like women in general—received no such rights and remained unable to vote until 1918" (Gillerman, "Germany: 1750–1945").

BIBLIOGRAPHY

Baader, Benjamin Maria, *Gender, Judaism and Bourgeois Culture in Germany 1800–1870* (Bloomington: Indiana University Press 2016).

Biale, Rachel, *Women and Jewish Law* (New York: Schocken Books, 1984).

Blaschke, Olaf, "Bürgertum und Bürgerlichkeit im Spannungsfeld des neuen Konfessionalismus von den 1830 bis zu den 1930iger Jahren," in *Juden, Bürger, Deutsche: zur Geschichte von Vielfalt und Differenz 1800–1933*, ed. Andreas Gotzmann, Rainer Liedcke, and Till van Rahden (Tübingen: Mohr Siebeck, 2001), 33–66.

Boyarin, Daniel, *Unheroic Conduct: The Rise of Heterosexuality and the Invention of the Jewish Man* (Berkeley: University of California Press, 1997).

Brämer, Andreas, *Judentum und religiöse Reform. Der Hamburger Israelitische Tempel 1817–1938* (Hamburg: Dölling und Galitz, 2000).

Brumlik, Micha, "Gelehrte Frauen. Regina Jonas und ihre Vorgängerinnen," in *JMB Journal*, ed. Stiftung Jüdisches Museum Berlin (Berlin: Jüdisches Museum Berlin, 2014), 11–14.

de Beauvoir, Simone, *Le deuxième sexe* (Paris: Gallimard, 1949).

Deeg, Alexander, *Predigt und Derascha. Homiletische Textlektüre im Dialog mit dem Judentum* (Göttingen: Vandenhoeck & Ruprecht, 2006).

Eliav, Mordechai, *Jüdische Erziehung in Deutschland im Zeitalter der Aufklärung und Emanzipation* (Münster: Waxmann, 2001).

Epstein, I. (trans.), *The Babylonian Talmud* (London: Soncino, 1936).

Fonrobert, Charlotte Elisheva, "Frauen im Judentum," in *Handbuch zur Geschichte der Juden in Europa*, vol. 2, *Religion, Kultur, Alltag*, ed. Elke-Vera Kotowski, Julius H. Schoeps, and Hiltrud Wallenborn (Darmstadt: Primus Verlag, 2001), 79–88.

Frevert, Ute, "Bürgerliche Meisterdenker und das Geschlechterverhältnis. Konzepte, Erfahrungen, Visionen an der Wende vom 18. zum 19. Jahrhundert," in *Bürgerinnen und Bürger* (Göttingen: Vandenhoeck & Ruprecht, 1988), 17–48.

Gillerman, Sharon, "Germany: 1750–1945," in *Jewish Women: A Comprehensive Historical Encyclopedia*," March 1, 2009, Jewish Women's Archive, https://jwa.org/encyclopedia/article/germany-1750-1945).

Gilman, Sander, *Jewish Self-hatred: Anti-semitism and the Hidden Language of the Jews* (Baltimore: Johns Hopkins University Press, 1986).

Gotzmann, Andreas, "Zwischen Nation und Religion: Die deutschen Juden auf der Suche nach einer bürgerlichen Konfessionalität," in *Juden, Bürger, Deutsche: zur Geschichte von Vielfalt und Differenz 1800–1933*, ed. Andreas Gotzmann, Rainer Liedcke, and Till van Rahden (Tübingen: Mohr Siebeck, 2001), 241–62.

Grab, Walter, *Der deutsche Weg der Judenemanzipation* (München: Piper 1991).

Haarman, Julia, *Hüter der Tradition. Erinnerung und Identität im Selbstzeugnis des Pinchas Katzenellenbogen (1691–1767)* (Göttingen: Vandenhoeck & Ruprecht, 2013).

Heller, Birgit, "Gender und Religion," in *Handbuch Religionswissenschaft*, ed. Johann Figl, (Göttingen: Vandenhoeck & Ruprecht, 2003), 758–69.

Hertz, Deborah, *Jewish High Society in Old Regime Berlin* (New Haven and London: Yale University Press, 1988).

Heschel, Susannah, "The Impact of Feminist Theory on Jewish Studies," in *Modern Judaism and Historical Consciousness. Identities, Encounters, Perspectives*, ed. Andreas Gotzmann and Christian Wiese (Boston: Brill, 2007), 529–48.

Horch, Hans Otto, "Friedrich Schiller, die Juden und das Judentum," in *Aschkenas. Zeitschrift für Geschichte und Kultur der Juden*, vol. 16, ed. Hans Otto Horch, Robert Jütte, Miriam Rürup, and Markus J. Wenninger (Berlin: De Gruyter, 2007), 17–36.

Hübinger, Gangolf, "Kulturprotestantismus, *Bürgerkirche* und liberaler Revisionismus im wilhelminischen Deutschland," in *Religion und Gesellschaft im 19. Jahrhundert*, ed. Wolfgang Schieder (Stuttgart: Klett-Cotta, 1993), 272–99.

Hyman, Paula E., *Gender and Assimilation in Modern Jewish History: The Roles and Representations of Women* (Seattle: University of Washington Press, 1995).

Jensen, Uffa, *Gebildete Doppelgänger, Bürgerliche Juden und Protestanten im 19. Jahrhundert* (Göttingen: Vandenhoeck & Ruprecht, 2005).

Kaplan, Marion A., *The Making of the Jewish Middle Class: Women, Family, and Identity in Imperial Germany* (New York: Oxford University Press, 1991).

Katz, Jacob, *Aus dem Ghetto in die bürgerliche Welt. Jüdische Emanzipation 1770–1870* (Frankfurt am Main: Jüdischer Verlag, 1986).

Lässig, Simone, *Jüdische Wege ins Bürgertum. Kulturelles Kapital und sozialer Aufstieg* (Göttingen: Vandenhoeck & Ruprecht, 2004).

Lenzen, Verena, "Judentum zwischen Emanzipation, Akkulturation, Assimilation und jüdischer Renaissance," in *Integration durch Religion? Geschichtliche Befunde, gesellschaftliche Analysen, rechtliche Perspektiven*, ed. Edmund Arens, Martin Baumann, Antonius Liedhegener, Wolfgang W. Müller, and Markus Ries (Zürich: Nomos Verlag, 2014), 103–16.

Meyer, Michael A., "Jüdische Gemeinden im Übergang," in *Deutsch-jüdische Geschichte in der Neuzeit 1780–1871*, ed. Michael Brenner, Stefi Jersch-Wenzel, and Michael A. Meyer (München: C.H. Beck, 1996): 96–134.

Meyer, Michael A. *Response to Modernity: A History of the Reform Movement in Judaism* (Detroit: Wayne State University Press, 1995).

Richarz, Monika (ed.), *Jewish Life in Germany. Memoirs from Three Centuries* (Bloomington & Indianapolis: Indiana University Press, 1991).

Richarz, Monika, "Geschlechterhierarchie und Frauenarbeit in der jüdischen Geschichte," in *Deutsch-jüdische Geschichte als Geschlechtergeschichte. Studien zum 19. und 20. Jahrhundert*, ed. Kirsten Heinsohn and Stefanie Schüler-Springorum (Göttingen: Wallstein, 2006), 87–104.

Richarz, Monika, "In Familie, Handel und Salon. Jüdische Frauen vor und nach der Emanzipation der deutschen Juden," in *Frauengeschichte–Geschlechtergeschichte*, ed. Karin Hause and Heide Wunder (Frankfurt am Main: Campus, 1992), 57–66.

Sorkin, David, *The Transformation of the German Jewry, 1780–1840* (New York: Oxford University Press, 1987).

Volkov, Shulamit, *Das jüdische Projekt der Moderne* (München: C.H. Beck, 2001).

Volkov, Shulamit, "Die Erfindung einer Tradition. Zur Entstehung des modernen Judentums in Deutschland," in *Schriften des Historischen Kollegs*, ed. Stiftung des Historischen Kollegs (München, 1992), 1–30.

Wallach-Faller, Marianne, "Mirjam—Schwester unter Brüdern", in *Die Frau im Tallit. Judentum feministisch gelesen. Judentum feministisch gelesen*, ed. Doris Brodbeck and Yvonne Domhardt (Zürich: Chronos, 2000), 177–91.

Wolff, Eberhard, "Ankunft in der Moderne: Aufklärung und Reformjudentum," in *Die Geschichte der Juden in Deutschland*, ed. Arno Herzig and Cay Rademacher (Bonn: Ellert & Richter Verlag, 2008), 114–22.

Chapter Two

Patterns of Reform

Tracking Women's Changing Roles in Synagogues and Communal Life within Nineteenth-Century American and German Judaism

Karla Goldman

Tensions between traditional roles for women and changing gender expectations within modernizing societies have been a key element in shaping the historical development of patriarchal religions.[1] The response of male religious leaders to evolving identities for women speaks powerfully to their group's relationship to changing societal values. At the same time, the roles that women find and take for themselves speak to the spaces they find available at the intersection of their own group experience and the example of the surrounding culture. In terms of Jewish modernization, modes of accommodation to women's changing roles have served as important proxies for the embrace and/or rejection of the mores of the surrounding society. The place and roles offered to and adopted by women within historical American and German Judaism provide a suggestive comparison of two modernizing Jewish communities as they sought to balance historical continuity with the demands of a changing cultural environment.

Historians have long been interested in the relationship between nineteenth-century German and American Reform Judaism. In the popular imagination, German Reform is often portrayed as the primary source for American Reform Judaism. There is plenty of evidence for this: German Reform synagogue regulations were adopted almost verbatim by many early

American synagogues looking to create more decorous modes of synagogue behavior. A majority of members of many mid nineteenth-century American synagogues emigrated from German-speaking regions of Europe. Moreover, many of these same synagogues were shaped by the first generation of American rabbis from German-speaking lands, many of whom had at least some contact with the developing German Reform movement. As they arrived in American Jewish urban communities, they played an important role in helping Americanizing Jews identify modes of Jewish practice that could harmonize with their sensibilities as acculturated citizens of a modern society. As in German communities, rabbis were key players in adapting Jewish worship to the new environment and in creating a formal and organized Reform movement.[2]

Still, German and American versions of Reform Judaism reflected very different political and social environments, which resulted in different versions of Reform Jewish aspirations and practice. Examining the different ways in which German and American reformers attempted to accommodate changing societal expectations for women offers an important lens for understanding the specific parameters that shaped these different experiences of modernization. In both American and German contexts, reformers had to adapt traditional roles for women to the expectations of the culture in which they hoped to find a home. The key defining dynamic for each movement, the achievement of *Bildung* (an educated refined culture) among German Jews and respectability among American Jews, could not be realized without finding roles for women that matched the ideals and expectations of the surrounding societies.

Differences in German and American Reform redefinitions of women's roles reflect basic structural differences limned by the different cultural contexts in which they developed. In general, the voluntary and pluralistic character of the American religious community allowed for far more radical innovations than were possible in German synagogues. American synagogue leaders could appeal to whichever sector of the community they chose with innovations geared to their interests and proclivities. German synagogue communities, organized and funded under the authority of local temporal leaders, were mandated to serve the whole range of Jewish community members. To shift resources away from the control of traditionalists, Reform leaders needed to win the support of a majority of local Jewish residents, leading to a tempering of their more radical proposals.[3] The effect of this difference can be seen in innovations absent in German settings but that ultimately became common in the United States, like the removal of head coverings for men, the elimination of second-day holiday observance, and most relevantly here, the introduction of mixed seating for men and women.

In the German context, it was possible to *propose* truly radical ideas such as Sunday Sabbaths or the elimination of ritual circumcision, but it was impossible to actually *introduce* what were really just symbolic changes—like the removal of head coverings—because those practices were understood as essential markers of Jewish practice. In the United States, innovations like these usually met strong opposition when initially proposed. However, with authoritative communal leaders arguing that such change was consistent with Jewish ideals, after a few years communities were able to accept the previously rejected practices—like worship with uncovered heads or the elimination of the second day of a holiday—with few qualms.[4] Once these innovations became familiar and thus apparently acceptable, they spread rapidly, becoming almost characteristic of acculturated American Jewish practice before the era of mass Eastern European Jewish migration began in the 1880s.[5]

Adjustments in the worship space assigned to women were among the first indications of the tendency of American synagogues to diverge from European models well before other reforming innovations began emerging in the 1850s. The rapid appearance of these innovations during the colonial era reflected an American concern for female religiosity and a general emphasis on public church worship that would shape what became distinctive about American Judaism. This is not to suggest that colonial or early national American churches offered a model of gender equity. Overall, American churches remained distinctly male-led bastions. Yet, the dominant presence of women has consistently defined the American church experience from its earliest colonial inception.[6] American synagogue-goers thus found themselves in an environment where the strong presence of women in public religious settings helped to frame critical appraisals of the space assigned to women in colonial American synagogues. This negative impression found expression in the written accounts of non-Jewish visitors to American synagogues, like one describing New York's Shearith Israel in 1744, which noted that the women "of whom some were very pritty [sic], stood up in the gallery like a hen coop."[7]

Given both the centrality of public worship in colonial America and of women's place within it, the nature of and space given to women's presence in early American synagogues quickly diverged from that found in contemporaneous European synagogues. Structural adjustments appeared already in the 1763 Newport synagogue, the second synagogue built in what later became the United States, and now the oldest existing synagogue building in the country. In the Newport synagogue, women sat behind a low balustrade, free of the opaque barriers of the European sanctuaries that would have served as models for the Newport congregation's design. Despite drawing upon the traditional plan of Sephardic synagogues in Amsterdam and London, the Newport gallery displays a significant adjustment to what otherwise appears to be a traditional synagogue design. This innovation was replicated in subsequent American synagogues, including Charleston's Beth Elohim (1794), New York's second Shearith Israel building (1818), and Philadelphia's second Mikveh Israel building (1824). Notably, contemporaneous German and other European traditional synagogues retained the opaque separation barrier shown in Amsterdam and London.[8]

The modified structure of Newport's women's gallery reflected the growing synagogue presence of Jewish women as they emulated the model of church attendance of their female neighbors. It also offered a response to disapproving assessments by non-Jews, who saw in women's relegation to the gallery the suggestion of lesser religious status. For a society that saw women as paragons of religious virtue and balconies as suitable for children, servants, and slaves, seating within closed galleries positioned Jewish women in an extremely unflattering light. Moreover, it confirmed portrayals of Judaism as an exotic oriental sect, segregating women and seemingly oblivious to the religious virtue of its female members, who were thus secluded, out of view.

American Jews realized quickly that acceptance among the cultured classes required their ability to highlight the virtue of and regard for their female adherents. In keeping with this expectation, nineteenth-century American synagogue design adjusted structurally in a steady advance toward increased inclusion for women. Beginning with Newport, most American synagogues removed the grill or latticework that defined the women's galleries of most European synagogues. By mid century, the processes of Americanization led to the replacement of women's galleries with family pews. By the 1870s, sanctuaries with family pews had become almost the hallmark of Americanized synagogues.[9]

The pressure to actually reconfigure synagogues in order to properly include women never became central to German or European Reform efforts. When the Hamburg Temple, the most radical Reform effort to date, was dedicated in 1818, its open gallery offered the same women's gallery design as those found in the most traditional contemporaneous American synagogues. Like their American counterparts, many acculturating Western European Jewish communities of the second half of the nineteenth century built increasingly ornate synagogues. These buildings featured well-appointed open balconies, but they remained women's galleries, with the men of the congregation seated in decorous rows in the sanctuary below.[10] Until World War I, mixed synagogue seating in European settings remained virtually nonexistent. This is not because reformers in Germany and elsewhere were unaware of or failed to critique what they understood as woman's unequal status in Judaism. Acculturating German Jews also found it necessary to adjust Jewish female religious identities in order to conform with the bourgeois cultural expectations of the surrounding society. It was only in the United States, however, that structural changes in women's place in the synagogue became a central aspect of a broad, synagogue-centered Reform program.

Jewish leaders in German lands also felt the need to address what they described as women's "oriental" and subservient role within traditional Judaism. In 1837, Rabbi Abraham Geiger, a pioneering German reformer, pointed to the fundamental respect accorded women within the Bible in contrast to what he saw as the deplorable exclusions from public worship enshrined within Talmudic law. Geiger advocated a reconfigured Judaism in which women would feel welcomed and valued.[11] In practice, Geiger and his even more radical colleagues were constrained in the degree of reform that they could bring to their communities. Despite declines in communal authority, German Jewish communities were invested with economic and juridical authority by the state. To control communal resources, Reform leaders had to win support from the majority of local Jewish residents. But even when they gained communal authority, they still had to meet the needs of the whole community, including residents who had no sympathy for a Reform program. Thus, whatever the extreme radicalism preached by German reformers, in practice, organized Jewish life continued much as it had been. Symbolic reforms, like the removal of head coverings or the abolition of women's sections, never came to the fore.[12] In the United States, competing congregations were free to alter their practices in order to appeal to those seeking less traditional (or, in some instances, more traditional) worship, without needing to worry about the wants of every Jewish resident.

This contrast between the theoretical radicalism of German thinkers and the practical reform possible in the United States is well illustrated by the contrasting German and American careers of Rabbi David Einhorn. In his address to the Third Assembly of German Rabbis meeting in Breslau in 1846, Einhorn, then a young rabbi in Birkenfeld, equated Judaism's treatment of women with political discrimination against Jews. In both cases, he suggested, rhetorical affirmations of equality were useless: "A mere theoretical recognition of women's disenfranchisement" gave "them as little satisfaction as the Israelites are given in civic matters."[13] Like German Jews, women had "received assurances of their capabilities without however being permitted to become emancipated."[14] In response, Einhorn called upon the assembly to declare "the complete religious equality of the female sex."[15] He demanded practical reforms that would include counting women in a minyan, omitting traditional prayers that disparaged women, equal educational opportunities, and assigning women the same rights and obligations as men.[16]

Einhorn's radical platform for women was scheduled to be taken up at the 1847 rabbis meeting, which was never convened. It would take another twelve years and a move to a congregation in Baltimore before Einhorn would again advocate publicly for equal rights and duties for women, condemning the "gallery cage" of the traditional synagogue. In the United States, Einhorn was able to translate his words into action, as his congregation soon brought women down from the women's gallery.[17]

Nineteenth-century German Reform synagogues never incorporated the kind of shifts in women's place and status that led to the reconfigured physical structure of acculturated American synagogues, but they nonetheless also became sites for reconfigured public religious identities for women. German reformers introduced stylistic and programmatic changes meant to attract or include women in ways that were substantively different from practices found in traditional synagogues. Historian Benjamin Baader points to the introduction of mixed-gender choirs and confirmation services for boys and girls as by-products of an effort to change Jewish culture from one in which male synagogue members acted as the sole protagonists to ones in which both men and women served (as in acculturated American synagogues) as relatively passive but now equal members of a congregational audience.[18]

German Jews, hoping to demonstrate that they were worthy not just of social acceptance, but also of political and civil rights, needed Jewish women to be able to show that they were worthy carriers and transmitters of public and domestic culture. Their ability to represent appropriate models of domestic piety was more important than their roles within public worship. As the synagogue declined in importance in the lives of many acculturating Jews, the domestic sphere became an imperative site for adjustment to the expectations of non-Jewish society and culture. German bourgeois society demanded that women serve as moral exemplars and the prime transmitters of religious values. Even if traditional Judaism assigned the responsibilities of religious education to fathers, the ability of mothers to take on this role allowed German Jewish women to connect their families to the emerging values of *Bildung* (the acquisition of culture through education) and bourgeois domesticity. As German Jewish men increasingly absented themselves from traditional spheres of worship, Jewish women took on more and more responsibility for their families' religious identity through their domestic duties and responsibility for child-rearing.[19]

Visibility for women within the synagogue was important to the process of overcoming the impression that Judaism represented a backward and "oriental" religious culture. But *the* essential site for constructing bourgeois Jewish female religiosity turned out to be the home. There, Jewish women could turn Jewish practice, ritual, and identity into solid emblems of bourgeois respectability. Historians Baader, Marion Kaplan, and Paula Hyman all present recollections from nineteenth-century German Jews sharing warm memories of tranquil homes where the mothers served as the central and virtuous purveyors of Jewish observance and practice. The ability of mothers to elevate and beautify the home while filling it with the clear bourgeois values of refinement, *Gemuetlichkeit* (hominess), and serenity became much more important than proper halakhic observance of Jewish law.[20]

Nineteenth-century German churches, like their American counterparts, became homes to increasing numbers of female congregants. As in the United States, nineteenth-century German society also developed a cultural ideal for women in which religious piety was fundamental. So, we might have expected that women's presence in German synagogues would have approached or exceeded the number of male congregants in attendance, as was the case in the United States. But despite the efforts of German synagogue leaders to reconfigure the practice and ethos of the synagogue to make it more welcoming and comfortable for women, we do not see the same shift in numbers or proportion of men and women present. Nor do we see any fundamental structural reorientation of the German synagogue to incorporate women's physical presence.[21] Our awareness that redefinitions of traditional Jewish female religiosity focused *on domestic Judaism in German lands* and *on public synagogue Judaism in the United States* alerts us to the distinctive framing contexts that shaped American and German Judaism.

Although German synagogues became more accessible to women, they did not become major sites for female religiosity. Given that many German churches maintained separate seating (on the same floor) of men and women, it is not surprising that German Jews were less likely to challenge the convention of separate seating. Still, if the synagogue had been seen as more important to Jewish women's religious identities, there might have been more challenge to the sequestering of women in synagogue balconies.[22]

As has been suggested, the lack of structural changes related to women's place in German synagogues may have reflected the fact that German synagogues were more resistant to change than were American synagogues. The introduction of family pews as seen in the United States would have seemed like too radical a departure in a setting intended to serve the whole community. It is likely, however, that the main distinction between American and German constructions of Jewish women's roles resulted from the differing salience of public worship in the two societies. As nineteenth-century German society moved in an increasingly secular direction, the church became less central relative to other societal institutions—becoming less important as a site to mark the attainment of bourgeois respectability. Despite attempts to adjust to the modern environment, the German synagogue receded in importance. For Jewish men, this led to a withdrawal of men from the traditional male spheres of Jewish life centered in the now devalued synagogue and study hall.[23]

The United States, of course, defined itself from the outset by its separation of church and state. Thus, the emergence of secular institutions did not necessarily challenge the pervasiveness of religious culture or imply a decline of religious institutions as it may have in Germany. While Americans also developed influential models of religious domesticity, the dominant expression of female religiosity remained in the church and in church-based institutions like temperance groups and missionary societies.[24] Structures of public worship remained the essential site for the formulation and expression of appropriate and expected female religious identities.

Women came to dominate American synagogue attendance in a fashion that found no parallel in European settings. It is true that the fuller integration of women into the American sanctuary took place in a setting where, as in German synagogues, the religious officiant was becoming more prominent and the role of the congregant was receding into a passive presence. Still, in the United States, even women's passive presence resulted in transformations that included the physical reconfiguration of the synagogue, the redefinition of Jewish female religious identity, and the end of male numeric dominance among regular synagogue worshippers.

Comparison of the ways in which Jewish communities adjusted to meet societal expectations for bourgeois respectability and identity illuminates both the centrality of negotiating appropriate roles for women within this process and the distinctive paths of American and German Reform Judaism. Such a comparison suggests that while their cultural background was important to how German Jews in America defined their Jewish identities, they were ultimately more attuned to the expectations of the society in which they lived than to any shared universal understanding of what the reform of Judaism should entail.

The analysis above suggests that the differing loci of Jewish women's religious presence in the United States and in German-speaking lands mainly reflected attempts to accommodate prevailing societal expectations for women's presence and behavior. Although not precisely equivalent to the religious culture of bourgeois Christian women, changing religious roles for Jewish women represented attempts to emulate the evolving values and behaviors for women they saw manifested in the surrounding society. In both settings—with Jewish communities deeply invested in seeing women take on roles appropriate to the society in which they hoped to take part—it was the relative centrality of the church or synagogue as a setting for female religiosity that appears to have defined the different trajectories and settings for Jewish women's religious presence and identity.

Beyond the synagogue and home, however, there was another important site for the development of a modernizing religious identity where patterns for Jewish women appear to have significantly diverged from that of bourgeois Protestant women. In looking at Jewish women's engagement in voluntary associations, we need to attend to differences both between that of American and German Jewish women and between Jewish women and non-Jewish women in each setting. Benjamin Baader points to the existence of more than 160 Jewish women's associations between 1745 and 1870 as one of the salient markers of the German Jewish community's transition from traditional patterns of religious life. Particularly striking is his observation that these mutual aid and charitable societies emerged not in imitation of German models of female associations, but according to a pattern established by Jewish men's organizations that began to form once prayer and study no longer constituted the core of male communal associational life.[25]

Baader's observations on the associational life of German Jewish women provide a critical context for understanding the emergence of women's groups in the formative American Jewish communities of the first half of the nineteenth century. It is easy to see these U.S. groups, which often used the title of Ladies' Hebrew Benevolent Society, as merely emulating an American female culture of denominationally-centered benevolence. The most conspicuous early examples of American Jewish women's organizations, like the Female Hebrew Benevolent Society (1819) and other groups founded by an activist group of acculturated Philadelphia Jewish women, do appear to have modeled themselves upon local Christian denomination-centered women's organizations.[26] Yet, many subsequent benevolent societies created around the country in the mid-nineteenth century by more recent immigrants from German lands seem more evocative of parallel organizations in Germany than of local models. Thus, the same women who formally constituted themselves as the Female Hebrew Benevolent Society of the City of Norfolk in 1867 were also known to themselves as the Israelitish Frauen Verein (Society of Israelite Women). Organizations like this responded to expectations framed both by American female association life and by those that may have been formed in German lands.[27]

Despite the relative sparseness of existing archival material documenting the existence of these societies, the shadow of their presence can be clearly seen in a number of communities and in the records of many male-led synagogues that often noted the receipt of loans of hundreds of dollars given by the ladies' benevolent societies associated with their congregations. Such funds were commonly used to secure building lots or begin synagogue construction, often at interest rates of 8–10 percent. Such societies were effective fundraisers in many communities, drawing upon not only monthly dues but also receipts from public balls that they sponsored.[28] They used their funds to assist congregations as well as to offer aid to needy, sick, or grieving Jews. But most importantly, the societies served as mutual aid societies for their members, on a model similar to those that Baader describes in German communities, as well as those seen in the mutual aid societies created by male Jewish immigrants. Members who fell ill could expect nursing visits from fellow members, as well as weekly payments to help with their care and the sustenance of their families. Those beyond hope could know that members of their society would watch over them when they died, staying with them until burial as was the traditional Jewish practice.[29]

Although such societies would have played an appreciably different social and economic role in the lives of recent immigrants to the United States than for those who lived among more grounded institutions of religious authority in Europe, it does not appear that their essential purposes and frameworks differed appreciably between American and German communities. Still, the trajectory of these institutions evidenced both marked parallels and variations in the different national settings. Sometimes even when the trajectory may appear similar, the explanation for parallel shifts may differ. Here too, it is important to attend to the ways that the organizational patterns of Jewish women's lives may have differed from those of non-Jewish women in their communities.

Baader illustrates that Jewish women's societies arose earlier than and independently of Catholic and Protestant women societies in German communities. He finds that they were characterized by a stronger tradition of female leadership than the Christian societies, which featured greater degrees of male participation and oversight. By 1870, however, most Jewish women's organizations had lost their independent quality or faded away. In many cities, women turned to men and the local Jewish community to take over management of their organizations. The male-run communal institutions, backed as they were by state-sanctioned control over Jewish communal life, were well positioned to push women out of positions of leadership in many of the charitable areas that they had shaped. By the 1870s, women who had been vitally engaged workers in addressing the welfare and needs of their community and co-religionists were relegated to the position of bystanders, now considered *Ehrendamen*, "honorary ladies," in the movements they had pioneered.[30]

Baader suggests that the diluted presence of Jewish women's organizations in civil Jewish life was a function of acculturation to the German bourgeois values of *Bildung*, or domestic piety. As bourgeois domesticity became more central to acceptable German identities, female public leadership within associational life became more problematic and difficult to sustain. In some communities, it became harder to find women willing to serve in public roles; in others, women found themselves under pressure from male community leaders to yield funds and direction to centralized male authorities. As an increasingly precise set of bourgeois values designated public space as male, independent public identities for women and women's groups became less tenable and went into retreat. Going forward, women were able to operate publicly only on the basis of distinctive feminine qualities, which had not been part of the initial rationale for the creation of female mutual aid societies or charitable work.[31]

A similar pattern of diminution also characterized Jewish women's organizations in the United States, though for different reasons. Many of the women's organizations such as Ladies' Hebrew Benevolent Societies that had been associated with congregations seemed to fade into irrelevance after the Civil War or disappear completely. Extant records of Ladies' Hebrew Benevolent Societies and similar groups that continued into or were founded during the 1860s, 1870s, and early 1880s portray associations lacking a clear sense of purpose or confidence around their communal role. There are likely many groups whose activities remain hidden to us because their records were not preserved, but the outlines of their impact on the Jewish community are not so readily apparent as they were in the pre–Civil War era. We can trace women's presence *within* their synagogue pews as well as their role in many successful fundraising efforts in response to the requests of male leaders. Their collective identity as public actors, however, actually seems to have shrunk as the Jewish communities after mid century proved increasingly successful at acculturation and Americanization. Given the rise of strong national organizations among Christian women during this period, the weak presence of Jewish women's organizations and collective identity is especially curious.[32]

While emerging bourgeois values in Germany may have made female associational life less attractive overall, in the United States Jewish women's retreat from civil religious life came just as Christian women began elaborating a vital institutional life, which increasingly shaped the agenda of their churches and communities. These local organizations, in turn, coalesced quickly into broader regional and national organizations, which buttressed influential public identities for Christian women. In particular, woman-powered temperance and missionary movements were the most influential, most vital, grassroots movement in the country in the decades after the Civil War.[33] Their example raises important questions about why Jewish women's associational life did not follow the model provided by those whom, we generally assume, Jewish women hoped to emulate socially and aesthetically.

The early women's societies in American Jewish life proved a useful vehicle for the broader effort to replicate traditional models of Jewish life while also adapting to the structures and values of contemporary American middle-class society. In the movement of women from the gallery to the family pew, we saw that traditional structures sometimes had to yield in order to accommodate emerging understandings of appropriate American configurations of female identity, place, and worth. Ironically, perhaps, it was this Americanizing transfer of women from the gallery to the pew that undermined the ability of Jewish women to create associations that could reflect their strong Americanized collective voice in a manner akin to that of Christian women.

We have already seen how the growing centrality of the synagogue in Americanizing versions of Judaism led to increased visibility and presence for women—ultimately leading to the restructuring of the synagogue itself with the introduction of family pews. An American Jewish Reform movement emerged as congregational leaders succeeded in creating synagogues able to attract adherence and support from upwardly mobile Americanizing Jews. Yet, the Reform movement's success in creating settings for elegant worship yielded a curious result. By privileging the synagogue at the expense of other institutions or expressions of Jewish life, American Jewish communities grew in the absence of firmly grounded traditional institutions of Jewish practice and observance. Communities built around the centrality of the synagogue focused more on the presentation and style of worship and less upon fostering a community engaged in religious life. Thus, it is not surprising that women would shift their religious expression toward synagogue attendance and away from work that fostered Jewish practice and community outside of the congregation.

As the network of communal and associational life around the synagogue weakened, women lost access to a realm of public Jewish life that they could shape themselves. Despite the advance to public religious identity seemingly offered by the family pew, synagogue lay and religious leadership remained exclusively male. This is not to say that Jewish women were inactive during this period. Most of their post–Civil War communal activity focused on raising money—often with great success. But such funds were quickly turned over to male organizing bodies. They might raise thousands of dollars but still lack sustained purpose or any authority over the proceeds associated with their work. To the extent that Jewish women had been active in an organized way outside of synagogues in addressing the needs of the poor or vulnerable in their community, women's organizations were often subsumed into federated or united efforts to centralize Jewish charities in different cities. Even the mutual aid benefit and energy of the early societies receded as families became more prosperous, with less need for the small-scale safety net that such organizations provided.[34]

As congregational energies became more and more centered on the sanctuary, nonworship activities weakened. As male leaders sought to bring centralized efficiency to communal benevolent work, women lost their own institutional base outside of the synagogue. Women did not have the cross-city networks to form secular Jewish organizations that could match the vitality of the B'nai B'rith, with its provision of extra-synagogal communal space for men.[35] Nor, given the historically male institutional structure of the synagogue, were they able to find roles within synagogue leadership. It is important, of course as well, that the causes that were galvanizing so many American women were not ones that Jews could easily embrace. Both temperance and Christian missionary work forwarded Christian values and identity in a manner that did not easily translate into activities for Jewish women. Thus, even as American Jews became more successful in their campaign for prosperous American identities, women were left with little to do as Jews beyond sit and rise as members of the congregation.

In the United States, this story shifted in the late 1880s with the emergence of a strong phalanx of empowered Jewish women's organizations. The turning point in Jewish women's activism hinged on the arrival of large numbers of impoverished and vulnerable Jewish immigrants beginning in the early 1880s. The swift local, then national, rise of women's groups to meet these immigrants' needs began to change the equation for acculturated Jewish women. Once these women began to organize, they quickly found a lot to do. In fact, their work rapidly spread beyond the needs of immigrants, leading to the organization of the first truly national Jewish women's organizations and an infusion of women's energies into Jewish communal life.[36] Once they found a *Jewish* cause for women's work, they had a platform upon which they could begin to emulate their activist Christian counterparts, transforming Jewish philanthropy, synagogue life, and American Jewish community in the process.

What are we to make ultimately of the similarities and contrasts that emerge in examining Jewish women's roles in the context of American and German experience? Both settings offer examples of communities deeply invested in the project of finding workable models for bourgeois identity—a project in which women's roles and behaviors became particularly sensitive markers of gentility. Looking across the two national cultures, it is striking to see the similarity in patterns of activism and decline in the creation of Jewish women's organizations in both the United States and Germany even if the influences shaping these patterns seem to have been quite different.

While German women's associations emerged from the model of male associations created within a Jewish context, the American version found its basis in the pattern of German Jewish women's groups as well as in the example of American Christian associations. The decline of the German Jewish women's societies accelerated in tandem with the rising centrality of bourgeois domestic piety as Jewish women accommodated to the model of their non-Jewish counterparts. The relative inactivity of American Jewish women's societies after the Civil War, by contrast, reflected the barriers that Jewish women faced in embodying the ideals for female character and behavior manifested in middle-class American. They receded from view in a manner contrary to their aspirations for acculturation. They were only able to embrace a more activist identity when they were able to identify suitably Jewish causes that could justify their public activism in Jewish philanthropic and institutional work.[37]

As an American Jewish historian, my explanations for the behavior and identities of American Jews too often point to efforts to emulate or adapt to bourgeois Christian models and behavior. Study of women's nineteenth-century organizational life offers an intriguing space in which to engage the complications of assimilation in societies that were, at once, both accepting and excluding. It also helps us identify the key institutional differences that may have yielded different versions of Jewish acculturation in these different cultural milieus. This comparative examination enables us to see that in both American and German settings, the distinctive historical experience of Jewish communities shaped the way they interacted with the surrounding culture.

Shifting identities for women in the Jewish communities of Germany and the United States emerged as part of a broad negotiation with the expectations of bourgeois culture as they attempted to refit Jewish life to a post-traditional world. While they encountered differing cultural forces, the impulses influencing the response of these Jewish communities were quite similar. Both German and American Jews had a deep investment in finding roles for women that would be suited to the broader societies in which they found themselves. The changing patterns of American Jewish and German Jewish women's organizational life in the nineteenth century suggest that attempts to respond to the breakdown of the traditional Jewish social order and the demands of acculturation did not always result in emulation of the surrounding society, even among those most seeking inclusion.

There is still much to explore in the emergence of public identities for American and German Jewish women, but, as we have seen, such study can illuminate how vital communal concerns like the centrality and architecture of public worship, aspirations to *Bildung* and respectability, and the imperatives of bourgeois domesticity could become determinative in shaping distinctive national expressions of Jewish worship, community, and culture.

NOTES

1. The first half of this chapter draws upon an essay published as "Beyond the Synagogue Gallery? Women's Changing Roles in Nineteenth-Century American and German Reform Judaism," in *American Jewry: Transcending the European Experience?*, ed. Christian Wiese and Cornelia Wilhelm (New York: Bloomsbury Academic, 2017), 159–68.

2. On regulations, see, for example, synagogue regulations proposed in Bene Israel Trustee minutes, February 12, 1848, Cincinnati, Ohio—Bene Israel Collection, Collection #24, American Jewish Archives, Cincinnati, Ohio (AJA); B'nai Yeshurun minutes, February 10, 1848; February 27, 1848, Cincinnati, Ohio—Bene Yeshurun Collection, Collection #62, American Jewish Archives, Cincinnati, Ohio. Much of the content and language of the plans considered by these congregations echoes the *Synagogenordnungen*, or plans for synagogue regulation, collected by Jakob J. Petuchowski in *Prayerbook Reform in Europe: The Liturgy of European Liberal and Reform Judaism* (New York: World Union for Progressive Judaism, 1968), 105–27. On places of origin, see Alan Silverstein, *Alternatives to Assimilation: The Response of Reform Judaism to American Culture, 1840–1930* (Hanover: Brandeis University Press by University Press of New England, 1994), 12–13; Hasia Diner, *The Jews of the United States, 1654–2000* (Berkeley: University of California Press, 2004); and Avraham Barkai, *Branching Out: German-Jewish Immigrants to the United States* (New York: Homes & Meier, 1994). On rabbinic authority, see Leon Jick, *The Americanization of the Synagogue, 1820–1870* (Hanover: Brandeis University Press, by the University Press of New England, 1976); Karla Goldman, "The Path to Reform Judaism: An Examination of Religious Leadership in Cincinnati, 1841–1855," *American Jewish History* 90 (2002): 35–50; and Zev Eleff, *Who Rules the Synagogue? Religious Authority and the Formation of American Judaism* (New York: Oxford University Press, 2016).

3. See Robert Liberles, "Emancipation and the Structure of the Jewish Community in the Nineteenth Century," *Leo Baeck Institute Year Book* 31 (1986): 61–65; Max Wiener, *Abraham Geiger and Liberal Judaism: The Challenge of the Nineteenth Century* (Cincinnati: Hebrew Union College Press, 1981), 89.

4. For a discussion of one evolving consideration of banning head covering during worship, see Jonathan D. Sarna and Karla Goldman, "From Synagogue-Community to Citadel of Reform: The History of K. K. Bene Israel (Rockdale Temple) in Cincinnati, Ohio," in *American Congregations*, vol. 1, *Portraits of Twelve Religious Communities*, ed. James P. Wind and James W. Lewis (Chicago: University of Chicago Press, 1995), 177.

5. Karla Goldman, *Beyond the Synagogue Gallery: Finding a Place for Women in American Judaism* (Cambridge: Harvard University Press, 2000), 132–33, 172–73.

6. Ann Braude, "Women's History *Is* American Religious History," in *Retelling U.S. Religious History*, ed. Thomas Tweed (Berkeley: University of California Press, 1997), 87–107.

7. Quoted in David de Sola Pool and Tamar de Sola Pool, *An Old Faith in a New World: Portrait of Shearith Israel, 1654–1954* (New York: Columbia University Press, 1955), 453.

8. Goldman, *Beyond the Synagogue Gallery*, 40–46.

9. Goldman, *Beyond the Synagogue Gallery*, 129–33; Jonathan Sarna, "The Debate Over Mixed Seating in the American Synagogue," in *The American Synagogue: A Sanctuary Transformed*, ed. Jack Wertheimer (Cambridge: Cambridge University Press, 1987), 363–93.

10. Benjamin M. Baader, *Gender, Judaism, and Bourgeois Culture in Germany, 1800–1870* (Bloomington: Indiana University Press, 2006), 152–53; Carol Herselle Krinsky, *Synagogues of Europe: Architecture, History, Meaning* (Mineola: Dover Publications, 1985), 63, 279, 284, 299, 416.

11. Abraham Geiger, "Die Stellung des weiblichen Geschlechtes in dem Judenthume unserer Zeit," *Wissenschaftliche Zeitschrift für jüdische Theologie* 3 (1837): 1–14.

12. Robert Liberles, *Religious Conflict in Social Context: The Resurgence of Orthodox Judaism in Frankfurt Am Main, 1838–1877* (Westport: Greenwood Press, 1985), 165–72.

13. David Einhorn, quoted in *The Rise of Reform Judaism: A Sourcebook of Its European Origins*, ed. W. Gunther Plaut (New York: World Union for Progressive Judaism, 1963), 253–55.

14. Ibid.

15. Ibid.

16. Ibid.

17. David Einhorn, "Predigt vom Herausgeber dieser Blätter gehalten im Tempel der Har-Sinai-Gemeinde," *Sinai* 3 (February 1858): 824; David Einhorn, "Über Familiensitze in den Synagogen," *Sinai* 6 (August 1861): 205–7.

18. Baader, *Gender, Judaism, and Bourgeois Culture in Germany*, 146; Goldman, *Beyond the Synagogue Gallery*, 133–34.

19. See Marion A. Kaplan, *The Making of the Jewish Middle Class: Women, Family and Identity in Imperial Germany* (New York: Oxford University Press, 1991); Paula E. Hyman, *Gender and Assimilation in Modern Jewish History: The Roles and Representation of Women* (Seattle: University of Washington Press, 1995).

20. See especially Baader, *Gender, Judaism, and Bourgeois Culture*, 212–16.

21. Baader, *Gender, Judaism, and Bourgeois Culture*, 152–53.

22. Ibid.

23. Baader, *Gender, Judaism, and Bourgeois Culture*, 212, 216–19.

24. See, for example, Patricia R. Hill, *The World Their Household: The American Woman's Foreign Mission Movement and Cultural Transformation, 1870–1920* (Ann Arbor: University of Michigan Press, 1985); Peggy Pascoe, *Relations of Rescue: The Search for Female Moral Authority in the American West, 1874–1939* (New York: Oxford University Press, 1990); Anne Firor Scott, *Natural Allies: Women's Associations in American History* (Urbana: University of Illinois Press, 1992); and Ruth Bordin, *Women and Temperance: The Quest for Power and Liberty, 1873–1900* (Philadelphia: Temple University Press, 1984). On American religious domesticity, see Colleen McDannell, *The Christian Home in Victorian America, 1840–1900* (Bloomington: Indiana University Press, 1986).

25. Baader, *Gender, Judaism, and Bourgeois Culture*, 161–62.

26. Goldman, *Beyond the Synagogue Gallery*, 60–61; see also Diane Ashton, *Rebecca Gratz: Women and Judaism in Antebellum America* (Detroit: Wayne State University Press, 1997), on Philadelphia's Female Hebrew Benevolent Society, Hebrew Sunday School, and Jewish Foster Home.

27. Goldman, *Beyond the Synagogue Gallery*, 64, 233 (see note 93). The society's name deviates from standard German and may reflect an Americanized German.

28. Goldman, *Beyond the Synagogue Gallery*, 64–67.

29. Baader, *Gender, Judaism, and Bourgeois Culture*, 167–71; Goldman, *Beyond the Synagogue Gallery*, 64.

30. Baader, *Gender, Judaism, and Bourgeois Culture*, 171–74; Benjamin Baader, "Jewish Women in Germany Between Community and Domesticity," Association for Jewish Studies conference paper, December 1998.

31. Marion A. Kaplan documents the reemergence of a powerful German Jewish women's movement in *The Jewish Feminist Movement in Germany: The Campaigns of the Jüdischer Frauenbund, 1904–1938* (Westport: Greenwood Press, 1979).

32. Goldman, *Beyond the Synagogue Gallery*, 137–49.

33. On their role, see for example, Bordin, *Women and Temperance*; Hill, *The World Their Household*; Edward J. Blum, *Reforging the White Republic: Race, Religion, and American Nationalism, 1865–1898* (Baton Rouge: Louisiana State University Press, 2005).

34. Goldman, *Beyond the Synagogue Gallery*, 139–42, 147.

35. Cornelia Wilhelm details the rapid growth of the male fraternal order the Independent Order of the B'nai B'rith (founded in 1843). She also details the related organization, the Independent Order of True Sisters (founded in 1846), but makes clear that the True Sisters grew in a much more limited fashion in membership and chapters, without the kind of impact or salience that the B'nai B'rith achieved. Cornelia Wilhelm, *The Independent Orders of B'nai B'rith and True Sisters: Pioneers of a New Jewish Identity, 1843–1914* (Detroit: Wayne State University Press, 2011).

36. Goldman, *Beyond the Synagogue Gallery*, 175–99.

37. Large numbers of young Eastern European Jewish immigrant female workers took a leading role in sparking a more activist U.S. labor movement in the early twentieth century. Among more acculturated women whose families had a longer history in the United States, engagement in Jewish communal work was often a necessary springboard for engagement in broader social concerns. On Eastern European Jewish women activists, see Susan Glenn, *Daughters of the Shtetl: Life and Labor in the Immigrant Generation* (Ithaca: Cornell University Press, 1990); and Annelise Orleck, *Common Sense and a Little Fire: Women and Working-Class Politics in the United States, 1900–1965* (Chapel Hill: University of North Carolina Press, 1995). For the institutional basis of the activism of more acculturated women, see Melissa R. Klapper, *Ballots, Babies, and Banners of Peace: American Jewish Women's Activism, 1890–1940* (New York: New York University Press, 2013).

BIBLIOGRAPHY

Ashton, Diane, *Rebecca Gratz: Women and Judaism in Antebellum America* (Detroit: Wayne State University Press, 1997).

Baader, Benjamin M., *Gender, Judaism, and Bourgeois Culture in Germany, 1800–1870* (Bloomington: Indiana University Press, 2006).

Barkai, Avraham, *Branching Out: German-Jewish Immigrants to the United States* (New York: Homes & Meier, 1994).

Blum, Edward J., *Reforging the White Republic: Race, Religion, and American Nationalism, 1865–1898* (Baton Rouge: Louisiana State University Press, 2005).

Bordin, Ruth, *Women and Temperance: The Quest for Power and Liberty, 1873–1900* (Philadelphia: Temple University Press, 1984).

Braude, Ann, "Women's History *Is* American Religious History," in *Retelling U.S. Religious History*, ed. Thomas Tweed (Berkeley: University of California Press), 87–107.

De Sola Pool, David and Tamar, *An Old Faith in a New World: Portrait of Shearith Israel, 1654–1954* (New York: Columbia University Press, 1955).

Diner, Hasia, *The Jews of the United States, 1654–2000* (Berkeley: University of California Press, 2004).

Einhorn, David, "Über Familiensitze in den Synagogen," *Sinai* 6 (August 1861): 205–7.

Einhorn, David, "Predigt vom Herausgeber dieser Blätter gehalten im Tempel der Har-Sinai-Gemeinde," *Sinai* 3 (February 1858): 824.

Eleff, Zev, *Who Rules the Synagogue? Religious Authority and the Formation of American Judaism* (New York: Oxford University Press, 2016).

Geiger, Abraham, "Die Stellung des weiblichen Geschlechtes in dem Judenthume unserer Zeit," *Wissenschaftliche Zeitschrift für jüdische Theologie* 3 (1837): 1–14.

Glenn, Susan, *Daughters of the Shtetl: Life and Labor in the Immigrant Generation* (Ithaca: Cornell University Press, 1990).

Goldman, Karla, "The Path to Reform Judaism: An Examination of Religious Leadership in Cincinnati, 1841–1855," *American Jewish History* 90 (2002): 35–50.

Goldman, Karla, *Beyond the Synagogue Gallery: Finding a Place for Women in American Judaism* (Cambridge: Harvard University Press, 2000).

Hill, Patricia R., *The World Their Household: The American Woman's Foreign Mission Movement and Cultural Transformation, 1870–1920* (Ann Arbor: University of Michigan Press, 1985).

Hyman, Paula E., *Gender and Assimilation in Modern Jewish History: The Roles and Representation of Women* (Seattle: University of Washington Press, 1995).

Jick, Leon, *The Americanization of the Synagogue, 1820–1870* (Hanover: Brandeis University Press, by the University Press of New England, 1976).

Kaplan, Marion A., *The Making of the Jewish Middle Class: Women, Family and Identity in Imperial Germany* (New York: Oxford University Press, 1991).

Kaplan, Marion A., *The Jewish Feminist Movement in Germany: The Campaigns of the Jüdischer Frauenbund, 1904–1938* (Westport: Greenwood Press, 1979).

Klapper, Melissa R., *Ballots, Babies, and Banners of Peace: American Jewish Women's Activism, 1890–1940* (New York: New York University Press, 2013).

Krinsky, Carol Herselle, *Synagogues of Europe: Architecture, History, Meaning* (Mineola: Dover Publications, 1985).

Liberles, Robert, "Emancipation and the Structure of the Jewish Community in the Nineteenth Century," *Leo Baeck Institute Year Book* 31 (1986): 61–65.

Liberles, Robert, *Religious Conflict in Social Context: The Resurgence of Orthodox Judaism in Frankfurt Am Main, 1838–1877* (Westport: Greenwood Press, 1985).

McDannell, Colleen, *The Christian Home in Victorian America, 1840–1900* (Bloomington: Indiana University Press, 1986).

Orleck, Annelise, *Common Sense and a Little Fire: Women and Working-Class Politics in the United States, 1900–1965* (Chapel Hill: University of North Carolina Press, 1995).

Pascoe, Peggy, *Relations of Rescue: The Search for Female Moral Authority in the American West, 1874–1939* (New York: Oxford University Press, 1990).

Petuchowski, Jakob J., *Prayerbook Reform in Europe: The Liturgy of European Liberal and Reform Judaism* (New York: World Union for Progressive Judaism, 1968).

Plaut, W. Gunther (ed.), *The Rise of Reform Judaism: A Sourcebook of Its European Origins* (New York: World Union for Progressive Judaism, 1963).

Sarna, Jonathan D., and Goldman, Karla, "From Synagogue-Community to Citadel of Reform: The History of K. K. Bene Israel (Rockdale Temple) in Cincinnati, Ohio," in *American*

Congregations, vol. 1, *Portraits of Twelve Religious Communities*, ed. James P. Wind and James W. Lewis (Chicago: University of Chicago Press, 1995), 159–220.

Sarna, Jonathan, "The Debate Over Mixed Seating in the American Synagogue," in *The American Synagogue: A Sanctuary Transformed*, ed. Jack Wertheimer (Cambridge: Cambridge University Press, 1987), 363–93.

Scott, Anne Firor, *Natural Allies: Women's Associations in American History* (Urbana: University of Illinois Press, 1992).

Silverstein, Alan, *Alternatives to Assimilation: The Response of Reform Judaism to American Culture, 1840–1930* (Hanover: Brandeis University Press by University Press of New England, 1994).

Wiener, Max, *Abraham Geiger and Liberal Judaism: The Challenge of the Nineteenth Century* (Cincinnati: Hebrew Union College Press, 1981).

Wilhelm, Cornelia, *The Independent Orders of B'nai B'rith and True Sisters: Pioneers of a New Jewish Identity, 1843–1914* (Detroit: Wayne State University Press, 2011).

Chapter Three

Women Students at the Berlin Hochschule für die Wissenschaft des Judentums

Esther Seidel

Scholars have largely examined and identified the historical and philosophical forces prevalent in Germany during the nineteenth century that, after having brought about a *Wissenschaft des Judentums* (a scholarly investigation into Judaism at large in all its various disciplines), eventually led to the establishment of the first rabbinical seminaries in Europe. Although, according to Richard Schaeffler, "*Wissenschaft des Judentums* is as old as Judaism itself," it was in its particular German understanding of *Wissenschaft* a specific product of nineteenth-century German *Geistesgeschichte*.[1] In this essay, I will briefly discuss the careers of eight pioneering women who studied at the renowned Hochschule für die Wissenschaft des Judentums in Berlin.

Since its foundation in 1872, the Hochschule für die Wissenschaft des Judentums in Berlin was a groundbreaking institution of academic excellence in all the disciplines of *Wissenschaft des Judentums* and the forerunner of all subsequent Jewish studies. During its seventy flourishing years, until it was closed by the Nazis in 1942, it brought forth some of the most eminent Jewish scholars of their age. It also recruited and trained rabbis who have left us a unique heritage of Jewish and general scholarship, combining the highest ideals of the nineteenth-century *Wissenschaft* with a deep love of their Jewish traditions. A spiritual center of Liberal Judaism, it also attracted numerous women students to its doors, who aspired to become teachers of religion. To put their achievements in context, let us first have a look at the historical development.

The Enlightenment had brought the Jews the promise of full economic and political integration into society. In Germany, this integration proceeded step by step, or rather by steps forward and then back, because rights were given and then taken away. Nonetheless, the German Jews succeeded by advancing themselves through *Bildung* (formation) and *Wissenschaft* (scholarship). The first generation of Jewish scholars was deeply committed to *Bildung*. It was on this concept that Wilhelm von Humboldt created Germany's education system in the nineteenth century. *Bildung*, through high school education, and *Wissenschaft* as a methodology of scholarship made the German university the world's leading institution of the age.

The new academic study of Judaism brought forth a new historical consciousness, which differed substantially from traditional Jewish learning. Jewish sources were now examined, taking into account their origin and development over centuries, so that the traditional and "timeless" idea within Jewish history was replaced by a new and dynamic approach. Free inquiry was allowed to challenge traditionally held beliefs and refute prejudgment. The former spontaneous and associative exegesis was now expanded, as a scholarly enterprise, to embrace a problem-oriented, systematic, and ultimately synthetic approach to textual studies.

While *Wissenschaft des Judentums* gave German Jewry the key to recognition in society through scholarly work on all aspects of Judaism, it would renew Judaism from within. But there were also pressures from outside: spurred on by the expectation of many Germans that Jews should convert to Christianity, the resulting Jewish identity crisis also had positive effects. And by clarifying its contribution to world history and culture, it would at the same time renew Judaism from within. Thus a new Judaism would be created, through study and reform and through the institutions, including the Hochschule and the Jüdisch-Theologisches Seminar of Breslau (Jewish Theological Seminary of Breslau), founded in 1854, that were pledged to implement "*neue Wissenschaft*" into their study program.

Both the Hochschule and the Breslau seminary owed their existence to Rabbi Dr. Abraham Geiger (1810–1874). A great scholar of the nineteenth century, Geiger deeply believed in the freedom of conscience and belief, the freedom of *Wissenschaft*, and the freedom of its peoples.[2] His unique contribution to Judaism was, according to Max Wiener, to have based Jewish life "on the clear, unbiased knowledge and understanding of indigenous history" and to have liberated it "for a rejuvenated presence and future."[3]

In the course of the nineteenth century, Jews now began to question their Judaism and to reflect on the essence of Judaism's inner core, what it meant to adhere to it, and what it had contributed over the millennia to the world spirit at large, to put it in Hegelian terms. In other words, German Jews were looking for a new Jewish self-definition.

1. UNIVERSITY EDUCATION FOR JEWISH WOMEN

Meanwhile, Jewish participation in the newly devised general education system could not be stopped. Already as early as 1886, Jewish students represented 10 percent of the student body at Prussian universities—proof of how eager Jews were to take up the promises of higher education and advance themselves in society. But these students were all men.[4]

World War I produced an era of inner turmoil and estrangement. People were less optimistic now, looking back on the Wilhelmine era as materialistic and artificial. During these years, many of our later Hochschule students were in their teens, full of existential anxieties and lack of purpose, with a disregard for religious values. Here the newly created youth movements stepped in, rescuing the young by, as Rabbi Paul Lazarus put it, creating "a new attitude towards the self and the world around it."[5] These German Jewish *Jugendverbände* (Unions of German Jewish Youth) indeed revitalized German Jewry, with their mixed offers of nature, sport, and communal and religious experiences. They offered to the young an array of idealistic ideologies, ranging from German nationalism to Zionist orientation, providing impetus and motivation to focus on their selected aims. These youth unions thus encouraged young Jews, both boys and girls, to study with diligence. They also instilled in young Jews a love for Jewish tradition, inspiring them to deepen and expand their Jewish knowledge. Also, for the first time, women as well as men were doing the studying.

Rabbi Paul Lazarus (1888–1951) was active in Wiesbaden from 1918 until 1938, when he and his family escaped to Haifa. In 1921, he had founded a *Jüdisches Lehrhaus* to follow the example set by Franz Rosenzweig's idea for "a new type of learning" and to combat "the secular environment of the 1920s. . . . Religious liberalism was failing. It was more concerned with secularizing faith than with penetrating life with faith."[6]

In Germany from 1865 onward, there were leagues and organizations like the *Allgemeiner Deutscher Frauenverein* (General German Women's Association) that aimed to discuss how education for girls could be improved.[7] They had to confront and overcome obstacles and opinions literally carved in stone. In 1871, for example, the university administration of Heidelberg issued a statement in which it declared that "it had never before come to pass that a woman [*Frauenzimmer*] had been matriculated or completed her doctorate."[8] However, in 1893, Germany's first high school for girls was opened in Karlsruhe, and there a Jewish girl, Rahel Goitein (1880–1963), the daughter of the local Orthodox rabbi Gábor Goitein, was the first to gain her *Abitur* (baccalaureate) in 1899. In 1900, Goitein became the first matriculated woman student at the University of Heidelberg. Having enrolled herself in the philosophy faculty, she soon gained admission to the medical faculty. She was the first woman to complete her medical studies in Germany. She started practicing in Munich, where she was married to lawyer Dr. Elias Straus, president of the Jewish Community of Munich, Israelitische Kultusgemeinde München.[9]

In her graduation speech, Goitein explained her own motivation and that of other girls in her class and why they were all keen to obtain higher education: "We wanted to learn how one learns, how one becomes independent through knowledge and inwardly free. . . . However, the second and stronger reason was the thought [that] we would like to have a profession, we would like to take up some position in life."[10] Dr. Rahel Goitein Straus died in 1963 in Jerusalem, where she had settled thirty years before and continued to devote her energies to Jewish causes. One obituary reads: "The memory of this wise and warmhearted woman will be honored by a wide circle of friends and admirers."[11]

The pioneers that Harriet Pass Freidenreich identifies as the first generation of Jewish university women are art historian Julie Braun-Vogelstein (Stettin 1883–New York 1971); historian Hedwig Hintze, née Guggenheimer (Munich 1884–Utrecht 1943); physician and professor of medicine Rahel Hirsch (Frankfurt am Main 1870–London 1953); physicist Lise Meitner (Vienna 1878–Cambridge 1968); philologist Elise Richter (Vienna 1865–Theresienstadt 1943); social reformer Alice Salomon (Berlin 1872–New York 1948); economist Frieda Wunderlich (Berlin 1884–East Orange, New Jersey 1965) and her sister, art historian Eva Wunderlich (Berlin 1889–East Orange, New Jersey 1968); and physician Helene Stöltzner, née Ziegelroth (Warsaw 1866–Berlin 1961).[12] By 1911, Jewish women represented almost 12 percent of all German women high-school graduates, while Jews were only 1 percent of Germany's population. When women were finally admitted to German universities between 1899 and 1908, they all too often had to endure sexist jokes and marginalization from male students and professors alike. In spite of such setbacks, women entered the universities. Of the 11,000 women who were studying in Germany in 1911, a high proportion, 11.2 percent, were Jewish.[13] However, not one of them decided to pursue a career as a Jewish scholar. In many cases, these Jewish women students sought to acquire *Bildung* and emancipation.

In 1907, a new chapter opened when a small band of women entered the Hochschule for the first time, wanting to become teachers of the Jewish religion in schools. However, although some women audited courses and others were admitted as part-time students in the teacher-training program, women were not accepted as full-time students before 1921. In that year, 5 percent of all the Hochschule students were women; in 1929 the percentage rose to 15 percent, and in 1931 to 18 percent. These students were the first to attempt something completely new for women: to study Judaism in all its various aspects—historical, philological, philosophical—and to study it as a living tradition in a scholarly way. To appreciate how daring their ambition was, we must remember that these women, and indeed women in general, had only recently been given access to higher learning and university studies.

This development correlated with the transformation of the German rabbinate in the Weimar Republic, which provided new perspectives for women, too. With the profession in transition, new fields of occupation opened up, including pastoral care and chaplaincy, thus enhancing so-called female skills. Walter Homolka has analyzed this development toward the occupational profile of today's community rabbi.[14]

Regina Jonas (1902–1944), who matriculated at the Hochschule für die Wissenschaft des Judentums in 1924, qualified first as a high school teacher, then as an academically trained teacher of religion, and eventually as the first ordained woman rabbi in the world. She never attended university, unlike most male rabbis of her time who graduated with an advanced degree (*Doktorrabbiner*). In 1937, Jonas accepted a position offered by the Jewish Community of Berlin (Jüdische Gemeinde zu Berlin). While her contract called her a "religion teacher with academic qualifications," she was expected "to provide rabbinical pastoral care in the social institutions of the community" and to meet the spiritual needs of patients in five hospitals and old-age homes run by the Jewish community.[15]

A number of studies on Regina Jonas have appeared recently that acknowledge her significance to modern Jewish rabbinical life.[16] As the school offered female students only teaching degrees, it is clear that all of Jonas's fellow women students were studying for an academic teacher's certificate. Let me introduce eight women pioneers of Jewish learning whose stories and achievements are largely unrevealed or unknown. All these biographical sketches reflect a range of significant attempts to cope with the problem of formation of Jewish identity and religion in the interwar years from a female perspective. They are substantially revised and extended versions of portrays I presented in my study on women pioneers of Jewish learning in 2002.[17]

2. BIOGRAPHICAL SKETCHES

2.1. Perle Haskel Gold

One of the first full-time students at the Hochschule was Perle Haskel (later Perle Gold), who arrived, at the age of seventeen, from Lithuania and lived with her aunt in Berlin in the 1920s.[18] Most of her male co-students were at least ten years older than her and had a rigorous religious training. However, she later recalled that "Professor Leo Baeck always remarked that I knew the Bible much better than all the other students."[19] This story was reported by Perle Gold in a letter sent to Leonard Baker in 1974, who also quotes her remark that "he [Baeck] was one of the leaders in German Jewry in insisting that women achieve the same rights within the religion as did men."[20] In his biography of Baeck, Leonard S. Baker describes an encounter of the venerated rabbi and scholar with Perle Haskell: "Once Baeck came into the school and found a number of male students paying court to her. 'Now,' he said, smiling, 'I understand why little Perle is coming to our school.'"[21] The patronizing, if not slightly sexist and condescending, tone might be a projection of Baker's own attitude. It tells a lot about the male gaze; to our ears today, it almost sounds like mockery. On the other hand, Baker reminds us of the fact that Leo Baeck did not neglect the education of Jewish women. "He was one of the leaders in German Jewry in insisting that women achieve the same rights within religion as did men. In Düsseldorf he introduced the process of confirmation for girls."[22] However, as a pulpit rabbi in Berlin, Baeck was thoroughly opposed to mixed synagogue seating.[23] Unfortunately, we do not know much more about the story of Perle Gold neé Haskel. The situation is quite different in the following cases.

2.2 Ellen Littmann

Ellen Littmann (Danzig 1909–London 1975) was the first woman to complete the Hochschule's academic program. She had been encouraged by Baeck to come to the Hochschule when she was only twelve years old, "enthralled" by Leo Baeck's *Essence of Judaism*.[24] Later she did come, though against the wishes of her parents. However, Baeck eventually won them over by guaranteeing her a teaching position after her successful graduation. Ellen Littmann must have studied at the Hochschule from 1922 onward, because in that year, and again in 1930, she received the annual prize in a Hochschule competition. In 1922, it was the Moritz-Meyer-Preis, and in 1930 the Moses-Mendelssohn-Preis.[25] After obtaining her doctor of philosophy degree in 1928 from the University of Cologne for "A Study on the Readmission of the Jews into German Towns after the Black Death,"[26] she did indeed become a teacher of religion: the forty-eighth annual report of the Hochschule from 1931 lists Dr. Ellen Littmann and Regina Jonas as having passed their examination as academically trained teachers of religion.[27]

Later, in London, Ellen Littmann taught Bible studies at the Leo Baeck College, where the later principal of the college, Rabbi Dr. Jonathan Magonet, was one of her students: "My Bible teacher at Leo Baeck College, Dr. Ellen Littmann, was quite scathing about rabbis who did not prepare their sermons properly. She noted that when you shake a sermon out of your sleeve, all you get is dust!"[28]

2.3 Lea Goldberg

Lea Goldberg (Königsberg 1911–Jerusalem 1970), born to a Lithuanian family from Kaunas, came to the Hochschule with a thorough knowledge of Hebrew. In 1926, when she was fifteen years old, she wrote in her personal diary, "The unfavourable condition of the Hebrew writer is no secret to me. . . . Writing in a different language than Hebrew is the same to me as not writing at all. And yet I want to be a writer. . . . This is my only objective."[29] She began her university studies in Kovno and then went on to study in Berlin from fall 1930. She successfully completed her studies toward her master's degree on March 14, 1932 and proceeded from there to her doctoral studies at Bonn University, completing a doctorate in Semitic studies in 1933.[30] Her dissertation about the Samaritan Targum of the Pentateuch was published two years later.[31] She studied only for a very short period at the Hochschule, where she "gained access to Western Jewish emancipation."[32]

Goldberg's erudition and renown was such that a leading newspaper in Palestine excitedly reported her plans to immigrate to that country.[33] In 1935, she settled in Tel Aviv. In her well-known essay "The Courage of the Ordinary" (1938), Goldberg champions a life and literature centered around "hard everyday work that demands concentration and precision"—work that "does not involve any great celebrations of glowing ideals and colored lights."[34] In addition to her poetry, she wrote songs for children, a novel, and a play, which was staged in Tel Aviv. She also worked on many translations from a number of languages into Hebrew. In 1954, Goldberg took up a position as lecturer in European literature at the Hebrew University in Jerusalem, where she eventually became a professor. She is remembered as "an extravagantly popular lecturer with hundreds of students flocking to her lectures, which she delivered in a voice characterized as strange and smoke-filled."[35] In her posthumously published novel *Avedot: Mukdash le'Antonia* (Losses: dedicated to Antonia), Goldberg describes the hubbub of Berlin's linguistic diversity of this time.[36]

2.4 Nechama Leibowitz

Like Goldberg, Nechama Leibowitz (Riga 1905–Jerusalem 1997) emigrated soon after receiving her doctorate. Born to Orthodox Jewish parents, she moved with her family to Berlin in 1919. She studied at the University of Berlin from 1925 to 1930 and simultaneously continued her Jewish studies at Hochschule für die Wissenschaft des Judentums. Professor Ismar Elbogen, who taught history, Bible exegesis, and liturgy at the Hochschule from 1904 to 1938, used to say that she was the best student he had ever had.[37]

In 1930, Leibowitz received a doctorate from the University of Marburg for her thesis, *Techniques in the Translations of German-Jewish Biblical Translations*.[38] In her thesis, she explored the Yiddish translations of the Hebrew Bible, based on manuscripts in the Parma and Berlin libraries. Her scholarly interests ran the gamut from Jewish classical commentaries, Hebrew philology, and pedagogy to Germanics and literature. In the same year, 1930, she immigrated to Mandate Palestine, where she made a name for herself as a leading Bible scholar, enthusiastically educating generations of students and teachers. "Why did she go?" biographer Hayuta Deutsch jokes, but with a serious point intended. "Since she wasn't going to be accepted to Beit Medrash L'Rabbanim (the Rabbinical Seminary)."[39]

Nechama Leibowitz taught at a religious Zionist teachers' seminar for the next twenty-five years. In 1957, she began lecturing at Tel Aviv University and became a full professor eleven years later. She also gave classes at the Hebrew University of Jerusalem and other educational institutions around the country. Her volumes in the study of the weekly Torah portions were translated into various languages, and in 1957 she was awarded the Israel Prize for Education. Regrettably, her entry in volume 10 of the *Encyclopaedia Judaica*, published in 1972, is only an attachment to the longer article on her more famous brother, Yeshayahu Leibowitz. In the Encyclopaedia Judaica's 2007 edition, David Derovan finally honored the life and work of Nechama Leibowitz in a separate article.[40]

2.5 Helene (Leni) Westphal Yachil

Helene (Leni) Westphal (Düsseldorf 1912–Israel 2007) is another student of the Hochschule who made a name for herself as a scholar in Israel. Known as Leni Yachil, she taught Holocaust studies, first at the Hebrew University of Jerusalem and later at Haifa University. Her masterwork, in terms of content and scope, was *The Holocaust: The Fate of European Jewry (1932–1945)*, published in Hebrew (1987), English (1990), and German (1998). Her scholarly work and legacy have been recognized in a biographical overview by Tikva Fatal-Kna'ani.[41]

Born to an affluent German Jewish family, Westphal was a sixth-generation descendant of Moses Mendelssohn from her father's side; her mother was a daughter of cotton magnate and benefactor James Simon. After completing her matriculations in Potsdam, where she had been raised, she studied history at the Universities of Munich and Berlin. She was enrolled at the Hochschule from autumn 1932 to the summer of 1934; at the same time, she devoted herself to the Jewish youth movement *Werkleute* (Workmen) of young socialist-oriented liberals, becoming one of its leaders in Berlin. "As far as knowledge is concerned, those Hochschule years certainly were most significant for me!" she recalled later.[42] Westphal immigrated to Palestine in 1934 with other members of the movement, who lived as a group in Haderah before their future settlement, Kibbutz Hazorea, was established. In 1940, she completed her master's degree at the Hebrew University, with her thesis "The Concept of Democracy in Tocqueville."

In 1942, Leni Westphal married Dr. Chaim Hoffman (later Yachil), director of the United Nations Relief and Restitution Agency. In 1947, she joined him in Munich, where he served as head of the Jewish Agency welfare units of the displaced persons (DP) camps in occupied Germany, and from 1953 to 1954, the family resided in Cologne, where Chaim Yahil represented the

Foreign Ministry as a deputy leader of the Israeli delegation. In 1965, Leni Yahil received her doctorate from the Hebrew University for her dissertation "The Jews of Denmark during the Holocaust." From the early 1960s onward, Yahil was involved in academic activity with Yad Vashem; until 2004, she was a member of the editorial board of *Yad Vashem Studies*.

2.6 Susi (Shoshana) Elbogen Ronen

In 1931–1932, Leni Westphal had studied together with Susi (Shoshana) Elbogen (Berlin 1912–Kfar Shmaryahu 2005) at Professor Elbogen's house for their entrance examination to the Hochschule. The daughter of eminent scholar and Rabbi Ismar Elbogen and his wife Regina, née Klemperer, Shoshana remembered how on Shabbat afternoons, the students came around to the house for biscuits,[43] while the students remember how much they were made to feel welcome. Professor Elbogen also organized, "as a favor to Susi," evening discussions at his house for groups of students.[44] The family's home was in Bundesratsufer 2, "Haus Lessing."[45]

Susi Elbogen enrolled at the Hochschule in 1931–1932, then studied during the summer of 1932 for one semester at the Jewish Theological Seminary of Breslau, which had admitted women students only from 1930 onward, and continued to study at the Hochschule until spring 1933. She also studied history and English language and literature at Berlin's Friedrich Wilhelm University.[46] Much to the dismay of her parents, she married another Hochschüler and rabbi, Dr. Manfred Rosenberg.

The couple moved to Göttingen in fall 1933; in 1935, they relocated to Worms. The Rosenbergs made *aliyah* in summer 1937, after Shoshana had undertaken further studies at Göttingen University and at Kings College, London. In 1946, Manfred and Shoshana Rosenberg, now Ronen, got divorced. Shoshana Elbogen Ronen became a teacher of English and was running her own publicity agency in Israel.

2.7 Hannah Stein Landau and Ruth Capell Liebrecht

The next two women I would like to introduce feature in a photograph from the early 1930s: Hannah Stein (Karlsruhe 1912–Jerusalem 1936) and Ruth Liebrecht (Wiesbaden 1911–London 1998). They studied together at the Hochschule and were bosom friends who shared accommodation in Berlin.

Hannah Stein's grandfather, Dr. Alexander Stein, had been a rabbi in Worms, and her father, Professor Dr. iur. Nathan Stein, was an economist.

From 1922 until 1931, Hannah attended the Lessingschule (*Höhere Mädchenschule*) in Karlsruhe. She was also a member of Kadimah, a Zionist youth group, where she may have met her future husband, Gustav Landau. After receiving her Abitur in 1931, she enrolled at the Friedrich-Wilhelms-University and at the Hochschule. Her study book records all the courses she attended: eighteen weekly hours at the university alone, where she read history, philosophy, and German languages, in addition to the Hochschule courses. Together with her future husband, she left for Palestine, where other members of the Landau family had already settled, in October 1933. A daughter was born to them in 1935, but tragically Hannah succumbed to a grave illness only one year later, leaving her baby in her husband's care. Fellow students remember her as an eager and very capable student and an excellent sportswoman.[47]

Ruth Liebrecht née Capell, was raised in Wiesbaden, where her father Edmund Isaak Capell served as a cantor for the liberal Jewish community and as a teacher of religion. She too belonged in her teens to a German Jewish youth movement, the *Kameraden* (Comrades), who strongly believed in a cultural symbiosis of Germanness and Jewishness. Ruth Capell took up her studies at the Hochschule in 1930 and studied the same subjects as Hannah at the university. Her aim was to become a teacher of the Jewish religion.[48]

Capell got married to Heinz Liebrecht, an engineer, in 1935. Two days before the war started, at the end of August 1939, she managed to flee with her little son to England, where her husband, who had been released from Dachau in April 1939, was waiting for her. In London, she retreated into the spiritual world of the immigrant. Events had been traumatic and wounding. She continued to suffer because of her rejection as a Jew in Germany. She gave music lessons and sought companionship in books and like-minded people, but she never recovered from the humiliation that Germany had inflicted on her. And yet, she continued also with her inner spiritual life that tied her to German Jewish culture and to her time of intense study at the Hochschule. She was proud that as a woman, she had asserted herself by being allowed to study. According to Shoshana Elbogen Ronen, Ruth Liebrecht's legacy was "Be positively Jewish! Profess Judaism and take an interest in it."[49]

3. CONCLUSION

One may ask what made me write a book about the Hochschule's women students and about one of them in particular, Ruth Liebrecht.[50] Ruth had died in London before I could meet her, but both her husband and son were keen for me to research her time at the Hochschule. This made me wonder what had been its spiritual climate and also what had been the women students' motivation to study there. How many women students were there at the Hochschule, and had they regarded themselves as pioneers by studying subjects that had been the prerogative of men for centuries? Did they hope to have an impact on other Jewish women or on Jewish society at large? How did they view the role of Jewish women in society? Did they wish to pursue a career, and how did they rate their chances of employment? Did they feel supported by their male co-students and male professors? And what did their own families think of their ambitions? It was indeed a great privilege, and a personal enrichment, for me to meet some of the women students of the Hochschule as well as a number of their male fellow students personally. In all the students I met in the late 1990s, the Hochschule lived on and beyond as an unforgettable symbol of German Jewish scholarship. It renewed and revitalized Judaism in all its disciplines and furthered its recognition, leaving an abundant heritage of exemplary scholarship and deep humanity.

"We didn't aspire to the rabbinate," explained Shoshana Ronen in 1999, commemorating her Hochschule years as a student.[51] Although several dozen women studied at the Hochschule to become teachers during the interwar years, only a few of them completed the program. This indicates how difficult it actually was for a young Jewish woman to create a career of her own. We have to keep in mind that in Weimar Germany, only the unmarried woman was free to choose a career. It seems likely that a major share of young women studied at the Hochschule to gain Jewish knowledge for its own sake, rather than in preparation for a teaching career.

My conversations with women students of the Hochschule gave testimony to the unique flourishing of an extraordinary institution of German Jewish life. We mourn its passing, but we hope also to gain inspiration from it to refresh our heritage, for Europe and beyond, and to build upon it. However, many issues remain, and many questions are still open. We need to discuss the ways in which German Jewish women saw themselves as such, how they were seen by others. Was it at all possible to reconcile women's aspirations and their career prospects? How did these different perspectives influence each other? None of the women students at the Hochschule had thought of themselves as pioneers or as special achievers, although they were at the forefront of Jewish education and scholarship, whether they aimed for the rabbinate, as Regina Jonas did, or for a teaching position, or whether they were there simply for their love of Judaism. It is through this love of Jewish learning that they keep inspiring us and continue to set an example for us.

NOTES

1. "Die Wissenschaft des Judentums ist einerseits ebenso alt wie das Judentum selbst—in der Gestalt, die es mit der Zerstörung des Zweiten Tempels angenommen hat," in Richard Schaffler, "Die Wissenschaft des Judentums in ihrer Beziehung zur allgemeinen Geistesgeschichte im Deutschland des 19. Jahrhunderts," in *Wissenschaft des Judentums. Anfänge der Judaistik in Europa*, ed. Julius Carlebach (Berlin: De Gruyter, 1992), 113.

2. Israel O. Lehman, "Lehrer und Schüler an der Hochschule für die Wissenschaft des Judentums in Berlin," *Tradition und Erneuerung* 34 (1972): 3.

3. Max Wiener, *Abraham Geiger and Liberal Judaism: The Challenge of the Nineteenth Century* (Philadelphia: Jewish Publication Society of America, 1962), 77.

4. Keith H. Pickus, *Constructing Modern Identities: Jewish University Students in Germany 1815–1914* (Detroit: Wayne State University Press, 1999).

5. Herbert A. Strauss, "The Jugendverband: A Social and Intellectual History," *Leo Baeck Institute Year Book* 6 (1961): 231.

6. Strauss, "The Jugendverband," 230.

7. Marion A. Kaplan, "Her Sisters Keeper: Women's Organizations from the Chevra to Feminism," in idem, *The Making of the Jewish Middle Class: Women, Family, and Identity in Imperial Germany* (New York: Oxford University Press, 1991), 192–227, here 207.

8. *Universitätsmuseum Heidelberg, Begleitheft zur Ausstellung*, ed. Matthias Untermann (Heidelberg, 2006), 63.

9. Cf. Kerstin Wolff, "Straus, Rahel/verheiratete," in *Neue Deutsche Biographie 25* (München: Historische Kommission bei der Bayerischen Akademie der Wissenschaften, 2013), 495–497.

10. See Monika Richarz, in Meyer III, 85. *Wir lebten in Deutschland: Erinnerungen einer deutschen Jüdin* (Stuttgart: 1961).

11. *AJR Information* 18, no. 7 (July 1963): 12.

12. Harriet Pass Freidenreich, *Female, Jewish, and Educated: The Lives of Central European University Women* (Bloomington: Indiana University Press, 2002), 232, n. 30.

13. Kaplan, *The Making of the Jewish Middle Class*, 138; Claudia Huerkamp, "Frauen, Universitäten und Bildungsbürgertum. Zur Lage studierender Frauen 1900–1930," in *Bürgerliche Berufe: zur Sozialgeschichte der freien und akademischen Berufe im internationalen Vergleich, acht Beiträge*, ed. Hannes Siegrist (Göttingen: Vandenhock & Ruprecht, 1988), 208.

14. See Walter Homolka, "The Modern Community Rabbi in Germany: Towards the Development of a Contemporary Occupational Profile," in *Rabbi—Pastor—Priest: Their Roles and*

Profiles through the Ages, ed. Walter Homolka, Heinz-Günther Schöttler (Berlin: De Gruyter, 2013), 327–354; Walter Homolka, *Der Moderne Rabbiner. Ein Rollenbild im Wandel* (Berlin: Hentrich & Hentrich, 2012).

15. Einstellungsurkunde, CJA [=Centrum Judaicum Archive] 1, 75 DJo 1, Nr. 14, f. 31–32.

16. See Katharina von Kellenbach, "'God Does Not Oppress Any Human Being': The Life and Thought of Rabbi Regina Jonas," in *Leo Baeck Institute Year Book* 39 (1994): 213–25; Elisa Klapheck, *Rabbiner Jonas: The Story of the First Woman Rabbi* (San Francisco: Jossey-Bass/John Wiley & Sons, 2004).

17. Esther Seidel, *Women Pioneers of Jewish Learning: Ruth Liebrecht and her Companions at the Hochschule des Judentums in Berlin 1930–1934* (Berlin: Jüdische Verlagsanstalt Berlin, 2002).

18. Her name is also listed by Irene Kaufmann, *Die Hochschule für die Wissenschaft des Judentums 1872–1942* (Berlin: Hentrich & Hentrich, 2006), 27, and mentioned by Herbert A. Strauss, "Die letzten Jahre der Hochschule (Lehranstalt) für die Wissenschaft des Judentums, Berlin: 1936– 1942," in Carlebach, *Wissenschaft des Judentums*, 36.

19. Leonard S. Baker, *Days of Sorrow and Pain: Leo Baeck and the Berlin Jews* (New York: Macmillan, 1978), 102.

20. Baker, *Days of Sorrow and Pain*, 103.

21. Ibid., 102f.

22. Ibid., 52.

23. Leo Baeck, "Das Zusammensitzen von Männern und Frauen in der Synagoge Prinzregentenstraße in Berlin," in *Leo Baeck Werke*, vol. 6, ed. Michael A. Meyer (Gütersloh: Gütersloher Verlagshaus, 2006), 507.

24. Baker, *Days of Sorrow and Pain*, 102.

25. *40. Bericht der Hochschule für die Wissenschaft des Judentums in Berlin* (Berlin: 1922), 17; *47. Bericht der Hochschule für die Wissenschaft des Judentums in Berlin* (Berlin: 1930), 9.

26. Ellen Littmann, *Studien zur Wiederaufnahme der Juden durch die deutschen Städte nach dem schwarzen Tode: ein Beitrag zur Geschichte der Judenpolitik der deutschen Städte im späten Mittelalter* (Breslau: Th. Schatzky, 1928).

27. *48. Bericht der Hochschule für die Wissenschaft des Judentums* (Berlin: 1931), 9.

28. Jonathan Magonet, "The Jewish Sermon," in Die Predigt des Alten Testaments . Beiträge des Symposiums *"Das* Alte *Testament und die Kultur der Moderne,"* ed. Wallace J. Alston et al. (Münster: Lit Verlag, 2003), 94.

29. Rachel and Arie Aharon, eds., *Leah Goldberg's Diaries* (Bnei Brak/Tel Aviv: Sifriat Poalim–Hakibbutz Hameuchad, 2005), 9.

30. Yfaat Weiss, *Lea Goldberg, Lehrjahre in Deutschland 1930–1933* (Göttingen: Vandenhoeck & Ruprecht, 2010).

31. Lea Goldberg, *Das* samaritanische *Pentateuchtargum. Eine Untersuchung seiner handschriftlichen Quellen* (Stuttgart: W. Kohlhammer, 1935).

32. "Für beide war die Hochschule das Tor, das ihnen den Weg zur westlichen jüdischen Emanzipation öffnete." Conversation with Shoshana Ronen, June 16, 2000.

33. Akin Ajayi, "The Diplomats of the Literary World," *Jerusalem Post*, December 29, 2011.

34. Ma'ayan Harel, "Lea Goldberg," in *Jewish Women: A Comprehensive Historical Encyclopedia*, 27 February 2009, Jewish Women's Archive, https://jwa.org/encyclopedia/article/goldberg-lea.

35. Lea Goldberg, *Selected Poetry and Drama*; poetry translated and introduced by Rachel Zvia Back; drama translated by T. Carmi and introduced by Matti Megged (New Milford, CT: Toby Press, 2006), 13.

36. Rachel Seelig, *Strangers in Berlin: Modern Jewish Literature Between East and West, 1919–1933* (Ann Arbor: University of Michigan Press, 2016), 47.
37. Fax from Shoshana Ronen, June 16, 2000.
38. Nechama Leibowitz, *Die Übersetzungstechnik der jüdisch-deutschen Bibelübersetzungen des 15. und 16. Jahrhunderts dargestellt an den Psalmen* (Marburg: Niemeyer, 1931).
39. See Hayuta Deutsch, Nehama: *The Life of Nehama Leibowitz* (Tel Aviv: Yedioth Ahronoth and Chemed Books, 2008).
40. *Encyclopaedia Judaica*, vol. 10 (Jerusalem: Keter, 1972), 1588; David Derovan: "Leibowitz, Nechama," *Encyclopaedia Judaica*, vol. 12 (Detroit: Macmillan Reference USA, 2007), 621–22.
41. Tikva Fatal-Kna'ani, "Leni Yahil," *Jewish Women: A Comprehensive Historical Encyclopedia*, March 1, 2009, Jewish Women's Archive, https://jwa.org/encyclopedia/article/yahil-leni [March 13, 2019].
42. Conversation with Leni Yahil in Jerusalem, May 31, 1999.
43. Conversation with Shoshana Ronen, December 27, 1998.
44. Abraham Wolff, unpublished memoirs, 7; see Esther Seidel, *Women Pioneers of Jewish Learning: Ruth Liebrecht and Her Companions at the "Hochschule für die Wissenschaft des Judentums" in Berlin 1930–1934* (Berlin: Jüdische Verlagsanstalt Berlin, 2002), 111.
45. *Jüdisches Adressbuch für Gross-Berlin, Ausgabe 1931* (Berlin: Godega Verlagsgesellschaft, 1931), 83.
46. Conversation with Shoshana Ronen, May 31, 1999.
47. Cf. Leo Baeck Institute–Center for Jewish History, *Guide to the Papers of Gustav and Hannah Landau 1923–1933* (AR 25357/MF 1052), http://digifindingaids.cjh.org/?pID=560451 [March 13, 2019].
48. See Seidel, *Women Pioneers of Jewish Learning*.
49. Conversation with Shoshana Elbogen Ronen, December 25, 1998.
50. Seidel, *Women Pioneers of Jewish Learning*.
51. Shoshana Elbogen Ronen, "We Didn't Aspire to the Rabbinate," *Bet Debora Journal* 1 (2000), 16.

BIBLIOGRAPHY

Aharon, Rachel and Arie (eds.), *Leah Goldberg's Diaries* (Bnei Brak/Tel Aviv: Sifriat Poalim–Hakibbutz Hameuchad, 2005).
Ajayi, Akin, "The Diplomats of the Literary World," *Jerusalem Post*, December 29, 2011.
Baeck, Leo, "Das Zusammensitzen von Männern und Frauen in der Synagoge Prinzregentenstraße in Berlin," in *Leo Baeck Werke*, vol. 6, ed. Michael A. Meyer (Gütersloh: Gütersloher Verlagshaus, 2006).
Baker, Leonard S., *Days of Sorrow and Pain: Leo Baeck and the Berlin Jews* (New York: Macmillan, 1978).
Derovan, David, "Leibowitz, Nechama," *Encyclopaedia Judaica*, vol. 12 (Detroit: Macmillan Reference USA, 2007), 621–22.
Deutsch, Hayuta, *Nehama: The Life of Nehama Leibowitz* (Tel Aviv: Yedioth Ahronoth and Chemed Books, 2008).
Elbogen Ronen, Shoshana, "We Didn't Aspire to the Rabbinate," *Bet Debora Journal* 1 (2000), 16.

Fatal-Kna'ani, Tikva, "Leni Yahil," *Jewish Women: A Comprehensive Historical Encyclopedia*, March 1, 2009, Jewish Women's Archive, https://jwa.org/encyclopedia/article/yahil-leni [March 13, 2019].

Freidenreich, Harriet Pass, *Female, Jewish, and Educated: The Lives of Central European University Women* (Bloomington: Indiana University Press, 2002).

Goldberg, Lea, *Das samaritanische Pentateuchtargum. Eine Untersuchung seiner handschriftlichen Quellen* (Stuttgart: W. Kohlhammer, 1935).

Goldberg, Lea, *Selected Poetry and Drama*; poetry translated and introduced by Rachel Zvia Back; drama translated by T. Carmi and introduced by Matti Megged (New Milford, CT: Toby Press, 2006).

Harel, Ma'ayan, "Lea Goldberg," in *Jewish Women: A Comprehensive Historical Encyclopedia*, 27 February 2009, Jewish Women's Archive, https://jwa.org/encyclopedia/article/goldberg-lea.

Homolka, Walter, "The Modern Community Rabbi in Germany: Towards the Development of a Contemporary Occupational Profile," in *Rabbi—Pastor—Priest: Their Roles and Profiles through the Ages*, ed. Walter Homolka, Heinz-Günther Schöttler (Berlin: De Gruyter, 2013), 327–54.

Homolka, Walter, *Der Moderne Rabbiner. Ein Rollenbild im Wandel* (Berlin: Hentrich & Hentrich, 2012).

Huerkamp, Claudia, "Frauen, Universitäten und Bildungsbürgertum. Zur Lage studierender Frauen 1900–1930," in *Bürgerliche Berufe: zur Sozialgeschichte der freien und akademischen Berufe im internationalen Vergleich, acht Beiträge*, ed. Hannes Siegrist (Göttingen: Vandenhock & Ruprecht, 1988).

Kaplan, Marion A., "Her Sisters Keeper: Women's Organizations from the Chevra to Feminism," in idem, *The Making of the Jewish Middle Class: Women, Family, and Identity in Imperial Germany* (New York: Oxford University Press, 1991), 192–227.

Kaufmann, Irene, *Die Hochschule für die Wissenschaft des Judentums 1872–1942* (Berlin: Hentrich & Hentrich, 2006).

Klapheck, Elisa, *Fräulein Rabbiner Jonas: The Story of the First Woman Rabbi* (San Francisco: Jossey-Bass/John Wiley & Sons, 2004).

Lehman, Israel O., "Lehrer und Schüler an der Hochschule für die Wissenschaft des Judentums in Berlin," *Tradition und Erneuerung* 34 (1972).

Leibowitz, Nechama, *Die Übersetzungstechnik der jüdisch- deutschen Bibelübersetzungen des 15. und 16. Jahrhunderts dargestellt an den Psalmen* (Marburg: Niemeyer, 1931).

Littmann, Ellen, *Studien zur Wiederaufnahme der Juden durch die deutschen Städte nach dem schwarzen Tode: ein Beitrag zur Geschichte der Judenpolitik der deutschen Städte im späten Mittelalter* (Breslau: Th. Schatzky, 1928).

Magonet, Jonathan, "The Jewish Sermon," in *Die Predigt des Alten Testaments. Beiträge des Symposiums "Das Alte Testament und die Kultur der Moderne,"* ed. Wallace J. Alston et al. (Münster: Lit Verlag, 2003).

Pickus, Keith H., *Constructing Modern Identities: Jewish University Students in Germany 1815–1914* (Detroit: Wayne State University Press, 1999).

Richarz, Monika, in Meyer III, 85. *Wir lebten in Deutschland: Erinnerungen einer deutschen Jüdin* (Stuttgart: 1961).

Schaffler, Richard, "Die Wissenschaft des Judentums in ihrer Beziehung zur allgemeinen Geistesgeschichte im Deutschland des 19. Jahrhunderts," in *Wissenschaft des Judentums. Anfänge der Judaistik in Europa*, ed. Julius Carlebach (Berlin: De Gruyter, 1992).

Seelig, Rachel, *Strangers in Berlin: Modern Jewish Literature Between East and West, 1919–1933* (Ann Arbor: University of Michigan Press, 2016).

Seidel, Esther, *Women Pioneers of Jewish Learning: Ruth Liebrecht and Her Companions at the "Hochschule für die Wissenschaft des Judentums" in Berlin 1930–1934* (Berlin: Jüdische Verlagsanstalt Berlin, 2002).

Strauss, Herbert A., "The Jugendverband: A Social and Intellectual History," *Leo Baeck Institute Year Book* 6 (1961).

Untermann, Matthias (ed.), *Universitätsmuseum Heidelberg, Begleitheft zur Ausstellung* (Heidelberg, 2006).

von Kellenbach, Katharina, "'God Does Not Oppress Any Human Being': The Life and Thought of Rabbi Regina Jonas," in *Leo Baeck Institute Year Book* 39 (1994): 213–25.

Weiss, Yfaat, *Lea Goldberg, Lehrjahre in Deutschland 1930–1933* (Göttingen: Vandenhoeck & Ruprecht, 2010).

Wiener, Max, *Abraham Geiger and Liberal Judaism: The Challenge of the Nineteenth Century* (Philadelphia: Jewish Publication Society of America, 1962).

Wolff, Kerstin, "Straus, Rahel/verheiratete," in *Neue Deutsche Biographie 25* (München: Historische Kommission bei der Bayerischen Akademie der Wissenschaften, 2013), 495–97.

Chapter Four

"The Woman in the House of God" (1926) Revisited

Hartmut Bomhoff

"I think there is a pressing need for women to come down from your synagogue galleries to enter into the life of the synagogue," so British reformer and social activist Lilian (Lily) Helen Montagu urged her audience in Berlin on January 27, 1930.[1] Montagu was the driving force behind the World Union for Progressive Judaism, and her historic challenge was met with open ears. A good three years before, in fall 1926, the Vereinigung für das liberale Judentum in Deutschland (Union for Liberal Judaism in Germany) had sponsored a symposium to discuss the role of Jewish women in the synagogue sanctuary and beyond, "Die Frau im Gotteshaus" ("The Woman in the House of God").[2] The discussion reflects the zeitgeist as well as the mutability of Liberal Judaism in Weimar Germany.

The Vereinigung was founded in 1908 by Bernhard Breslauer (1851–1928), who became its first chairman. The union included progressive communities of the major cities, rabbis of the Vereinigung der liberalen Rabbiner Deutschlands (Union of Liberal Rabbis in Germany), founded in 1899 by Rabbi Hermann Vogelstein, as well as individuals. Vogelstein was also one of the founders of the Union for Liberal Judaism; however, the lay element was traditionally predominant in the governing bodies of the organization, which numbered about 10,000 members.

The 1926 symposium comprised ten statements, seven of them by women, which were printed by *Jüdisch-Liberale Zeitung*, the union's newspaper. It was published in Breslau between 1920 and 1936 and testified to the vibrant progressive Jewish community in Germany at that time. Historian Michael A. Meyer has briefly dealt with the proceedings of the symposium. He summarizes the statements as follow: "Not only did the participants, almost without exception, call for expanded activity by women in community and synagogue governance, but most insisted on enhanced participation inside the sanctuary as well. Of the seven women, four specifically raised the possibility of women rabbis. Their feminine talents, two of them argued, would be especially useful in the area of pastoral work."[3]

A close reading of the proceedings of the 1926 symposium and an examination of its impact are still due. To put them in a wider context, it might be helpful to recall the developments prior to that time.

Liberal Judaism in Germany had addressed women's equality in terms of religious practice already in the early nineteenth century. In 1837, Rabbi Abraham Geiger at the rabbinic conference in Wiesbaden said:

> Let there be from now on no distinction between duties for man and woman, unless flowing from the natural laws governing the sexes; no assumptions of the spiritual minority of woman, as though she were incapable of grasping the deep things in religion; no institution of the public service, either in form or content, which shuts the doors of the temple in the face of women; no degradation of woman in the form of our marriage service, and no application of fetters which may destroy woman's happiness. Then will the Jewish girl and the Jewish woman, conscious of the significance of our faith, become fervently attached to it, and our whole religious life will profit form the beneficial influence which feminine hearts will bestow upon it.[4]

In 1846, the liberal-minded rabbis met for a conference in Breslau, which was chaired by Abraham Geiger. In its proceedings, it reads: "The Rabbinical Conference wants to declare the female sex to be religiously [as] equally obligated and entitled as the male [sex]."[5] The question that must be asked is why it took nearly a century, from 1837 to 1935, when the first woman rabbi worldwide was ordained, to achieve that equality.

It was not until 1871 that women's religious status, and marital matters in particular, were widely discussed. The Second Israelite Synod of liberal-minded German rabbis and lay leaders, with Abraham Geiger as its vice president, was held in Augsburg July 11–17 and passed resolutions concerning, for example, the religious wedding ceremony, the validity of civil marriage, and the ceremony of *halizah*.[6]

Rabbi Meyer Kayserling (1829–1905) was the first scholar to write a history of Jewish women. A son-in-law of the liberal rabbi, scholar, and publisher Ludwig Philippson, he was elected rabbi of the Neolog Pest Jewish community in Hungary in 1870. In 1879, he published *Die Jüdischen Frauen in der Geschichte, Literatur und Kunst*, highlighting Jewish women's contributions to history, literature, and art from the Talmudic period to the present. His 375-page-long book is, however, a conversation about women from a man's perspective. It was only in Weimar Germany that access to university education expanded leadership opportunities for Jewish women, who were now welcomed into the workforce.

Michael A. Meyer reasons:

> With one notable exception, the German Reform movement in succeeding years did little collectively to advance the cause of Jewish women. The exception was its full support of the right of women to vote in Jewish community elections and also to run for office. In contrast to the statute of the Hamburg Jewish community, the 1924 regulations of the Hamburg Reform Temple granted women equal membership rights with men. The Liberal Jewish party, which had long supported Jewish community voting rights for women, that same year threw its support behind a "Jewish Women's Voting Rights Week" organized by the League of Jewish Women to "finally" achieve that end.[7]

It was the conviction of the League of Jewish Women's founder, Bertha Pappenheim (1859–1936) that women, when granted equality, would return to Judaism and thus reinvigorate Jewish life.[8]

One of the promising new employment opportunities for Jewish and non-Jewish women at the turn of the century was social work. Formulated as an extension of the domestic sphere, social work involved, in the words of Alice Salomon (1872–1948), "an assumption of duties for a wider circle than are usually performed by the mother in the home."[9] Salomon was one of the great pioneers of modern social work, called during her lifetime "the Jane Addams of Germany," referring to the saintly American founder of Chicago's Hull House.[10] Her biographer Adriane Feustel explains that *tzedakah* was a fundamental motivation for Salomon, whose conversion to Protestantism during World War I "was by no means a rejection of Judaism in principle."[11]

Seven years after her conversion, Salomon explains in her remarks about the history of welfare among the people of Israel that social care derives from the Jewish sources, first of all from the concept of *tzedakah*.[12] To quote

Bertha Falkenberg (1876–1946), an activist who was third on the list of Liberal candidates for the Berlin Jewish representative assembly in 1930, "Social work means the fulfillment of true Judaism. The obligation of the Liberal associations is not fulfilled by arousing religious feelings through worship. It is just as necessary to sharpen the social conscience, for only out of the union of both does true religious Judaism arise."[13] This resonates with the ideas of Bertha Pappenheim, stated in a paper read at the Women's Congress at Munich, 1912: "Feeding the hungry, nursing the sick, caring for the orphan, endowing the bride, performing the last rites for the dead—all these works Jewish women can and should be ever willing to perform."[14]

Pappenheim concluded her paper "The Jewish Woman in Religious Life" as follows:

> Had the Jewish woman been able to expend her energies and capabilities in communal work, and been given her rightful position and status in the congregation, we should not have had to lament the loss of so many, who in their justifiable longing for useful activity and self-development, have broken the bands which held them to their community, and have sought salvation elsewhere. Full participation in all humanitarian objects is at once the final aim of the woman's movement and the meeting point of all religions. The Jewish religion makes such demands of character and courage that all the majority of Jewish women can find their high vocation anew within their own race and religion, and draw thence their truest inspiration.[15]

In a broader sense, the emphasis on humanitarian causes brings to mind the works of Émile Durkheim (1858–1917), who defined the social as the sacred. The son, grandson, and great-grandson of rabbis, Durkheim demonstrated that religious phenomena stemmed from social rather than divine factors.[16]

In conjunction with the transformation of voluntary charity into paid social work, both the recognition of feminine skills as well as the urge for female empowerment laid the foundations for the very conceivability of female clergy in Weimar, Germany. Women were beginning to play a larger role in Christian denominations, even as candidates for preaching positions in the Evangelical Church. In 1925, the Association of Protestant Women Theologians in Germany (Verband Evangelischer Theologinnen Deutschlands) was founded in Marburg, and a special ministry for women was discussed. This special ministry was intended only to support the male ministry, but not to act independently.[17]

It is a widely shared assessment that Rabbi Regina Jonas (1902–1944) pursued her rabbinic ordination in 1935 on her own accord. However, we can assume that Lily Montagu served as a catalyst to enhance women's participation inside the sanctuary. In 1918, Montagu preached her first sermon at London's Liberal Jewish Synagogue.[18] On August 19, 1928, Montagu delivered the first sermon ever given by a woman from the pulpit of a German synagogue—an event that found great attention, was covered by liberal Jewish papers,[19] and even picked up by the Zionist press.[20] During the conference, the minutes recall, "Frau Ollendorff (Breslau) began by thanking Miss Montagu in the name of the German Jewish women who regarded her as an example and an inspiration."[21]

However, there might have been one more concrete role model, as a former pupil of Jonas, Inge Kallman, was told by her teacher that "apart from a woman rabbi in America, she—Jonas—was the only woman rabbi in her time."[22] This other woman might have been either Martha Neumark (1904–1981), who requested ordination in 1922 (which was approved by the faculty of Hebrew Union College but turned down by the college's Board of Governors) or Helen Levinthal (1910–1989), who in 1939 became the first woman to complete the rabbinical course at Rabbi Isaac Meyer Wise's Jewish Institute of Religion. She was hailed in the press at the time as the "the first woman Rabbi" (even if not ordained) and took over rabbinical tasks for a period in her father's congregation.[23]

The proceedings of the 1926 symposium, however, give us the opportunity to put the story of Regina Jonas in a wider context. Concurrently with developments in the German Protestant Church, or in response to it, more and more Jewish lay leaders discussed the role of women in the sanctuary, including the issue of women in the rabbinate.

In Germany, the subject of women rabbis had come up much earlier, in April 1897. A Jewish newspaper, *Berliner Vereinsbote*, covered the story of Hannah Greenebaum Solomon (1858–1942) of Chicago, who had delivered a sermon at Temple Sinai. The paper called her a female rabbi and assumed that she very soon would find employment: "Die Probepredigt des weiblichen Rabbi fiel so glänzend aus, das seine Anstellung demnächst erfolgen dürfte."[24] Hannah Solomon, however, continued her career as a lay leader, social reformer, and the founder of the National Council of Jewish Women, the first national association of Jewish women in the United States (1893). It was in her capacity as the council's first president that Solomon was invited to preach from many synagogue pulpits. As for public discourse in the German Jewish arena, it remained with this one example for another three decades.

Although women associated with Liberal and Reform Judaism in Germany played increasingly active roles in various Jewish communities and denominations during the Weimar years, not one of them considered herself a candidate for the rabbinate, and none would be ordained as a rabbi anywhere—until the appearance of Regina Jonas. The female participants of the 1926 symposium were closely connected with the social work sector. Sharon Gillerman explains:

> Among those Jewish women who trained as social workers, some elected to work with the working class, lower middle class and east European Jewish population sectors within the Jewish community that required, in the view of their middle-class patrons, the provision of health services, job training and "moral reform." From their roles as organizers of mutual assistance and charitable work in the eighteenth century, middle-class Jewish women became, by the Weimar period, the agents of a rationalized and "scientific" social work, one that was viewed by its practitioners as the modern-day realization of the traditional Jewish ethic of charity. As a gendered sphere of Jewish communal activity, the social arena became not only a site where those in need received assistance, but also a form of Jewish social commitment, like social action, or *tikkun olam*, today. About one third of the leading German women's rights activists were of Jewish origin.[25]

The symposium's convener, however, was a man: Rabbi Dr. Hermann Vogelstein (1870–1942), a Hebrew scholar standing for a conscious modernization of the Jewish worship service and the chief rabbi of the Liberal synagogue in Breslau. He was flanked by two male representatives of the Union for Liberal Judaism in Germany, lawyer Dr. Moritz Galliner (1884–1942), of the Jewish Reform Congregation of Berlin, and industrialist Emil Blumenau (1856–1932), chairman of the board of the Jewish Community of Cologne.

Born in Pilsen, Czechoslovakia in 1870, Dr. Vogelstein was raised in Stettin and received his higher education at the Universities of Berlin and Breslau. In 1895, he became the rabbi in Oppeln, and from 1897 he served as rabbi at Königsberg, East Prussia, for twenty-three years, until 1920, when he assumed the post at Breslau. There, during the pogroms of 1938, he saw his synagogue blown up and in flames. He left Germany the same year with the permission of the Nazi authorities and immigrated to New York, where he died in 1942.[26]

Vogelstein's special focus was the role of women in the synagogue, as is evident by his articles in the Jewish press. Here again he represented a liberal tradition that had been founded in Breslau by Abraham Geiger. Himself profoundly influenced by Geiger's thought, Vogelstein demanded in 1926 that parents should pay more attention to the "Mädchenkonfirmation": "The establishment of the confirmation for girls is a generally valuable and essential measure of the first reform period."[27]

Some of the seven women who contributed to the 1926 symposium are still well known today, while the memory of others has almost vanished. Who were these pioneering women?

Else Dormitzer (1877–1958) had a writing career that can be traced back to the beginning of the twentieth century, and her long list of publications includes children's books and stories, translations, essays, as well as newspaper articles on various topics in different outlets.[28] She wrote passionately on the role of women in liberal Judaism for newspapers and magazines such as the *Jüdisch-Liberale Zeitung* and *Liberales Judentum* and regularly contributed articles to the widely read *Berliner Tageblatt*. Dormitzer was a member and supporter of the Union for Liberal Judaism in Germany and took on an active role both in the regional branch of the Central Association of German Citizens of Jewish Faith (Central-Verein Deutscher Staatsbürger Jüdischen Glaubens), and on its national level. According to historian Kerry Wallach, she "played a key role in rallying women to become active members of the Central-Verein."[29]

As part of her volunteer work, Dormitzer gave numerous talks, often geared toward a female audience, and traveled to different cities in Germany. In 1925, the Central-Verein published her essay *Berühmte jüdische Frauen in Vergangenheit und Gegenwart*, which enjoyed widespread popularity. In 1922, she was the first woman elected to the administrative board of the Jewish Community of Nuremberg, which in 1933 numbered 10,000 members.

In the symposium, Dormitzer stated:

> If one further considers that there are enough learned Jewish women who are able to read our sacred writings in the language of our ancestors, are well acquainted with Talmud and Torah, and if one further considers the natural eloquence of the woman who, filled with the spirit of true piety would surely be capable of preaching the word of God to her brothers and sisters, then one would have to admit that objectively she possesses the requisite qualities for the elevated vocation.[30]

Much less is known about the second speaker, Hedwig Riess. The only reliable information is her entry as a member of the Jewish Reform Congregation of Berlin in 1926.[31] There are also references to a Hedwig Riess who received her doctorate degree in philosophy from the University of Freiburg. Her dissertation, *Motive des patriotischen Stolzes bei den deutschen Humanisten*, was published in Berlin in 1934.

Henriette May née Lövinson (1862–1928) was quoted as saying that "only by making others happy can one achieve happiness."[32] She attended a teacher's seminary, later working as an educator in Berlin and London. In retrospect, she perceived herself as having been equipped for life by a "good Prussian drill at home, at school and at the seminary."[33] When the Jüdischer Frauenbund (League of Jewish Women) was established in 1904, Henriette May became a board member and editor. Formerly herself a teacher, she felt strong sympathy for Jewish women teachers who were unemployed or unprovided for in old age. This led her to establish a home for Jewish women teachers in Berlin. In addition, she was a prominent member of numerous welfare institutions and served as a member of the business-operating subcommittee of the Hilfsverein der Deutschen Juden (Relief Organization of German Jews) and as treasurer of the Zentralwohlfahrtsstelle der deutschen Juden (Central Welfare Board of Jews in Germany). She was a founder, board member, and, from 1918, an honorary member of the Central-Verein Deutscher Staatsbürger Jüdischen Glaubens (Central Association of German Citizens of Jewish Faith), the largest organization of Jews in Germany, where she was the first female board member. In 1929, a memorial book was published by her family, the League of Jewish Women, and the Central-Verein to pay tribute to the late activist.[34]

Let us turn to Minna Schwarz (1859–1936). On Brunnenstrasse 41 in Berlin, a glass plate serves as a memorial of what once was a Jewish institution. In 1888, Minna Schwarz founded the first B'nai B'rith Lodge for women in Berlin with eventually 6,000 members, who created at her initiative a kindergarten for abandoned children and a refuge for single mothers. Between 1932 and 1940, the "Heim" was named after the founder, who dedicated her time and energy to help women and children in need. To mark her seventieth birthday in 1929, she was honored with a memorial plaque: "Unserer Minna Schwarz / Es töne hinfort ihr Motto, ihr Rat: Vom Gedanken zum Wort / Vom Wort zur Tat." On December 29, 1936, the Jewish Telegraphic Agency news reported: "Minna Schwarz, B'nai B'rith Women's

Leader, Dead. Minna Schwarz, president of the Women's Union of B'nai B'rith, died today in the age of 78."[35]

"I can claim that women have gained themselves their right to vote in community elections and that we have achieved this through peaceful means," said Bianka Hamburger (1877–1942) in 1926.[36] Hamburger has only recently been rediscovered. A women's rights activist in the Weimar Republic, she was among the first elected female board members of the Jewish Reform Congregation of Berlin and a leader in Jewish communal politics. She also served as the administration manager of the Jewish Hospital of Berlin. In her contribution to the 1926 symposium, she said:

> Under pressure of economic worries and occupational burdens, leading Jewish community leaders now often complain that they can no longer cope with all their volunteer work and the demands on time and strength associated with it. Accordingly, it was admitted that there was a demand for co-workers. Nevertheless, enormous difficulties had to be overcome until women were granted the participation they desired. Anyone familiar with the development of the Jewish Reform Congregation of Berlin in the eighty years of its existence will be astonished to learn that this community has also done pioneering work in relation to the position of women. At their place of worship women were always equal to men: there were never barred women's seats and designated women's galleries, and as far as room allocation permits, as in the High Holidays services in the more modern halls in the western part of the city, women and men, husband and wife, parents and children do sit together. Already years ago, the same suffrage was introduced in this community. . . . [Women] had proved so successful as members of the various commissions that their male colleagues wished to work with them on the board and in the college of representatives. Thus, as a longtime member of the Reform Congregation of Berlin, I welcome with particular joy and satisfaction that women are being given more and more opportunities to serve their faith community in a truly loyal performance of duties.[37]

Much less is known about Martha Coblenz, née Jacobsohn (1870–1940), who died in London and is buried in Bocklemünd, Cologne. She was the wife of the headmaster of the Jewish School of Cologne, Bonnevit (Bernhard) Coblenz (1861–1932), and sister-in-law of a well-known Reform rabbi, Felix Coblenz (1863–1923). She is briefly mentioned in a newspaper article in 1927, "Die jüdische Frau und das jüdische Haus" (The Jewish woman and the Jewish home).[38] According to the article, Coblenz designed and organized the same-named exhibition on behalf of Cologne's B'nai B'rith sisterhood to reinvigorate Jewishness in the family, displaying the Jewish home as a site for religious practice. Coblenz is frequently named in the sisterhood's magazine *Die Logenschwester Mitteilungsblatt des Schwesternverbandes der U.O.B.B Logen*; she took care of the children of sisterhood members in Cologne, while Minna Schwarz was the contact person in Berlin.[39]

"We need love and creative imagination to do constructive work," Paula Ollendorff (1860–1938) wrote in 1928.[40] The most prominent female contributor to the symposium, she served also as a link to the Women's League of the United Synagogue of America and to the B'nai B'rith sisterhoods in the United States. The Jewish Telegraphic Agency called her in 1934 "the noted German feminist."[41]

Paula Ollendorff was born in Kostenblut near Breslau in 1860, and she would spend much of her life in that city.[42] By profession a teacher, she had finished the teacher's seminary of Fräulen Berta Lindner. When she was eighteen years old, Ollendorff left for Hungary and later moved to England, making a living as a governess and, until 1887, a language instructor. In 1888, she married civil rights lawyer Isidor Ollendorff, apparently a distant relative, and after his death in 1911 she continued many of his social engagements. In Breslau, she built homes for Jewish infants and girls, a kindergarten for illegitimate children, as well as a school for domestic workers. She was also a leader in the German Democratic Party, representing the DDP in the Breslau municipality—Stadtverordnetenversammlung—from 1918, thus being the first woman in Germany to hold the office of city councilor.

In 1920, Ollendorff had become president of Germany's League of Jewish Women (Jüdischer Frauenbund), an organization of 60,000 members, and in 1936 vice president of the International Jewish Women's Federation. From 1926 to 1936, she served as an executive board member of the World Union for Progressive Judaism. On August 21, 1928, the Jewish Telegraphic Agency reported on the World Union for Progressive Judaism's international conference in Berlin:

> Madame Ollendorff of Breslau paid tribute to the activities of the American Jewish women, members of the Liberal congregations and of the sisterhoods. In the United States the Jewish women frequently visit the Liberal synagogue and engage in extensive social service work through the sisterhoods. Synagogue attendance by women is not as frequent in Europe, she stated, urging European women to take their sisters as an example.[43]

Ollendorff dwelled on the work of American Jewish women, who were at once idealistic and practical.

To mark her seventieth birthday in 1930, a library and a home economics institute were named after Ollendorff, and an award was donated, the Paula-Ollendorff-Preis für jüdische Sozialarbeit.[44] In 1935, she was recognized as an elder of the Jewish community of Breslau.

Paula Ollendorff immigrated to Palestine in 1937, where she reunited with her son, Friedrich Ollendorff, and she died in Jerusalem in 1938. Her obituary was written by Rabbi Hermann Vogelstein.[45] Today, the Fundacja Ollendorff in Wroclaw (formerly Breslau) keeps her memory and legacy alive. The Paula Ollendorff Foundation was established to run the Jewish primary school Szalom Alejchem in Wrocław, founded in 1998. It is not a religious school and is open to both Jewish and non-Jewish students. The philosophy of the school is to foster in students a sensitivity to other cultures, while at the same time developing their social skills and competences.

While Regina Jonas discussed matters of religious authenticity and authority, the women who participated in the 1926 symposium appeared to be less demanding. The areas crucial for them were balance, a sense of familiarity, and empowerment (mainly religious education), active participation in religious life, and political representation, which would eventually lead to the need and the recognition of a women's rabbinate. In this sense, the 1926 symposium demonstrated that Jewish women were ready for widespread change, ready to create alternatives. And despite their divergent attitudes, Regina Jonas and the social welfare activists had one impetus in common: to authorize and empower themselves as carriers of a Judaism they wanted to develop from a women's perspective and on their own responsibility.

However, the innovative voices of the seven pioneering women introduced above were gradually silenced. At the September 1928 women's meeting of the DDP, the German Democratic Party, Paula Ollendorff summarized party attitudes toward female candidates, which applied also to attitudes within the wider Jewish community: When newly enfranchised, women were courted, but with the rising dominance of special interests, "Male party leaders . . . sacrificed women first."[46] "Jewish women must cultivate a Jewish social life if Judaism is to continue," she explained at the turn of the year 1932, contrasting the modern Jewish woman with the Jewish woman of the ghetto: "The walls of the ghetto preserved the Jewish people by compelling Jews to live together. When these walls are down their function must be maintained. The Jewish woman must create a warm congeniality in social intercourse that will keep Jewish life in existence."[47]

In February 1929, the *Jüdisch-Liberale Zeitung* addressed the role of women in synagogue life anew, although from a different perspective: mixed seating in the sanctuary. While the front-page headline reads "Erfüllung einer liberalen Forderung," the rabbinical statements are much less affirmative. Again, it was historian Michael A. Meyer who called attention to this issue, albeit in a footnote: "Rabbinical opinion on this subject, even among Liberal rabbis, was divided: Three rabbis favored mixed seating: Louis Blumenthal, Julius Galliner, and Max Weyl; three were opposed to it: Juda Bergmann, Julius Lewkowitz, and Malwin Warschauer. Max Wiener and Leo Baeck took intermediate positions. Baeck favored a synagogue that had sections for those who wanted to sit together and for those who wanted to sit separately. The Orthodox rabbis were unanimously opposed."[48] Opened on September 16, 1930, the huge temple in Prinzregentenstrasse with its 2,300 seats was the first community-run synagogue in the city where men and women sat together—an issue discussed by Rabbi Leo Baeck in a responsum.[49] Before, mixed seating was only introduced by private initiatives like the Liberale Synagoge Norden, founded in 1923 by Hermann and Bertha Falkenberg, or the grassroots congregation that met at the Cecilienschule in Berlin's Wilmersdorf neighborhood and attracted 350 people for its first service in 1927.[50]

The participants of the 1926 symposium must have raised their eyebrows at this all-male expertise that didn't embrace the new profile of Jewish women formulated by them and their peers. Separate seating remained standard practice in Germany's Reform temples down to the 1930s. Even in the Reform Congregation of Berlin, which mandated "the seating of men and women on the same floor," the congregation continued to preserve the principle of sexual separation during worship: men occupied the left side of the auditorium, women the right.[51] And yet, drawing upon the discussions of the 1920s, women demanded their right to perform religious functions in the synagogues. In 1930, Martha Ehrlich (1896–1942) officiated as the first woman board member, or *gabbait*, in Berlin's Rykestrasse synagogue. It was synagogue president Hugo Alexander who had convinced the congregants to elect Ehrlich as the presumably first woman in Germany into this office. She participated equally in synagogue decisions and tasks, except in calling congregants up to read the Torah.[52]

However, such a new departure was a rare exception. Still in 1935, Michael A. Meyer points out, the Liberal rabbi of Frankfurt an der Oder, Ignatz Maybaum (1897–1976) expressed the view that allowing men and women to sit together was distinctly Christian and allowing women to become religious leaders characteristically pagan.[53]

While the 1920s had brought new understanding of the role of women in religious life, the societal changes in the last years of the Weimar Republic narrowed the opportunities for Jewish women. As Esther Seidel puts it:

> In the 1930s, while the female Hochschule students were enjoying the benefits of Jewish higher education, the Jewish League of Women still hesitated to encourage wives and mothers to seek employment and reminded women of the double burden of housework and career. Doubtless, male unemployment at the time may also have been an important factor. The Jewish wife and mother was seen to be responsible for maintaining the equilibrium of the home, and there was no question that she could also have a career.[54]

From 1933 on, the political development and the exclusion of the Jewish population from public life signaled the demise of German Jewry. Under Nazi rule, women were generally expected to stay at home and look after the family. Confronted with anti-Jewish legislation, discrimination, and persecution, Jewish women now had to struggle for survival and often remained their families' primary source of support. This time, it was the hardships that Jews encountered under Nazi oppression that altered the traditional role models.[55]

NOTES

1. *Lily Montagu: Sermons, Addresses, Letters and Prayers*, ed. Ellen Umansky (Lewiston: Edwin Mellen Press, 1985), 168; *Jüdisch-Liberale Zeitung* 10 no. 5 (January 30, 1930): 5.

2. *Jüdisch-Liberale Zeitung* 6, no. 45 (November 5, 1926): 1–4.

3. Michael A. Meyer, "*Gemeinschaft* within *Gemeinde*: Religious Ferment in Weimar Liberal Judaism," in *In Search of Jewish Community: Jewish Identities in Germany and Austria, 1918–1933*, ed. Michel Brenner and Derek J. Penslar (Bloomington: Indiana University Press, 1998), 21; Michael A. Meyer, *Judaism within Modernity: Essays on Jewish History and Religion* (Detroit: Wayne State University Press, 2001), 262.

4. Abraham Geiger, "Zur Stellung des weiblichen Geschlechts in dem Judenthume unserer Zeit," in *Wissenschaftliche Zeitschrift für jüdische Theologie* 3 (1837): 1–14, quoted in David Philippson, *The Reform Movement in Judaism* (London: Macmillan, 1907), 354, n. 1.

5. Protokolle der 3. Versammlung der deutschen Rabbiner, Breslau, den 13. bis 24. Juli 1846, Fünfzehnte Sitzung (Breslau: Leuckart, 1847), 265.

6. Verhandlungen der zweiten israelitischen Synode zu Augsburg vom 11. bis 17. Juli 1871 (Berlin: Louis Gerschel, 1873), 159ff.

7. Michael A. Meyer, "Women in the European Jewish Reform Movement," in *Gender and Jewish History*, ed. Marion A. Kaplan and Deborah Dash Moore (Bloomington: Indiana University Press, 2011), 145.

8. See footnote 15.

9. Ann Taylor Allen, *Feminism and Motherhood in Germany 1890–1914* (New Brunswick, NJ: Rutgers University Press, 1991), 213–14.

10. Benjamin Ivry, "Pioneering Social Worker Alice Salomon," *Forward*, January 5, 2012, https://forward.com/schmooze/149002/pioneering-social-worker-alice-salomon/.

11. Adriane Feustel, *Das Konzept des Sozialen im Werk Alice Salomons* (Berlin: Metropol, 2011), 114.

12. Cf. Alice Salomon, *Leitfaden der Wohlfahrtspflege* (Leipzig: Teubner, 1928), 86f.

13. Meyer, "*Gemeinschaft* within *Gemeinde*," 15–35, n. 63.

14. Bertha Pappenheim, "The Jewish Women in Religious Life," reprinted from the *Jewish Review* (January 1913), trans. Margery Bentwich, in *Four Centuries of Jewish Women's Spirituality: A Sourcebook*, ed. Ellen M. Umansky and Dianne Ashton (Waltham: Brandeis University Press, 2009), 158–63.

15. Pappenheim, "The Jewish Women in Religious Life," 163.

16. Cf. Émile Durkheim, *The Elementary Forms of Religious Life* (London: George Allen & Unwin, 1912).

17. Hannelore Erhart, "Die Theologin im Kontext von Universität und Kirche," in *Theologische Fakultäten im Nationalsozialismus, ed.* Leonore Siegele-Wenschkewitz and Carsten Nicolaisen (Göttingen: Vandenhoeck und Ruprecht, 1993): 235ff.

18. Lily H. Montagu, "Kinship with God: A Sermon Preached at the Liberal Jewish Synagogue," June 15, 1918, 7 pages.

19. "Die liberale Weltkonferenz in Berlin. Die Konferenzberatungen des Sonntags," *Jüdisch-Liberale Zeitung* 8, no. 34 (August 24, 1928): 5; Julius Lewkowitz, "Die Tagung des Weltverbandes für religiös-liberales Judentum," *Der Morgen* 4, no. 4 (October 1928): 410.

20. Bertha Badt-Strauss, "Eine Frau predigt," *Jüdische Rundschau* 67 (August 24, 1928): 480.

21. Proceedings of the First Conference of the World Union for Progressive Judaism, Berlin 1928, 111.

22. Inge Kallman, letter to Jonathan Magonet, January 4, 1994, in Elizabeth Tikvah Sarah, "Fraulein Rabbiner Regina Jonas, 1902–1944" (Regina Jonas Lecture, February 23, 2009), n. 22, Rabbi Elli Sarah, http://www.rabbiellisarah.com/rabbi-regina-jonas-lecture-23rd-february-2009-by-ets/.

23. Cf. Michael A. Meyer, *Response to Modernity: A History of the Reform Movement in Judaism* (New York: Oxford University Press, 1988), 379.

24. *Berliner Vereinsbote. Central-Organ für die jüdischen Vereine Berlins* 3, no. 16 (April 16, 1897): 7.

25. Sharon Gillerman, "Germany: 1750–1945," in *Jewish Women: A Comprehensive Historical Encyclopedia*," March 1, 2009, Jewish Women's Archive, https://jwa.org/encyclopedia/article/germany-1750-1945.

26. See "Hermann Vogelstein," Biographisches Handbuch *der Rabbiner*, vol. II.2, 546–548; cf. Hermann Vogelstein, "Ohne Vorbild (Zur JLZ-Umfrage: Einsegnung der Mädchen?)," *JLZ* 14, no. 56 (July 13, 1934): 5.

27. "Die Einrichtung der Mädchenkonfirmation ist eine überaus wertvolle und wesentliche Maßnahme der ersten Reformzeit," *JLZ*, November 5, 1926, 1.

28. Cf. Sandra Alfers, *weiter schreiben. Leben und Lyrik der Else Dormitzer* (Berlin: Hentrich und Hentrich, 2015).

29. Kerry Wallach, Paths of Modernity: *Jewish Women in Central Europe* (West Sussex: Wiley-Blackwell, 2012), 425.

30. Michael A. Meyer, "Women in the Thought and Practice of the European Jewish Reform Movement," in Kaplan and Moore, *Gender and Jewish History*, 152.

31. Simone Ladwig-Winters, *Freiheit und Bindung. Zur Geschichte der Jüdischen Reformgemeinde zu Berlin von den Anfängen bis zu ihrem Ende 1919*, ed. Peter Galliner (Teetz: Hentrich & Hentrich, 2004), 304.

32. Bettina Kratz-Ritter, "Henriette May," in *Jewish Women: A Comprehensive Historical Encyclopedia*, March 1, 2009, Jewish Women's Archive, https://jwa.org/encyclopedia/article/May-Henriette.

33. Kratz-Ritter, "Henriette May."

34. Zentralwohlfahrtsstelle, ed., *Henriette May zum Gedächtnis. Gewidmet von ihrer Familie in Gemeinschaft mit der Zentralwohlfahrtsstelle der deutschen Juden und dem Jüdischen Frauenbund* (Berlin, 1929), 58 pages.

35. "Minna Schwarz, B'nai B'rith Women's Leader, Dead," Jewish Telegraphic Agency, December 30, 1936, https://www.jta.org/1936/12/30/archive/minna-schwarz-bnai-brith-womens-leader-dead.

36. My own translation.

37. *Jüdisch-Liberale Zeitung* 5 (November 1926): 4; my translation.

38. Joseph Freimark, "Die jüdische Frau und das jüdische Haus," *Menorah* 5, no. 8 (August 1927): 489f.

39. Cf. Nr. 11, 4. Jg. (November 15, 1931), https://archive.org/stream/DieLogenschwester/Jg.%204%2C%20Nr.%2011%20%281931%29_djvu.txt.

40. *Das Jahr des Jüdisches Frauenbundes* (Frankfurt am Main, 1928).

41. "Women's Synagogue League," Jewish Telegraphic Agency, October 5, 1934, https://www.jta.org/1934/10/05/archive/womens-synagogue-league.

42. Cf. Maciej Łagiewski, *Breslauer Juden 1850–1944* (Wrocław: Muzeum Historyczne, 1996), 67.

43. "Three Americans Elected on Board of World Union for Progressive Judaism," Jewish Telegraphic Agency, August 22, 1928, https://www.jta.org/1928/08/22/archive/three-americans-elected-on-board-of-world-union-for-progressive-judaism.

44. The Paula-Ollendorff-Haus was located in Schweidnitzer Stadtgraben 28, opposite Liebichshöhe, today's Wzgórze Partyzantów.

45. Hermann Vogelstein, "Paula Ollendorf zum Gedächtnis," *Jüdisches Gemeindeblatt für die Synagogen-Gemeinde Breslau* 15, no. 20 (October 25, 1938): 1.

46. Julia Sneeringer, *Winning Women's Votes: Propaganda and Politics in Weimar Germany* (Chapel Hill: University of North Carolina Press, 2002), 192.

47. "Urges Jewish Women to Cultivate Jewish Social Life," Jewish Telegraphic Agency, January 1, 1933, https://www.jta.org/1933/01/01/archive/urges-jewish-women-to-cultivate-jewish-social-life.

48. Meyer, "*Gemeinschaft* within *Gemeinde*," 23, n. 35.

49. Leo Baeck, "Das Zusammensitzen von Männern und Frauen in der Synagoge Prinzregentenstraße in Berlin," in *Jüdisch-Liberale Zeitung* 9 (August 1929): 2.

50. Meyer, "*Gemeinschaft* within *Gemeinde*," 29.

51. Jonathan D. Sarna, "The Debate over Mixed Seating in the American Synagogue," in *The American Synagogue: A Sanctuary Transformed*, ed. Jack Wertheimer (New York: Cambridge University Press, 1987), 364.

52. Elisa Klapheck, *Fräulein Rabbiner Jonas: The Story of the First Woman Rabbi* (San Francisco: Jossey-Bass, 2004), 31.

53. See Ignaz Maybaum, *Parteibefreites Judentum. Lehrende Führung und priesterliche Gemeinschaft* (Berlin: Philo Verlag, 1935), 55–56.

54. Esther Seidel, *Women Pioneers of Jewish Learning: Ruth Liebrecht and Her Companions at the "Hochschule für die Wissenschaft des Judentums" in Berlin 1930–1934* (Berlin: Jüdische Verlagsanstalt Berlin, 2002), 122.

55. Cf. Marion A. Kaplan, *Between Dignity and Despair: Jewish Life in Nazi Germany* (New York: New York University Press, 1998).

BIBLIOGRAPHY

Alfers, Sandra, *Weiter Schreiben. Leben und Lyrik der Else Dormitzer* (Berlin: Hentrich und Hentrich, 2015).

Allen, Ann Taylor, *Feminism and Motherhood in Germany 1890–1914* (New Brunswick, NJ: Rutgers University Press, 1991).

Badt-Strauss, Bertha, "Eine Frau predigt," *Jüdische Rundschau* 67 (August 24, 1928): 480.

Baeck, Leo, "Das Zusammensitzen von Männern und Frauen in der Synagoge Prinzregentenstraße in Berlin," in *Jüdisch-Liberale Zeitung* 9 (August 1929).

Durkheim, Émile, The *Elementary Forms of Religious Life* (London: George Allen & Unwin, 1912).

Erhart, Hannelore, "Die Theologin im Kontext von Universität und Kirche," in *Theologische Fakultäten im Nationalsozialismus*, ed. Leonore Siegele-Wenschkewitz and Carsten Nicolaisen (Göttingen: Vandenhoeck und Ruprecht, 1993): 235ff.

Feustel, Adriane, *Das Konzept des Sozialen im Werk Alice Salomons* (Berlin: Metropol, 2011).

Freimark, Joseph, "Die jüdische Frau und das jüdische Haus," *Menorah* 5, no. 8 (August 1927): 489f.

Geiger, Abraham, "Zur Stellung des weiblichen Geschlechts in dem Judenthume unserer Zeit," in *Wissenschaftliche Zeitschrift für jüdische Theologie* 3 (1837): 1–14.

Gillerman, Sharon, "Germany: 1750–1945," in *Jewish Women: A Comprehensive Historical Encyclopedia*," March 1, 2009, Jewish Women's Archive, https://jwa.org/encyclopedia/article/germany-1750-1945.

Ivry, Benjamin, "Pioneering Social Worker Alice Salomon," *Forward*, January 5, 2012, https://forward.com/schmooze/149002/pioneering-social-worker-alice-salomon/ .

Kaplan, Marion A., *Between Dignity and Despair: Jewish Life in Nazi Germany* (New York: New York University Press, 1998).

Klapheck, Elisa, *Fräulein Rabbiner Jonas: The Story of the First Woman Rabbi* (San Francisco: Jossey-Bass, 2004).

Kratz-Ritter, Bettina, "Henriette May," in *Jewish Women: A Comprehensive Historical Encyclopedia*, March 1, 2009, Jewish Women's Archive, https://jwa.org/encyclopedia/article/May-Henriette.

Ladwig-Winters, Simone, *Freiheit und Bindung. Zur Geschichte der Jüdischen Reformgemeinde zu Berlin von den Anfängen bis zu ihrem Ende 1919*, ed. Peter Galliner (Teetz: Hentrich & Hentrich, 2004).

Łagiewski, Maciej: *Breslauer Juden 1850–1944* (Wrocław: Muzeum Historyczne, 1996).

"Three Americans Elected on Board of World Union for Progressive Judaism," Jewish Telegraphic Agency, August 22, 1928, https://www.jta.org/1928/08/22/archive/three-americans-elected-on-board-of-world-union-for-progressive-judaism .

Lewkowitz, Julius, "Die Tagung des Weltverbandes für religiös-liberales Judentum," *Der Morgen* 4, no. 4 (October 1928): 410.

Maybaum, Ignaz, *Parteibefreites Judentum. Lehrende Führung und Priesterliche Gemeinschaft* (Berlin: Philo Verlag, 1935).

Meyer, Michael A., "Women in the European Jewish Reform Movement," in *Gender and Jewish History*, ed. Marion A. Kaplan and Deborah Dash Moore (Bloomington: Indiana University Press, 2011).

Meyer, Michael A., *Judaism within Modernity: Essays on Jewish History and Religion* (Detroit: Wayne State University Press, 2001).

Meyer, Michael A., "Gemeinschaft within Gemeinde: Religious Ferment in Weimar Liberal Judaism," in *In Search of Jewish Community: Jewish Identities in Germany and Austria, 1918–1933*, ed. Michel Brenner and Derek J. Penslar (Bloomington: Indiana University Press, 1998).

Meyer, Michael A., *Response to Modernity: A History of the Reform Movement in Judaism* (New York: Oxford University Press, 1988).

Montagu, Lily H., "Kinship with God: A Sermon Preached at the Liberal Jewish Synagogue," June 15, 1918.

Pappenheim, Bertha, "The Jewish Women in Religious Life," reprinted from the *Jewish Review* (January 1913), trans. Margery Bentwich, in *Four Centuries of Jewish Women's Spirituality: A Sourcebook*, ed. Ellen M. Umansky and Dianne Ashton (Waltham: Brandeis University Press, 2009), 158–163.

Philippson, David, *The Reform Movement in Judaism* (London: Macmillan, 1907).

Proceedings of the First Conference of the World Union for Progressive Judaism, Berlin 1928.

Salomon, Alice, *Leitfaden der Wohlfahrtspflege* (Leipzig: Teubner, 1928).

Sarah, Elizabeth Tikvah, "Fraulein Rabbiner Regina Jonas, 1902–1944" (Regina Jonas Lecture, February 23, 2009), n. 22, Rabbi Elli Sarah, http://www.rabbiellisarah.com/rabbi-regina-jonas-lecture-23rd-february-2009-by-ets/ .

Sarna, Jonathan D., "The Debate over Mixed Seating in the American Synagogue," in *The American Synagogue: A Sanctuary Transformed*, ed. Jack Wertheimer (New York: Cambridge University Press, 1987), 364.

Seidel, Esther, *Women Pioneers of Jewish Learning: Ruth Liebrecht and Her Companions at the "Hochschule für die Wissenschaft des Judentums" in Berlin 1930–1934* (Berlin: Jüdische Verlagsanstalt Berlin, 2002).

Sneeringer, Julia, *Winning Women's Votes: Propaganda and Politics in Weimar Germany* (Chapel Hill: University of North Carolina Press, 2002).

Umansky, Ellen (ed.), *Lily Montagu: Sermons, Addresses, Letters and Prayers* (Lewiston: Edwin Mellen Press, 1985).

Vogelstein, Hermann, "Paula Ollendorf zum Gedächtnis," *Jüdisches Gemeindeblatt für die Synagogen-Gemeinde Breslau* 15, no. 20 (October 25, 1938): 1.

Vogelstein, Hermann, "Ohne Vorbild (Zur JLZ-Umfrage: Einsegnung der Mädchen?)," *JLZ* 14, no. 56 (July 13, 1934).

Wallach, Kerry, *Paths of Modernity: Jewish Women in Central Europe* (West Sussex: Wiley-Blackwell, 2012).

Chapter Five

Paving the Road to Women Rabbis, 1889–2015

Pamela S. Nadell

"With the ordination of Rabbi Sally Priesand," in June 1972, "Judaism learned that a great religious debate over women in the pulpit had been settled before it began," proclaimed a journalist.[1] A reporter is no historian, and this one had no idea that a great debate over women in the pulpit, Christian and Jewish, had been underway for more than a century by the time he wrote these words. Had he asked, rather than surmising from his own observations, this anonymous journalist could have learned from Rabbi Priesand that she had uncovered that the history of the quest for women's rabbinic ordination went back, as far as she knew, half a century. Rabbi Priesand could have explained that when Reform rabbis first debated the matter in 1922, they well understood that the "ordination of woman as rabbi is a modern issue, due to the evolution in her status in our day."[2]

Interestingly, newspapers were broadcasting a far bigger women's story in the spring of 1972. On March 22, the U.S. Congress had, at last, passed the Equal Rights Amendment (ERA). Introduced into every session of Congress since 1923, the ERA read: "Equality of rights under the law shall not be denied or abridged by the United States or by any State on account of sex."[3] Now Congress sent the proposed Twenty-Seventh Amendment to the U.S. Constitution out to the states for ratification. No one could have predicted then, in this era of headlines announcing women's almost daily advances into new frontiers, including reports of the first woman rabbi in history, that the ERA would fail to win ratification by the states.[4]

Champions of the ERA had trod a long road to congressional approval.[5] It seemed, at least to our reporter, that the first woman rabbi had not marched down a similarly long path. But, as this chapter demonstrates, the debate over women's rabbinic ordination has ebbed and flowed in every stream of American Judaism, and indeed in Jewish communities in Europe and Israel too, for more than a century. The men of Reform Judaism's Central Conference of American Rabbis discussing the question back in 1922 grasped that once U.S. women had won the vote—which had occurred but two years before—the moment seemed poised to revolutionize American women's social, legal, economic, and political status. Among the transformations evidently underway and widely reported in the news were more and more women entering into the learned professions. In hindsight we know just how small their numbers actually were, but that was not readily apparent then.[6] If women could become doctors, lawyers, and ministers, then could they also become rabbis? That today more than a thousand women hold this title tells us that ultimately they did.[7]

But how this came to be is a much older story than even Rabbi Priesand, let alone our mistaken journalist, realized back in 1972. In fact, the story of the quest for women's rabbinic ordination goes back further in time than the introduction of the Equal Rights Amendment into Congress. The ERA first surfaced on the coattails of the Nineteenth Amendment to the U.S. Constitution granting women suffrage. But the first glimmer of the demand for women's rabbinic ordination dates back to 1889, when, on the front page of Philadelphia's Jewish newspaper, the *Jewish Exponent*, writer Mary M. Cohen asked, "Could not—our *women*—be ministers?"[8] That question launched the debate over women's right to rabbinic ordination.

1. OPENING THE PATH: 1890s–1930s

This story of women's road to ordination is largely an American story, one that sits squarely against the backdrop of the nineteenth-century U.S. women's rights movement. Although best known for demanding female suffrage, the women's rights movement, launched at the Seneca Falls Convention in New York in 1848, was even then railing against men for monopolizing the learned professions. In the nineteenth century, a few courageous women managed to break into them, becoming the first female doctors, lawyers, and even ordained Protestant clergy.

The notion of seeing women enter into the male bastion of the rabbinate just as a few American women were crashing the barriers to these other professions, struck a chord, particularly among American Reform Jews. Leaders of Reform Judaism had long boasted of how their movement had emancipated women in the synagogue and of Reform's progressive stance on women's equality. They pointed proudly to men and women sitting together in their synagogues and singing together in their choirs. They touted their invention of confirmation, a ceremony in which girls as well as boys demonstrate their commitment to their faith. In 1892, echoing the prophet Isaiah (40:3–4), Adolph Moses, a Reform rabbi who led congregations in Alabama and Kentucky, proclaimed, "Make a highway for woman, remove every obstacle from her path, let every mountain of inequality and injustice be made level, let every valley of ignorance and prejudice be raised. . . . Let all her powers grow and expand, and be added to the working forces of civilization."[9]

As Rabbi Moses called for "all avenues of human activity"[10] to be opened to women, he may not have envisaged the woman rabbi. Yet, others were already pointing her way. In the pages of the *American Jewess*, the first Jewish woman's magazine in the United States, Henry Berkowitz, a Philadelphia Reform rabbi with deep interests in social reform, gushed that women were becoming "physicians, preachers, dentists, lawyers, journalists, compositors, typewriters, bookkeepers, sales women, telephone and telegraph operators. . . . Every day a bolt is wrenched off, bars are pulled down, and an entrance to some new occupation is being forced open for women."[11] Pulling down the bar against the woman rabbi surely could not be far behind, the next logical step to making women fully equal within Reform Judaism.[12]

Yet, while some girls and women found their way into classes at Hebrew Union College (HUC) in its first decades after the Reform rabbinical seminary was established in Cincinnati in 1875, none seems to have ever been considered a serious candidate for ordination. This includes Ray Frank (Litman), dubbed by the press "the girl rabbi of the golden west" for her lay preaching, teaching, and leading of religious services in the 1890s.[13] Nevertheless, Hannah Solomon, a proud Reform Jew and the founding president of the National Council of Jewish Women, the first nationwide American Jewish women's club, boasted in 1895, "We are receiving every possible encouragement from our rabbis, and should women desire to enter the ministry, there will be no obstacles thrown in their way."[14] Yet, not until the 1920s, during the era of rising expectations for women's new opportunities following the ratification of the woman suffrage amendment, did women seeking ordination begin carving out a trail that others could follow. These pioneers pushed the debate about women rabbis from the realm of the abstract to the domain of the actual.

The first was Martha Neumark (Montor). The daughter of Hebrew Union College professor David Neumark had matriculated, as had other young women, as a special student in HUC's Preparatory Division. There she studied Bible, Hebrew, Aramaic, rabbinics, liturgy, and Jewish history. In 1921, after three years of study, seventeen-year-old Neumark asked the college for a High Holiday pulpit. Every fall, small Jewish communities scattered across America invite rabbinical students to lead them in prayer on the holiest days of the year. Neumark wanted the same opportunity her male classmates would soon have—to lead and to preach to Jews in the American hinterlands. She thus raised the very real question of what would happen if she completed the nine-year rabbinical course. Would the college ordain her?

For the next two years, college faculty, alumni, and trustees debated women's ordination. Delving into the classical texts of Jewish tradition, scholars lined up on opposite sides, shaping the lines of the debate that would, in decades to come, echo throughout American Jewish life. Some believed Jewish law unequivocally prohibited women rabbis. Others argued that nothing in Judaism forbade this, in large measure because the sages of old had simply never considered the question. Even so, argued others, the notion of a woman rabbi was "contrary to all Jewish tradition," an "absurd and ridiculous" innovation that would "outrage the feelings of a large part of the Jewish people."[15] In New York, Cyrus Adler, president of the Conservative movement's Jewish Theological Seminary (JTS), weighed in: his seminary "would not entertain the idea for a moment."[16] In the end, the HUC Board of Governors voted, six laymen to two rabbis, to exclude women from the rabbinate. Martha Neumark would not become a rabbi.

Yet, even as her hopes were quashed, another seminary was already facing the same question. New York's Jewish Institute of Religion (JIR) was a nondenominational but decidedly liberal school founded by Rabbi Stephen S. Wise, the Zionist leader and a towering figure of his generation. By the time Irma Levy Lindheim joined JIR's inaugural class in the fall of 1922, this mother of five and wife of a JIR trustee was a deeply committed Zionist who wanted higher education to fill in the gaping holes in her knowledge of Jews and Judaism. A semester later, shortly after HUC decided that it would limit "to males the right to matriculate for the purpose of entering the rabbinate,"

Lindheim asked the JIR to change her status from that of a special student to that of rabbinical student.[17] The faculty yielded, and JIR announced that it trained men *and women* for the Jewish ministry.

Nevertheless, Lindheim failed to complete the rabbinical course. Instead, a few years later she became president of Hadassah, the Women's Zionist Organization of America, an organization of 30,000 members established in 1912. As she prepared to succeed its founder Henrietta Szold, the journalist, educator, and icon of American Jewish womanhood for her generation and beyond, Lindheim wrote, "If, at the Convention, the decision of the National Board is confirmed, I shall feel that I have been ordained, more truly so, even, than had I been confirmed as a rabbi."[18] In 1926, Lindheim could not become a rabbi in America. She could not lead Jewish men and women as rabbi, teacher, and preacher. But she could lead the women of Hadassah and did so until she settled in Palestine and dedicated the remainder of her life to Zionism and building up the State of Israel.

However, Lindheim was not the only woman at the Jewish Institute of Religion aiming for ordination. Dr. Dora Askowith, who had earned a doctorate from Columbia University for a dissertation on Jews in the ancient Roman Empire, was in her class. Later, after also failing to advance toward ordination, Askowith explained, "I took the work at the Institute because of my deep interest in Judaica and Hebraica rather than because I sought to enter the ministry though I hoped to open the road for women who might be desirous of being ordained."[19]

In the 1930s at JIR, there was indeed another woman "desirous of being ordained." Helen Levinthal (Lyons) was the daughter of one of the most highly regarded Conservative rabbis of his day, Israel Levinthal, and the granddaughter of Bernard Levinthal, the founder of the Union of Orthodox Rabbis, the Agudat ha-Rabbanim. She grew up receiving the intensive Jewish education typical of rabbis' children. After college and graduate school, she joined a number of Jewish women's organizations and, perhaps to occupy her time, enrolled first as an auditor at JIR and then as a rabbinical student. Since other women before her had come and gone at JIR without ever reaching the point of ordination, the problem of whether to ordain Helen Levinthal only became real as she approached her final year of study. In December 1937, the faculty debated the matter: would they ordain her if she finished the coursework? Ultimately, they decided that they could not see any reason to break with tradition in the case of "Miss Levinthal," whom they considered, despite her deeply researched, closely argued thesis "Woman Suffrage from the Halachic Aspect," "an average student with no special qualifications."[20] Contravening the seminary's own mission that stated that it trained men and women for the ministry, JIR refused to ordain Helen Levinthal.

In 1939, as her classmates became rabbis, Helen Levinthal graduated with a master of Hebrew literature and a special certificate recognizing her accomplishments. *Time* magazine ordained her "as near to being a rabbi as a female might be." She told the press, "It is all a process of evolution. . . . Some day there will be women rabbis."[21] Apparently, neither she nor the press knew then that already one woman had indeed become the first woman rabbi in the world.

In 1935 in Germany, Regina Jonas became the first woman rabbi. Because her story is told more fully elsewhere in this book, this chapter covers just the outline of her journey to ordination. As a student at Berlin's Hochschule für die Wissenschaft des Judentums, she sought ordination and wrote a thesis titled "Can a Woman Hold Rabbinic Office?" There she argued that the weight of tradition and precedents in the history of Jewish women proved that the woman rabbi was "merely the elongation of a line which is sketched already by our scriptures."[22] Her thesis was accepted by Professor Eduard Baneth, the Hochschule's distinguished scholar of Talmudic and rabbinic literature, but before he could administer the required oral exam, he died. Whether Baneth would have acted upon the conclusion of the thesis that he accepted remains unknown, but the other faculty refused to do so. Instead of becoming a rabbi then, Jonas graduated in 1930 with the only diploma women could earn, that of academic teacher of religion. But she still hoped to pursue the profession that she loved. Five years later, Rabbi Max Dienemann, one of the leaders of German Liberal Judaism, gave her an oral exam in Jewish law and signed her rabbinic diploma. Although he cautioned her against using the title "rabbi" until she consulted with other authorities, from then, in Berlin and in the notorious Nazi ghetto of Theresienstadt, some called her, until she was murdered in Auschwitz in fall 1944, "Rabbiner Doktor Regina Jonas."

What joins the 1920s and 1930s pioneers of women's ordination to those who followed them and to those who argued their cause before them is that all believed Jewish tradition permitted women to be rabbis. Each on her own, and largely unaware that others had already made similar arguments, turned to the Jewish past, especially to the history of women in Judaism, to find support in Jewish tradition for her aims—even though, as a woman who wanted to be a rabbi, she seemed destined to overturn that very tradition. Martha Neumark, Irma Levy Lindheim, Dora Askowith, Helen Levinthal, and Regina Jonas, and those who championed their cause all pointed to the prophetesses Miriam, Deborah, and Hulda, claiming that their religious leadership proved unequivocally that Judaism permitted women rabbis. They brought forth—in articles and speeches, in student sermons, and, for Levinthal and Jonas, in their theses—remarkable medieval and modern Jewish women, those who taught, who founded schools, and who knew Jewish law, including several accepted by their contemporaries as "*rabbinim.*" In the end, they argued, as Regina Jonas had in her thesis, that "other than prejudice and unfamiliarity, almost nothing opposes a woman holding the rabbinical office "*halakhically*," that is in terms of Jewish law.[23]

Finally, what binds the pioneers of the 1920s and 1930s is that each—with the tragic exception of Jonas, whose voice the Nazis silenced—would again take up the cause of women's ordination. In decades to come, these women wrote seminary faculty and presidents, and even the press, trying to "complete the circle" of the path they had laid out for the women who followed them and who wanted to be rabbis.[24]

2. THE ROAD ENDS IN REFORM JUDAISM

In 1947, another woman applied to the Jewish Institute of Religion bent on becoming a rabbi. This time the seminary, which once boasted it trained women for the ministry, responded that it was impossible to admit female students. That seemed to close the door on women rabbis. Yet, during the 1950s the debate about women's ordination continued.

The decade opened with the extraordinary case of a woman succeeding her husband as rabbi. In 1924, when Temple Beth Israel in Meridian, Mississippi, called Rabbi William Ackerman to its pulpit, his wife, Paula Herskovitz Ackerman, was by his side. The rebbetzin, the rabbi's wife, was traditionally a full partner in her husband's rabbinate and was crucial to his success.[25] Ackerman was no exception. She taught Sabbath school and was active in the National Federation of Temple Sisterhoods, today known as the Women of Reform Judaism. When her husband was ill or away, she often substituted for him in the pulpit.

In November 1950, her husband of thirty-one years died. Temple Beth Israel's president asked the widow to lead them until they could find a new rabbi, something that they expected could take some time in this early postwar era when, as Jews left the cities for the suburbs, they were founding hundreds of new congregations, and there were just not enough rabbis for all of their pulpits.

Ackerman fully comprehended what this meant: "I also know how revolutionary the idea is . . . if perhaps it will open a way for women students to train for congregational leadership—then my life would have some meaning."[26] Leading Reform rabbis opposed her. She was not ordained. She did not have the right education. She set a dangerous precedent. Would other rabbis' wives assume that they could follow in her footsteps? In spite of their opposition, from December 1950 until the fall of 1953, Paula Ackerman was Temple Beth Israel's "rabbi."

Disapproval of Ackerman did not mean, however, that Reform rabbis opposed women's ordination in principle. In the mid 1950s, these rabbis returned again to the matter many had supported back in the 1920s. This time, they were propelled by the news that the Presbyterian Church, one of the largest and most important of the mainline Protestant denominations, had decided, in 1955, to ordain female clergy and also that Harvard Divinity School would soon begin accepting female students.

In response, Reform's Central Conference of American Rabbis created a commission to study the issue. Its 1956 "Report on the Ordination of Women" recognized that "in view of woman's parity with man, we believe that the unwarranted and outmoded tradition of reducing woman to an inferior status with regard to ordination for the rabbinate be abandoned." It called for admitting women to study for the rabbinate and ordaining them "if and when" they completed the course of study.[27]

Yet the rabbis were convinced that the matter was purely hypothetical—there were no female candidates for the rabbinate, or so they presumed. But they were wrong. Other young women were poised to set out on the path plowed by the women who would have been rabbis if they could have been rabbis in the 1920s and 1930s.

This time, the journey started at the University of Cincinnati. In 1957, HUC-JIR—the two seminaries had merged in 1950—offered to University of Cincinnati students, whose campus was just up the hill, the chance to complete the first-year rabbinical curriculum as undergraduates. The seminary hoped to speed young men on the road into the rabbinate in this era when American Judaism was exploding and in need of more rabbis. Several scores of students took advantage of this opportunity. Among them were a dozen women. Some of the coeds saw this higher Jewish education as the path to religious school teaching or scholarship; some made it their path to becoming rebbetzins. A few wanted to be rabbis.

Among them was Sally Priesand. As a teenager at Cleveland, Ohio's Beth Israel–The West Temple and at Reform's Goldman Union Camp Institute at Zionsville, Indiana, Priesand had found herself deeply attached to Judaism. Her camp friends knew that she hoped one day to become "Rabbi Sally."

In her junior year of high school, Priesand wrote to HUC-JIR to find out what she needed to do to get in. College officials responded cautiously. The school had never ordained a woman. Most women preferred the field of Jewish education. Nevertheless, in 1964, when Priesand entered her freshman year at the University of Cincinnati, she enrolled at HUC-JIR as an undergraduate. Already, her hometown paper, the *Cleveland Plain Dealer*, was announcing: "Girl Sets Her Goal to Be 1st Woman Rabbi."[28]

By 1968, when Priesand graduated from the University of Cincinnati with her BA and entered the regular rabbinical program at HUC-JIR, the question of women's ordination had become inextricably tied to the new wave of American feminism. Just as in the nineteenth century where the notion of women's ordination was set against the backdrop of the women's rights movement, now, in the 1960s, the swelling second wave of American feminism propelled forward the issue of women rabbis.

Feminism seemed to be bursting forth everywhere. In 1961, President John F. Kennedy convened the Commission on the Status of Women. Its report, issued two years later, documented widespread discrimination against women in the workplace and called for equal employment opportunity for women. That same year, journalist and housewife Betty Friedan published her clarion call *The Feminine Mystique*, chronicling the discontent of her generation of female college graduates whose talents and educations were wasted on their suburban homes, which she shockingly called "comfortable concentration camps."[29] A year later, Title VII of the 1964 Civil Rights Act prohibited discrimination in employment on the basis of race and, perhaps more astonishingly, sex.

These events galvanized American women to push anew on multiple frontiers and all at once for political, social, and economic equality. In the annals of American Judaism, Priesand appeared unique. But in the annals of the new wave of feminism, her ambition to become the first woman rabbi appeared but part of a larger story of tremendous changes underway for all American women, a story that would, by 1972, push the ERA, after fifty years of debate, through Congress. As headlines blazoned "Women's 'Lib' on the March in the Churches" and reported more Protestant denominations ordaining women, *Time* and *Newsweek* magazines covered "Rabbi Sally" in her student pulpits.

This publicity was crucial to Priesand's ultimate success. The attention of the press not only helped to sustain her but also to convince others to champion her cause. It guaranteed that, in the end, if she finished rabbinical school, whatever HUC-JIR did would make national headlines.

The publicity led synagogues and Jewish groups to invite rabbinical student Priesand to come and speak. With sermons with titles like "A Woman Rabbi. . . . Her Prerogatives, Principles, and Problems," Priesand affirmed that during these turbulent years in American life—as liberal movements, like women's rights and civil rights, took radical turns, and as rage against the Vietnam War erupted on campuses and in the streets—Judaism, too, was "a-changin'" with the times.

Yet, in her speeches, Priesand was always careful to distance herself from the radical wing of the women's rights movement, dubbed "women's libbers" and inaccurately, but persistently, "bra burners." She championed a different strain of feminism, the liberal one that called for the right of men—and of women—to fulfill their potential. Having spoken her piece on feminism, she turned next to what was really important to her, to Judaism—to God, Torah, and the Jewish people, and to how she hoped to become a rabbi, to spend her life serving and guiding her people. She intended to preserve and uphold Jewish tradition, not to overthrow it, even if ordaining her a rabbi seemed to others a terrible violation of that very tradition.

As Priesand entered her last year of rabbinical school, one major hurdle remained—her thesis. She decided to research and write "Toward a Course of Study for Reform High School Youth Dealing with the Historic and Changing Role of the Jewish Woman," a curriculum that surveyed Jewish women from the biblical era to the present. She seems, however, to have been utterly unaware that all who had championed women rabbis before her had also turned to Jewish women in the past, seeking, consciously or not, role models. Now she turned over a few pages in the history of the women who would have been rabbis if they could have been rabbis. She discovered the debate around Martha Neumark. She learned that in 1963 the members of the National Federation of Temple Sisterhoods had resolved in favor of women's ordination. Discovering Regina Jonas's life let her claim that she "was not truly the first woman rabbi," that she was "actually the second woman rabbi," but that she was the first ordained by a seminary.[30]

On June 3, 1972, the high school junior of a decade before who had written, "Although I am a girl, I would like very much to study for a rabbinical degree," was ordained rabbi, teacher, and preacher.[31] The first American woman had become a rabbi. The road to women's ordination in Reform Judaism had closed, and a new road opened, one that the first women to become Reform rabbis would pave.

3. THE ROAD BECOMES A HIGHWAY: RECONSTRUCTIONIST AND CONSERVATIVE JUDAISM

The debate over women's ordination was never confined exclusively to Reform Judaism. Mary M. Cohen, who first raised it, was not a Reform Jew. She was an active member of Philadelphia's traditionalist congregation Mikveh Israel.

Unsurprisingly, each time the controversy about women's ordination had swelled in Reform circles, it had spilled over to other sectors of American Jewish religious life. The Jewish Theological Seminary's president Cyrus Adler had weighed in on the question when the Reform movement was first debating it in the early 1920s. A quarter century later, his successor, Louis Finkelstein, wrote to a young woman, Gladys Citrin. Her superb Jewish education had begun at the Shulamith School for Girls, the first Orthodox elementary school for girls in the United States, whose dean, Judith Berlin Lieberman, was also the wife of the renowned JTS Talmud professor Saul Lieberman. Finkelstein responded to this young woman that the seminary would not admit her to study for the rabbinate because the "place of women in religion is to be high priestesses in the sanctuary of their home and we want them to become good wives and good mothers in Israel."[32]

By the 1970s, as Sally Priesand's ordination was imminent and with the feminist movement urging forward all sorts of demands for full equality for women everywhere in American life, the question of women's ordination, which had periodically surfaced in Conservative Judaism in the past, emerged anew and for far longer than a moment. Those raising the issue in this branch of American Judaism then also knew that the Reconstructionists would soon also ordain their first female rabbi.

Reconstructionist Judaism was for many decades the liberal wing of the Conservative movement. A response to the complexities of modern American Jewish life, Reconstructionist Judaism was the brainchild of JTS professor Mordecai M. Kaplan. Over the course of several decades, Kaplan's acolytes had gradually developed a set of Reconstructionist institutions, distinct from those of the Conservative movement. The split between the two became final when, in 1968, its leaders opened their own rabbinical seminary, the Reconstructionist Rabbinical College (RRC), in Philadelphia.

From the first, the RRC admitted women and men. In the fall of 1969, Sandy Eisenberg, who, although raised a Reform Jew, had become intrigued with Reconstructionist ideology, enrolled. Like her contemporary Sally Priesand, and like those who had traveled this road before her, she too found herself speaking and writing widely about women in Jewish tradition and calling for that tradition to which she would dedicate her life to create "full opportunity for women in all areas of Jewish life."[33] In 1974, having married her classmate Dennis Sasso, she became not a rebbetzin, but the first Reconstructionist female rabbi. Three years later, in the fall of 1977, the Rabbis Sasso were hired by Indianapolis's Beth El Zedeck, a congregation affiliated with both the Reconstructionist and the Conservative movements. Sandy Eisenberg Sasso thus became the first woman rabbi in a Conservative congregation. By then, the furor over women's ordination was well underway in Conservative Judaism.

In the spring of 1972, committed, Conservative Jewish—and passionately feminist—women began vociferously demanding religious equality in their movement. Three months before Sally Priesand was ordained, a group of these women, calling themselves Ezrat Nashim (referring both to "the help of women" and to the women's court in the ancient Jerusalem Temple) sounded off. They were tired of men's apologetics and their parades of the great Jewish women of the past. Decrying women's "separate but equal," second-class status in their stream of American Judaism, they demanded full religious equality, including the admission of women to rabbinical school.[34]

At the same time, other young women were already applying to JTS's rabbinical school. Over the course of the next decade, as more and more such women kept writing for applications, they compelled seminary leaders to keep confronting the question. Some entered other JTS graduate programs, pursuing as masters and doctoral candidates as much of the rabbinical curriculum as they could on their own, hoping that when, in the near future, the faculty would accept women into the rabbinical school, they would already be well on their way to becoming rabbis.

Conservative leaders continued to struggle with the question. For a long decade between 1972 and 1983, the issue both drained and electrified Conservative rabbis, JTS faculty and students, the women who would be rabbis if they could be rabbis, and their supporters and opponents out in Conservative congregations across America. Some young women reluctantly abandoned their movement and were ordained at other seminaries. Meanwhile, Conservative leaders engaged in an intricate political dance of shifting alliances, studies undertaken, commissions formed, hearings held, motions tabled, and votes counted.

To give but one example, the Conservative movement convened the Commission for the Study of the Ordination of Women as Rabbis in December 1977. Its members wrote papers examining all aspects of the question and even convened public hearings in five North American synagogues to take the pulse of Conservative laity.[35] At the end of its deliberations, eleven commission members agreed that, since Jewish law offered no direct objection to women's ordination, they recommended that the movement train women to become rabbis. Three members dissented, portending a schism in the movement if it took this irrevocable, radical step.

By December 1979, as the JTS faculty prepared to vote on the issue, the decision proved so fraught that the faculty Senate decided to table the decision, that is, it refused to vote yea or nay on admitting women to the rabbinical school and called for yet another study, this time "a balanced committee of Talmudic scholars" to convene and rule. One professor predicted that this meant the end of "the issue of the ordination of women for at least fifty years, if not forever."[36]

Professors are not prophets. Less than four years later, after the intricate dance of just who held the reins of power in the movement over women rabbis—the JTS alumni in their rabbinical organization who were about to admit to their ranks a female rabbi, a graduate of HUC-JIR who would have been ordained at JTS if she could have been ordained at JTS, or the seminary—JTS faculty voted to admit women to the rabbinical school. A year later, Amy Eilberg, one of the women who had been waiting in the wings biding her time by taking as much of the curriculum necessary for ordination as she could as a doctoral student, entered rabbinical school in the first class to include women. In May 1985, JTS chancellor Gerson Cohen, who had personally shifted his view on women's ordination over the course of the heated debate, ordained her a rabbi.

4. BYWAYS OFF THE HIGHWAY: ORTHODOXY

As the Conservative movement concluded its debate over women rabbis, Orthodox Jews launched theirs. Even before Amy Eilberg was ordained, the leading Orthodox feminist activist Blu Greenberg was asking, "Will there be Orthodox women rabbis?"[37] The answer is yes. In the less than two decades since I published *Women Who Would Be Rabbis* in 1998, a sea change in the Orthodox world has occurred. The first generation of Orthodox women who preach, teach, and rule on matters of Jewish law now stand among us. But they do so under a variety of titles: maharat, rabba, rabbanit, and even rabbi. Yet, no matter the title, whose adaptations reflect in part the fact that Hebrew is a gendered language, with no neuter gender, today some sectors of the Orthodox world have embraced the modern notion of the woman rabbi.

It is difficult, however, to decide just who can claim to be the first Orthodox female rabbi, and not only because of these different titles. Orthodox Judaism encompasses an extraordinarily wide spectrum of voices and views, from those who one historian has styled as "accommodators"—Orthodox Jews who observe halakhah but whose dress, education, and employment integrate them fairly well into the modern world—to the "resisters"—whose distinctive dress, educational patterns, and rigid gender roles limit, as much as possible, interactions with contemporary culture.[38]

In the past decades, some sectors of the "accommodationist" Orthodox, in both the United States and in Israel, began experimenting with innovative strategies for opening byways toward women's religious leadership. They permitted women who have the requisite training to become legal advisors to answer questions women pose about observing the laws of family purity, that is, those governing marital relations, and to deal with issues related to female fertility and sexuality. In Israel, women who had mastered Jewish legal texts have been accepted as advocates for women appearing before rabbinical courts, the only courts allowed to deal with issues of Jewish marriage and divorce. In the United States, some Orthodox rabbis appointed female congregational interns, whose responsibilities for teaching and preaching are analogous to those of rabbis.[39]

These and other paths led some women to aspire to greater authority, that of the rabbinate. The first among them sought, as Regina Jonas had, private ordination. In 1994, Mimi Feigelson, known as Reb Mimi, was ordained by disciples of the charismatic neo-Hasidic rabbi Shlomo Carlebach, and ever since then, she has called herself, in English, an Israeli Orthodox woman rabbi, and, in Hebrew, rabba. "Rabba" is one way of rendering in Hebrew the feminine of "rabbi," the title, from the Hebrew word *rav*, meaning "master," conferred upon men at ordination.[40]

Another who ultimately received what she has termed private ordination is Haviva Ner-David. In 1993, as Haviva Krasner-Davidson, she applied to New York's Yeshiva University's rabbinical school, the flagship of modern American Orthodoxy. Not surprisingly, her application was ignored.[41] She then moved to Israel and pursued an independent course of study. In 2006, in Israel, Rabbi Aryeh Strikovsky granted her what she calls private *semikhah*, that is, Orthodox ordination, but what he characterizes as "more an official recognition of her studies and was not intended to be construed as an ordination." Because Strikovsky also affirmed that she had "covered exactly the tractates and the issues that men have to master in order to get ordination," Ner-David took this as a signal that she could "act in the role of a rabbi" if her community recognized her as one.[42]

Meanwhile, in the United States, another young woman set off along a divergent byway. In 2003, Sara Hurwitz had been hired as a congregational intern by maverick New York Rabbi Avi Weiss. But she too yearned to study, to master Jewish law, and to exercise the authority such knowledge confers. Six years later, having completed an extensive program of text study, she was ordained, in a public ceremony, by Rabbi Weiss with the title "maharat," a term that he had invented, an acronym of the Hebrew for female leader of Jewish law, spirituality, and Torah. At the time, the event scarcely made the news. A few months later, Rabbi Weiss and Maharat Hurwitz opened Yeshivat Maharat, a seminary offering women "an official path for gaining the skills, training, and certification they need to become spiritual leaders within the Modern Orthodox community."[43]

As its first semester came to a close, Weiss decided to clarify Hurwitz's position in his synagogue, where she visited the sick and conducted funerals. He changed her title to "rabba," unleashing a firestorm of condemnation in the Orthodox world.[44] In its wake, Weiss promised his Orthodox colleagues that he would not use the title again in the future. But since then, Yeshivat Maharat permits its ordainees—as of 2016, there were fourteen—to choose their honorific. In the class that graduated in 2015 some took the title "rabba," one took the title "maharat," and, for the first time, one, Lila Kagedan, took the title "rabbi."

Meanwhile, in Israel some learned women prefer another title, that of "rabbanit," which is another way to render "rabbi" in the feminine. Historically, "rabbanit" has designated the wife of a rabbi. However, these women, who complete rigorous programs of Jewish legal textual study on their own and in seminaries, like Har'el Beit Midrash, are being ordained with the title "rabbanit."[45]

Orthodox women have thus plowed several byways off the highway of women's ordination. Rabba Hurwitz's participation in several public programs featuring the first female rabbis finds her standing proudly alongside the other firsts—Rabbis Priesand, Sasso, and Eilberg.[46] Yet opposition to female religious leadership in most of the Orthodox world remains fierce. America's main Modern Orthodox rabbinical association, the Rabbinical Council of America, has banned its members from hiring female clergy, "regardless of the title used."[47]

So where does this leave us? No matter the title—rabba, maharat, rabbanit, rabbi—the first generation of women to become Orthodox rabbis have created facts on the ground. They preach, teach, act as legal decisors, and are paving the road into the Orthodox rabbinate for those who come after them.

5. THE ROAD TAKEN

The women who, in the end, became rabbis or rabba or maharat or rabbanit set out on trails laid by others, but they completed the course. As they reached the end of the journey to women's ordination, they looked behind them to see that the road that the firsts had forged had expanded into a highway and that more than a thousand women have already traveled it.

At the end of this road to ordination, the first women rabbis halted before setting out on a new and unmapped pathway, one that they and those behind them would pave. There they would encounter new questions and issues. How would women rabbis be received out in the congregations? What challenges would their presence pose to their seminaries, congregants, and male colleagues? What would bringing women's voices and perspectives to bear on an ancient, androcentric tradition mean? These and other matters would line the surface of the road opening into the future paved by the women who had become rabbis.

NOTES

1. Quoted in Pamela S. Nadell, *Women Who Would Be Rabbis: A History of Women's Ordination, 1889–1985* (Boston: Beacon Press, 1998), 1. This chapter is largely based on my book *Women Who Would Be Rabbis: A History of Women's Ordination, 1889–1985*.
2. Quoted in Sally Priesand, *Judaism and the New Woman* (New York: Behrman House, 1975), 62. This book is a revision of her 1972 rabbinical thesis, "Toward a Course of Study for Reform High School Youth Dealing with the Historic and Changing Role of the Jewish Woman."
3. Eileen Shanahan, "Equal Rights Amendment is Approved by Congress," *The New York Times*, 22 March, 1972, 1, https://archive.nytimes.com/www.nytimes.com/learning/general/onthisday/big/0322.html#article.
4. Thirty-five states voted for ratification, three short of the necessary thirty-eight.
5. For an excellent analysis of the debates over the first ERA, see Rebecca DeWolf, "Gendered Citizenship: The Original Conflict over the Equal Rights Amendment, 1920–1963" (PhD diss., American University, 2014).
6. William H. Chafe, *The Paradox of Change: American Women in the 20th Century* (New York: Oxford University Press, 1991), 100; Nancy Cott, *The Grounding of Modern Feminism* (New Haven: Yale University Press, 1987), 217–18; Barbara Miller Solomon, *In the Company of Educated Women* (New Haven: Yale University Press, 1985), table 5.
7. The current number is unavailable; Gerhard Falk, "The Rabbi Has No Beard," Jewish Buffalo on the Web, November 4, 2016, http://jbuff.com/c090607.htm, asserts that in 2007 there were 829 female rabbis.
8. Mary M. Cohen, "A Problem for Purim," *Jewish Exponent*, March 15, 1889, 1.
9. Adolph Moses, "The Emancipation of Women," in *Yahvism and Other Discourses*, ed. H. G. Enelow (Louisville: Louisville Section of the Council of Jewish Women, 1913), 104. Cf. Isaiah 40:3–4. On Adolph Moses, see the introduction by H. G. Enelow in Adolph Moses, *Yahvism and Other Discourses*, ed. H. G. Enelow (Louisville: Louisville Section of the Council of Jewish Women, 1903).
10. Ibid.
11. Henry Berkowitz, "Woman's Part in the Drama of Life," *American Jewess* 1, no. 2 (May 1895): 64.
12. Reform's stance on women's equality was largely rhetorical; see Karla Goldman, "Women in Reform Judaism: Between Rhetoric and Reality," in *Women Remaking American Judaism*, ed. Riv-Ellen Prell (Detroit: Wayne State University Press, 2007), 109–34.
13. Simon Litman, *Ray Frank Litman: A Memoir* (New York: American Jewish Historical Society, 1957); Reva Clar and William M. Kramer, "The Girl Rabbi of the Golden West: The Adventurous Life of Ray Frank in Nevada, California and the Northwest," *Western States Jewish History* 18 (1986): 99–111, 223–36, 336–51.
14. Hannah G. Solomon, "Council of Women, Washington, DC, February, 1895," in Solomon, *A Sheaf of Leaves* (Chicago: printed privately, 1911), 131–32.
15. American Jewish Archives (Cincinnati, Ohio) [hereafter AJA], Rabbis, F.F. Correspondence . . . readmission of women to the College for the Purpose of Ordination, 1921–22, Miscellaneous File: J. Lauterbach and Oscar Berman, "Minority Report of the Committee on the Question of Graduating Women as Rabbis," June 20, 1921.
16. AJA, Cyrus Adler Papers, Microfilm 517: Addresses, articles, biographical sketches, tributes, and miscellaneous items, 1909–34: "On the Woman Rabbi," typescript, n.d. but given as an interview, possibly to Leon Spitz of the Day and likely in the early 1920s.

17. Cited in Michael A. Meyer, "A Centennial History," in *Hebrew Union College–Jewish Institute of Religion: At One Hundred Years*, ed. Samuel E. Karff (Cincinnati: HUC Press, 1976), 99.

18. Irma L. Lindheim, *Parallel Quest: A Search of a Person and a People* (New York: Thomas Yoseloff, 1962), 201–3.

19. AJA, Ms. Col. #19, JIR 1921–50, Dora Askowith Correspondence, 1948, 2/8; Letter from Dora Askowith to Stephen S. Wise, August 2, 1948.

20. Cited in Lester Lyons Collection [hereafter LLC], Letter from Alfred Gottschalk to Earl Stone, July 24, 1985.

21. "Religion," *Time*, October 2, 1939, 48; "Woman Passes Tests, but She Is Barred from Becoming a Rabbi because Talmud Doesn't Recognize Her Sex in Synagogues," *New York World-Telegraph*, May 29, 1939.

22. Katharina von Kellenbach, "'God Does Not Oppress Any Human Being': The Life and Thought of Rabbi Regina Jonas," *Leo Baeck Institute Year Book* 39 (1994): 215–19. I wish to thank Professor von Kellenbach for going over Jonas's thesis with me.

23. Askowith claimed to have published her student sermon, but I have not located this. Instead, this is drawn from Dora Askowith, "The Role of Women in the Field of Higher Jewish Education," *Judaism* 5 (1956): 169–72, where she discussed her research for that sermon; von Kellenbach, "Regina Jones," 215–19. On Jonas, see Elisa Klapheck, *Fräulein Rabbiner Jonas: The Story of the First Woman Rabbi* (San Francisco: Jossey-Bass, 2004).

24. AJA, New York World's Fair, 1964, Letter from Martha Neumark Montor to Jacob Rader Marcus, June 28, 1964.

25. Shuly Rubin Schwartz, *The Rabbi's Wife: The Rebbetzin in American Jewish Life* (New York: New York University Press, 2006).

26. AJA, Paula Ackerman, Correspondence File, Letter from JDS (Jacob D. Schwarz) to Mrs. William Ackerman, December 20, 1950.

27. "Report on the Ordination of Women," *Central Conference of American Rabbis Yearbook* 66 (1956): 93.

28. Jack Hume, "Girl Sets Her Goal to Be 1st Woman Rabbi," newspaper clipping, undated, but most likely *Cleveland Plain Dealer*, March–early April 1964. I am deeply grateful to Rabbi Sally J. Priesand for sharing this with me.

29. On this, see Kirsten Lise Fermaglich, "'The Comfortable Concentration Camp': The Significance of Nazi Imagery in Betty Friedan's *the Feminine Mystique* (1963)," *American Jewish History* 91, no. 2 (2003): 205–32.

30. Sally J. Priesand, *Judaism and the New Woman* (New York: Behrman House, 1975), 62, 67.

31. Hebrew Union College–Jewish Institute of Religion Sally Priesand Registrar File: Letter from Sally J. Preisand to Sir, June 14, 1963; "1st Woman Rabbi in U.S. Ordained," *New York Times*, June 4, 1972.

32. Courtesy of the Ratner Center for the Study of Conservative Judaism, the Jewish Theological Seminary of America (JTSA), Records, RG 1M, Box 153: Letter from Louis Finkelstein to Gladys Citrin, May 28, 1957.

33. Sandy Eisenberg Sasso, Rabbi, Congregation Beth El Zedeck, Files: "Presentation to American Jewish Committee," May 1972.

34. "Ezrat Nashim, Jewish Women Call for Change," in *American Jewish History: A Primary Source Reader*, ed. Gary Phillip Zola, Marc Dollinger (Brandeis University Press: Boston 2014), 363f.

35. These papers have been published; Simon Greenberg, ed., *The Ordination of Women as Rabbis: Studies and Responsa* (New York: Jewish Theological Seminary of America, 1988).

36. Joel Roth, "Statement to the Faculty Senate, 20 December 1979," *Ikka d-Amrei: A Journal of the Students of the Jewish Theological Seminary of America* 2, no. 1 (January 1980): 58–60.

37. Blu Greenberg, "Will There Be Orthodox Women Rabbis?," *Judaism* 33, no. 1 (Winter 1984): 23–33.

38. Jeffrey S. Gurock, "Resisters and Accommodators: Varieties of Orthodox Rabbis in America, 1886–1983," in *American Rabbinate: A Century of Continuity and Change, 1883–1983*, ed. Jacob Rader Marcus and Abraham J. Peck (Cincinnati: American Jewish Archives, 1985), 10–97.

39. For an excellent discussion of Orthodoxy and feminism, see the chapter "Open and Closed to Feminism," in Jeffrey S. Gurock, *Orthodox Jews in America* (Bloomington: Indiana University Press, 2009), 273–311.

40. For Feigelson's story, see Mimi Feigelson, "The Matmida," *Eretz Acheret* [in Hebrew], December 2005. The spelling of the title varies (rabba/rabbah) among those holding it and others using it.

41. Haviva Ner-David, *Life on the Fringes: A Feminist Journey toward Traditional Rabbinic Ordination* (Needham: JFL Books, 2000).

42. Strikovsky quoted in Gurock, *Orthodox Jews in America*, 281–82. For Ner-David's claim that she has "*semikhah*," see Haviva Ner-David, "Orthodox Women Rabbis: It's About Time," *Jerusalem Post*, December 3, 2010, http://www.jpost.com/LandedPages/PrintArticle.aspx?id=170763.

43. Rabba Hurwitz is dean of Yeshivat Maharat, which is "the first institution to train Orthodox women as spiritual leaders and halakhic authorities"; http://yeshivatmaharat.org/, accessed October 31, 2012.

44. Ben Harris, "Maharat Becomes Rabbah," Jewish Telegraphic Agency, January 27, 2010, https://www.jta.org/2010/01/27/news-opinion/the-telegraph/maharat-becomes-rabbah; Debra Nussbaum Cohen, "Woman 'Rabba' Roils Orthodox World," *Forward*, March 3, 2010, http://forward.com/articles/126454/woman-rabba-roils-orthodox-world/.

45. In Israel, Rabbi Daniel Landes ordained eight women in July 2016; Elhanan Miller, "Go East Young Woman, If You Want to Be a Rabbi," *Forward*, July 15, 2016, 11. See also, Ner-David, "Orthodox Women Rabbis: It's About Time."

46. "Leading the Way: America's First Women Rabbis," National Museum of American Jewish History, June 4, 2012, parts 1 and 2, available from http://www.nmajh.org/publicprograms/.

47. Rabbinical Council of America, "2015 Resolution RCA Policy Concerning Women Rabbis." October 31, 2015.

BIBLIOGRAPHY

Askowith, Dora, "The Role of Women in the Field of Higher Jewish Education," *Judaism* 5 (1956): 169–72.

Berkowitz, Henry, "Woman's Part in the Drama of Life," *American Jewess* 1, no. 2 (May 1895): 63–66.

Chafe, William H., *The Paradox of Change: American Women in the 20th Century* (New York: Oxford University Press, 1991).

Clar, Reva, and Kramer, William M., "The Girl Rabbi of the Golden West: The Adventurous Life of Ray Frank in Nevada, California and the Northwest," *Western States Jewish History* 18 (1986): 99–111, 223–36, 336–51.

Cohen, Mary M., "A Problem for Purim," *Jewish Exponent* (March 15, 1889), 1.
Cott, Nancy, *The Grounding of Modern Feminism* (New Haven: Yale University Press, 1987).
DeWolf, Rebecca, "Gendered Citizenship: The Original Conflict over the Equal Rights Amendment, 1920–1963" (PhD diss., American University, 2014).
Falk, Gerhard, "The Rabbi Has No Beard," Jewish Buffalo on the Web, November 4, 2016, http://jbuff.com/c090607.htm.
Feigelson, Mimi, "The Matmida," *Eretz Acheret* [in Hebrew], December 2005.
Fermaglich, Kirsten Lise "'The Comfortable Concentration Camp': The Significance of Nazi Imagery in Betty Friedan's *the Feminine Mystique* (1963)," *American Jewish History* 91, no. 2 (2003): 205–32.
Goldman, Karla, "Women in Reform Judaism: Between Rhetoric and Reality," in *Women Remaking American Judaism*, ed. Riv-Ellen Prell (Detroit: Wayne State University Press, 2007), 109–34.
Greenberg, Blu, "Will There Be Orthodox Women Rabbis?," *Judaism* 33, no. 1 (Winter 1984): 23–33.
Greenberg, Simon (ed.), *The Ordination of Women as Rabbis: Studies and Responsa* (New York: Jewish Theological Seminary of America, 1988).
Gurock, Jeffrey S., *Orthodox Jews in America* (Bloomington: Indiana University Press, 2009).
Gurock, Jeffrey S., "Resisters and Accommodators: Varieties of Orthodox Rabbis in America, 1886–1983," in *American Rabbinate: A Century of Continuity and Change, 1883–1983*, ed. Jacob Rader Marcus and Abraham J. Peck (Cincinnati: American Jewish Archives, 1985), 10–97.
Harris, Ben, "Maharat Becomes Rabbah," Jewish Telegraphic Agency, January 27, 2010, https://www.jta.org/2010/01/27/news-opinion/the-telegraph/maharat-becomes-rabbah.
Klapheck, Elisa, *Fräulein Rabbiner Jonas: The Story of the First Woman Rabbi* (San Francisco: Jossey-Bass, 2004).
Lindheim, Irma L., *Parallel Quest: A Search of a Person and a People* (New York: Thomas Yoseloff, 1962), 201–3.
Litman, Simon, *Ray Frank Litman: A Memoir* (New York: American Jewish Historical Society, 1957).
Meyer, Michael A., "A Centennial History," in *Hebrew Union College–Jewish Institute of Religion: At One Hundred Years*, ed. Samuel E. Karff (Cincinnati: HUC Press, 1976), 3–283.
Miller Solomon, Barbara, *In the Company of Educated Women* (New Haven: Yale University Press, 1985).
Miller, Elhanan, "Go East Young Woman, If You Want to Be a Rabbi," *Forward*, July 15, 2016, 11.
Moses, Adolph, "The Emancipation of Women," in *Yahvism and Other Discourses*, ed. H. G. Enelow (Louisville: Louisville Section of the Council of Jewish Women, 1913), 104.
Nadell, Pamela S., *Women Who Would Be Rabbis: A History of Women's Ordination, 1889–1985* (Boston: Beacon Press, 1998).
Ner-David, Haviva, "Orthodox Women Rabbis: It's About Time," *Jerusalem Post*, December 3, 2010, http://www.jpost.com/LandedPages/PrintArticle.aspx?id=170763.
Ner-David, Haviva, *Life on the Fringes: A Feminist Journey toward Traditional Rabbinic Ordination* (Needham: JFL Books, 2000).
Nussbaum Cohen, Debra "Woman 'Rabba' Roils Orthodox World," *Forward*, March 3, 2010, http://forward.com/articles/126454/woman-rabba-roils-orthodox-world/.
Priesand, Sally J., *Judaism and the New Woman* (New York: Behrman House, 1975).

Roth, Joel, "Statement to the Faculty Senate, 20 December 1979," *Ikka d-Amrei: A Journal of the Students of the Jewish Theological Seminary of America* 2, no. 1 (January 1980): 58–60.

Schwartz, Shuly Rubin, *The Rabbi's Wife: The Rebbetzin in American Jewish Life* (New York: New York University Press, 2006).

Shanahan, Eileen, "Equal Rights Amendment is Approved by Congress," *The New York Times*, 22 March, 1972, 1. https://archive.nytimes.com/www.nytimes.com/learning/general/onthisday/big/0322.html#article

Solomon, Hannah G, "Council of Women, Washington, DC, February, 1895," in Solomon, *A Sheaf of Leaves* (Chicago: printed privately, 1911), 131–32.

Von Kellenbach, Katharina, "'God Does Not Oppress Any Human Being': The Life and Thought of Rabbi Regina Jonas," *Leo Baeck Institute Year Book* 39 (1994): 215–19.

Zola, Gary Phillip, and Dollinger, Marc, (eds.), "*Ezrat Nashim*, Jewish Women Call for Change," in *American Jewish History: A Primary Source Reader* (Brandeis University Press: Boston 2014).

Part II

Three Pioneers of Female Leadership

Henrietta Szold, Margarete Susman, and Regina Jonas

Chapter Six

Henrietta Szold: A "Pretty Certain Miriam"

Gail Twersky Reimer

Henrietta Szold has long been acknowledged as one of the greatest Jewish women leaders of all time.[1] The subject of numerous full-length biographies, museum exhibitions, films, PhD dissertations, and scores of local community pageants, Szold is mostly celebrated as a secular Zionist leader and an organizational visionary—the founding mother of Hadassah and the force behind Youth Aliyah.[2] While some attention has been given to Szold's religious outlook, particularly as it developed under the early tutelage of her father Benjamin Szold, only recently have we begun to appreciate Szold's pioneering role in laying the groundwork for the entry of women into the rabbinate as well as into communal positions of leadership.

Interest in Szold's religious thought has mostly crystallized around a 1916 letter to Haym Peretz in which Szold asserts her right to honor her mother's memory by reciting the *Kaddish*, the Jewish mourner's prayer for the dead traditionally recited only by men.[3] The letter has achieved almost iconic status among feminists and liberal Jewish rabbis interpreting halakhah for contemporary times. Even America's Chief Justice Ruth Bader Ginsburg, who claims Henrietta Szold as an important role model, frequently cites this particular letter for its tolerance and appreciation of "the differences among us concerning religious practice."[4]

Szold's application in 1903 to be a full-time student at the Jewish Theological Seminary of America has also elicited interest from Jewish feminist activists and scholars.[5] They point to it as an early dent, if not quite a crack, in the wall barring women from ordination by the Conservative movement. And yet even as they acknowledge Szold as a "groundbreaker" and a woman who "personally transcended the customary roles of Jewish woman,"[6] they all conclude that on the question of women rabbis, Szold held the conventional view that this exalted vocation was reserved for males.

A closer look at Szold's early thinking about religious leadership reveal Szold's struggle with conventional views of women as unsuited for religious leadership as well as her growing skepticism about the American rabbinate as an exalted vocation. The task of this essay is to trace this early thinking through a focus on three revealing documents from Szold's pre-Hadassah years. The documents were written within a ten-year period, but the story they tell begins when Henrietta Szold turned twenty-one and visited the Alt-Neu Shul in Prague in the company of her father, Rabbi Benjamin Szold.

Hungarian-born Benjamin Szold emigrated to the United States along with his wife Sophia in 1859. Trained at Breslau's rabbinical seminary, Szold came to America to serve as rabbi of Baltimore's Oheb Shalom synagogue. His first child, Henrietta, was born one year after her parents arrived in the United States. Like many first-born daughters, she was educated by her father to be his spiritual and intellectual heir. She proved a worthy student and by her teens was translating and editing her father's works, as well as teaching Hebrew, Jewish history, and Bible in his congregation's religious school.

Henrietta excelled as a student at school as well as at home and graduated at the top of her class at Baltimore's Western Female High School. Higher education was just beginning to open some doors to women, but Szold ended her formal schooling upon receiving her high school diploma. Her father's needs for her assistance and companionship very likely stood in the way of her going to college. Those same needs, as well as his continued investment in Henrietta's education, led Rabbi Szold to propose to Henrietta that she accompany him on a trip to Europe when she turned twenty-one. Szold's was not a typical "grand tour," though she did visit the great centers of Western culture—Berlin, Vienna, Prague, Paris, and London. But they also visited Bremen, Hamburg, Dresden, Pressburg, and other cities where she was introduced to the Szolds' many relatives and friends. Wherever she and her father went, their visits to museums, monuments, and opera houses were supplemented with visits to Jewish synagogues, sites, and homes.

Upon their return to Baltimore, Henrietta wrote about her travels in a series of pieces titled "Reminiscences," published in the *Jewish Messenger* under her pen name "Sulamith."[7] Some ten years after her trip to Europe, Szold would hark back to it and to one of the synagogues that made an especially strong impression on her in a lecture she delivered in 1891 before the Hebrew Literary Society of Baltimore titled "Tales of Good Women: Sound Advice for Women of All Conditions of Life."[8]

The opening of the "Tales of Good Women" lecture is generally read as Szold's "disavowal of any intention of being a female rabbi."[9] Twelve years after delivering this lecture, her hand forced by the leadership of the Jewish Theological Seminary, Szold would indeed disavow her intention of being a female rabbi. But in 1891, a younger Szold, who at that time was editing and translating major works in Jewish history and thought for the newly formed Jewish Publication Society, contributing essays to various national Jewish publications, and occasionally delivering lectures to a variety of adult groups, seemed to be developing a broad conception of herself as a religious leader, one not confined to a narrow notion of ordained clergy leading congregations.

1. "TALES OF GOOD WOMEN: SOUND ADVICE FOR WOMEN OF ALL CONDITIONS OF LIFE"

"I know that usually Jewish women do not take the office of rabbis nor do I mean to give you a regular learned sermon, with a verse from the Bible as a text and illustrations from the Talmud and Rashi. It will not be that sort of sermon."[10] The lecture opens with a significant qualification. Szold announces that she knows that "*usually* Jewish women do not take the office of Rabbis."[11] In other words, it isn't common—but it also is not not done. Szold, who received an intensive Jewish education from her Breslau-trained rabbi father, was an unusually learned woman. Unsaid but implied is the possibility that unusual women might very well do unusual things, including take the office of rabbi. They might also carry out the responsibilities of that office in unusual or different ways. Rather than giving a "regular learned sermon" whose purpose is to expound and explain a biblical text, they might engage their congregation in a different way: "If you have listened to many sermons," she continues, "you will remember that usually the preacher tells a story, a *moshal*, and then at the end of the sermon he uses that story to give some good advice. That is all I am going to do."[12]

Framing her lecture as a narrative sermon in which "the preacher" tells a story or series of stories in order to make a particular moral point, Szold goes on to tell the stories of Rebecca Gratz, Penina Moise, and Emma Lazarus—three American Jewish women, devoted to their religion and their people, and celebrated for their significant contributions to improving the lives of their co-religionists.

But the very first story Szold tells is autobiographical—the story of her visit to the Altneu Shul in Prague—a story whose point is to underscore the legitimacy of women serving as religious leaders. Szold recalls visiting the synagogue, "finding everything in it interesting," and after looking at it all, seeing "high up on the wall, a small window through which no light came." When told that this was "the window of the room where the women said their prayers" Szold remembers suddenly comprehending "what [she] had often heard of—that in some places the women had a chazzan of their own."[13] Szold was referring to the *zogerke*, or *zagerin*, an honored role in Eastern European synagogues usually filled by the most learned woman in the community. "She it is," Szold continues, "who stands at the window and inspired by what goes on inside and below in the men's *shule*, reads for her sisters the prayers that are being read there too."[14]

The discourse of recollection (or the autobiographical story) seamlessly leads into a discourse on women's religious leadership (the moral of the story): "Now if a Jewish woman could be a substitute chazzan I do not see why a Jewish woman in these modern times when Rabbis preach cannot be a substitute rabbi."[15]

It seems clear from the context that "substitute rabbi" here carries the meaning of "alternative rabbi" rather than "stand in for the rabbi." Szold continues, reaching back to the Bible for a more authentic proof-text: "When Moses and the children of Israel had passed over the red sea safely, they sang a song—I will sing unto the Lord and when the beautiful song was ended Moses' sister Miriam led the women and said 'Sing ye to the Lord."[16] The recollection of the Altneu Shul with its *zogerke* culminates in Szold imagining herself as a religious leader in the tradition of Miriam. It may be a circumscribed leadership—one in which the leader, like Miriam, is not an originator but rather one who says "over again what others have said" and one who speaks "to and for the women only."[17] But it is religious leadership nonetheless.

Miriam is not the only biblical figure or religious leader whom Szold invokes in this lecture/sermon. After discussing Gratz, Moise, and Lazarus, Szold notes that it is not just the comfortable and well-off women who have made significant contributions to American Jewish life: "If you will read the history of the Jews of this country, you will see that no congregation was started, no school funded, no charitable undertaking begun, without the help of the women. I indeed sometimes think that *the men were the helpmates of the women and not the women the helpmates of the men* as the Bible says they should be."[18]

Here Szold quietly shifts the conventional view that nothing could be done without the *help* of women to the subversive claim that it is men who are the helpmates of women. This, in turn, leads to, for its time, some rather radical readings of biblical women, beginning with Eve and culminating with Deborah, whose story Szold claims "shows exactly how much interest a Jewish woman may take and where she must stop."[19]

The only place a Jewish woman must stop, Szold's telling of Deborah's story suggests, is in claiming full credit for what she alone has achieved. Deborah is the "man" who stands up where there are no men—advising the paralyzed general Barak and accompanying him when he refuses to go without her into the battle that saves Israel. With a dose of irreverence, Szold sums up this part of the story, extolling Deborah for not holding back: "Now if she had been like those who object to such things as un-Jewish, she would have refused and Barak would have been beaten and Israel lost."[20]

Szold moves on to Deborah's husband, Lapidoth, noting that "although he never did anything for his people," he is always mentioned together with her "to show that she did not neglect her little duties in doing her great ones."[21] In a related vein, when Deborah sings her song of victory, Szold writes, "the Bible is careful to say that she sang it with Barak, *who had really done nothing.*"[22] Though she emphasizes the fact that Deborah is anything but a helpmate, Szold concludes this section by noting that "the lesson is thus taught that Deborah considered herself only a helpmate."[23] Szold is pointing to the significant distinction between Deborah's accomplishments and Deborah's sense of self-importance. In Deborah, leadership and modesty are not at odds. Rather, combined they become a new model for leadership—leadership without ego.[24]

Once we recognize what one scholar has referred to as Szold's "epiphany" at the Altneu Shul, we begin to see that the European trip she took at age twenty-one in the company of her father was no less important to her future as a leader than the famous 1909 trip to Palestine, taken together with her mother, in which her Zionist calling began to crystallize.[25]

In her father's company, Szold had the opportunity to meet important members of the various European Jewish communities that they visited. She was charmed by the highly educated Jewish women she met in Austro-Hungary who could converse "in most elegant Hebrew, quoting copiously and with ease from the Bible and other Hebrew works."[26] Even the ordinary Pressburg Jewess, she added, "would be ranked by most American born and bred Jewesses as prodigies, savants, learned enough to occupy a Western Jewish pulpit."[27]

Szold's admiration for the learning available to European women both in the home and beyond carries with it an implicit critique of the inadequate Jewish knowledge most American Jewish women possessed and an explicit critique of the American rabbinate. She expands that critique in an article titled "Thoughts on European Judaism." "The European Rabbi," she wrote, is "the intellectual leader of Jews and not the priestly guide of laymen." The American rabbi, on the other hand, hears in place of religious questions and hair's breadth differences of opinion, this one proposed to him:

> Dr. Why do you not visit us? You went to see so and so and passed right by our house. When once consolatory, congratulatory and social visits are paid off and he turns for a moment to his thoughts and books, he finds that he has nearly consumed the store of ideas with which his university career has stocked him. More than that he is appalled to find that he is no longer trained to study. But he consoles himself, he has a hold on his people even without erudition and is content to drop into slovenly careless habits of thought and action. Finally they come to rely upon catchwords of reform to dazzle their audiences.[28]

Both the respect for learning and disdain for the superficiality of Reform rabbis that Szold shared with her father are clearly in evidence here. Szold had written on both topics before traveling to Europe and would continue to write about them over the next two decades. Feeding her early efforts to define a religious leadership role for herself are the low estimation in which she held American rabbis, her own thirst for learning and high regard for the learned, and the distinction she makes in this essay between intellectual leader and priestly guide.

2. WHAT JUDAISM HAS DONE FOR WOMEN

A few years after she returned from her "European tour," Szold was asked to join the nine-member publication committee of the newly formed Jewish Publication Society. Five years later, her volunteer position became a paid position. Though given the title and salary of secretary, it was she and she alone who shepherded the books from manuscript to publication, serving as translator, indexer, fact checker, proofreader, and editor.[29]

In the same year that Szold became JPS's first paid employee, she was invited to address the Parliament of Religions at the World Columbian Exposition in Chicago.[30] The whole of her lecture, titled "What Judaism Has Done for Women," can be read as a prolegomenon to the lecture's final paragraph, an elaborate excursus designed to buttress the claims made in answer to the question with which the final paragraph opens: With what fitness to meet nineteenth-century demands has Judaism endowed her daughters?

> The 19th century Jewess is wholly free to do as and what she wishes, nor need she abate a jot of her Judaism. Judaism does not, indeed, bid her become a lawyer, a physician, a bookkeeper, or a telegraph operator, *nor does it forbid her becoming anything for which her talents and her opportunities fit her.* It simply says nothing of her occupations. . . . *Judaism permits her daughters to go forth into this new world of ours to assume new duties and responsibilities and rejoice in its vast opportunities.* But it says "beware of forfeiting your dignity."[31]

It is easy to be swept away by what Szold is saying and miss the significance of how she says it. Nothing in Judaism, Szold claims, directs women to pursue a particular profession, nor does anything in Judaism inhibit them from going forth to assume new duties and responsibilities and take advantage of the opportunities of a new age. But her broader claim here is that in the absence of an explicit prohibition, the fact that there is no historical precedent should have no bearing on what women are permitted to do or not do, or on what professions or vocations they pursue. We cannot know for sure whether Szold had in mind the rabbinate as she spoke these words. But given the circumstances in which she gave this lecture, it is hard to imagine Szold not thinking of the rabbinate, women, and religious leadership. As Pamela Nadell reminds us in a footnote to her discussion of this closing paragraph, there was a striking disparity in the professional status of the Jewish male and Jewish female presenters at the Columbian Exposition. Nearly all the men were ordained rabbis and scholars, while the women had no formal professional training or credentials. The "juxtaposition of largely leisured middle-class women displaying their informally acquired knowledge of Judaism versus the representatives of the learned Jewish profession pointed subtly, but surely, to the question of women in the rabbinate."[32]

Szold's comments on Deborah in the earlier essay offer a useful gloss on the warning to Jewish women that closes "What Judaism Has Done for Women." "Beware of forfeiting your dignity" could be read as a backing away from claims made earlier in the essay regarding Jewish women's rights to pursue what vocation they will. Or the warning might rather be intended as a reminder to women that even as they assume new duties and responsibilities, like the biblical Deborah, they must remain modest. Far from retreating into a conventional stance on women's modesty, Szold is arguing, as she did in the earlier essay, that, for women, leadership and modesty must go hand in hand; that modesty or lack of ego may even be a unique and defining characteristic of women's leadership.[33]

3. WOMEN IN THE SYNAGOGUE

At the 1893 Chicago Columbian Exposition, Szold was one of only two Jewish women to address the official Parliament of Religions. But elsewhere at the exposition, she joined some two dozen Jewish women from across North America who, over four days, lectured on Jewish women's roles in religion, history, and philanthropy to the audience of women gathered at the unprecedented Jewish Women's Congress.

Four years later, many of the speakers, including Szold, were invited to participate in the print symposium "Women in the Synagogue" convened by one of the leading figures in the Reform movement and the editor of the *Reform Advocate*, Rabbi Emil G. Hirsch. Hirsch asked the invited women to respond to five specific questions, the last of which was "Should [women] occupy the pulpit?"[34]

Hirsch had been public about his own views on "woman in the pulpit." In an editorial with that title, published in 1893, he declared that woman is "as much in place there as she is in any other profession" but that the exalted profession of rabbi also required that its occupant have "a comprehensive knowledge of the literature and history of Judaism."[35]

A few symposium participants, like Esther Ruskay and Katherine de Sola, rejected Hirsch's position and responded with an emphatic *no*.[36] Most, however, saw the absence of any prohibition against woman becoming anything for which her talents and her opportunities fit her, coupled with clear evidence of women's success in the professions they had by this time entered, as sufficient reason for answering the question in the affirmative—albeit, like

Hirsch, a qualified affirmative. All would set the bar for a woman who would be a rabbi very high.

Szold's symposium response harked back to her earlier lecture/essay "Tales of a Good Woman" in two important ways. First, here as there, she resisted a simple answer and instead offered a qualified yes. Second, here as there, she invoked both Deborah and Miriam.[37]

> Woman can best serve the interests of the synagogue by devoting herself to her home . . . and by occupying the pulpit only when her knowledge of the law, history, and literature of Judaism is masterful and her natural gift so extraordinary as to forbid hesitation, though even then it were the part of wisdom not to make a profession of public preaching and teaching, the old Jewish rule of not holding women responsible for religious duties performed at definite times having a deep seated rational basis and wide applicability. . . . In other words, the Deborahs and Miriams need not hide their light under a bushel, but they and the world must be pretty sure that they are Deborahs and Miriams, not equally admirable Hannahs and Ruths.[38]

Here Szold deftly shifted the terms of the symposium, ignoring the question of whether a woman should occupy the pulpit and reframing the conversation as one about the woman who would occupy the pulpit. Such a woman, Szold declared, must be absolutely certain that she has this gift for leadership and must also be sufficiently learned in Jewish law, history, and literature to be able to respond to religious questions. While one could argue that Szold was setting impossibly high standards for the female aspirant to the rabbinate, I would suggest that what she was doing was setting what she believed were appropriate standards for a rabbinate to which women would want to aspire. For women to become rabbis of limited learning, forced like their male counterparts to "rely upon catchwords of reform to dazzle their audiences,"[39] would only swell the ranks of mediocrity in the American rabbinate. She wanted women to aspire to something better—to the kind of intellectual leadership that she associated with her European-trained father and with the European rabbis she met while traveling in Europe.

One such learned European rabbi would soon be recruited to head the Jewish Theological Seminary in New York, with the goal of making that kind of rigorous rabbinic training available in America. Shortly after Solomon Schechter arrived at JTS, Henrietta Szold, though working full-time at the Jewish Publication Society, applied to be a full-time student at JTS.

The seminary application, Szold's biographers tell us, resulted from her mother's suggestion, following Rabbi Szold's death in 1902, that Henrietta organize her father's papers and prepare them for publication. As the story goes, the suggestion appealed to Szold, but she worried that she did not have sufficient mastery of rabbinics to do justice to her father's writings. Her mother saw this as an obstacle easily surmounted. Solomon Schechter, a friend of the family and an advocate for women, had just assumed leadership of the newly reorganized JTS and had recruited several brilliant young scholars to its faculty.[40] Szold could study there and gain the mastery she needed to edit and complete her father's unfinished work.

What is puzzling about this narrative is Szold's failure to anticipate a major obstacle to her mother's suggestion of how she gain the mastery she was seeking. The Jewish Theological seminary was a rabbinical school and did not admit women students. Only after Szold agreed not to be "an aspirant after Rabbinical honors" did Dr. Schechter pass her request for admission on to the seminary's board of directors.[41]

Did Dr. Schechter's request take Szold by surprise? Had her own sense of herself as a "Miriam" blinded her to the resistance her application to study at the Jewish Theological Seminary would engender? Notification regarding her application, which came in the form of a letter from Cyrus Adler, the seminary's chair of the board, emphasized that Szold was being accepted as a special student and not a candidate for a degree.[42]

Was Szold disappointed by the terms of her admission to JTS? She never spoke of disappointment, though she took a peculiar pleasure in the notices in the Jewish and Yiddish press about her studying at the seminary, with their speculations and insinuations. For three years she studied diligently alongside the rabbinical students at New York's Jewish Theological Seminary, tutored its faculty in English, and assisted many of them with the editing and translating of their work. But far from feeling jealousy as fellow students were granted ordination, Szold found her conversations with them on the topic of rabbinical service singularly uninspiring. "It is hopeless," she wrote to Louis Ginzberg, referring to "the Seminary, the students there and the work it is supposed to stand for." "The whole business has no vitality, no viability—no spring, no compelling force."[43]

Before coming to JTS, Szold had blamed Reform Judaism for the lack of vitality in both the rabbinate and the communities led by its rabbis. She believed, however, that the influx of immigrant scholars and rabbis created the conditions for a revitalization. "The one great spiritual current rejuvenating the Jewish world of our day," she wrote in 1899, "flows not from American Temples, a la Pittsburgh, but from Talmudists' back rooms in Polish and Russian Jewish Streets."[44] By 1907, the high regard in which she held the mostly foreign-born JTS faculty notwithstanding, Szold recognized the limits of their influence. The problem, she came to see, was not the superficiality of Reform Judaism as practiced in the United States, but the American rabbinate writ large.

The foundation for Szold's journey to JTS was laid in the study of her Baltimore home, where her rabbi father taught her as he would have taught a son. But the journey itself began with the vision of herself as a religious leader in the tradition of Miriam that Szold first had when visiting the Altneu Shul in Prague. That vision was honed and tested over the next two decades. In her work at JPS, making the best works in Jewish thought and history available and accessible to American Jews, and in her preaching, teaching and writing, Szold transmitted to others the Jewish knowledge she'd been taught first by her father and which she then continued to deepen however and wherever she could.

Ironically, her time at the Jewish Theological Seminary turned out to be a detour rather than the ultimate step toward proving to herself and the world that she was indeed a Miriam. Not only was she denied the option of earning the degree that would allow her to follow in her rabbi father's footsteps, but her own voice grew increasingly silent. The skilled teacher and amateur preacher who entered JTS spent her time there editing and revising the work of its faculty. It would take another trip abroad, this one to Palestine in the company of her mother, for Szold to stop hiding her light under a bushel and emerge as a confident and fearless spiritual leader whose congregation without walls grew to include a membership in the hundreds of thousands.

NOTES

1. Work on this project was made possible thanks to a research fellowship at the Jacob Rader Marcus Center of the American Jewish Archives. I would like to thank the center's director, Dr. Gary P. Zola, and its senior archivist, Kevin Proffitt, for their generous support and indispensable assistance as I completed this project.

2. The standard biographies are Marvin Lowenthal, *Henrietta Szold: Life and Letters* (New York: Viking Press, 1942); Alexandra Lee Levin, *The Szolds of Lombard Street* (Philadelphia: Jewish Publication Society of America, 1960); Irving Fineman, *Woman of Valor: The Life of Henrietta Szold 1860–1945* (New York: Simon and Schuster, 1961); Joan Dash, *Summoned to Jerusalem: The Life of Henrietta Szold* (New York: Harper and Row, 1979). See also *Daughters of Zion: Henrietta Szold and American Jewish Womanhood*, exhibition catalogue, Jewish

Historical Society of Maryland, 1995; and "Henrietta Szold," Jewish Women's Archive, accessed August 11, 2018, https://jwa.org/womenofvalor/szold.

3. Letter from Henrietta Szold to Haim Peretz, September 16, 1916, in *Henrietta Szold: Life and Letters*, ed. Marvin Lowenthal (New York: Viking, 1942).

4. "Ruth Bader Ginsburg," Jewish Women's Archive, accessed August 11, 2018, https://jwa.org/feminism/ginsburg-bader-ruth.

5. See, for example, Susan Dworkin, "Henrietta Szold," in *The Jewish Woman: New Perspectives*, ed. Elizabeth Koltun (New York: Schocken Books, 1976), 164–70; Anne Lapidus Lerner, "On the Rabbinic Ordination of Women," in *The Ordination of Women as Rabbis: Studies and Responsa*, ed. Simon Greenberg (New York: Jewish Theological Seminary of America, 1988); Pamela S. Nadell, *Women Who Would Be Rabbis: A History of Women's Ordination 1898–1985* (Boston: Beacon Press, 1998), 56–59.

6. Nadell, *Women Who Would Be Rabbis*, 58.

7. Fineman, *Woman of Valor*, 58.

8. The Hebrew Literary Society, as Szold would describe it years later, was Baltimore's version of a YMHA. Organized by a group of young Jewish immigrants, it housed a library of Hebrew, Yiddish, and English books, and its activities included lectures on Jewish topics, classes for the study of Bible in Hebrew, and regular discussion groups on Zionism. Two years after its establishment, Szold, a passionate advocate for the refugees from Russian pogroms arriving in Baltimore, proposed to the society that they add to their program evening classes in English for recent Russian immigrants. One of the first immigrant night schools in America, Szold's Russian Night School became the model for the institution of night schools across the United States.

9. Fineman, *Woman of Valor*, 88–89.

10. "Tales of Good Women: Sound Advice for Women of All Conditions of Life," *Jewish Exponent*, March 6, 1891, 5.

11. "Tales of Good Women," 5, emphasis added.

12. Ibid.

13. Ibid.

14. Ibid.

15. Ibid.

16. Ibid.

17. Ibid.

18. "Tales of Good Women," 5, emphasis added.

19. Ibid.

20. Ibid.

21. Ibid.

22. Ibid.

23. Ibid.

24. Ibid.

25. Joyce Antler, "Zion in [Our] Hearts: Henrietta Szold and the American Jewish Women's Movement," in *Daughters of Zion*, exhibition catalogue, 37.

26. "Tales of Good Women," 5.

27. Ibid.

28. "Thoughts on European Judaism," *Jewish Messenger* 52 (September 13, 1882): 4–5.

29. See Jonathan Sarna, *JPS: The Americanization of Jewish Culture, 1889–1989: A Centennial History of the Jewish Publication Society* (Philadelphia: Jewish Publication Society of America, 1989); 47–94. Alexandra Lee Levin, "Henrietta Szold as Essayist," *Jewish Heritage*, Winter 1961, 38–42.

30. "What Has Judaism Done for Women?," in *The World's Congress of Religions*, ed. J.W. Hanson (Vancouver: J.M. MacGregor Publishing Co., 1894), 587–93. *Judaism at the World's Parliament of Religions: Comprising the Papers on Judaism Read at the Parliament, at the Jewish Denominational Congress, and at the Jewish Presentation* (Cincinnati: Union of American Hebrew Congregations, 1894), 304–10.

31. See Nadell, *Women Who Would Be Rabbis: A History of Women's Ordination 1898–1985*, 56 [emphasis added]. In a footnote to the quotation from Szold's address, Nadell explains that there seem to be two versions of Szold's presentation at the World's Congress of Religions, one of which omits entirely this final paragraph.

32. See Nadell, *Women Who Would Be Rabbis*, 235, n. 82.

33. It is interesting to note that throughout her rabbinic thesis, "Can a Woman Be a Rabbi According to Halakhic Sources?" Regina Jonas also emphasized the traditional value of modesty (*tzeniut*)—not as something to prevent women's participation in religious life, but rather as a value essential to women in the rabbinic role: "That something such as zniut should prevent her from preaching is also not acceptable, for certainly in her dress she would not be taken in by the "fashionable frivolity" to which unfortunately the world of our women today have surrendered, as she must wear the clothing befitting to her job. Her hair likewise is covered." See Elisa Klapheck, *Fraulein Rabbiner Jonas: The Story of the First Woman Rabbi*, (San Francisco: Jossey-Bass, 2004) 161.

34. Emil G. Hirsch, "Woman in the Synagogue," *Reform Advocate*, February 20, 1897, 7.

35. Emil G. Hirsch, "Woman in the Pulpit," *Reform Advocate*, November 11, 1893, 201.

36. Nadell, *Women Who Would Be Rabbis*, 52–53.

37. It is also worth noting that after her trip to Europe, Szold began supplementing the "Baltimore Letters" that she had been writing for the *Messenger* under the pen name Sulamith, with similar letters to the *Jewish Exponent* under the pen name Miriam.

38. Henrietta Szold, "Woman in the Synagogue," *Reform Advocate*, February 20, 1897, 9.

39. Thoughts on European Judaism," *Jewish Messenger* 52 (September 13, 1882): 4–5.

40. Baila Shargel, *Lost Love: The Untold Story of Henrietta Szold* (Philadelphia: Jewish Publication Society, 1997), 5.

41. Jewish Museum of Maryland, MS 38—Henrietta Szold Papers, Box 1, Folder 20—Correspondence 1903—Letter from Henrietta Szold to Judge Mayer Sulzberger, February 14, 1903.

42. Jewish Museum of Maryland, MS 38—Henrietta Szold Papers, Box 1, Folder 20—Correspondence 1903—Letter from Cyrus Adler to Henrietta Szold, February 22, 1903.

43. Letter from Henrietta Szold to Louis Ginsburg August 18, 1907, *Henrietta Szold Papers*, Microfilm no. 1012, American Jewish Archives, Cincinnati, Ohio.

44. Henrietta Szold, "Catholic Israel," *American Hebrew*, May 12, 1899, 11.

BIBLIOGRAPHY

Dash, Joan, *Summoned to Jerusalem: The Life of Henrietta Szold* (New York: Harper and Row, 1979).

Dworkin, Susan, "Henrietta Szold," in *The Jewish Woman: New Perspectives*, ed. Elizabeth Koltun (New York: Schocken Books, 1976), 164–70.

Fineman, Irving, *Woman of Valor: The Life of Henrietta Szold 1860–1945* (New York: Simon and Schuster, 1961).

Hanson, J.W. (ed.), *The World's Congress of Religions*, (Vancouver: J.M. MacGregor Publishing Co., 1894).

Hirsch, Emil G., "Woman in the Synagogue," *Reform Advocate*, February 20, 1897.
Hirsch, Emil G., "Woman in the Pulpit," *Reform Advocate*, November 11, 1893, 201.
Klapheck, Elisa, *Fraulein Rabbiner Jonas: The Story of the First Woman Rabbi* (San Francisco: Jossey-Bass, 2004).
Lapidus Lerner, Anne, "On the Rabbinic Ordination of Women," in *The Ordination of Women as Rabbis: Studies and Responsa*, ed. Simon Greenberg (New York: Jewish Theological Seminary of America, 1988), 93–106.
Lee Levin, Alexandra, "Henrietta Szold as Essayist," *Jewish Heritage*, Winter 1961, 38–42.
Lee Levin, Alexandra, *The Szolds of Lombard Street* (Philadelphia: Jewish Publication Society of America, 1960).
Lowenthal, Marvin (ed.), *Henrietta Szold: Life and Letters* (New York: Viking, 1942).
Nadell, Pamela S., *Women Who Would Be Rabbis: A History of Women's Ordination 1898–1985* (Boston: Beacon Press, 1998).
Sarna, Jonathan, *JPS: The Americanization of Jewish Culture, 1889–1989: A Centennial History of the Jewish Publication Society* (Philadelphia: Jewish Publication Society of America, 1989).
Shargel, Baila, *Lost Love: The Untold Story of Henrietta Szold* (Philadelphia: Jewish Publication Society, 1997).
Szold, Henrietta, "Catholic Israel," *American Hebrew*, May 12, 1899.
Szold, Henrietta, "Woman in the Synagogue," *Reform Advocate*, February 20, 1897.

Chapter Seven

The Religious as the Political in Margarete Susman

Elisa Klapheck

For much too long, Margarete Susman (Hamburg 1872–Zurich 1966) has been known only to a tiny circle of German theologians and scholars. A reassessment is overdue, as she deserves to be ranked alongside Martin Buber, Franz Rosenzweig, and all the other celebrated Jewish thinkers of her time.

A writer, she began her career as a poet and never ceased weaving her figurative style into the religious-political themes of her essays. While some readers most admired her lyrical flair, others appreciated her affection for Christianity, which always shone through her writings about Judaism. This made her an ideal interlocutor for Christian-Jewish dialogue.[1] Jews, however, often considered Susman merely an ambiguous personality in the history of German Jewry. After her death, she was soon forgotten. The extent to which she remains unknown today is revealed by the treatment of Gershom Scholem's oft-cited letter "Against the Myth of a German-Jewish 'Dialogue.'" In it, he contests the idea that there ever was such a thing as a German-Jewish symbiosis, and although the text is clearly directed against Susman, she is never mentioned when the letter is quoted.[2]

Nearly unknown today are Susman's major essays on the religious-political meaning of Judaism in Germany. Yet, these writings have inspired many protagonists of the Jewish Renaissance and secular messianism over the years. Better known, however, is Susman's 1946 publication, *The Book of Job and the Destiny of the Jewish People* (*Das Buch Hiob und das Schicksal des jüdischen Volkes*), often considered her magnum opus.[3] It represents the first attempt to apply a religious interpretation to the Shoah, long before the birth of a "Shoah theology." Susman's book, however, would only strengthen Jewish ambivalence toward its author, as she reintroduced the ancient theological concept of an interrelationship between Jews' divine designation as the "Chosen People" and the persecution necessarily following from it—a linkage that, especially after the Shoah, most Jews were no longer willing to accept. Instead, they thought the issue had been laid to rest by the State of Israel's founding and its subsequent military and political achievements.

In the 1990s, Susman would be rediscovered as a Jewish philosopher by a few researchers in women's studies. Credit is due to Ingeborg Nordmann and Barbara Hahn for drawing renewed attention from readers and reviewers to Susman's writings.[4] Unfortunately, they read Susman selectively in the light of their own criticism of male dominance in intellectual history, thereby also acknowledging German guilt around National Socialism. By using Susman to distance themselves from mainstream German philosophical traditions that had not managed to prevent the country's slide into the National Socialist abyss, they failed to sufficiently appreciate Susman's religious contribution to *Judaism*—of significance in its own right.

A fresh reading of Susman's work from a Jewish-rabbinic perspective, however, reveals a profound awareness of the political dimensions of religion—a consciousness that not only addressed the dark powers of those times in which Susman lived, but also contained a stand-alone religious-political message.[5] This aspect of Susman's work, which simultaneously reveals her Jewish approach, should prove of particular interest today given renewed reflection on the relationship between politics and religion.

Even if Susman has been long forgotten, she stands shoulder-to-shoulder with other major Jewish figures of the Jewish Renaissance movement and the secular messianism of her time: Martin Buber, Ernst Bloch, Gustav Landauer, Franz Rosenzweig, and many others. These men were close friends of Susman and engaged with her as intellectual partners. Yet, Susman's work follows an original course. Next to Zionism or secular socialism and liberalism, it stands for another political Judaism *in and for Germany* and Europe, self-confident in referencing its religious origins. Different from the two alternative political paths that many Jews of that time had chosen—secular engagement in liberal and socialist parties, or Zionism aimed at establishing a Jewish homeland in Palestine—Susman's conception of a European Judaism stands as a counterweight. Her understanding of Judaism, based on Germany as it was before 1933, identified the desired reorganization of German society as a Jewish task, that is, one that would be fulfilled from a Jewish point of view. The precondition for this stance was a positive interpretation of Jewish exile; in other words, a yes to the Jewish Diaspora.

Now, Susman did not reject Zionism per se. Rather, her opinion of a return to Zion was more ambivalent.[6] This was due to her political interpretation of the Jewish religion. Her focus on the religious-political value of "community" building stood in a critical tension with the idea of establishing a state. In her 1916 article "Ways of Zionism" ("Wege des Zionismus"), she applauded the cultural Zionism of Ahad Haam and Martin Buber, while at the same time fearing that gathering Jews from all over the world and yoking them to the establishment of a Jewish national state would by-pass the unique spiritual expectations and requirements of Judaism.[7] She predicted spiritual impoverishment for a Judaism lived as part of "the mechanisms of modern statehood and with it a dominance of the profane," which would deplete Judaism's religious power.[8] This aspect of her thought anticipated many arguments brought forward by contemporary post-Zionist thinkers, which is yet another reason why her writing should be understood not only within the context of her times but also within the discourse of today.[9]

First, however, let us look at the relevant biography. Susman's very long life—she died at the age of ninety-four—spanned four eras of German history: the German Empire, the Weimar Republic, the Nazi regime, which Susman survived in Switzerland, and the period after the Shoah, in which she refused to ever again set foot on German soil.

Only belatedly did Susman develop a fruitful relationship with her Jewish heritage. She was born in Hamburg in 1872 as the daughter of an affluent German Jewish family assimilated into the dominant Christian culture. The household celebrated Christmas; it was the nanny who first informed little Margarete that she was Jewish,[10] and it would not be until after her father's death in 1894 that Margarete Susman, already in her twenties, would first take lessons in Judaism, with Rabbi Caesar Seligmann. However, before her wedding in 1906, she was still prepared to convert to Christianity as a concession to the family of her fiancé, painter Eduard von Bendemann.[11] Yet, like Franz Rosenzweig, at the last minute she called off the baptism and from that time forward turned to Judaism. This about-face notwithstanding, throughout her life she held Christianity in high regard and consistently sought to associate both faiths in a productive and harmonious rapport.

Despite her extraordinary poetic and artistic talent, Susman was allowed to study only after her father's death. She first lived for a year in Düsseldorf as a student of painting and then in Munich, where, as a poet, she associated with the circle around the cult figure Stefan George and his most important promoter, the Jewish poet Karl Wolfskehl.[12] Around the turn of the twentieth century, together with her friend, poet and art historian Gertrud Kantorowicz, she moved to Berlin to study philosophy with Georg Simmel.[13] Simmel was deeply impressed with Susman, so much so that he dedicated to her and Gertrud Kantorowicz his 1906 book on religion.[14] His description of Susman as a "center without periphery" became famous.[15] Participating in recurring salons at Simmel's home, Susman attracted many of his students, who admired her spiritual-intellectual capacity as much as her beauty. Among them were Bernhard Groethuysen, Georg Lukács, Ernst Bloch, and Martin Buber, whose works Susman reviewed in the *Frankfurter Zeitung*.[16] But also other protagonists of the German Jewish avant garde, such as the anarchist Gustav Landauer and Franz Rosenzweig, founder of the Jewish Lehrhaus in Frankfurt, where Susman also taught, must be named as her close friends.[17] Ernst Bloch apparently fell in love with her. During the first World War, when Susman was living with her son in Switzerland, Bloch moved nearby to discuss his writing of *Spirit of Utopia* (*Geist der Utopie*) with her.

Already before World War I, Susman had made a name for herself with two major publications: a 1910 treatise on modern German poetry in which she coined the concept of a "lyrical 'I,'" and a 1912 metaphysical analysis of love titled *The Meaning of Love* (*Vom Sinn der Liebe*).[18] With Heinrich Simon, editor-in-chief of the *Frankfurter Zeitung* and another of Susman's admirers, she edited the unfinished book of her friend Erwin Kircher after his premature death, *Philosophy of Romanticism* (*Philosophie der Romantik*).[19] Heinrich Simon provided an additional platform for Susman's work—the *Frankfurter Zeitung*. In its pages in 1907, Susman's first article appeared—a critical review of Jakob Fromer's then-scandalous book *Judaism and Culture* (*Judentum und Kultur*). In that work, Fromer, best known as a modern Talmudist, called for a total assimilation of Jews to the supposedly higher German culture. Susman reacted with an indignant denunciation of this call. Her critique of Fromer was simultaneously her first public yes to Judaism.[20] The article marks the beginning of her path toward redefining the meaning of Judaism for the present day.

Susman took Spinoza's philosophy as her starting point. In 1913, the Zionist Bar Kochba student association in Prague published an edited volume, *On Judaism* (*Vom Judentum*). The book, which attracted considerable attention, contained essays by many contemporary supporters and masterminds of the Jewish Renaissance movement.[21] As the only woman among them, Susman contributed an essay titled "Spinoza and the Jewish Sense of the World" ("Spinoza und das Jüdische Weltgefühl"). It revealed what would characterize all subsequent Susman texts, her typical *religious* and simultaneously *secular* understanding of Judaism.[22]

The concept introduced in the title—*Weltgefühl*, or "sense of the world"—held the religious yet secular key. Susman understood Spinoza's epistemology, his fixation on "laws," as a mode of thought whose origin lay in the Jewish religion as a revelation of "God's law"—be it as laws of nature or as ethical laws.

The inner nexus of religious and secular thought would from then on determine Susman's understanding of divine law and thus of Judaism. In subsequent essays on Judaism, many of which appeared in the liberal Jewish newspaper *Der Morgen* as well as in Buber's magazine *Der Jude*, Susman interpreted God's law as critical for religiously motivated political thought. Gradually, she moved away from understanding the Jewish view of divine law as an instrument to coerce spiritual obedience, as she had done in her Spinoza essay, and increasingly saw it in political terms: as a vehicle for secular liberation from oppression and thus at the same time a redemptive, messianic means of working toward a better future.

In this context, she highlights differences between the Hebrew Bible and Greek philosophy. Plato's Idea refers to memory and is drawn from bygone days; in contrast, "the commandment: the revealed divine law" points toward a messianic future:

> In contrast to a focus on the past, memory and observation, concepts inherent in Plato's Idea, the divine commandment of the Bible gestures toward the future, hope, and action. In the words of Isaiah, "Remember ye not the former things, neither consider the things of old," we find in pure form what is required of Jewish people and the Jewish spirit. . . . That the *time* of Judaism is the *future* and that the highest *value* is accorded to the *deed*—they are one and the same.[23]

Susman, who had opposed the first World War, aligned herself in 1918 with the November Revolution and the proclamation of the socialist-anarchist Bavarian Republic of Councils by her friend Gustav Landauer.[24] Similar to Hannah Arendt later, Susman called on German Jews to become more political, yet in contrast to Arendt she deployed a religiously motivated argument—to understand civic participation as a Jewish religious duty.

In her 1919 pamphlet "The Revolution and the Jews" ("Die Revolution und die Juden"), Susman perceived a revolutionary identification among Jews with the social redesign of the prostrate Germany:

> In their attitudes toward the German revolution, Jews who had truly experienced it were certainly not divided as they were in their opinions of the war. In this instance, they felt an immediate, weighty responsibility for the life and destiny of Germany. And here also that conflicting, constricted moment ceased—the desire, no matter what the cost, to be German. Although the required tasks included the hardest sacrifice, here was a mission passionately seized.[25]

According to Susman, Judaism itself provided the religious-political rationale behind what she perceived as a revolutionary responsibility. For her, "revolution" meant the realization of the Jewish concept of atonement—*teshuvah*. In other words, "atonement" was not understood in Christian terms as "punishment," but rather given a Jewish inflection as "repentance" and "change," that is, a positive possibility realized by means of a cathartic, expiatory transformation of the political present.[26]

For today's contestations swirling around the relationship between the political and the transcendent, Susman's religious thinking is interesting in that she attempts to redefine Jewish responsibility in Europe without implying any fixed pious identity. Susman's thought boils down neither to any sort of orthodox theocracy nor to a religious ethics expressed in liberal and social clichés. Rather, Susman drafted something resembling an open religious-political platform in which divine law was revealed as the bedrock of democracy. She interpreted Jewish thought as both religious and political, beyond the reach of theocratic appropriation. More fundamental than the dogmas of institutionalized religion, it exposes a religious grounding of democracy. As she wrote in her later interpretation of the prophet Ezekiel: "It is no longer theocracy as in the early days, God's rule as in the ancient cultic society, in which each individual was immersed in communal service to God; it is God's rule in precisely the opposite sense: as a calling to each to be oneself; to assume one's own responsibility. It is theocracy as *democracy*."[27]

Susman understood theocracy's metamorphosis into democracy as a shifting of the idea of God's rule to the primacy of the individual's own relationship with God. The starting point of all religious experience and thought lay for Susman not in existing theology, nor in pre-scripted devout identity, but rather solely in the spiritual experience of each individual soul. Only the soul could enjoy the human-God relationship, but this in turn implied that each soul performed a *political* function, namely to make the experienced relationship concrete in the real world by building "community"—for Susman, the ultimate meaning of politics:

> Politics is clearly the cocoon of the human soul that does not yet allow flight to her own pure realm, yet the threads have been spun by the soul itself. Because politics is nothing other, nor can it be anything other, than a search for the true aims of human community, a quest impeded, however, by a thousand hurdles stumbled over again and again, and derailed by lapses and error.[28]

Susman's idea of a "politics of the soul" was linked to her understanding of the political meaning of Judaism. The Torah, the "divine law," she wrote, revealed the "community."[29] Here, we have the core of Susman's religious-political understanding. In her view, the true religious or political community was a bond between people, committed to each other by means of the very foundation of the human-God relationship in each unique soul. In other words, the human-God relationship, which is rooted in the individual, also reaches out beyond the limits of the individual to form a community with other individuals. According to Susman, the relationship between the individual and God was reflected in the divine law and concretized in laws that build community. The religious-political potential of the community has to be seen in the context of the socialist ideas of Susman's time, but it also prefigured aspects of the debate about communitarianism today.

The political potential of community was yet another aspect of Susman's thought. She saw the political function of the soul in its moment of resistance, which places the soul in a critical tension with the "state," with "society," or with "history."[30] As Susman wrote in her 1926 essay "What Can the Bible Mean for Us Today?" ("Was kann uns die Bibel heute noch bedeuten?"), only in this resistant impulse of the soul vis-à-vis the state can "history" arise—a narrative that earned the right to be called "history" because it chronicled not the "simple unfolding of events," but rather arose from an inner, rebellious sentiment of the soul inspired by God, directing each individual toward a deeper sense of history made concrete.[31]

> The current of life that eternally sustains, carries, and runs through us is sucked up and, wrenching around itself, whirling and funneling from below

and inside, drives the self from a simple movement toward progress in another direction foreign to that current. Alone the march of life through the depths of the subject can create historical truth. Resistance to the course by the force of the self is in fact our history.[32]

The Bible serves as witness to this moment of the soul's resistance, shaped in keeping with the story of one people—Israel—buttressed by divine law, a struggle inflamed at that instant of the soul's opposition that culminates in the form of community. "Nowhere is the truth of history that is rooted in the individual human being clearer and more convincing than in Israel's chronicle with its roots in meta-history, its origin in the God of truth."[33]

Susman saw God's law not as legislation consigned to the past. Instead, it manifested in the present as driven by the future—hence the timeless eternity of the Jewish people—with its tight grasp on a past that actually resides in a revolutionary-messianic future:

> And even those who have fallen away from the law are bound to one another by common descent from it. The law also accounts for the peculiar responsibility that every Jew feels for every other Jew. And in this heritage lies another key to that curious puzzle, that each Jew, the abiding person [relating] to God's law, the conservative person as such, is in truth the real revolutionary, radical person, the pure person of the future. . . . This direction drawn from divine law with regard to its absolute fulfillment has been indelibly impressed on every Jew moving toward completion. . . . And therefore all must, for the sake of divine law and its fulfillment, adopt a revolutionary outlook vis-à-vis human arrangements. Because the law is not of this world, it must force a revolution against all limiting earthly order.[34]

All the prophets had been "revolutionaries in the most profound way": "People of the future, of the idea, blasting, pushing forward, arousing other human beings. Yet none of the prophets were revolutionaries vis-à-vis the law; it was imperturbable, all held tight to it, for even Christ had not come to break the law but to ensure its fulfillment."[35]

Judaism's secular messianism motivated another aspect of Susman's religious-political viewpoint. Judaism was only thinkable in connection to other peoples, just as others could not exist without Judaism. Her essay "The Bridge" ("Die Brücke"), published in 1925, said that the homeless, otherworldly, formless Jewish people go through their lives in all eras, challenged to find another people with a homeland and history with whom they can connect, in order that God's law may unfold and prepare them for the messianic future.[36] Envisioning a "bridge" in which Christians and Jews approach one another from opposite sides, the Christians from an earthly-historical homeland and the Jews from a homeless eternity, Susman sees them each giving meaning to the other.[37] While the Jews relinquish their mode of homeless eternal wandering to become an earthly-historical people, Christians, by virtue of their Jewish elements "expressed in their attitude to Christ," break through the boundaries of nations to reach humanity's eternal realm.[38] This meeting point would be essential for the course of humanity.

Increasingly, Susman interpreted divine law as the absolute negation of the emerging Nazi regime. Today, engaging with Susman's understanding of God's law entails exploring the relevance of her interpretation for legislation in democratic states. For her, God's law has been realized throughout history by the *laws of atonement*—that is, statutes that enable *teshuvah*, repentance, and reparation by means of secular rulings passed by political institutions. Susman's theory of divine law thus embraced the *religious share* that civic jurisprudence can contain and revealed the religious dimension of politics. She saw the religious-political potential of Jewish thought for secular reality.

Susman's commitment to law was a commitment to the Torah—a Torah, however, that should first be understood as the law *anterior to* legislation, decreed in every age and constantly regained by religious-secular revelation, situating Jewish tradition in an active relation to political history. Religious patterns of meaning, like the Jewish paradigm of exile and return, held for Susman a specific epistemological potential—that is, a special mode of revelation. Susman's reinterpretation of Jewish exile as a positive way of being proves fruitful for today's discourses on the Diaspora. According to Susman, Jewish revelation presupposed an understanding of the existential homelessness of all the world's people—exile as a shared state of being, starting with Adam's expulsion from Paradise. As Susman wrote in her 1932 essay "Judaism as a World Religion" ("Das Judentum als Weltreligion") and in her interpretation of the prophet Ezekiel, the Jewish people have taken individual human exile and turned it into a collective way of life, thereby gaining deeper insight into this original condition.[39] Susman understood exile as the will of God—and as such, it was recognized by Ezekiel as Israel's proper way of life. We find in her essay on Ezekiel:

> In exile, dispersed among other peoples with their lighter, brighter, more enticing cultural offerings, the danger grew exponentially that the Jews would be taken up and dissolved. At that moment of greatest peril, however, the prophet appeared. The family tree had been uprooted from its familiar ground; it no

longer grew or sent its shoots into the soil. Of this fact, Ezekiel was certain: seeds planted failed to take root. And now the most tremendous thing occurred: the prophet's powerful hand grabbed the floating tree, ripped it the rest of the way out of the exhausted earth, turned it upside down, and replanted it in a direction counter to all natural rules of growth, with its roots in the air. Thus transplanted, this form of anchoring in God would provide Israel's most intimate reason for being.[40]

As a result of Ezekiel's intervention, for once in the history of humanity, it was possible to turn around a national catastrophe, one that would normally splinter the group into a soulless mass, leading it instead into a deeper humanity and giving the people a new lease on life. But this required a historical decision of the highest magnitude: embracing exile—detaching from everything beyond the group's own power and reality—and making the Diaspora the entire raison d'être of the tribe. But does this state not contain a general human truth? Is not exile an expression of human destiny *as such*? Are not *all* people unattached, homeless, and wandering the earth?[41]

The simultaneously religious and political revelation of Jewish exile is expressed in the *Sh'ma Yisrael*—"Hear, O Israel. The Eternal is our God, the Eternal is One!"[42] Susman describes the call to "hear" as an act performed in a spirit of conscious self-alienation from the world. Only this makes possible the revelation of the "nearly inaudible":

> Because this kind of hearing is no easygoing, casual listening: it does not imply that same faculty of receiving what people say or what obviously enters my ears from the babble around me. It means the opposite, that I can only hear when I do not hear all that white noise, but instead I become all ears only for the One. Only when I am no longer drowned and confused by millions of competing voices and trivial things can the almost entirely inaudible from the depth of all depths penetrate my mind.[43]

The Jewish rule against depicting God in images was also linked in Susman's thought to exile as a precondition for revelation. She described this ban as a commandment to destroy all pictures of God.[44] Number one among God's laws, the commandment is directed against idolatry and the mystification of worldly "powers":

> Our handiwork always contains something of the idol; we cannot help serving the powers of this world when we create. For that reason, we are forbidden to invest our *creativity* in producing pictures of God, but rather the opposite: the

deepest imaginative impulse of the Jew is the elemental power to destroy the image in order to arrive at truth.[45]

In the prohibition against picturing God, Susman identified three aspects:

1. The rule against making an "image of God from earthly substances."[46]
2. The command to destroy all images of God (*destructive*).
3. The "task of forming the human being in the image of God" (*constructive*).[47]

Ultimately, exile and its corollary, the prohibition against picturing God, prove to contain the secret to human freedom:

> Thus we understand humanity's proto-state as one in which men and women, distinct from other creatures, can leave a place both physically and imaginatively; they can set out for a destination, moving forward; they can transform themselves incessantly and go beyond multiple entanglements to answer the call and realize in themselves the image of the One.[48]

Margarete Susman produced an oeuvre consisting of 17 books and about 250 articles and essays. These contain numerous themes and approaches that one could also pursue to gain an understanding of her thought. At the same time, as concerned as she was with Judaism, she also penned essays on women's emancipation.[49] Shortly after her divorce, she published a book in 1929 titled *Women of the Romantic Era* (*Frauen der Romantik*).[50] It contains portraits of female authors from the period, ranging from Caroline Schlegel-Schelling to Rahel Levin von Varnhagen. The book revealed a covert debate between Christianity and Judaism, but also a spiritual self-portrait of Susman's own conflicting motives as a female philosopher, independent writer, former wife, and Jew coping with the tides of life.[51] That same year witnessed the publication of her trail-blazing essay "The Problem of Job in the Work of Franz Kafka" ("Das Hiob-Problem bei Franz Kafka"); the text was considered a pioneering, first-ever interpretation of Kafka.[52] Another interesting way of getting to know Margarete Susman would be through her many friendships and correspondence with other philosophers and writers. Among them was also the poet Paul Celan, who visited her regularly in Zurich and wrote two poems for her, which were published in an anthology in honor of her ninetieth birthday.[53]

But it is truly her texts on Judaism that retain a particular boldness for today's reader, because they unfold an imperative that did not end with the

Shoah. In them, Susman posits a religious-political nexus of exile, revelation, Torah as God's law, and a revolutionary-messianic future as the never-ceasing Jewish contribution to the history of humanity.

After the Nazis came to power, Susman left Frankfurt, where she had lived since her divorce in 1928, and emigrated to Switzerland. Susman had a son, Erwin von Bendemann, who fled the Nazi regime to England. Many of Susman's friends and relatives were murdered or died in the persecutions— among them Susman's sister Paula and her friend Gertrud Kantorowicz. For the rest of her life until her death in 1966, she never returned to Germany but resided in Zurich, where she joined the Religious Socialism movement founded by Protestant pastor Leonhard Ragaz. For its journal *New Paths* (*Neue Wege*), Susman continued writing extensively on religious-philosophical themes. During the second World War, she also produced her magnum opus, *The Book of Job and the Destiny of the Jewish People* (*Das Buch Hiob und das Schicksal des jüdischen Volkes*). However, the theodicy in it, presented so soon after the murder of millions of European Jews, would fail to convince at the time. Critics of Susman, above all Gershom Scholem, accused her of trying to merge Christian with Jewish thought. Susman, however, described her book as a "Jewish confession."[54] It contained not only a few critical passages about Christianity, but went further to underscore "that Jesus himself, were he to encounter a Jew engaged in the weighty process of choosing his life's path, would not direct him toward the open and shining church but rather toward the darkness of a people bleeding from thousands of wounds."[55]

It is astonishing to discover that this and other similar passages failed to disturb Susman's Christian reviewers, who instead consistently emphasized the Christian content of her thought.[56] But half a century later, scholars of women's studies acknowledged only remotely the meaning of the Jewish religion for Susman and at times even removed her from the Jewish context altogether. Thus, Ingeborg Nordmann, who published an important anthology of Susman's essays, emphasized that Susman saw "neither in Zionism nor in the Jewish community a place for herself," nor could "her religious avowal be inserted into any tradition."[57] The meaning Judaism had for Susman then, and could have again today, is drowned in such statements. Beside the fact that for Zionism, this observation is false, Susman's critical relationship to an institutionalized Jewish religion corresponded to that of many other Jews of her generation, who strove for a Jewish Renaissance independent of religious denominations and congregational authority. Barbara Hahn, in turn, placed

Margarete Susman within a "dead, . . . bygone culture" of Jewish women writers in Germany about whom, in eternal mourning, Hahn wrote a book as a *Kaddish*.[58] Here, too, we can see how differently Susman's work will be understood if read through a Jewish lens and her interpretations applied to the present.

A Jewish reading of Susman asks once again how religious and political ideas are linked. For Susman, religious experience focuses on secular reality, imbuing the secular with a spiritual dimension while not necessarily justifying holy dogma. Yet, this dimension is not all there is. It is only a part, the part representing atonement—*teshuvah*—with political guidelines and legislation scripted by human hands. The question that arises next, as to *how* reparation or expiation can be achieved, Susman still has not answered, although the issue does appear in her work. It reads like a call for active involvement—not within organized religion, but rather in a sociopolitical context. In sum, Margarete Susman has derived this perspective from her thought about Judaism, thereby preserving its religious-political relevance for readers today.

NOTES

1. A good illustration is the 1965 anthology of essays by Margarete Susman, *Vom Geheimnis der Freiheit. Gesammelte Aufsätze 1914–1964*, ed. Manfred Schlösser (Darmstadt/ Zürich: Agora, 1965).

2. Gershom Scholem, "Wider den Mythos vom deutsch-jüdischen 'Gespräch'" (Against the Myth of a German-Jewish "Dialogue"), in *Auf gespaltenem Pfad (zum 90. Geburtstag von Margarete Susman)*, ed. Manfred Schlösser (Darmstadt: Erato-Presse, 1964), 229–32; again in Gershom Scholem, *Judaica 2* (Frankfurt am Main: Suhrkamp, 1970), 7–11.

3. Margarete Susman, *Das Buch Hiob und das Schicksal des jüdischen Volkes* (Zürich: Steinberg, 1946; Frankfurt am Main: Jüdischer Verlag, 1996).

4. Ingeborg Nordmann, "Wie man sich in der Sprache fremd bewegt. Zu den Essays von Margarete Susman," in Margarete Susman, *" Das Nah- und Fernsein des Fremden "* (Frankfurt am Main: Jüdischer Verlag, 1992); Barbara Hahn, *Die Jüdin Pallas Athene. Auch eine Theorie der Moderne* (Berlin: Berlin Verlag, 2002); Barbara Hahn and Anke Gilleir, eds., *Grenzgänge zwischen Dichtung, Philosophie und Kulturkritik. Über Margarete S usman* (Göttingen: Wallstein, 2012).

5. Elisa Klapheck, *Margarete Susmans jüdischer Beitrag zur politischen Philosophie* (Berlin: Hentrich & Hentrich, 2014).

6. See also Micha Brumlik, the chapter on Margarete Susman in *Kritik des Zionismus* (Hamburg: Europäische Verlagsanstalt, 2007), 116–20.

7. Margarete Susman, "Wege des Zionismus—Achad Haam: 'Am Scheidewege, Martin Buber: Die jüdische Bewegung,'" *Frankfurter Zeitung*, September 17–19, 1916, 1.

8. Margarete Susman, "Die Revolution und die Juden," *Das Forum*, September 1919; again in Susman, *Vom Geheimnis der Freiheit*, 122–43.

9. Zionism, however, of which Susman approved, was consistently linked to social criticism. "Zion is not the destination but the path; not the answer but the question, an open query about the future for the people to answer. It is put to the test in a wholly secular world, yet Zionism's task is limited to the realm of salvation: only in a restructuring of society, a renewal of the community, a new, lively representation of humanness. . . . Zionism without change in the derelict economic and social configurations could not be true Zionism allowing the people's humanness to shine through." Susman, *Das Buch Hiob*, 118.

10. For all biographical data, see Margarete Susman's autobiography, *Ich habe viele Leben gelebt. Erinnerungen* (Stuttgart: Deutsche Verlags-Anstalt, 1964).

11. The Bendemanns, a famous family of artists, were also of Jewish heritage but had converted to Protestantism two generations back.

12. In 1901, Susman's collection of poems *Mein Land, Gedichte* appeared in the publishing house Schuster & Loeffler (Berlin/Leipzig). Ute Oelmann and Ulrich Raulff draw attention to the astonishing number of Jewish women in the circle around Stefan George. See Ute Oelmann and Ulrich Raulff, *Frauen um Stefan George* (Göttingen: Castrum Peregrini, Wallstein, 2010).

13. On the friendship between Susman and Kantorowicz, see *Der abgerissene Dialog, Die intellektuelle Beziehung Gertrud Kantorowicz—Margarete Susman. Oder Die Schweizer Grenze bei Hohenems als Endpunkt eines Fluchtversuches*, ed. Petra Zudrell (Innsbruck, Wien: Studien Verlag, 1999).

14. Georg Simmel, *Die Religion*, vol. 2, *Die Gesellschaft*, Sammlung sozialpsychologischer Monographien, ed. Martin Buber (Frankfurt am Main: Rütten & Loening, 1906).

15. Walter Nigg, *Heilige und Dichter* (Zürich: Diogenes, 1991), 181.

16. Margarete Susman, "Die Seele und die Formen" (zu Georg Lukács: "Die Seele und die Formen"), *Frankfurter Zeitung*, 5.9.1912, 1; also in Margarete Susman, *Das Nah- und Fernsein des Fremden*, 15–21; "Die Theorie des Romans" (zu Georg von Lukács: "Die Theorie des Romans, Ein geschichtsphilosophischer Versuch über die großen Formen der Epik," 1916), *Frankfurter Zeitung* 16.8.1921, 1; "Von der Verwirklichung" (zu Martin Buber: "Daniel—Gespräche von der Verwirklichung," 1913), *Frankfurter Zeitung* 28.5.1914; also as "Martin Buber—Der Philosoph mit der Lyra," in Susman, *Vom Geheimnis der Freiheit*, 1965, 144–54; "Wege des Zionismus"—Achad Haam: "Am Scheidewege," Martin Buber: "Die jüdische Bewegung," *Frankfurter Zeitung* 17./19.9.1916, 1; "Geist der Utopie" (zu Ernst Bloch: "Geist der Utopie"), *Frankfurter Zeitung* 12.1.1919, 1; also in: Susman, *Das Nah- und Fernsein des Fremden*, 22–30; "Der Bürger in Frankreich" (zu Bernhard Groethuysen: "Die Entstehung der bürgerlichen Welt- und Lebensanschauung in Frankreich," Bd. 1, *Frankfurter Zeitung* 2.9.1928, Beilage, 1; "Der Bürger in Frankreich" (zu Bernhard Groethuysen: "Die Entstehung der bürgerlichen Welt- und Lebensanschauung in Frankreich," Bd. 2, *Frankfurter Zeitung* 16.11.1930, Literaturblatt, 1.

17. Margarete Susman, "Gustav Landauer (Nachruf)," in *Das Tribunal*, I, 6, Darmstadt 1919; also in Susman, *Vom Geheimnis der Freiheit*, 255–66 and as "Zu den Revolutionsbriefen," 266–70 (zu Landauers Werk "Briefe aus der französischen Revolution"v. 1919) in Susman, *Das Nah- und Fernsein des Fremden*, 129–39; "Gustav Landauers Briefe" (Rezension zu "Gustav Landauer. Sein Lebensbild in Briefen." Unter Mitwirkung von Ina Britschgi-Schimmer hrsg. v. Martin Buber 1929), *Der Morgen*, V, 2, June 1929, 194–98; "Der Stern der Erlösung," *Der Jude*, 1921/22, No. 4, 259–64; "Franz Rosenzweig (Nachruf)," *Frankfurter Zeitung* 22.12.1929, 1; "Stern der Erlösung," *Der Morgen* VII, 4, Berlin, Oct. 1931, 379–80; "Die neue Übersetzung der Heiligen Schrift" (zu Martin Buber—Franz Rosenzweig, "Die Schrift," Berlin 1927), *Basler Nachrichten* 18.2.1928, also in Susman, *Das Nah- und Fernsein des Fremden*, 204–208.

18. Margarete Susman, *Das Wesen der modernen deutschen Lyrik* (Stuttgart: Strecker & Schröder, 1910); Margarete Susman, *Vom Sinn der Liebe* (Jena: Eugen Diederichs, 1912).
19. Erwin Kircher, *Philosophie der Romantik.* Aus dem Nachlaß herausgegeben v. Margarete Susman u. Heinrich Simon (Jena: Eugen Diederichs, 1906).
20. Margarete Susman, "Judentum und Kultur" (zu Jakob Fromer, "Vom Ghetto zur modernen Kultur"), *Frankfurter Zeitung*, May 16, 1907.
21. Robert Weltsch, "Erinnerungen an ein vergessenes Buch (Nach fünfzig Jahren)," in Schlösser, *Auf gespaltenem Pfad.*
22. Margarete Susman, "Spinoza und das jüdische Weltgefühl," in *Vom Judentum. Ein Sammelbuch*, ed. Hans Kohn, Verein jüdischer Hochschüler, "Bar Kochba" in Prag (Leipzig: Kurt Wolff Verlag, 1913), 51–70; and in Margarete Susman, *Vom Geheimnis der Freiheit*, 85–104.
23. Margarete Susman, "Der jüdische Geist," *Blätter des jüdischen Frauenbundes für Frauenarbeit und Frauenbewegung* 9 (1933): 11; also in *Vom jüdischen Geist, Aufsatzsammlung des Jüdischen Frauenbundes*, 1934; again in Susman, *"Das Nah- und Fernsein des Fremden,"* 210.
24. See, for example, Susman's articles and essays "Aufblick," *Frankfurter Zeitung*, November 15, 1918, 1 and as "Zur Revolution von 1918" in Margarete Susman, *"Das Nah- und Fernsein des Fremden,"* 105–106; "Gustav Landauer (Nachruf)," in *Das Tribunal* 1, no. 6 (Darmstadt, 1919); again in *Vom Geheimnis der Freiheit*, 255–66. Also "Der Sinn des Anarchismus," in *Neue Wege* 41 (1947): 1–3, 5–10, 67–73, 110–20; again as "Der Versuch des Anarchismus," in Susman, *Gestalten und Kreise* (1954), 136–59.
25. Margarete Susman, "Die Revolution und die Juden," in *Das Forum*, ed. Wilhelm Herzog, Munich, 3/12 (September 1919): 921–48, again in Susman, *Vom Geheimnis der Freiheit*, 128.
26. See the chapter "Umkehr—*Teschuwa*—Revolution," in Klapheck, *Margarete Susmans jüdischer Beitrag zur politischen Philosophie*, 114–51.
27. In her interpretation of Ezekiel, Susman described the prophet's aim to transform the theocracy into a religiously motivated democracy. Margarete Susman, "Ezechiel—Der Prophet der Umkehr," *Neue Wege* 7, no. 8 (1942): 14–15 (emphasis in the original); again in Susman, *Deutung biblischer Gestalten*, 61–95.
28. Margarete Susman, "Die Schicksalsstunde der deutschen Juden (ca. 1933)," unpublished manuscript, Bl. 4, Deutsches Literaturarchiv, Marbach.
29. Margarete Susman, "Leben," *Züricher Jüdische Pressezentrale*, May 1, 1939, 12.
30. See Margarete Susman, "Einzelmoral und Staatsmoral," *Frankfurter Zeitung*, November 17, 1915, 1; again as "Der Einzelne und der Staat," in Susman, *Vom Geheimnis der Freiheit* (1965), 49–55.
31. Margarete Susman, "Was kann uns die Bibel heute noch bedeuten?," *Der Morgen*, August 1926, 299–310.
32. Susman, "Was kann uns die Bibel," 301.
33. Ibid., 302–3.
34. Margarete Susman, "Die Revolution und die Juden" (1919), in Margarete Susman, *Vom Geheimnis der Freiheit*, 139–40.
35. Susman, "Die Revolution und die Juden," 139.
36. Margarete Susman, "Die Brücke," *Der Jude*, 1925, 76–84; see also "1. Teil" (1921) of "Die Brücke zwischen Judentum und Christentum," in Susman, *Vom Geheimnis der Freiheit*, 15–26.
37. Susman, "Die Brücke," 76–84.
38. Ibid., 83–84.

39. Margarete Susman, "Das Judentum als Weltreligion," *Mitteilungsblatt der jüdischen Reformgemeinde Berlin*, 1.7.1932; again in Margarete Susman, *Vom Geheimnis der Freiheit*, 105–21.
40. Susman, "Ezechiel"; again in Susman, *Deutung biblischer Gestalten*, 62–63.
41. Susman, "Ezechiel," 80–81 (emphasis in the original).
42. Susman, "Das Judentum als Weltreligion"; again in Susman, *Vom Geheimnis der Freiheit*, 107.
43. Susman, "Das Judentum als Weltreligion," 107–8; see also "Der jüdische Geist," in *Blätter des jüdischen Frauenbundes für Frauenarbeit und Frauenbewegung* (1933); also in *Vom jüdischen Geist* (1934), 49; again in Susman, *" Das Nah- und Fernsein des Fremden,"* 209–23.
44. Susman, "Der jüdische Geist" (1933), in *Vom jüdischen Geist* (1934), 50; and "Das Judentum als Weltreligion" (1932), in Susman, *Vom Geheimnis der Freiheit*, 111.
45. Susman, "Der jüdische Geist" (1933), in *Vom jüdischen Geist* (1934), 50 (emphasis in the original).
46. Susman, "Das Judentum als Weltreligion" (1932), in Susman, *Vom Geheimnis der Freiheit*, 110.
47. Susman, "Das Judentum als Weltreligion," 119.
48. Ibid., 119.
49. See also Susman's essays "Die Revolution und die Frau," in *Das Flugblatt*, Nr. 4 (Frankfurt am Main: Tiedmann and Uzielli, 1918), and "Das Frauenproblem in der gegenwärtigen Welt," *Der Morgen* 5 (December 1926): 431–52, both in Susman, *" Das Nah- und Fernsein des Fremden"* (1992). See also Susman, "Auflösung und Werden in unserer Zeit," *Der Morgen* 4 (October 1928): 335–53; Susman, "Frau und Geist," *Die Literarische Welt*, Berlin, March 20, 1931; Susman, "Wandlungen der Frau," *Die Neue Rundschau*, January 1933, 105–24, also in Susman, *Gestalten und Kreise*, 160–77. See also Susman's *Vom Sinn der Liebe*.
50. Margarete Susman, *Frauen der Romantik* (Jena: Eugen Diederichs, 1929).
51. See my interpretation in "Das Gesetz der Welt selbst mitzugestalten," in Klapheck, *Margarete Susmans jüdischer Beitrag zur politischen Philosophie*, 215ff.
52. Margarete Susman, "Das Hiob-Problem bei Franz Kafka," *Der Morgen* 5, no. 1 (April 1929): 31–49; again as "Früheste Deutung Franz Kafkas," in Susman, *Gestalten und Kreise*, 348–66, and in Susman, *" Das Nah- und das Fernsein des Fremden,"* 183–203.
53. Paul Celan, "Zwei Gedichte," in Schlösser, *Auf gespaltenem Pfad*, 75.
54. Susman, *Das Buch Hiob*, 25.
55. Ibid., 132.
56. See Erwin von Bendemann, "Margarete Susman im Licht ihrer Korrespondenz," unpublished manuscript, legacy of Margarete Susman, Deutsches Literaturarchiv Marbach.
57. Ingeborg Nordmann, "Wie man sich in der Sprache fremd bewegt. Zu den Essays von Margarete Susman," in Susman, *"Das Nah- und Fernsein des Fremden,"* 259 and 235.
58. Hahn, *Die Jüdin Pallas Athene*, 13.

BIBLIOGRAPHY

Brumlik, Micha, *Kritik des Zionismus* (Hamburg: Europäische Verlagsanstalt, 2007).
Hahn, Barbara, and Gilleir, Anke, (eds.), *Grenzgänge zwischen Dichtung, Philosophie und Kulturkritik. Über Margarete S usman* (Göttingen: Wallstein, 2012).

Hahn, Barbara, *Die Jüdin Pallas Athene. Auch eine Theorie der Moderne* (Berlin: Berlin Verlag, 2002).
Kircher, Erwin, *Philosophie der Romantik*. Aus dem Nachlaß herausgegeben v. Margarete Susman u. Heinrich Simon (Jena: Eugen Diederichs, 1906).
Klapheck, Elisa, *Margarete Susmans jüdischer Beitrag zur politischen Philosophie* (Berlin: Hentrich & Hentrich, 2014).
Nigg, Walter, *Heilige und Dichter* (Zürich: Diogenes, 1991).
Nordmann, Ingeborg, "Wie man sich in der Sprache fremd bewegt. Zu den Essays von Margarete Susman," in Margarete Susman, *"Das Nah- und Fernsein des Fremden"* (Frankfurt am Main: Jüdischer Verlag, 1992), 229–67.
Oelmann, Ute and Raulff, Ulrich, *Frauen um Stefan George* (Göttingen: Castrum Peregrini, Wallstein, 2010).
Scholem, Gershom, "Wider den Mythos vom deutsch-jüdischen 'Gespräch'" ("Against the Myth of a German-Jewish "Dialogue"), in *Auf gespaltenem Pfad (zum 90. Geburtstag von Margarete Susman)*, ed. Manfred Schlösser (Darmstadt: Erato-Presse, 1964), 229–32; again in Gershom Scholem, *Judaica 2* (Frankfurt am Main: Suhrkamp, 1970), 7–11.
Simmel, Georg, *Die Religion*, vol. 2, *Die Gesellschaft*, Sammlung sozialpsychologischer Monographien, ed. Martin Buber (Frankfurt am Main: Rütten & Loening, 1906).
Susman, Margarete, *Vom Geheimnis der Freiheit. Gesammelte Aufsätze 1914–1964*, ed. Manfred Schlösser (Darmstadt/ Zürich: Agora, 1965).
Susman, Margarete, *Ich habe viele Leben gelebt. Erinnerungen* (Stuttgart: Deutsche Verlags-Anstalt, 1964).
Susman, Margarete, "Der Sinn des Anarchismus," in *Neue Wege* 41 (1947): 1–3, 5–10, 67–73, 110–20.
Susman, Margarete, *Das Buch Hiob und das Schicksal des jüdischen Volkes* (Zürich: Steinberg, 1946).
Susman, Margarete, "Ezechiel—Der Prophet der Umkehr," *Neue Wege* 7, no. 8 (1942): 14–15.
Susman, Margarete, "Leben," *Züricher Jüdische Pressezentrale*, May 1, 1939, 12.
Susman, Margarete, "Der jüdische Geist," in *Blätter des jüdischen Frauenbundes für Frauenarbeit und Frauenbewegung* (1933).
Susman, Margarete, "Die Schicksalsstunde der deutschen Juden (ca. 1933)," unpublished manuscript, Bl. 4, Deutsches Literaturarchiv, Marbach.
Susman, Margarete, "Der jüdische Geist," *Blätter des jüdischen Frauenbundes für Frauenarbeit und Frauenbewegung* 9 (1933): 11.
Susman, Margarete, "Wandlungen der Frau," *Die Neue Rundschau*, January 1933, 105–24.
Susman, Margarete, "Das Judentum als Weltreligion," *Mitteilungsblatt der jüdischen Reformgemeinde Berlin*, 1.7.1932.
Susman, Margarete, "Stern der Erlösung," *Der Morgen* VII, 4, Berlin, Oct. 1931, 379–80.
Susman, Margarete, "Frau und Geist," *Die Literarische Welt*, Berlin, March 20, 1931.
Susman, Margarete, "Der Bürger in Frankreich" (zu Bernhard Groethuysen: "Die Entstehung der bürgerlichen Welt- und Lebensanschauung in Frankreich," Bd. 2, *Frankfurter Zeitung* 16.11.1930, Literaturblatt, 1.
Susman, Margarete, "Franz Rosenzweig (Nachruf)," *Frankfurter Zeitung* 22.12.1929, 1.
Susman, Margarete, "Gustav Landauers Briefe" (Rezension zu "Gustav Landauer. Sein Lebensbild in Briefen." Unter Mitwirkung von Ina Britschgi-Schimmer hrsg. v. Martin Buber 1929), *Der Morgen*, V, 2, June 1929, 194–98.
Susman, Margarete, "Das Hiob-Problem bei Franz Kafka," *Der Morgen* 5, no. 1 (April 1929): 31–49.
Susman, Margarete, *Frauen der Romantik* (Jena: Eugen Diederichs, 1929).

Susman, Margarete, "Auflösung und Werden in unserer Zeit," *Der Morgen* 4 (October 1928): 335–53.
Susman, Margarete, "Der Bürger in Frankreich" (zu Bernhard Groethuysen: "Die Entstehung der bürgerlichen Welt- und Lebensanschauung in Frankreich," Bd. 1, *Frankfurter Zeitung* 2.9.1928, Beilage, 1.
Susman, Margarete, "Die neue Übersetzung der Heiligen Schrift" (zu Martin Buber–Franz Rosenzweig, "Die Schrift," Berlin 1927), *Basler Nachrichten* 18.2.1928.
Susman, Margarete, "Was kann uns die Bibel heute noch bedeuten?," *Der Morgen*, August 1926, 299–310.
Susman, Margarete, "Das Frauenproblem in der gegenwärtigen Welt," *Der Morgen* 5 (December 1926): 431–52.
Susman, Margarete, "Die Brücke," *Der Jude* (1925): 76–84.
Susman, Margarete, "Der Stern der Erlösung," *Der Jude* (1921/22): 259–64.
Susman, Margarete, "Die Theorie des Romans" (zu Georg von Lukács: "Die Theorie des Romans, Ein geschichtsphilosophischer Versuch über die großen Formen der Epik," 1916), *Frankfurter Zeitung* 16.8.1921, 1.
Susman, Margarete, "Gustav Landauer (Nachruf)," in *Das Tribunal*, I, 6, Darmstadt 1919.
Susman, Margarete, "Die Revolution und die Juden," in *Das Forum*, ed. Wilhelm Herzog, Munich, 3/12 (September 1919): 921–48.
Susman, Margarete, "Gustav Landauer (Nachruf)," in *Das Tribunal* 1, no. 6 (Darmstadt, 1919).
Susman, Margarete, "Geist der Utopie" (zu Ernst Bloch: "Geist der Utopie"), *Frankfurter Zeitung* 12.1.1919, 1.
Susman, Margarete, "Die Revolution und die Frau," in *Das Flugblatt*, Nr. 4 (Frankfurt am Main: Tiedmann and Uzielli, 1918).
Susman, Margarete, "Aufblick," *Frankfurter Zeitung*, November 15, 1918, 1.
Susman, Margarete, "Wege des Zionismus"—Achad Haam: "Am Scheidewege," Martin Buber: "Die jüdische Bewegung," *Frankfurter Zeitung* 17./19.9.1916, 1.
Susman, Margarete, "Wege des Zionismus—Achad Haam: 'Am Scheidewege, Martin Buber: Die jüdische Bewegung,'" *Frankfurter Zeitung*, September 17–19, 1916, 1.
Susman, Margarete, "Einzelmoral und Staatsmoral," *Frankfurter Zeitung*, November 17, 1915, 1.
Susman, Margarete, "Von der Verwirklichung" (zu Martin Buber: "Daniel—Gespräche von der Verwirklichung," 1913), *Frankfurter Zeitung* 28.5.1914.
Susman, Margarete, "Spinoza und das jüdische Weltgefühl," in *Vom Judentum. Ein Sammelbuch*, ed. Hans Kohn, Verein jüdischer Hochschüler, "Bar Kochba" in Prag (Leipzig: Kurt Wolff Verlag, 1913), 51–70.
Susman, Margarete, "Die Seele und die Formen," *Frankfurter Zeitung*, 5.9.1912, 1.
Susman, Margarete, *Vom Sinn der Liebe* (Jena: Eugen Diederichs, 1912).
Susman, Margarete *Das Wesen der modernen deutschen Lyrik* (Stuttgart: Strecker & Schröder, 1910).
Susman, Margarete, "Judentum und Kultur" (zu Jakob Fromer, "Vom Ghetto zur modernen Kultur"), *Frankfurter Zeitung*, May 16, 1907.
Susman, Margarete, *Mein Land, Gedichte* (Berlin/ Leipzig: Schuster & Loeffler, 1901).
von Bendemann, Erwin, "Margarete Susman im Licht ihrer Korrespondenz," unpublished manuscript, legacy of Margarete Susman, Deutsches Literaturarchiv Marbach.
Zudrell, Petra (ed.), *Der abgerissene Dialog, Die intellektuelle Beziehung Gertrud Kantorowicz—Margarete Susman. Oder Die Schweizer Grenze bei Hohenems als Endpunkt eines Fluchtversuches*, (Innsbruck, Wien: Studien Verlag, 1999).

Chapter Eight

Remembering Regina Jonas

On the Intersectionality of Women's, Jewish, German, and Holocaust History

Katharina von Kellenbach

How could the memory of Rabbi Regina Jonas have been lost? Born in 1902 in Berlin into a poor merchant's family, Regina Jonas grew up pious, fatherless, and convinced that women could become rabbis. Her thesis "Can a Woman Hold Rabbinic Office?" argued that there were no religious laws to preclude women's rabbinic ordination.[1] The death of her Talmud teacher at the Hochschule für die Wissenschaft des Judentums, Eduard Baneth, foiled her graduation as an ordained rabbi in 1933. She was reexamined by Max Dienemann, the director of the *Liberaler Rabbinerverband*, in Offenbach and was ordained by him on December 27, 1935. She struggled for recognition as a congregational rabbi in Berlin and was assigned by the Jewish community to teach in Jewish schools and preach in the Jewish hospital, senior citizen homes, and institutions for the disabled. Her sermons became legendary, especially once her male rabbinic colleagues were arrested or left Germany into exile. In the fall of 1942, she was deported to Theresienstadt, where she continued to preach and provide pastoral care until she was transported to Auschwitz, where she was murdered on arrival, probably on October 12, 1944.[2]

If someone of her stature could have been "written out of history," how many more women's lives of piety and leadership, vision and learning are lost to the religious traditions?[3] In 1990, Shulamit Magnus, who was at the time director of the Program of Modern Jewish Civilization at the Reconstructionist Rabbinical College in Philadelphia, wrote a stinging indictment of Jewish historiography, "For all of our impressive studies of Jewish society and culture, an enormous area of inquiry has not been touched. More, its very existence has barely been acknowledged. That area concerns half of Jewish society in all classes and countries throughout the ages: women."[4]

I had taken Shulamit Magnus's course on Jewish women's history at the Reconstructionist Rabbinical College but was still stunned to realize that there were no scholarly publications about Regina Jonas to be found. Forgetting and remembering Regina Jonas occurred at the intersection of Jewish history and women's history and was further complicated by German and Holocaust history. It is this division of women's historical reality into different "ghettos" warily watched by guardians of scholarly method and religious, national, and gender identity that conspires to render women's religious subjectivity invisible. The memory of Regina Jonas was recovered because the borders between East and West, Jewish and Christian, male and female religious worlds cracked open. I offer my experience of crossing disciplinary, religious, and national boundaries in search of Regina Jonas's rabbinic ordination to reflect on some of the factors that render women mute and the need for feminist solidarity to overcome silence and invisibility across religious boundaries.[5]

The name of Regina Jonas was spoken on my very first day as a graduate student in the Religion Department of Temple University in Philadelphia. I had crossed the Atlantic Ocean on a DAAD scholarship to study abroad for one year in 1983, and we were asked to introduce ourselves to our classmates. I introduced myself as an exchange student from West Berlin who was studying Protestant theology at the Kirchliche Hochschule in order to become a minister. My neighbor Joanna Katz continued and said, "I am also studying theology, and I will become a rabbi." I was astonished and responded with conviction, "That is impossible, there are no female rabbis." Like most Germans born after the war, I had never met a Jew, and certainly no Jewish feminists. But despite my complete ignorance, I felt absolutely sure that Judaism, unlike Christianity, would never accommodate women's ordination and religious leadership. Then Joanna Katz challenged me: "You come from Berlin but don't know your own history; the first rabbi was ordained in Berlin in the 1930s, and her name was Regina Jonas." This first embarrassing exchange with Joanna Katz, who was later ordained as a Reconstructionist rabbi, blossomed into a friendship. My embarrassment became the impetus to document anti-Judaism in Christian feminist writings in my dissertation.[6] I felt the need to trace the roots of my deep-seated conviction that Christianity was somehow more progressive, feminist, and open to change than Judaism. I enrolled in classes at the Reconstructionist Rabbinical College (RRC) in Philadelphia and began to examine anti-Jewish tropes in Christian feminist theological writings, which I had unquestioningly absorbed. Upon graduation from Temple University in 1990, I turned to the *Encyclopaedia Judaica* to look up the entry on Rabbi Regina Jonas. In her comment, Joanna Katz had challenged the limitations of my knowledge of German history, and I assumed that my lack of knowledge was a result of skewed German history that marginalizes Jewish history. On that view, I also assumed that Jonas's memory was well preserved within the perimeters of Jewish history. But, as we know, there was no entry in the *Encyclopaedia Judaica*.

When I began my search in earnest, I found a grand total of three written references. Sally Priesand, who was ordained in the Reform movement in 1972, mentions Regina Jonas in *Judaism and the New Woman* (1975).[7] Alexander Guttmann, whose wife Manya Kampf had graduated from the Hochschule, mentions Regina Jonas in his *Hochschule Retrospective*, published in 1972.[8] The *Aufbau* published a letter to the editor in November 1970 titled "Ein weiblicher Rabbiner in Berlin."[9] Other than these, there was nothing.

On what grounds did I, as a German Christian feminist scholar of religion, have the right or the responsibility to pursue a historical project that documents the life of a Jewish woman in Berlin? In the end, there were two reasons that overcame any qualms I felt over my authority and competence to research and interpret the biography of Regina Jonas. First, as a feminist scholar in religion, I approached her disappearance as one of many examples of women whose stories, writings, and achievements have been excised from memory across the great world religions. Over the course of the last decades, feminist scholars in religion have mined the archives and reread ancient texts in a herculean effort to unearth their stories and, whenever possible, to publish their words and document their accomplishments.[10] Since Virginia Woolf complained a century ago about the one-sided nature of the storehouse of knowledge in the British Library, feminist scholars have worked tirelessly to retrieve the history of women, including in all of the religions.[11]

But Regina Jonas was not only a woman whose religious calling was deemed unfitting and subsequently ignored by her male peers. She was murdered by her government, betrayed by her country, and abandoned by her neighbors. As a German, I felt implicated in Nazi Germany's mass murder of

European Jews and its attempt to consign Jewish life to oblivion. Retracing Regina Jonas's steps in Berlin under Nazi rule to Theresienstadt and to Auschwitz constituted an act of restitution and of commemorative resistance. The least I could do as a postwar-born German was to restore her memory and make her writings available to the American feminist Jewish community that was often loath to learn the German language and was effectively disconnected from the history of the German Jewish women's movement because of the Holocaust.[12]

I am not a trained historian, and I proceeded in an unorthodox fashion, which may explain why I was able to succeed where others had failed. I began by contacting Michael A. Meyer at Hebrew Union College in Cincinnati, who gave me a list of HUC faculty members who had graduated from the Hochschule für die Wissenschaft des Judentums and were old enough to remember Regina Jonas.[13] One of them, Herbert A. Strauss, replied on April 3, 1991, "You are asking questions we have been asking ourselves the last few years without reference to women's studies. . . . You are not the first person asking about Jonas. I don't recall their names but you probably know them."[14]

His response suggested that better-qualified people had already tried and failed because there was nothing to find. His colleague's response however, made me more determined to proceed. Professor Israel Otto Lehman from HUC, ordained a rabbi in Berlin in 1939, wrote:

> Under the orthodox *halakhah* the ordination of women is inadmissible. No woman was ever ordained at the *Hochschule* nor did any faculty members, including Dr. Baeck, lend their hands to that. . . . The ordination of Miss Jonas was based on a pious tradition that three rabbis may ordain a person, obviously on the assumption that the traditional *halakhah* was strictly observed. Miss Jonas therefore, had to find some rabbis with very liberal views, of whom Dr. Dienemann was one, to accede to her request. I remember the dispute well. She never became a *Gemeinderabbiner* [congregational or pulpit rabbi], but if I remember correctly, merely a preacher in an old age home, what is done in the U.S.A. usually by student rabbis. Miss Jonas certainly was what you call a "loner," which had some psychological consequences also.[15]

The dismissive tone of this letter challenged me to craft a scholarly rebuttal that would prove him wrong. I realized that I would need documentary evidence to demonstrate that Jonas not only officially carried the title, but also that she legitimately performed rabbinic functions in wartime Berlin and later Theresienstadt.

I looked in the Leo Baeck Institute archives in New York and the Gratz College Holocaust archives in Philadelphia. All I could find were fragmentary references in memoirs and survivor accounts from Theresienstadt, which described her sermons and collaboration with psychiatrist Viktor Frankl.[16] I put an appeal in the *Aufbau* and received responses from her former students who had taken religion lessons from Jonas,[17] among them Pnina Navè-Levinson, who wrote that that she was "profoundly influenced in her interests" but that others in Berlin considered Jonas a "joke [*Witzfigur*]."[18] Most of these letters were written by women, such as Margaret Collin, who sang in the Oranienburger Strasse synagogue choir and wrote, "My uncle, Prof. Rabbi Dr. Leo Hohenstein, pointed to Rabbi Jonas as a role model and told me repeatedly: 'If Regina Jonas can be a rabbi, then you can be cantor' but in 1938 there were no cantors in America, and now that it is possible, I am too old, I am 78 years old."[19]

In the summer of 1991, I visited Vienna and, on a lark, checked the phone book for the telephone number of Viktor Frankl.[20] I was shocked when he simply picked up the phone and requested an hour lead time in order to organize his recollections and began to tell me about his role in the department of health and hygiene, which tried to maintain people's emotional and mental health upon their arrival in the hell of Theresienstadt.[21] I made notes while he was talking. Later I checked up on his information with well-known Theresienstadt scholar Susan Cernyak-Spatz, who had never come across references to Regina Jonas.[22]

These phone conversations and letter exchanges with Holocaust survivors involved navigating the betrayals of the German Jewish "symbiosis."[23] My last name is identifiably German and non-Jewish. And there was always an unspoken question in the room: who is she, and why is she doing this? Viktor Frankl, for instance, wanted to know what I thought of his acclaimed book *Man's Search for Meaning*. When I told him that I considered it one of the most profound, moving, and empowering books, he replied that he had written the manuscript in one week and been persuaded by friends to publish it. Now he was unsure whether it should have been published. I was deeply unsettled by this conversation. My praise of the book seemed hollow and inadequate in the face of his doubts. Were they rooted in survivor guilt? And how should I, struggling with my own "guilt by association," react to his conflicts over this book?[24]

Attending the first Annual Holocaust Survivor Gathering in Philadelphia in 1985 had forced me to recognize that my lack of historical and personal knowledge of my family's whereabouts during the Holocaust was not innocent. What exactly was hiding behind this veil of silence? National Socialism had erected a rigid boundary between "Jewish" and "German" identities. On the one side, "non-Aryans" were dehumanized, degraded, expropriated, deported, and killed, while those living on the other side of the line were inducted into the perpetration of unspeakable cruelty and genocidal violence. After 1945, shattered lives were rebuilt on the basis of silence. Survivors shielded their families from extreme trauma, while perpetrators protected their identities by denying any participation in the defeated National Socialist project. As the second generation met each other in facilitated and spontaneous dialogue, we realized that we shared experiences of running into walls of silence as well as eruptive revelations. Generally, second-generation Jews knew more about their families' past than second-generation Germans, who benefitted from silence and denial. I realized that my cluelessness would not absolve me from the obligation to account for my family. This project, however, involved archival research, since my questions to members of my family were met by stony silence and deceitful denial. Eventually, I gained access to privacy-protected trial records that involved a great uncle, Alfred Ebner, who was responsible for the ghettoization of more than 28,000 Belorussian Jews and for their mass execution that lasted three days between October 30 and November 1, 1942. As a member of the SS, he was sent to Pinsk with the Civil Administration and became the responsible official for "Jewish affairs" as vice commissioner of Pinsk.[25] While this research into family and perpetrator history occurred separate from the scholarship on Regina Jonas, it has colored the public perception and narrative of the recovery of her materials.[26] Holocaust history, in my view, is inclusive of German (perpetrator) and Jewish (victim) perspectives at both the methodological and personal levels. The same archives store the documents required to reconstruct the biographies of both victims and perpetrators. Their memory is always emotionally fraught and more than "just the facts." Their stories of survival *in extremis* question identity, entail obligations, and demand ethical responses.

Since I am not trained as a historian, my forays into the archives felt more like detective work than actual historical scholarship. For instance, desperate to find proof of Jonas's official use of the professional title as a rabbi, I turned to the *Bundesversicherungsanstalt für Angestellte*, West Germany's public pension authority. I wondered whether she had paid into social security and pension funds while she was employed as a rabbi. The official on the phone was startled and defensive. I used all of my phone etiquette to reassure him I was not a relative of Regina Jonas, that I had no intention of claiming restitution, and that I was only interested in her professional employment history. What title had she used, what professional position did she hold? Eventually, I was informed that she paid into the fund between October 1923 and December 1936 as *Lehramtskandidatin* (candidate for teaching certificate).[27] Disappointed, I continued on to *Landesarchiv Berlin* in the Kalckreuthstrasse to look for her deportation file, which was filed under her mother's name. In this file, which recorded her belongings and deportation, dated November 3, 1942, I first held written proof that she used the title "Fräulein Rabbiner Jonas" in official paperwork.[28]

The archives of the Hochschule für die Wissenschaft des Judentums were destroyed, and I knew that it would be impossible to place Jonas's educational and professional career within the context of the other 27 "girls," to quote Guttmann, who had studied "as regular students and often constituted a sizable part of the student body. In the summer of 1932, for example, a student body of 155 included 27 women. Most of these women studied for the degree of an Academic Teacher of Religion."[29] Throughout her twelve semesters at the Hochschule, Jonas supported herself teaching in girls' high schools (*Lyzeen*), for which she had been certified in 1924. (Her father had died in 1913, leaving her and her brother Abraham Jonas without many financial resources.) Yet, for Jonas, teaching was only a steppingstone. She aimed for the rabbinate and fought hard to break out of the teaching career that was the only generally accepted "woman's profession."

Although I was aware that the archives of the Hochschule were lost, I decided to visit the Neue Synagoge in Oranienburger Strasse. In 1991, the synagogue was a construction site, and I climbed the stairs blocked by scaffolding. It was my first visit to the newly unified city after the fall of the Berlin Wall in 1989. I was greeted by Dr. Hermann Simon and asked for permission to look through the archives of the *Israelitisches Familienblatt*, hoping to find a press release about her ordination. Sure enough, there was an article from 1935 that announced her ordination in a somewhat polemic tone. I asked Dr. Simon whether he knew where the *Gesamtarchiv der Juden in Deutschland* was located, and he sent me to the *Bundesarchiv* in Coswig, Saxony. But, he said, "you are not the first to look for Regina Jonas, and you will not find anything."

Upon contacting the Bundesarchiv in Coswig by mail, I was informed on September 23, 1991, that the archive held fourteen files of "relevant material," but that I would need permission from the director of the *Stiftung Neue*

Synagoge, Dr. Simon.[30] That permission, it turned out, would take an entire year and the intercession of numerous well-known Jewish scholars.

As I was waiting impatiently, I speculated about the reasons for the reluctance to grant me access to the papers. I could think of several possibilities. It could have been an East-West conflict, as the East German Jewish community asserted control over documents of the communal *Gesamtarchiv der Juden in Deutschland*, which was being integrated into the federal (West German) *Bundesarchiv*. It could have been an attempt to control publicity of the first female rabbi, whose existence might be considered embarrassing, politically explosive, and religiously heterodox. It could have been a German-American conflict and a wish to protect German Jewish history from American cultural hegemony. In retrospect, I believe it was the Jewish-Christian dynamic, which rendered my credentials, intentions, and perspectives suspicious. Who was this young German Christian feminist theologian employed by St. Mary's College of Maryland, which sounds Catholic even though it is the public honor's college of the state of Maryland, to claim authority to document and interpret the work and life of the first female rabbi?

Many Jewish scholars intervened on my behalf: Abraham Peck from the American Jewish Archives in Cincinnati, Julius H. Schoeps from Potsdam,[31] Professors Liliane Weisberg and Marion Kaplan, Fred Grubel from the Leo Baeck Institute, Rabbi Elizabeth Tikvah Sarah from London, and survivors who knew Dr. Hermann Simon personally. By March 1992, I was informed that I would receive copies of Regina Jonas's birth certificate, rabbinic diploma, Hochschule transcripts, and final thesis at the same time as Daniela Thau, who was at the time studying for the rabbinate in London. When the files arrived in April, the package contained numbers 3, 4, 5, and 14. I asked for an explanation of the criteria for this selection. After more delays and interventions, in July 1992, a year after I first received notice, I held the microfilm of her archived papers (*Nachlass*) in my hands, except for one file, which contained letters of an intimate nature. It took another year to receive a copy of the photographs, and I have never seen the file containing the personal letters.

My subject position as an outsider to the Jewish religious tradition and community affected not only the retrieval of historical documents but also their interpretation and publication. Despite my classes on Jewish history at the Reconstructionist Rabbinical College and Temple University, I felt insecure about my grasp of German Jewish history, and I had no halakhic training and little credibility to present Jonas's halakhic thesis on the ordination of women. I worked hard to overcome these shortcomings and relied on the advice of Jewish friends, teachers, and colleagues, who supported the effort of documenting Jonas's life. I planned to submit my biographical essay to the *Leo Baeck Institute Year Book* and sent it off in July 1992. In November 1992, I received the reviewer's letter, which I have shared quite often with junior colleagues as an example of a devastating reader review. Rabbi Julius Carlebach wrote:

> As the associate editor of the *Year Book*, I've been asked to look at your manuscript on the life and thought of Rabbi Regina Jonas and . . . although we are very interested in the subject of your paper and would very much like to see an essay on this historically important person, your paper presents a number of problems which we feel would have to be resolved before publication could be considered. The biggest problem is that Rabbi Jonas is presented without the kind of context, which could make her position and her difficulties intelligible. I would have to write another paper to explain all the things, which worry us and think it would be a much better idea if I could put you in touch with a colleague who has worked extensively on the lives and histories of students at the Hochschule. Her name is Irene Kaufmann, Heidelberg . . . and I would suggest you write to her if you are interested in extending your own research.[32]

This letter confirmed my worst fears, and I questioned my ability to proceed with this project. I sent for comment my essay and Carlebach's letter to Professor Marion Kaplan, as the most eminent and respected historian of the German Jewish women's movement, who also served on the board of the *Year Book*. She replied immediately: "I am enclosing the THIRD version of the letter I finally sent to Grenville. The first two would have burned the envelope in which they were placed. I actually asked someone to tune it down for me."[33] By February 12, 1993, John Grenville, the editor of the *Year Book*, had changed his mind: "My feeling now is that we will publish your article, with some revisions as indicated above, irrespective of the Kaufmann article. Hence, you should not wait for her article."[34] The essay appeared with minor revisions in the *Year Book* in 1994.[35]

For Kaplan, Carlebach's negative review was connected to his "distaste/disdain for feminist interpretations." But Carlebach was right to be troubled by the historical matrix in which I had placed Jonas's struggle for ordination. I had compared her struggle for ordination to Protestant and Catholic women who were graduating at the same time from German universities with academic degrees in theology and philosophy. Carlebach correctly noted that I transgressed the boundaries of Jewish religious history because I described Regina Jonas as a member of the first generation of German women who earned graduate degrees and confronted religious leaders with their academic credentials and requests for leadership positions in the church and the synagogue.[36] Furthermore, I pointed out that the rise of National Socialism, which mobilized male clergy for military service and forced rabbis into exile, especially after the November pogrom of 1938, created a crisis that put women into leadership positions. While I certainly never claimed that the Holocaust was good for Jonas's career, I wanted to disprove Professor Israel O. Lehmann's point that Jonas remained in auxiliary positions and never performed more than what "student rabbis" are allowed to do in the United States. Her assignments and responsibilities grew as the situation of Jews in Berlin became catastrophic. As one survivor wrote in a letter to me, "After Kristallnacht in November 1938, she [Jonas] preached in various synagogues in Berlin, often replacing rabbis who were thrown into concentration camps or had emigrated."[37] Gender conventions collapse in times of war and calamity that force women out of the private realm into the public world of religion and politics.

In light of these parallels, I was also interested in the secret file containing Jonas's private letters. The newly designed contracts that regulated the congregational service of ordained Protestant women in the various regional churches during the 1930s included a celibacy clause, which automatically dismissed them in case of marriage.[38] I naturally wanted to know whether a similar celibacy provision existed, which might have kept Jonas from marrying. I also speculated whether had she survived the war, she would have been reinstated as a rabbi or whether she would have been dismissed, as happened to the Protestant vicars, who were forced to vacate their congregational positions once their male colleagues returned from war.[39] Their ordination became void. It was not until the 1970s that regional Protestant churches in Germany took up the ordination of women again, around the same time as Sally Priesand's ordination in 1972. It was only the second wave of the women's movement that permanently broke gender barriers, which had been reestablished in the immediate postwar period both in the United States and in Europe.

My work on Regina Jonas challenged the boundaries of Jewish history, women's history, Holocaust history, and German history. And it raised the question of ownership of the memory of Regina Jonas. Is she a Jew, a

German, a woman of faith, a feminist? Who is allowed to write her history? When I presented my paper "Denial and Defiance in the Work of Rabbi Regina Jonas," which analyzed her sermons and pastoral work in Berlin and Theresienstadt, at a conference on religion and genocide organized at the United States Holocaust Memorial Museum in 1997, Susannah Heschel questioned my ability to interpret the resistance Jonas encountered from her male rabbinic colleagues.[40] She raised an excellent point. For Jewish feminists, Jonas's trials and triumphs within the Jewish community provide a vital link to Jewish women's piety and religious leadership across the generations. For me, however, Regina Jonas is an equally vital and integral link to the German women's movement that broke gender barriers in universities, professions, and religious institutions. Her life unfolded at the crossroads of German and Jewish history and is instructive of the particular linguistic, social, and political conventions of Germany, as well as of her Jewish religious and communal identity.

1. JEWISH-CHRISTIAN FEMINIST SOLIDARITY

Identity politics has created historical sub-disciplines in order to expand boundaries and include the experiences and perspectives of silenced people in marginalized communities. At the same time, we need to beware of increasing fragmentation into black, Jewish, Latina, German, lesbian, transgender sub-histories. For all of our obvious differences, our histories are connected. We would do well to develop models of commemorative practices that generate feminist solidarity across religious, national, and ethnic boundaries. All of the world religions are patriarchal and enshrine women's inferior, private, silent role to support male religious leadership in public. The feminist vision of gender justice is global and has been interreligious from the beginning. Feminists of faith have supported each other, and feminist hermeneutics and arguments that were developed in one religious context have traveled into others. Most recently, just before the conference on women's religious leadership convened in Berlin in November 2015, the mother of Rabbi Sally Priesand published an opinion piece in the *Forward* titled "What a Catholic Mom Wants the Pope to Learn from Her Rabbi Daughter." She recounted her youngest daughter's "leaving for Jerusalem" and expressed her "sadness and frustration that she is not likely to rub shoulders with a female priest anytime soon."[41] Patriarchy is a global religious reality, as is women's struggle to break gender barriers and gain public recognition for women's religious faith and practice.

There is not one shred of historical evidence that Regina Jonas received practical, political, or theological support from non-Jewish or Christian women. The German women who fought for leadership positions in the church or synagogue apparently saw no connections across the religious and denominational lines. Even at the height of Nazi persecution, there is no indication that Jonas sought or obtained assistance from offices such as the Protestant *Büro Grüber* or the Catholic *Bischöfliche Hilfstelle* in Berlin. These relief organizations were predominantly staffed by women, many of whom were themselves "non-Aryan" Christians.[42] The emergence of Jewish-Christian dialogue occurred only after 1945. While some of the seeds of solidarity were sown by activists such as Gertrud Luckner, interreligious relations and dialogue across religious borders were a fruit of repentance in the Christian churches facing their catastrophic failure during the Holocaust. Recognition of complicity resulted in changes to centuries-old habits of anti-Jewish theology, liturgy, and politics.[43]

Against this backdrop, the collaboration between Rabbi Elisa Klapheck and myself serves as a model for a feminist practice of solidarity that crosses the Jewish-Christian borderline. While I had resisted the heavy-handed suggestions of Hermann Simon and Julius Carlebach to coordinate my scholarship with Daniela Thau and Irene Kaufmann (neither of whom I knew), because they considered them more trustworthy or better qualified, I felt no such qualms when Elisa Klapheck approached me. Luckily, she contacted me before I received a letter from Hermann Simon in 1998 informing me that "we have been able to persuade Ms Klapheck to prepare an edition of Jonas's work for publication."[44] It was Elisa Klapheck's feminist Jewish practice and commitment to build an egalitarian minyan and to nurture a feminist German Jewish community back to life that convinced me to hand over my documentary materials.

As feminists, Elisa and I were keenly aware of the forces that deride, minimize, and erase women's scholarly and religious accomplishments. While Regina Jonas did not and would not have called herself a feminist, she was intensely conscious of the forces that conspired to expunge her life and her memory. She made sure to collect and submit the written records of her life to the archive. Elisa and I both wanted to salvage Jonas's memory from the ruins of that annihilation. But we were also committed to honor each other's work and to refuse to succumb to the competitive gamesmanship that characterizes academia. As a matter of faith and feminist principle, we wanted to find a different way. Rabbi Dr. Elisa Klapheck is rightly credited with bringing public recognition to Rabbi Regina Jonas and rekindling European Jewish feminist communal life.[45] She published the edited halakhic thesis of Regina Jonas and made her biography widely available.[46] She also conscientiously footnoted unpublished materials that I had shared with her from my previous search. What we achieved in our collaboration is a restoration of trust between women who have been taught to distrust each other by virtue of our religious affiliations, our marginalization as women scholars in religion, and the trauma of the Holocaust. The rediscovery of Regina Jonas should be framed not only against the historical background of the Holocaust, but also against a future of feminist solidarity and interreligious collaboration that strives to respect religious difference while opposing systems of power that denigrate and dismiss women's contributions to religious life.

NOTES

1. Elisa Klapheck, *Fräulein Rabbiner Regina Jonas: Kann die Frau das rabbinische Amt bekleiden?* (Berlin: Hentrich & Hentrich Teetz, 1999).

2. Cf. Katrin Nele Jansen, "Regina Jonas" in *Biographisches Handbuch der Rabbiner, Vol. 2, Die Rabbiner im Deutschen Reich 1871–1945*, ed. Michael Brocke and Julius Carlebach (München: K.G. Saur, 2009), 312f.

3. Cf. Emily Taitz, *Written Out of History: Our Jewish Foremothers* (New York: Bloch, 1990).

4. Shulamit Magnus, "Out of the Ghetto': Integrating the Study of Jewish Women into the Study of 'The Jews,'" *Judaism* 39, no. 1 (Winter 1990): 28–36, 28.

5. There are different accounts of the so-called "discovery" of Jonas's papers: Aryeh Dayan, "A Forgotten Myth," *Haaretz*, May 25, 2004, http://www.haaretz.com/print-edition/business/a-forgotten-myth-1.123526; Rabbi James Rudin, "Obscure No More: World's First Woman Rabbi Receives Recognition," *Washington Post*, July 7, 2014, https://www.washingtonpost.com/national/religion/commentary-obscure-no-more-worlds-first-woman-rabbi-receives-recognition/2014/07/25/f0efe7dc-1433-11e4-ac56-773e54a65906_story.html. For a fictionalized account, see Clémence Boulouque, *Nuit Ouverte* (Paris: Flammarion, 2007). Stefanie Sinclair was the only author who actually talked to me: "Regina Jonas: Forgetting and Remembering the First Female Rabbi," *Religion* 43, no. 4 (2013): 541ff.

6. Katharina von Kellenbach, *Anti-Judaism in Feminist Religious Writings* (New York: Oxford University Press, 1994).

7. Sally Priesand, *Judaism and the New Woman* (New York: Behrman House, 1975), 67.

8. Alexander Guttmann, "Hochschule Retrospektive," *CCAR Journal*, Autumn 1974, 74.

9. *Aufbau*, November 6, 1970, with a response by Alexander Guttman.

10. Fortunately, the list of publications exceeds one footnote; among the path-breaking scholars were Ross Kraemer, *Her Share of the Blessings: Women's Religions among Pagans, Jews, and Christians in the Greco-Roman World* (New York: Oxford University Press, 1994).

11. Virginia Woolf cursed the library and thought about "the effect of tradition and the lack of tradition upon the mind of the writer." Virginia Woolf, *A Room of One's Own* (San Diego: Harcourt Brace, 1989), 24.

12. Exceptions include an outstanding group of feminist historians of German Jewish life meeting in New York, including Marion Kaplan, *The Jewish Feminist Movement in Germany: The Campaigns of the Jüdischer Frauenbund, 1904–1938* (Westport: Greenwood Press, 1979); Marion Kaplan, Renate Bridenthal, and Atina Grossmann, eds., *When Biology Became Destiny: Women in Weimar and Nazi Germany* (New York: Monthly Review Press, 1984); Atina Grossmann, *Jews, Germans, and Allies: Close Encounters in Occupied Germany 1945–1949* (Princeton: Princeton University Press, 2007).

13. Letter, Michael A. Meyer, March 18, 1991, personal archive.

14. Letter, Herbert A. Strauss, April 3, 1991, personal archive.

15. Letter (original English; "*Gemeinderabbiner*" in the original), I. O. Lehmann, June 1992, personal archive.

16. Cf. Leo Baeck Institute Archive, New York: Richard Ehrlich Collections (AR C.Z.4 11); Jacob Jacobson, *Bruchstücke 1939–1945* (1965): 33. Collection of Gratz Center Holocaust Archive, Philadelphia: Hardy Kupferberg; Susan Neulaender Faulkner; letter, Pnina Navè Levinson, January 12, 1994, personal archive: "In Theresienstadt arbeitete sie mit Victor [*sic*] Frankl zusammen, der hohes Lob über sie aussprach (Radio-Vortrag? Wien? Vor Jahren)."

17. Katharina von Kellenbach, "Wer kannte Frl. Rabbiner Regina Jonas," *Aufbau*, September 13, 1991, 23; Katharina von Kellenbach, "Die Majorität ist gegen Sie: Der Leidensweg der Regina Jonas, Rabbinerin in Nazi-Deutschland," *Aufbau*, March 12, 1993.

18. Letter, Pnina Nave Levinson, January 12, 1994, personal archive.

19. Letter, Margaret Collin, March 26, 1993, personal archive.

20. Phone conversation, Victor Frankl, June 6, 1991.

21. *Abteilung Gesundheitswesen und Fürsorge*.

22. Letter, Susan Czerniak-Spatz, June 15, 1992, personal archive.

23. Leslie Morris and Jack Zipes, *Unlikely History: The Changing German-Jewish Symbiosis: 1945–2000* (New York: Palgrave, 2002); Dan Diner, "Negative Symbiosis"; Enzo Traverso, *The Jews and Germany: From the "Judeo-German Symbiosis" to the Memory of Auschwitz*, trans. Daniel Weissbort (Lincoln: University of Nebraska Press, 1995).

24. Howard Ball, *Prosecuting War Crimes and Genocide: The Twentieth Century Experience* (Lawrence: University of Kansas, 1999).

25. Katharina von Kellenbach, "Vanishing Acts: Perpetrators in Postwar Germany," *Journal of Holocaust and Genocide Studies* 17, no. 2 (2003): 305–29; Katharina von Kellenbach, *The Mark of Cain: Guilt and Denial in the Lives of Nazi Perpetrators* (New York: Oxford University Press, 2013).

26. In his opening paragraph in *Haaretz*, Aryeh Dayan frames the story: "In 1991, two years after the fall of the Berlin Wall, and immediately after the reunification of Germany, a wave of researchers and professors began to visit East Berlin and the other major cities that had been part of East Germany. They came from all over the world, looking for material and documents hidden in various archives of the communist state that had just ceased to exist. One of them was Dr. Katerina [sic] von Kellenbach, a researcher and lecturer in the department of philosophy and theology at St. Mary's College of Maryland, a small Christian college. Von Kellenbach was born in Germany and immigrated to the United States after one of her uncles, who was the deputy governor of Pinsk in Poland during World War II, was tried for crimes against the Jewish population in that city. . . . In a small and remote archive in East Berlin, she found an envelope containing a document, written in German and Hebrew, entitled 'Teaching certificate'" (Dayan, "A Forgotten Myth").

27. Letter, Bundesversicherungsanstalt für Angestellte, August 29, 1991, personal archive.
28. Landesarchiv Berlin Rep. 92 Acc. 3924.
29. Alexander Guttmann, "Hochschule Retrospektive," *CCAR Journal*, Autumn 1974, 74.
30. Letter, Bundesarchiv Coswig, September 23, 1991, personal archive.
31. Letter, Julius H. Schoeps, May 1992, personal archive.
32. Letter, Julius Carlebach, November 19, 1992, personal archive.
33. Letter, Marion Kaplan, December 22, 1992, personal archive.
34. Letter, John Grenville, February 12, 1993, personal archive.
35. Katharina von Kellenbach, "God Does Not Oppress Any Human Being: The Life and Thought of Rabbi Regina Jonas," *Leo Baeck Institute Year Book* 39 (1994): 213–25.
36. Katharina von Kellenbach, "Fräulein Rabbiner Regina Jonas: Eine religiöse Feministin vor ihrer Zeit," *Schlangenbrut* 38 (1992): 35–39; Katharina von Kellenbach, "Fräulein Rabbiner Regina Jonas (1902–1945): Lehrerin, Seelsorgerin, Predigerin," in *Yearbook of the European Society of Women in Theological Research* (Kampen: Kok Pharos, 1994), 97–102.
37. Letter, personal archive.
38. Dietlinde Cunow, "Im Falle einer Eheschließung endet das Dienstverhältnis: Rückblick auf die Zölibatsklausel bei Pastorinnen," in *Querdenken: Beiträge zur feministisch-befreiungstheologischen Diskussion*, ed. Frauenforschungsprojekt zur Geschichte der Theologinnen, Göttingen (Pfaffenweiler: Centaurus, 1992), 307–10.
39. Ilse Härter, "Die Weiterentwicklung der Berufsgeschichte der Theologinnen nach 1945," in *Darum wagt es Schwestern: Zur Geschichte evangelischer Theologinnen*, ed. Frauenforschungsprojekt zur Geschichte der Theologinnen, Göttingen (Neuenkirchen-Vluyn: Neukirchener Verlag, 1994), 263–84.
40. Katharina von Kellenbach, "Denial and Defiance in the Work of Rabbi Regina Jonas," in *In God's Name: Genocide and Religion in the 20th Century*, ed. Phyllis Mack and Omar Bartov (New York: Berghahn Books, 2001), 243–59; Katharina von Kellenbach, "Reproduction and Resistance during the Holocaust," in *Women and the Holocaust*, ed. Esther Fuchs (Lanham: University of America Press, 1999), 19–33.
41. Cindy Skrzycki, "What a Catholic Mom Wants the Pope to Learn from Her Rabbi Daughter," *Forward*, September 21, 2015.
42. Hartmut Ludwig, *An der Seite der Entrechteten und Schwachen: Zur Geschichte des Büro Pfarrer Grüber* (Berlin: Logos Verlag, 2009); Katharina von Kellenbach, "Dialogue in Times of War: Christian Women's Rescue of Jews in Hitler's Germany," in *Women in Interreligious Dialogue*, ed. Catherine Cornille (Portland: Cascade Books, Wipf & Stock, 2013), 77–80.
43. Elias H. Füllenbach, "Shock, Renewal, Crisis: Catholic Reflections on the Shoah," in *Antisemitism, Christian Ambivalence and the Holocaust*, ed. Kevin P. Spicer (Bloomington: Indiana University Press, 2007), 201–37; John Connelly, *From Enemy to Brother: The Revolution in Catholic Teaching on the Jews 1933–1965* (Cambridge: Harvard University Press, 2012).
44. Letter, Hermann Simon, 1998, personal archive.
45. As founding member of Bet Debora, http://www.bet-debora.net.
46. Klapheck, *Fräulein Rabbiner Regina Jonas*.

BIBLIOGRAPHY

Ball, Howard, *Prosecuting War Crimes and Genocide: The Twentieth Century Experience* (Lawrence: University of Kansas, 1999).

Boulouque, Clémence, *Nuit Ouverte* (Paris: Flammarion, 2007).
Connelly, John, *From Enemy to Brother: The Revolution in Catholic Teaching on the Jews 1933–1965* (Cambridge: Harvard University Press, 2012).
Cunow, Dietlinde, "Im Falle einer Eheschließung endet das Dienstverhältnis: Rückblick auf die Zölibatsklausel bei Pastorinnen," in *Querdenken: Beiträge zur feministisch-befreiungstheologischen Diskussion*, ed. Frauenforschungsprojekt zur Geschichte der Theologinnen, Göttingen (Pfaffenweiler: Centaurus, 1992), 307–10.
Dayan, Aryeh, "A Forgotten Myth," *Haaretz*, May 25, 2004, http://www.haaretz.com/print-edition/business/a-forgotten-myth-1.123526 .
Füllenbach, Elias H., "Shock, Renewal, Crisis: Catholic Reflections on the Shoah," in *Antisemitism, Christian Ambivalence and the Holocaust*, ed. Kevin P. Spicer (Bloomington: Indiana University Press, 2007), 201–37.
Grossmann, Atina, *Jews, Germans, and Allies: Close Encounters in Occupied Germany 1945–1949* (Princeton: Princeton University Press, 2007).
Guttmann, Alexander, "Hochschule Retrospektive," *CCAR Journal*, Autumn 1974, 74.
Härter, Ilse, "Die Weiterentwicklung der Berufsgeschichte der Theologinnen nach 1945," in *Darum wagt es Schwestern: Zur Geschichte evangelischer Theologinnen*, ed. Frauenforschungsprojekt zur Geschichte der Theologinnen, Göttingen (Neuenkirchen-Vluyn: Neukirchener Verlag, 1994), 263–84.
Jansen, Katrin Nele, "Regina Jonas," in *Biographisches Handbuch der Rabbiner, Vol. 2, Die Rabbiner im Deutschen Reich 1871–1945*, ed. Michael Brocke and Julius Carlebach (München: K.G. Saur, 2009), 312f.
Kaplan, Marion, et al. (eds.), *When Biology Became Destiny: Women in Weimar and Nazi Germany* (New York: Monthly Review Press, 1984).
Kaplan, Marion, *The Jewish Feminist Movement in Germany: The Campaigns of the Jüdischer Frauenbund, 1904–1938* (Westport: Greenwood Press, 1979).
Klapheck, Elisa, *Fräulein Rabbiner Regina Jonas: Kann die Frau das rabbinische Amt bekleiden?* (Berlin: Hentrich & Hentrich Teetz, 1999).
Kraemer, Ross, *Her Share of the Blessings: Women's Religions among Pagans, Jews, and Christians in the Greco-Roman World* (New York: Oxford University Press, 1994).
Ludwig, Hartmut, *An der Seite der Entrechteten und Schwachen: Zur Geschichte des Büro Pfarrer Grüber* (Berlin: Logos Verlag, 2009).
Magnus, Shulamit, "'Out of the Ghetto': Integrating the Study of Jewish Women into the Study of 'The Jews,'" *Judaism* 39, no. 1 (Winter 1990): 28–36.
Morris, Leslie, and Zipes, Jack, *Unlikely History: The Changing German-Jewish Symbiosis: 1945–2000* (New York: Palgrave, 2002).
Priesand, Sally, *Judaism and the New Woman* (New York: Behrman House, 1975).
Rudin, James, "Obscure No More: World's First Woman Rabbi Receives Recognition," *Washington Post*, July 7, 2014, https://www.washingtonpost.com/national/religion/commentary-obscure-no-more-worlds-first-woman-rabbi-receives-recognition/2014/07/25/f0efe7dc-1433-11e4-ac56-773e54a65906_story.html.
Sinclair, Stefanie, "Regina Jonas: Forgetting and Remembering the First Female Rabbi," *Religion* 43, no. 4 (2013): 541–63.
Skrzycki, Cindy, "What a Catholic Mom Wants the Pope to Learn from Her Rabbi Daughter," *Forward*, September 21, 2015.
Taitz, Emily, *Written Out of History: Our Jewish Foremothers* (New York: Bloch, 1990).
Traverso, Enzo, *The Jews and Germany: From the "Judeo-German Symbiosis" to the Memory of Auschwitz*, trans. Daniel Weissbort (Lincoln: University of Nebraska Press, 1995).

von Kellenbach, Katharina, "Dialogue in Times of War: Christian Women's Rescue of Jews in Hitler's Germany," in *Women in Interreligious Dialogue*, ed. Catherine Cornille (Portland: Cascade Books, Wipf & Stock, 2013), 77–80.

von Kellenbach, Katharina, *The Mark of Cain: Guilt and Denial in the Lives of Nazi Perpetrators* (New York: Oxford University Press, 2013).

von Kellenbach, Katharina, "Vanishing Acts: Perpetrators in Postwar Germany," *Journal of Holocaust and Genocide Studies* 17, no. 2 (2003): 305–29.

von Kellenbach, Katharina, "Denial and Defiance in the Work of Rabbi Regina Jonas," in *In God's Name: Genocide and Religion in the 20th Century*, ed. Phyllis Mack and Omar Bartov (New York: Berghahn Books, 2001), 243–59.

von Kellenbach, Katharina, "Reproduction and Resistance during the Holocaust," in *Women and the Holocaust*, ed. Esther Fuchs (Lanham: University of America Press, 1999), 19–33.

von Kellenbach, Katharina, *Anti-Judaism in Feminist Religious Writings* (New York: Oxford University Press, 1994).

von Kellenbach, Katharina, "God Does Not Oppress Any Human Being: The Life and Thought of Rabbi Regina Jonas," *Leo Baeck Institute Year Book* 39 (1994): 213–25.

von Kellenbach, Katharina, "Fräulein Rabbiner Regina Jonas (1902–1945): Lehrerin, Seelsorgerin, Predigerin," in *Yearbook of the European Society of Women in Theological Research* (Kampen: Kok Pharos, 1994), 97–102.

von Kellenbach, Katharina, "Die Majorität ist gegen Sie: Der Leidensweg der Regina Jonas, Rabbinerin in Nazi- Deutschland," *Aufbau*, March 12, 1993.

von Kellenbach, Katharina, "Fräulein Rabbiner Regina Jonas: Eine religiöse Feministin vor ihrer Zeit," *Schlangenbrut* 38 (1992): 35–39.

von Kellenbach, Katharina, "Wer kannte Frl. Rabbiner Regina Jonas," *Aufbau*, September 13, 1991.

Woolf, Virginia, *A Room of One's Own* (San Diego: Harcourt Brace, 1989).

Chapter Nine

Memory and Identity

Female Leadership and the Legacy of Rabbi Regina Jonas

Stefanie Sinclair

Regina Jonas is now widely recognized as the first female rabbi in the world. Her story highlights particularly pertinent issues in historiography, especially with regard to the role of memory and identity. For almost fifty years following her murder at Auschwitz in 1944, Jonas remained a largely forgotten figure and received hardly any acknowledgment in published records, reference works, or scholarly literature. Until the early 1990s, it was widely assumed that Sally Priesand, who was ordained in the Reform movement in the United States in 1972, was the first female rabbi. However, Jonas's ordination had taken place in Nazi Germany—of all places—thirty-seven years earlier. How is it possible that Jonas was almost lost to historiography? And how is she remembered today? This chapter reflects on possible reasons why Jonas was "almost forgotten" and explores how she is remembered today in a range of different national contexts (with a particular focus on Germany, Britain, and the United States). My analysis centers on themes of memory and identity and highlights the significance of a sense of heritage in the process of inspiring and "naturalizing" female leadership within faith communities and beyond.

1. WHY WAS JONAS "ALMOST FORGOTTEN"?

While a range of complex factors were at play, gender bias and prejudice are likely to have played a role in Jonas's temporary disappearance from historiography. From this point of view, her case could be regarded as a classic example of women's "marginalization in the process of history making."[1] In historiography, "women's stories are particularly vulnerable since, until recently, [they] were not the keepers of these stories."[2] The opportunities Jonas had to ensure the preservation of her legacy were indeed very limited. Jonas was not only a woman in a world dominated by men, but a Jewish woman exposed to the persecution of the anti-Semitic policies of the Nazi regime, leading to her deportation, incarceration, and death. Nevertheless, a collection of her most important papers was preserved. This collection included her ordination certificate as well as a copy of her dissertation "Can a Woman Be a Rabbi According to Halakhic Sources?," letters, newspaper clips, and two photographs of Jonas. While the exact circumstances are not known, Jonas (or a trusted colleague or friend) brought these papers to the administration of the Jewish community in Berlin before she and her mother were deported to Theresienstadt in 1942.[3] However, after the fall of the Nazi regime and the end of the second World War, her papers disappeared in inaccessible archives controlled by the repressive policies of the government of the East German Democratic Republic (GDR). Her papers were only discovered in 1991, when access to East German archives was opened up following the fall of the Berlin Wall. Access to the archive where Jonas's records are currently held, the Centrum Judaicum, is now in the hands of leaders of the Jewish community in Berlin.[4]

Another factor contributing to Jonas's temporary disappearance from historiography was the fact that she had challenged and transgressed many different norms and boundaries and had not strongly associated herself with a particular movement, social class, or political organization. Jonas's approach was difficult to label, as it combined aspects of Orthodox and Liberal Judaism. She came from an Orthodox background but studied at a Liberal seminary and was ordained in a private ceremony by Rabbi Max Dienemann, executive director of the Conference of Liberal Rabbis (Liberaler Rabbinerverband) in Germany. Some of her contemporaries found Jonas's approach too radically reformist; others criticized her for not being radical enough. As Kellenbach notes, "Jonas' interpretation of Torah, Talmud, and halakhah in support of women's equality was unpopular on both the right as well as the left, among more conservative Jews as well as in more liberal circles."[5] While Jonas's story needs to be understood in the wider context of the Jewish women's movement, there is no evidence that Jonas was aware of or in contact with other contemporary women seeking to be ordained as rabbis in the United States or Britain—or vice versa.[6] Unlike most of these women, Jonas came from a poor background, with no other rabbis in her family. While there is evidence that Jonas gave lectures at meetings of the German League of Jewish Women (Jüdischer Frauenbund), the Women's International Zionist Organisation, and other women's organizations, there is no clear evidence that she strongly associated herself with these organizations or was a member. Jonas's biographer, Elisa Klapheck, argues that "it was important for her to be above political organisations."[7] However, that also meant that in the decades following her death, before the arrival of a new generation of female rabbis, there was no clear lobby or organization with a strong interest in promoting her legacy.

Jonas's temporary disappearance from historiography as well as her rediscovery as a significant historical figure have been deeply intertwined with turbulent social and political developments in German history and with dramatic changes in Jewish communities in Germany and beyond. As historian Yosef Hayim Yerushalmi points out, "'Forgetting' in a collective sense occurs when human groups fail—whether purposely, out of rebellion, indifference, or indolence, or as a result of some disruptive historical catastrophe—to transmit what they know out of the past to their posterity."[8] The devastating impact of the Shoah, the dispersal of Shoah survivors across the globe, the division of Germany into East and West, and the lack of trained teachers and rabbis with German roots in the small reemerging Jewish communities in postwar Germany created significant hurdles in the transmission of knowledge of the history of Jewish life, culture, and traditions in Germany—including knowledge of Jonas's ordination.[9] In spite of the Hebrew Bible's command to remember, many traumatized survivors of the Shoah simply found it too painful and tried their best to distance themselves from an "unmasterable past" to enable themselves to build a new future.[10]

Some did talk about Jonas. Hermann Simon, former director of the Centrum Judaicum in Berlin, recalls his mother talking about "Rabbinerin Jonas, who supposedly had lived in our city," but struggled to find out more about her from her surviving contemporaries.[11] Apparently, Berlin-born Rabbi Louis Gerhard Graf (1912–1987), who was a rabbi at the Cardiff New Synagogue, "often mentioned her and her work," and British rabbi Sybil Sheridan, who was ordained in 1981, remembers that stories about a "woman in Germany who studied to be a rabbi" were circulated in Jewish communities and colleges in Britain.[12] However, the lack of written evidence posed significant hurdles in the transmission of Jonas's story. Sheridan recalls, "As one of the first women ordained at Leo Baeck College, I had heard of her [Jonas]. The story I received was a strange and garbled one that made no mention of her ordination."[13] Sheridan also admits to a certain level of indifference about Jonas's story among British women seeking to be ordained as rabbis in the 1970s and early 1980s: "I can only think that our indifference grew out of an attempt to be like men. As we struggled to gain recognition and respect in the Jewish world, we thought that to reclaim the inheritance of other women would only serve to marginalize us and emphasize our differences from our male colleagues."[14]

2. NATIONAL AND GENERATIONAL TRAJECTORIES OF MEMORY

The first published posthumous acknowledgment of Jonas's ordination—that I am aware of—was in a newspaper article entitled "The First Woman Rabbi" by Rabbi Jacob R. Marcus (1896–1995), founding director of the American Jewish Archives, published in the *American Israelite* in 1972, written in response to Sally Priesand's ordination in the United States.[15] In this article, Marcus makes reference to Jonas as the first woman worldwide ordained as a rabbi. In her book *Judaism and the New Woman*, Priesand acknowledges herself that "I was actually the second woman rabbi, then, although I was the first to be ordained by a theological seminary."[16]

However, in the United Kingdom, the ordination of the first British female rabbi, Jackie Tabick, in 1975 was described by the secular newspaper *The Times* as "the first woman outside the United States to be ordained as a rabbi" and by the *Jewish Chronicle* as "the third woman rabbi in the world (two have been ordained in the United States)."[17] No reference to Jonas was made.

Incidentally, the scholar who initiated the successful search for Jonas's papers and was the first to publish her research on Jonas's life was not a Jewish scholar, but a German Christian feminist theologian, Katharina von Kellenbach, living in the United States.[18] While studying in the United States, she had heard rumors about Jonas and decided to further investigate, recognizing the new opportunities that the collapse of the GDR regime offered in terms of access to archives in East Germany. Her interest in Jonas's story was related to her research interest in the history of the ordination of women in the German Protestant Church. However, Kellenbach has also described her motivation for her work on Jonas as a "form of reparation" as a descendant of the perpetrators, reflecting Jürgen Habermas's view that "there is the obligation incumbent upon us in Germany—even if no one else were to feel it any longer—to keep alive, without distortion and not only in an intellectual form, the memory of the sufferings of those who were murdered by German hands."[19]

The news of the discovery of Jonas's papers has been of particularly great significance to a new generation of female rabbis, as it has given this group a new historical perspective. The discovery of Jonas's papers happened at a time when a growing number of female rabbis had established themselves more securely and confidently. Female rabbis had become "a fact of life" in the non-Orthodox world and become more confident in establishing a distinct sense of identity and tradition.[20] British Rabbi Sibyl Sheridan described the impact of the news of the discovery of Jonas's papers in the 1990s, as follows:

> It gave us a heritage. . . . Judaism itself has such a long tradition. You're always looking back at where you come from, at previous rabbis and their statements and their understanding, and there was nothing for women rabbis at all. There was just a blank page. And so really, the discovery of Rabbi Regina Jonas gave us the first link, as it were, to go back. And it also opened up the possibilities that since she, who had been ordained so recently within the living memory of people, could be forgotten, then how many more people could there be out there that we didn't know? It opened up a huge possibility to explore . . . women's leadership roles within Judaism that just wasn't there before.[21]

Sheridan's statement stresses the importance of the link between leadership, heritage, memory, and identity. While this link is not unique to Jewish communities, these concepts are of particularly great significance to a community that understands itself as a "community of memory." As Yerushalmi points out, the Hebrew Bible's "injunctions to remember are unconditional, and even when not commanded, remembrance is always pivotal. Altogether the verb *zakhor* [remember] appears in its various declensions in the Bible no less than one hundred and sixty-nine times."[22] So, from this point of view, the memory of Jonas's story helped to firm up and consolidate a growing female tradition of leadership in Jewish communities and served as an important point of identification for a new generation of female rabbis.

The news of the discovery of Jonas's papers inspired British rabbi Elizabeth Tikvah Sarah to travel to Germany to work with Jonas's papers and write one of the first accounts of Jonas's life in English.[23] Sarah felt a particularly strong resonance between Jonas's fight for recognition as a rabbi and her own experience as one of the first lesbian rabbis in Britain and identified with her struggle as someone who "had shown an enormous amount of determination."[24] Sheridan and Sarah are part of a group of female rabbis in the United Kingdom who contributed to a collection of essays dedicated to Jonas's memory commemorating the fiftieth anniversary of her death. This volume, *Hear Our Voice*, relates to Jonas's memory as a "missing link" with their past, but is equally "intent on destroying the myth that there is such a thing as an 'archetypal' woman rabbi" and highlights the rich variety of thoughts and diversity of experiences of female rabbis.[25]

The discovery of evidence certifying Jonas's ordination in the context of 1930s Germany was perhaps of even greater significance to members of Jewish communities in Germany, such as Elisa Klapheck, whose work on Jonas's biography played a significant role in her own decision to become a rabbi working in Germany. She explains:

> So we found out all of a sudden, hey, we don't have to go to the United States to find inspiration in the Liberal Jewish communities there. We have our own tradition. We even have our own rabbi. The first female rabbi was in Germany. And we can be proud about it. It was still an issue. Can you be a proud German Jew? That was a taboo in those days. But all of a sudden you can say, hey, we can be proud. We have fantastic forerunners, predecessors.[26]

The discovery of Jonas's papers coincided with a revival of Judaism in Germany and across Western and Eastern Europe. This "new chapter" in Jewish history[27] was triggered by the fall of the Berlin Wall and the end of the Cold War. Until that time, many members of Jewish communities in Germany had felt somewhat ambiguous or embarrassed that they had stayed in "the land of perpetrators." Leading Jewish figures of the survivor generation, such as Leo Baeck, had previously argued that there was no future for Jews in Germany and that following the trauma of the Shoah, "the history of German Judaism [had] definitely come to an end."[28] However, since the early 1990s, there has been a growing desire among new generations to reconnect with the history of Judaism in Germany, including its vibrant intellectual culture and heritage, and develop a new, more confident and positive sense of German Jewish identity not exclusively framed by the Shoah.[29] Klapheck regards the renewed interest in Jonas's story as "an expression of a greater development—the renewal of a German, a European

Jewry that no longer stands on the ruins of the Shoah, that is no longer imprisoned by the trauma of the destruction, that builds bridges to a great past."[30]

The establishment of Abraham Geiger College in Berlin in 1999, which ordained its first class of rabbis in 2006 and its first female rabbi in 2010, is a clear expression of this new chapter in German Jewish history and a sign of confidence in the lasting continuity of Jewish life, heritage, and culture in Germany. When I interviewed a group of women training to be rabbis at Abraham College in 2012, I noticed a further generational shift. While they clearly had a lot of respect for Jonas, this new generation of female rabbis finds it harder to identify with Jonas's struggle than had Rabbis Sarah, Sheridan, and Klapheck. As one of these students explained to me, Regina Jonas "certainly offers an opportunity to identify. But on the other hand, I feel like I'm not in her position anymore."[31] It is fair to say that members of this new generation of female rabbis can take knowledge of Jonas's ordination, and that of many other women since, for granted, feel a lot more secure in themselves, and see their situation in contemporary Germany as very different and far removed from that of Nazi Germany.

By contrast, Gail Twersky Reimer, the founding director of the Jewish Women's Archive, notices some hesitancy within the American context to view German Jewish history and identity beyond the context of the Shoah. She maintains that "to this day, for most American Jews, Germany is a place of catastrophe, and not a place to which they would look to claim a legacy."[32] Reimer argues that this has contributed to a "certain reluctance amongst Americans to make the German Jonas part of their story of women in the rabbinate."[33] She claims that this reluctance has led to a "pattern of acknowledging Jonas but 'keeping her in the shadows.'"[34] This reluctance to regard Jonas as a full member of the chain of female rabbis is, for example, reflected in the title of the recent volume commemorating the fortieth anniversary of Priesand's ordination: *The Sacred Calling: Four Decades of Women in the Rabbinate*.[35] While this volume includes several chapters referring to and reflecting on Jonas's story, the title of this volume refers to only four decades of women in the rabbinate and thus excludes Jonas's ordination and work as a rabbi in the 1930s and 1940s from this narrative, placing Priesand's ordination in 1972 as the first. Reimer concludes that in Germany, the absence of a usable past has shaped how Jonas is remembered, whereas in America her memory was shaped by the presence of a quasi-sacred narrative about women's ordination. In neither community was her memory shaped in a vacuum.

In both, present understanding and needs determined how the memory of Jonas was received as well as how it would be transmitted to future generations.[36]

3. FILLING THE GAPS

Jonas's story has been explored in a wide range of different contexts and interpreted in many different ways. Her story has not only been covered in Elisa Klapheck's biography *Fräulein Rabbiner Jonas* and an increasing range of academic publications, reference works, and newspaper articles, but also in Diana Groó's 2013 film *Regina*.[37]

Since the initial discovery of Jonas's papers, there has been further research into witness accounts, primarily conducted by Kellenbach and Klapheck, and further written evidence was found, including transcripts and notes of Jonas's sermons delivered in Theresienstadt and letters Jonas wrote to her fiancé Rabbi Joseph Norden. In preparation for her work on Jonas's biography, Klapheck placed ads in Jewish newspapers across the world in 1998 to locate and interview eyewitnesses, who had known Jonas.[38] She was surprised by the number of people who contacted her: "It was as if they all had been waiting to say something about Regina Jonas, whether good or bad. The story moved them in a way that the ordination of Sally Priesand had not, because Regina Jonas was ordained in Germany—specifically, in Berlin. It was a way for all these older people to reconnect with their own past."[39]

The accounts of the witnesses who contacted Klapheck reflect strong and sometimes conflicting views about the ordination of women in general and about Jonas in particular. Whereas some eyewitnesses remembered Jonas with much admiration and referred to her "very impressive personality," her gift for teaching and public speaking, her moving, popular sermons, her exceptional energy and dedication to her work, or the pleasant sound of her deep voice, others "described Jonas as a 'hysterical person' whose only goal was to 'show herself off against the men.'"[40] Many eyewitness accounts centered on Jonas's looks, clothes, and hairstyle. Some remembered her as "unforgettably beautiful"; others claimed that she "did not take care of herself, her wardrobe left much to be desired, and even her hair supposedly stood on end."[41] Klapheck comes to the conclusion that "often, the descriptions revealed more about the witnesses themselves than about Regina Jonas."[42] As Hermann Simon, the former director of the Centrum Judaicum, notes, "It is difficult to assign Rabbi Jonas to her proper place in Berlin

Jewish history: some reject her vehemently, while others raise her to the heavens and turn her into a cult figure."[43] However, what is her "proper" place in history? Who "owns" her story?

The space left by the relative scarcity of information about Jonas has often been filled with projections of people's own hopes, ideals, and fears.[44] So it is not surprising that in recent years, her story has also inspired a number of novels, including *Nuit Ouverte* by Clémence Boulouque and *The English German Girl* by Jake Wallis Simons, which both mix history with fiction.[45] The French novel *Nuit Ouverte* uses historical references to Jonas's life to explore themes of memory, the weight of the past, and guilt. It focuses on the fictional character Elise Lermont, an actress who plays Regina Jonas and enacts her life story on screen as a form of atonement for her grandparents' guilt as Nazi collaborators.[46] *The English German Girl* tells the story of the fictional character Rosa Klein, her Berlin childhood as a Jewish girl in Nazi Germany, and her escape to England on a Kindertransport. This novel only briefly mentions Jonas's work as a rabbi supporting the Jewish community in Berlin as part of a backdrop to the main character's story. Jonas is one of many real-life characters incorporated in this novel, including Rabbi Malvin Warschauer; Wilhelm Kruetzfeld, the German police lieutenant who saved the Neue Synagogue from being burned down during Kristallnacht; Norbert Wollheim, who played a key role in organizing the Kindertransports, which he often accompanied; Baron Rothschild, the French-born philanthropist who did much to help Jews during the war; and Clare Alexander, matron of the London Hospital. Eva Tucker's review of this novel in the *Jewish Chronicle* notes that the inclusion of these real-life characters enhances this novel's factual foundations.[47] It is fair to say that their inclusion also draws a wider audience's attention to the existence of these historical figures and the contributions they have made. This novel does not specifically focus on Jonas, but by including her as part of the wider picture of Jewish community life in Berlin at this time, it contributes to the wider acceptance and "naturalization" of her place in history as a religious leader and as the first woman to be ordained as a rabbi.

In Diana Groó's "poetic documentary" *Regina*, Jonas's story takes center stage. Hungarian director Groó was attracted to her story, as she felt that Jonas "was exactly what a leader should be . . . and it's really rare. I was really amazed how she was fighting, how many difficulties she had to face, but at the same time she concentrated on her work."[48] As critics have noted, this film "is not a Holocaust tale but a gracefully edited documentary of a woman who emerges as determined, fearless, with the true calling of rabbi."[49] In the production of this award-winning documentary, Groó faced a number of challenges due to the limited availability of visual material and the fact that none of the eyewitnesses were still alive. Only two photographs of Jonas are available to us today: one was taken in 1936 and the other three years later, but both show Jonas in a very similar pose, wearing rabbinic robes. In the absence of further visual clues, Groó used black-and-white archival footage to "evoke the atmosphere of Berlin in the first half of the 20th century" supported by musical recordings from the Weimar era.[50] However, since there was only limited archival film and photographic footage of Jewish life of Berlin at the beginning of the twentieth century, Groó took some artistic liberties and supplemented footage of Berlin with close-ups of Orthodox Jews in Warsaw and Krakow.[51] The trailer of this film highlights a poetic, mysterious scene from the film superimposing Jonas's photograph, almost floating, on black-and-white footage of a deserted street. Against the backdrop of melancholy music, a female voice is heard quoting an extract from an eyewitness account: "They say she walked on the streets like a mystical medieval figure, her gaze turned inward, her thoughts not on this world but on completely different things."[52] The set-up of this scene and the choice of words could suggest an almost hagiographic approach to Jonas; however, while the film conveys a deep emotional connection with its subject, it does "stay true to the hundreds of documents Regina Jonas managed to save for posterity."[53]

As none of the eyewitnesses were still alive when Groó made the film, she decided to use voice-overs reading out witness accounts as well as passages from letters that form part of the collection of Jonas's papers. Groó aimed to re-create the feeling of hearing "old ladies in the voice-overs, who would sound like real persons who used to know Regina Jonas."[54] It was particularly important to her to use the voice of someone who had firsthand experience of concentration camps, "who really knows what it is about . . . creating somehow the feeling that it is true . . . to keep this kind of natural, human part of this story."[55] The voice-overs were recorded in English, German, and Hungarian, with subtitles in many other languages. In all three versions, Groó used the voice of her own grandmother, who survived four concentration camps, to bring to life witness accounts, reflecting a particularly close emotional connection with the subject matter of the film. Groó notes that in terms of her grandmother's age, "if she had lived in Berlin she could have been one of the students of Regina Jonas."[56] A close personal connection was also reflected in the fact that well-known actress Rachel Weisz, who is the daughter of this film's producer, George Weisz, gives voice to Jonas's own accounts in the English-language version of the film. Groó initially had difficulties in finding producers until George Weisz decided to support the production of this film, as he wanted to "promote awareness of Jonas' work."[57] Weisz has Hungarian Jewish roots, but his family escaped to England in 1938. He made his debut as a producer with this documentary, but he is also considering making a feature film of Jonas's life story and already holds the rights for this.[58] In an interview with the German newspaper *Jüdische Rundschau* following the German premiere of the film in Berlin in 2015, Weisz explained that he felt that Jonas's story "was something that had to be preserved for the future."[59]

While the film *Regina* has been screened in many different countries, it was particularly warmly received in Berlin. As Weisz notes:

> Since 2013, we've been to Paris, the USA, Budapest, Hong Kong and London. We won various prizes. The reactions to the film have always been different. Perhaps that's why it was so important to us to come to Berlin today. Because you see in every face here that this story touches people in a special way. There's a special atmosphere here, a vibrancy, a vivid engagement. In London, for example, people seemed very distant.[60]

As the *Jüdische Rundschau* concludes, "Berlin is something very special because Regina Jonas is 'coming home.'"[61]

4. LOOKING AHEAD

Regina Jonas's story has offered female leaders in Jewish communities and beyond an important historical perspective, but it has also found strong emotional resonance with many people in a wider sense, either as a reminder of controversy, loss, or guilt or as a source of strength and inspiration for leadership, commitment, and faith in the face of adversity. The different national trajectories the memory of her story has taken since the discovery of her papers, certainly in the American, German, and British contexts, and the generational differences the memory of her story reflects are particularly fascinating. As Jonas's case illustrates, memory is a process that is shaped by and shapes national, generational, and gender identities. "'Remembering,' that is, the way a social group positions itself in a historical perspective, is an essential feature of identity."⁶² However, as Yerushalmi concludes, "Memory is always problematic, usually deceptive, sometimes treacherous."⁶³

As Jonas's case illustrates, written evidence can serve a crucial role in anchoring and shaping historiography. The lack of access to written evidence and the discovery of her papers have been important factors in her temporary disappearance from and reappearance in historiography. As Sally Priesand notes, had Jonas not given "her documents to the Berlin Jewish community for safekeeping . . . , we would know even less than we do now about her life and the significant contribution she made to the Jewish community."⁶⁴ In recognition of the significance of written evidence, Priesand has taken the initiative to protect the memory of her own legacy and that of other female rabbis: "When I retired from the active rabbinate, I announced that I would be donating my documents and papers to the American Jewish Archives in Cincinnati, and I encouraged all female rabbis to do the same."⁶⁵

In recent years, digital archives have been offering new important opportunities for the preservation of primary sources. The website of the Jewish Women's Archive, for example, offers "the world's largest collection of information on Jewish women, and draws more than one million visitors a year."⁶⁶ Digital archives allow previously marginalized groups and their leaders to take control of preserving and curating sources and grant public access to them, and thus transcend many of the bureaucratic, logistical, financial, and political hurdles that have restricted access to many archives in the past.⁶⁷ Hopefully, this means that current and future generations and their leaders will have more opportunities to protect evidence and secure their legacy than Rabbi Regina Jonas had.

NOTES

1. Gerda Lerner, *The Creation of Feminist Consciousness: From the Middle Ages to Eighteen-Seventy* (New York: Oxford University Press, 1993), 280–81.

2. Judith Abrams, "Who Controls the Narrative? A 'Stop Action' Analysis of the Story of Beruriah and the Implications for Women Rabbis," in *The Sacred Calling: Four Decades of Women in the Rabbinate*, ed. Rebecca Einstein Schorr and Alysa Mendelson Graf (New York: CCAR Press, 2016), 7.

3. Hermann Simon, foreword to *Fräulein Rabbiner Jonas: The Story of the First Woman Rabbi*, by Elisa Klapheck, trans. T. Axelrod (San Francisco: Jossey-Bass, 2004), ix; Hermann Simon, interview conducted by author, May 30, 2012.

4. Stefanie Sinclair, "Regina Jonas: Forgetting and Remembering the First Female Rabbi," *Religion* 43, no. 4 (2013): 543.

5. Katharina von Kellenbach, "Denial and Defiance in the Work of Rabbi Regina Jonas," in *In God's Name: Genocide and Religion in the Twentieth Century*, ed. Omer Bartov and Phyllis Mack (New York: Berghahn Books, 2001), 247.

6. Elisa Klapheck, "'Mir war nie darum zu tun, die Erste zu sein': Das Vermächtnis von Rabbinerin Regina Jonas," in *Bet Debora Journal: Engendering Jewish Politics* (Berlin: Hentrich and Hentrich, 2016), 24.

7. Elisa Klapheck, interview conducted by author, Berlin, May 30, 2012.

8. Yosef Hayim Yerushalmi, *Zakhor: Jewish History and Jewish Memory* (Seattle: University of Washington Press, 1996), 109.

9. Michael Brenner, *After the Holocaust: Rebuilding Jewish Lives in Postwar Germany*, trans. Barbara Harshav (Princeton: Princeton University Press, 1997).

10. Roger Frie, "Memory and Responsibility: Navigating Identity and Shame in the German-Jewish Experience," *Psychoanalytic Psychology* 29, no. 2 (2012): 208.

11. Simon, foreword to Klapheck, *Fräulein Rabbiner Jonas*, ix.

12. Rachel Montagu, "Comment: Shameful Silence," *Jewish Chronicle*, June 12, 2015, 37; Sybil Sheridan, preface to *Hear Our Voice: Women Rabbis Tell Their Stories*, ed. Sybil Sheridan (London: SCM Press, 1994), x.

13. Sheridan, preface to *Hear Our Voice*, x.

14. Ibid., x–xi.

15. Jacob R. Marcus, "The First Woman Rabbi," *American Israelite* 118, no. 34 (March 9, 1972): 1, 3.

16. Sally J. Priesand, *Judaism and the New Woman* (New York: Behrman House, 1975), 67.

17. "First Woman Rabbi in Britain," *Times*, June 30, 1975, 3; "Britain's First Woman Rabbi," *Jewish Chronicle*, July 4, 1975, 1.

18. Katharina von Kellenbach, "Frl. Rabbiner Regina Jonas: Eine religiöse Feministin vor ihrer Zeit," *Schlangenbrut* 38 (1992): 35–39; see also Kellenbach's contribution to this volume, "Remembering Regina Jonas; On the Intersectionality of Women's Jewish, German, and Holocaust History."

19. Katharina von Kellenbach, telephone interview conducted by author, July 9, 2012; Jürgen Habermas, *The New Conservatism: Cultural Criticism and the Historians' Debate*, ed. and trans. Shierry Weber Nicholsen (Cambridge: MIT Press, 1989), 233.

20. Sylvia Rothschild, "Why Aren't Women Viewed as 'Proper' Rabbis?," *Jewish Chronicle*, May 29, 2015, 37.

21. Sybil Sheridan in The Open University, "Track 2 Regina Jonas' Legacy: Stefanie Sinclair talks to Rabbi Elizabeth Tikvah Sarah and Rabbi Sybil Sheridan, discussing the significance of the first female rabbi, Regina Jonas, her life and legacy," *Regina Jonas: The First Female Rabbi*, OpenLearn, 2013, https://www.open.edu/openlearn/history-the-arts/religious-studies/regina-jonas-the-first-female-rabbi?track=2.

22. Yerushalmi, *Zakhor*, 5.

23. Elizabeth Tikvah Sarah, "Rabbiner Regina Jonas: Missing Link in a Broken Chain," in Sheridan, *Hear Our Voice*, 2–9.

24. Elizabeth Tikvah Sarah in The Open University, "Track 2 Regina Jonas' Legacy: Stefanie Sinclair talks to Rabbi Elizabeth Tikvah Sarah and Rabbi Sybil Sheridan, discussing the significance of the first female rabbi, Regina Jonas, her life and legacy," *Regina Jonas: The First Female Rabbi*, OpenLearn, 2013, https://www.open.edu/openlearn/history-the-arts/religious-studies/regina-jonas-the-first-female-rabbi?track=2.

25. Sheridan, *Hear Our Voice*; Valerie Monchi, "A Job for a Jewish Girl?," *Jewish Chronicle*, December 16, 1995, 25.

26. Elisa Klapheck, interview conducted by author, Berlin, May 30, 2012.

27. Ibid.

28. Leo Baeck, cited in Michael A. Meyer, "Denken und Wirken Leo Baecks nach 1945," in *Leo Baeck. 1873–1956. Aus dem Stamme von Rabbinern*, ed. Georg Heuberger and Fritz Backhaus (Frankfurt am Main: Jüdischer Verlag im Suhrkamp Verlag, 2001), 130; my translation from German original.

29. Elisa Klapheck, interview conducted by author, Berlin, May 30, 2012; see also Michal Y. Bodemann, "A Jewish Cultural Renascence in Germany?," in *Turning the Kaleidoscope: Perspectives on European Jewry*, ed. Sandra Lustig and Ian Levenson (New York: Berghahn Books, 2006), 164–75.

30. Klapheck, *Fräulein Rabbiner Jonas*, 14.

31. Student at Abraham Geiger College, interview conducted by author at Abraham Geiger College, Berlin, May 31, 2012.

32. Gail Twersky Reimer, "Regina Jonas: The Shifting Sands of Memory," in *Bet Debora Journal: Engendering Jewish Politics* (Berlin: Hentrich and Hentrich, 2016), 19.

33. Reimer, "Regina Jonas," 19.

34. Ibid., 18.

35. Rebecca Einstein Schorr and Alysa Mendelson Graf, eds., *The Sacred Calling: Four Decades of Women in the Rabbinate* (New York: CCAR Press, 2016).

36. Reimer, "Regina Jonas," 21.

37. Elisa Klapheck, *Fräulein Rabbiner Jonas: Kann die Frau das rabbinische Amt bekleiden?* (Teetz: Hentrich & Hentrich, 1999); Klapheck, *Fräulein Rabbiner Jonas*; Regina, directed and written by Diana Groó (UK: Malcah Production; Hungary: Katapult Film; Germany: Time Prints, 2013).

38. Kellenbach had done the same in 1991.

39. Klapheck, *Fräulein Rabbiner Jonas*, 10.

40. Ibid., 8, 11–14.

41. Ibid., 11.

42. Ibid.

43. Simon, foreword to *Fräulein Rabbiner Jonas*, xi.

44. Klapheck, *Fräulein Rabbiner Jonas*, 40; Sheridan, preface to *Hear Our Voice*, xvii.

45. Clémence Boulouque, *Nuit Ouverte* (Paris: Flammarion, 2007); Jake Wallis Simons, *The English German Girl* (Edinburgh: Polygon, 2007).

46. Isabelle Courty, "Nuit Ouverte," *Le Figaro Magazine*, October 4, 2007, http://www.lefigaro.fr/lefigaromagazine/2007/09/28/01006-20070928ARTMAG90501-nuit_ouverte.php .

47. Eva Tucker, "Review: The German English Girl—From Bicycle to Kindertransport," *Jewish Chronicle*, May 18, 2011, https://www.thejc.com/culture/books/review-the-english-german-girl-1.23101 .

48. Groó, cited in Ayelet Dekel, "Jerusalem Film Festival 2013: Diana Groó on Making Regina," *Midnight East: An Insider Perspective on Israeli Culture*, July 3, 2013, http://www.midnighteast.com/mag/?p=26893.

49. Amy Stone, "Meet on Screen the First Woman Rabbi," *Lilith*, February 12, 2014, http://lilith.org/blog/2014/02/meet-on-screen-the-first-woman-rabbi/.

50. Dekel, "Jerusalem Film Festival 2013: Diana Groó on Making Regina"; Kurt Brokaw, "New York Jewish Film Festival 2014—Critic's Choices: Regina," *The Independent*, January 15, 2014, http://independent-magazine.org/2014/01/new-york_jewish-film-festival_2014_kurt-brokaw/.

51. Dekel, "Jerusalem Film Festival 2013: Diana Groó on Making Regina"; Stone, "Meet on Screen the First Woman Rabbi."

52. Groó, *Regina*.

53. Stone, "Meet on Screen the First Woman Rabbi."
54. Groó, cited in Dekel, "Jerusalem Film Festival 2013: Diana Groó on Making Regina."
55. Ibid.
56. Ibid.
57. Ibid.
58. Jennifer Lipman, "Rachel Weisz' Father Makes His Movie Debut," *Jewish Chronicle*, May 31, 2013, 10.
59. Translated from the German original: "Und das ist etwas, was für die Zukunft bewahrt werden muss"; George Weisz, cited in Laura Külper, "Die erste Rabbinerin der Welt: Zum neuen Film über '*Fräulein Rabbiner Jonas*,'" *Jüdische Rundschau* 16, no. 12 (December 2015): 28.
60. Translated from German original: "Wir waren seit 2013 in Paris, den USA, Budapest, Hongkong und London und haben verschiedene Preise gewonnen. Die Reaktionen auf den Film waren immer anders, vielleicht war es uns deshalb so wichtig, heute in Berlin zu sein. Denn man sieht in jedem Gesicht hier, dass diese Geschichte berührt und das auf eine besondere Art. Da herrschte eine besondere Atmosphäre, ein Vibrieren, eine Lebendigkeit der Anteilnahme. In London zum Beispiel wirkten die Menschen sehr distanziert"; George Weisz, cited in Külper, "Die erste Rabbinerin der Welt."
61. Translated from German original: "ist Berlin etwas ganz besonderes, denn Regina Jonas 'kommt nach Hause'"; Külper, "Die erste Rabbinerin der Welt."
62. Translated from German original, Thomas Brechenmacher, "Identität und Erinnerung: Schlüsselthemen deutsch-jüdischer Geschichte und Gegenwart. Eine Einführung," in *Identität und Erinnerung: Schlüsselthemen deutsch-jüdischer Geschichte und Gegenwart*, ed. Thomas Brechenmacher (Munich: Olzog, 2009), 9–19.
63. Yerushalmi, *Zakhor*, 5.
64. Sally J. Priesand, foreword to Schorr and Graf, *The Sacred Calling*, xii.
65. Priesand, foreword to Schorr and Graf, *The Sacred Calling*, xii.
66. "Welcome to the Jewish Women's Archive!," Jewish Women's Archive, accessed April 4, 2017, https://jwa.org/aboutjwa.
67. Wolfgang Ernst, *Digital Memory and the Archive* (Minneapolis: University of Minnesota Press, 2013).

BIBLIOGRAPHY

Abrams, Judith, "Who Controls the Narrative? A 'Stop Action' Analysis of the Story of Beruriah and the Implications for Women Rabbis," in *The Sacred Calling: Four Decades of Women in the Rabbinate*, ed. Rebecca Einstein Schorr and Alysa Mendelson Graf (New York: CCAR Press, 2016).

Bodemann, Michal Y., "A Jewish Cultural Renascence in Germany?," in *Turning the Kaleidoscope: Perspectives on European Jewry*, ed. Sandra Lustig and Ian Levenson (New York: Berghahn Books, 2006), 164–75.

Boulouque, Clémence, *Nuit Ouverte* (Paris: Flammarion, 2007).

Brechenmacher, Thomas,"Identität und Erinnerung: Schlüsselthemen deutsch-jüdischer Geschichte und Gegenwart. Eine Einführung," in *Identität und Erinnerung: Schlüsselthemen deutsch-jüdischer Geschichte und Gegenwart*, ed. Thomas Brechenmacher (Munich: Olzog, 2009), 9–19.

Brenner, Michael, *After the Holocaust: Rebuilding Jewish Lives in Postwar Germany*, trans. Barbara Harshav (Princeton: Princeton University Press, 1997).

Brokaw, Kurt, "New York Jewish Film Festival 2014—Critic's Choices: Regina," *The Independent*, January 15, 2014, http://independent-magazine.org/2014/01/new-york_jewish-film-festival_2014_kurt-brokaw/ .

Courty, Isabelle, "Nuit Ouverte," *Le Figaro Magazine*, October 4, 2007, http://www.lefigaro.fr/lefigaromagazine/2007/09/28/01006-20070928ARTMAG90501-nuit_ouverte.php .

Dekel, Ayelet, "Jerusalem Film Festival 2013: Diana Groó on Making Regina," *Midnight East: An Insider Perspective on Israeli Culture*, July 3, 2013, http://www.midnighteast.com/mag/?p=26893 .

Einstein Schorr, Rebecca, and Mendelson Graf, Alysa (eds.), *The Sacred Calling: Four Decades of Women in the Rabbinate* (New York: CCAR Press, 2016).

Ernst, Wolfgang, *Digital Memory and the Archive* (Minneapolis: University of Minnesota Press, 2013).

Frie, Roger, "Memory and Responsibility: Navigating Identity and Shame in the German-Jewish Experience," *Psychoanalytic Psychology* 29, no. 2 (2012): 206–25.

Habermas, Jürgen, *The New Conservatism: Cultural Criticism and the Historians' Debate*, ed. and trans. Shierry Weber Nicholsen (Cambridge: MIT Press, 1989).

Klapheck, Elisa, "'Mir war nie darum zu tun, die Erste zu sein': Das Vermächtnis von Rabbinerin Regina Jonas," in *Bet Debora Journal: Engendering Jewish Politics* (Berlin: Hentrich and Hentrich, 2016).

Klapheck, Elisa, *Fräulein Rabbiner Jonas: Kann die Frau das rabbinische Amt bekleiden?* (Teetz: Hentrich & Hentrich, 1999).

Klapheck, Elisa, *Fräulein Rabbiner Jonas: The Story of the First Woman Rabbi*, trans. T. Axelrod (San Francisco: Jossey-Bass, 2004).

Külper, Laura, "Die erste Rabbinerin der Welt: Zum neuen Film über '*Fräulein Rabbiner Jonas*,'" *Jüdische Rundschau* 16, no. 12 (December 2015).

Lerner, Gerda, *The Creation of Feminist Consciousness: From the Middle Ages to Eighteen-Seventy* (New York: Oxford University Press, 1993).

Lipman, Jennifer, "Rachel Weisz' Father Makes His Movie Debut," *Jewish Chronicle*, May 31, 2013, 10.

Marcus, Jacob R., "The First Woman Rabbi," *American Israelite* 118, no. 34 (March 9, 1972).

Meyer, Michael A., "Denken und Wirken Leo Baecks nach 1945," in *Leo Baeck. 1873–1956. Aus dem Stamme von Rabbinern*, ed. Georg Heuberger and Fritz Backhaus (Frankfurt am Main: Jüdischer Verlag im Suhrkamp Verlag, 2001), 130.

Monchi, Valerie, "A Job for a Jewish Girl?," *Jewish Chronicle*, December 16, 1995, 25.

Montagu, Rachel, "Comment: Shameful Silence," *Jewish Chronicle*, June 12, 2015, 37.

Priesand, Sally J., *Judaism and the New Woman* (New York: Behrman House, 1975).

Reimer, Gail Twersky, "Regina Jonas: The Shifting Sands of Memory," in *Bet Debora Journal: Engendering Jewish Politics* (Berlin: Hentrich and Hentrich, 2016).

Rothschild, Sylvia, "Why Aren't Women Viewed as 'Proper' Rabbis?," *Jewish Chronicle*, May 29, 2015, 37.

Sheridan, Sybil (ed.), *Hear Our Voice: Women Rabbis Tell Their Stories* (London: SCM Press, 1994).

Sinclair, Stefanie, "Regina Jonas: Forgetting and Remembering the First Female Rabbi," *Religion* 43, no. 4 (2013): 543–63.

Stone, Amy, "Meet on Screen the First Woman Rabbi," *Lilith*, February 12, 2014, http://lilith.org/blog/2014/02/meet-on-screen-the-first-woman-rabbi/ .

Tucker, Eva, "Review: *The German English Girl*—From Bicycle to Kindertransport," *Jewish Chronicle*, May 18, 2011, https://www.thejc.com/culture/books/review-the-english-german-girl-1.23101.

von Kellenbach, Katharina, "Denial and Defiance in the work of Rabbi Regina Jonas," in *In God's Name: Genocide and Religion in the Twentieth Century*, ed. Omer Bartov and Phyllis Mack (New York: Berghahn Books, 2001), 243–59.

von Kellenbach, Katharina, "Frl. Rabbiner Regina Jonas: Eine religiöse Feministin vor ihrer Zeit," *Schlangenbrut* 38 (1992): 35–39.

Wallis Simons, Jake, *The English German Girl* (Edinburgh: Polygon, 2007).

Yerushalmi, Yosef Hayim, *Zakhor: Jewish History and Jewish Memory* (Seattle: University of Washington Press, 1996).

Part III

Personal Reflections

Chapter Ten

They Married What They Wanted to Be?

Rebbetzins and Their Unconventional Paths to Power

Shuly Rubin Schwartz

In the 2016 U.S. presidential election, countless commentators remarked on the unprecedented nature of Hillary Clinton's bid for president as the first female nominee of a major political party. Serving as a U.S. senator from the State of New York from 2001 to 2009 and as secretary of state in the Obama administration from 2009 to 2013, Hillary Clinton had honed her skills as a negotiator, policy maker, and administrator and was eminently qualified for the role. But many reporters also highlighted her earlier position as first lady of the United States during Bill Clinton's eight-year presidency and the access to power and experiences afforded by that role. They were right to do so, for marriage to a political figure has proved throughout history to be the most common way for women to assume political office.[1]

On the international arena, the first female president of Argentina was Isabel Martínez de Perón, who assumed the presidency after her husband's death in 1974. In the United States, Hattie Wyatt Caraway, the first woman elected to the U.S. Senate in 1932, succeeded her husband Senator Thaddeus Caraway upon his death and then won election in her own right a year later. Friends recalled the critical role she had played in her husband's political career, working on his campaign, speaking on his behalf, and serving as his closest political confidante. Constituents assumed that husbands consulted with their wives throughout their years in government and that the wives had gained knowledge and skills that would uniquely prepare them to function in the role themselves.[2]

For me, the political spouse role has always proved fascinating because it echoes on the national, civil stage what I have lived, breathed, and studied for most of my life—the special role and experiences of rabbis' wives. I was privileged to be in this role for twenty-four years, as my late husband was a congregational rabbi until his death. My father also served as a congregational rabbi for his entire career; my brother-in-law, uncles, and cousins have also been congregational rabbis. (This even continues to the next generation, as I am the mother of a rabbi—and mother-in-law of a rabbi's wife!) I thus grew up in a rabbinic home, saw other models of rabbinic couples within my family, and lived as half of a rabbinic couple for most of my adult life. These experiences initially drew me to contemplate this topic as one worthy of inquiry, and it is this personal connection that has hopefully given me the empathy and perspective to deeply understand it.

Growing up on Long Island in a rabbinic home, I saw at close range the success of rabbinic couples in cultivating postwar Jewish life in suburban America. I admired my mother and the work that she did as a congregational rebbetzin. A graduate of the Jewish Theological Seminary's Teachers' Institute who married her rabbinical student sweetheart, Gilla Pearlstein Rubin was eager to use her skills and talents to enrich the lives of Jews in the congregation and beyond. Though surely the exaggerated perspective of a proud mother, I often heard her boast that I, as a Hebrew-speaking toddler, avidly participated in the beginner's Hebrew classes that she taught in our living room. My parents regularly invited guests for Shabbat and holiday meals so that congregants could experience the warmth of traditional Jewish living. Particularly attuned to the challenges of individuation and Jewish identity, they hosted college students annually on Thanksgiving weekend, facilitating socialization and reflective conversation. In the synagogue, Rubin taught holiday workshops to women, hoping to infuse their home life with Jewish foods, songs, and rituals. A regular attendee at Shabbat services and Sisterhood meetings and events, Rubin would often counsel congregants informally before, during, and after. Individual students sought her out when they chose to write papers on Jewish topics, and she generously offered concrete suggestions and guidance. She also co-led with my father several congregational trips to Israel to deepen the connection between American Jews and the Jewish state. Closer to home, she galvanized congregational contingents to rally on behalf of Soviet Jewry and Israel. A sought-after public speaker, Rubin also offered reviews of contemporary American Jewish literature to women's groups throughout Long Island. All the while, she was serving as the primary parent rearing three children.

I came of age in the 1970s, as the Jewish feminist movement emerged and the struggle for women's ordination in the Conservative movement began in earnest. Studying for my PhD at the Jewish Theological Seminary, I found myself in classes with several bright, motivated, and accomplished women who took graduate school classes, hoping that they would be transferable to the rabbinical school as soon as JTS changed its policy to train women as well as men for ordination. During those years, people often assumed that I too yearned to be a rabbi and that studying Jewish history was a temporary endeavor. Amused by this supposition both because studying for a PhD is hardly something one does to bide one's time and because the thought of becoming a rabbi myself had never crossed my mind, I nevertheless began to view my talented female classmates with inquiring eyes. This led me to question where one would have found the bright, talented, educated Jewish women with a sense of calling prior to the mid-1970s. In what arenas did they serve in the era before ordination became an option?

As I began to explore these questions, I read many accounts of the crucial role played by rabbis in the flourishing of Jewish life in the United States but never found one that noted the significant efforts of their wives in helping to achieve this goal. This lacuna impelled me to study this issue in earnest not only to acknowledge the contributions of my mother and her generation of rabbis' wives, but also to redress what I had come to see as an egregious omission in American Jewish history. I knew personally that Jewishly educated women in past decades had pursued avenues short of ordination in which to serve effectively as religious leaders, and I felt driven to retrieve and share their stories.

At the same time, I myself became the wife of a rabbi when my late husband was ordained. Surely, I had witnessed the extent to which the role enriched my mother's life, but I also felt her frustrations with aspects of it. Moreover, I was training for and planned to pursue a career as an American Jewish historian. What place would the rebbetzin role play in my life? Gradually, I found my way. Building on my strengths, expertise, and interests, I tried to support my husband's rabbinate and address the needs of the congregation without erasing my own professional aspirations. For example, in the early years, I helped establish a babysitting co-op for young Jewish mothers that brought women into the congregational orbit in a nonthreatening manner by addressing a pressing need that we all shared. As we met to discuss the kind of group we hoped to establish, we also talked about Jewish parenting and how best to cultivate a Jewishly nourishing home. And as the co-op took hold, I hungrily used precious babysitting hours to furtively work on my dissertation.

As my career began to blossom, I offered in my own congregation annual scholar-in-residence talks on a wide range of topics which enabled me to share in my home community the teachings that I offered in synagogues around the country. I also worked to initiate and facilitate a Rosh Hodesh group, which brought together women of various ages and life stages to study and discuss issues pertaining to our place in Jewish life—past, present, and future. And throughout these years, just as my parents had done a generation earlier, my husband and I would host guests for Shabbat and holiday meals, help families feel more comfortable with Jewish living by modeling it, answering questions, and offering suggestions. In all my efforts, I strove to reach individuals in ways or venues that would have been inaccessible to my husband and to work together with him to complement his strengths with my own.

During the 1980s, I also belonged to a rebbetzins' group on Long Island, where seasoned rabbis' wives would offer advice and all could find camaraderie. Discussions focused on issues unique to the role, such as whether and how to invite the entire congregation to a child's bar/bat mitzvah, how often to entertain, and how to manage the reality of living in a parsonage where simple decisions about home decorating, repair, or improvement were subject to synagogue board approval. Rebbetzins craved support from peers who understood the unique circumstances of their lives and who were not congregants whose views or judgment could adversely affect a rabbinic family's future in the congregation. A variation on the consciousness-raising groups that grew out of the 1960s counterculture, such support groups—which existed in many communities around the country—proved to be a lifeline for many rabbis' wives.

By the 1990s, I had decided to write a book-length study of the rebbetzin experience in America. When I expressed this interest to my academic colleagues, the topic was met with enthusiasm but also with caution for fear of a dearth of sources. As with the field of women's studies in general, here, too, I was naming as a subject of serious study a topic that scholars had never focused on before. Would I find enough material to reach any broader conclusions or offer new insights? Writing an article seemed to be the way to start.

With insights garnered from contextualizing the role of the American rabbi's wife within the traditional Eastern European milieu, the American ministry, and the sociology of American women, I conducted oral interviews in the early 1990s with several postwar rebbetzins. Then to corroborate, deepen, and expand these findings, I turned my attention to the written record, hoping to find sources in unconventional places. And what a bounty I discovered! Synagogue flyers, histories, photographs, program books, magazines, and annual journals; rebbetzin's memoirs, articles, and books and more. All of this enabled me to contextualize, verify as far as possible, and enhance the oral interviews.

Focusing on my mother and her cohort of postwar rebbetzins, what I discovered is that many talented women had married what they wanted to be. I don't mean to suggest that they actually wanted to serve as ordained rabbis. Most would have found that suggestion preposterous. But many of these women did indeed want to serve as Jewish religious leaders. They cared passionately about enriching Jewish lives in the postwar period and wanted to share their love of *Yiddishkeit* with others. They intuitively if not consciously understood that they could most effectively accomplish this goal by marrying a rabbi. By working together with him, they could exercise religious leadership to advance Jewish life in their communities and beyond—leadership that would otherwise have been beyond their reach.

From the perspective of the twenty-first century where women hold leadership positions in a wide variety of careers, this two-person career model seems deeply discriminatory. The rabbi's wife gained status and a platform on which to effectively serve the community but without pay or adequate recognition for her efforts. Moreover, she was completely dependent on her husband for access to such a career. He provided the platform through which she acted. If he succeeded in the congregation, she, too, had the opportunity to minister to the congregation, albeit in a supportive, gender-appropriate manner. If he failed, she, too, lost her position and often her home.

Why then was this path to leadership through one's husband so coveted? For much of the twentieth century, women faced limited career options, especially because middle-class expectations encompassed the notion that careers were incompatible with marriage and family. As women struggled to find socially acceptable ways to cultivate and sustain meaningful lives—including consequential work and marriage—many women discovered that they could have both by marrying a man with a career to which they had an affinity. Their "wife of" status opened doors to the public domain, affording them otherwise unattainable access and power that enabled them to impact organizations, public policy, and the hearts and minds of thousands of men, women, and children over the course of their adult lives.

Because of this, until the third quarter of the twentieth century, marriage to a rabbi provided many women with a very gratifying life: rabbis' wives lived full, rich Jewish lives that many felt they would not have been able to do otherwise, they gained immediate status as community leaders, they were right in the middle of the action Jewishly, and they had a built-in audience for their leadership talents, often through Sisterhood. And congregations eagerly sought to hire married rabbis whose wives embraced the rabbinate as a two-person career. As synagogues sought to expand their membership and broaden the scope of what they offered, they were thrilled to get two for the price of one.

Sociologist Hanna Papanek first conceptualized the relationship of a wife to her husband's work as a "two-person single career" in which educated middle-class American wives found vicarious achievement through their husbands' work. Papanek understood that this phenomenon channeled women's occupational aspirations onto a noncompetitive track. Women gained praise for supportive behavior, while men garnered rewards for individual mastery. Because of this, women often sought to marry men who could provide position and status as well as security. They then channeled their energies into enhancing their husbands' careers. Such women, including the wives of corporate executives, army officers, physicians, politicians, and academics, have historically augmented their husbands' work through intellectual contributions, status maintenance, and public performance. In addition, certain two-person career expectations required specialized skills or knowledge unique to the man's profession. Ambassadors' wives, for example, had to master the symbolic nature of diplomatic interactions and hone skills of indirect political and social messaging. In the sphere of religion, marriage to a clergyman provided women who felt drawn to religious service a particularly meaningful outlet for their sense of calling. Such work—though unpaid and without formal title—provided wives with status, authority, and legitimacy that they would have been unable—no matter how talented or ambitious—to achieve on their own.[3]

By marrying a rabbi, an American rabbi's wife thus followed a pattern common to middle-class women. In addition, she also assumed a role with long-standing, rich historical associations, for Eastern European rabbis' wives were known for piety, scrupulous observance, leadership, and concern for the poor. Though plagued by derogatory, disparaging stereotypes that proved to be a source of pain and anxiety for the wives, on the positive side rabbis' wives were also known for frugality and business savvy, since they were tasked with supporting their families so that their husbands could learn Torah and minister to the community. Many rabbis' wives possessed deep Jewish knowledge, often because they had grown up in rabbinic homes. As rabbis' daughters, they not only were trained in running a Jewish home by their rebbetzin mothers, but they also absorbed a tremendous amount of traditional Jewish learning from their fathers. Jewishly educated daughters were especially common in families without sons, a phenomenon characteristic of general society as well. Serving as surrogate sons for intellectually driven fathers, such women had the opportunity to attain advanced knowledge in subject areas that were usually limited to men.

These rich associations were embedded in the special title reserved for Eastern European Jewish rabbis' wives, the Yiddish "rebbetzin." Eastern European Ashkenazi Jews then brought these assumptions about rabbis' wives with them in their collective consciousness when they immigrated to the United States in the late nineteenth and early twentieth centuries. As with everything else they brought with them, these images were then reshaped by the American environment that they encountered.[4]

In particular, the role of the rabbi's wife in America was influenced by expectations of Protestant clergy that had crystallized in the nineteenth century.[5] The notion of a minister's wife possessing a special sense of calling or performing discrete behaviors emerged in the mid 1800s with the spread of Methodism. The role also gained credence from the view, increasingly popular in the nineteenth century, that women harbored an innately religious nature that predisposed them to serve as society's moral guardians. This belief enabled women to take on public leadership roles on behalf of benevolent endeavors, and this work then afforded them personal authority in spheres that did not threaten male privilege. This idea reinforced clergy wives' efforts to assist their clergy husbands in their congregational work, and it justified their instrumental roles in founding women's societies that dispensed charity and served as auxiliaries for Bible and prayer book groups.

As the American rabbinate came into its own at the end of the nineteenth and early twentieth century, rabbis patterned their profession on what they observed in the Protestant pastors around them. In fact they came to see themselves as Jewish ministers—preachers, officiants, teachers, and community leaders. And their wives similarly learned much about how to serve as American rabbis' wives from their Christian counterparts. Since ministers' wives were playing a vital role in the life of the church as helpmeets to their husbands, choir leaders, hostesses, teachers, and more, so too did rabbis' wives begin to articulate a distinct position for themselves.

Three women—Carrie Simon, Mathilde Schechter, and Rebecca Goldstein—played critical roles in these early years by leveraging their positions as wives of prominent religious leaders to model religious leadership by founding the women's branch of their respective religious denominations: the Reform movement's National Federation of Temple Sisterhoods (1913), the Conservative movement's National Women's League (1918), and the Orthodox movement's Women's Branch of the Union of Orthodox Jewish Congregations of America (1923). These organizations gave each woman a national platform independent of her husband's rabbinate, affording her a unique venue through which to exercise religious leadership. Each sought independently of the others to educate and inspire a group of American Jewish women to lead more robust Jewish lives and deepen the Jewishness of their families. Similarly, many other rabbis' wives assumed leadership roles in these women's organizations, but they each worked individually rather than connecting as a cohort of rabbis' wives.

The recognition by rabbis' wives that they formed a discrete group with common goals and challenges can be traced to a 1925 special symposium on the rabbi's wife sponsored by the New York Board of Jewish Ministry. Rebekah Kohut delivered the keynote address. Wife, and then widow, of the renowned scholar and rabbi Alexander Kohut, Rebekah was herself accomplished as the founder of the Kohut School for Girls and as the longtime president of the New York section of the National Council of Jewish Women. In her remarks, Kohut spoke about the American rabbinate as a two-person career, with both husband and wife being essential to its success. Moreover, she shared the view that all rabbis' wives—not only the most educated and ambitious among them—ought to embrace the role. Articulating its primary aspects, Kohut noted that rabbis' wives should create an exemplary home characterized by "organization, cleanliness, simplicity and culture." They ought to be model mothers who filled their homes with moral and religious values that enabled them to rear exemplary children. Finally, it was imperative that rabbis' wives involve themselves in the life of the congregation by regularly attending services and engaging with congregants. If they have special training or knowledge, rabbis' wives should utilize them to enhance the life of the congregation. Kohut's vision assumed that this role, while rich and satisfying, would always be supportive to that of the rabbi. As her colleague at the symposium Sara Hyamson described it, the rabbi's wife "may be the power behind the throne, but she must be *behind* the throne and not apparent."[6]

Over time, rabbis' wives expanded on these components, taking on more public and activist roles both within and beyond their congregations. Rebecca Brickner was one of these activist rebbetzins.[7] She had a rich Jewish upbringing in Baltimore, Maryland; her parents were deeply involved in Jewish communal life, and they transmitted that love to her. Brickner also gained a rigorous Jewish education in a school whose principal was the young Jewish educator Samson Benderly. Here, Brickner was inspired to become a Jewish educator; she hoped to promote the Hebrew language, Jewish learning, and the Zionist cause among a wide range of individuals of all ages. She subsequently worked and studied with Benderly and others at Columbia University and the Jewish Theological Seminary's Teachers Institute. Despite her gender, Brickner was among the original group of maverick Jewish educators known as the "Benderly boys." So was her future husband, Barnett Brickner, whom she met in their shared classes. Ordained at Hebrew Union College in 1919, Barnett served as rabbi first in Toronto and then for decades at the Fairmount Temple in Cleveland. Rebecca played an active role in these communities, as both formal and informal educator, and though she never earned the title "rabbi," she and Barnett honed a rabbinic partnership that enhanced each other's strengths as leaders.

An inventory of the kind of work Rebecca Brickner did lends insight into the way that rabbis' wives could—despite the role's intrinsic limitations—exercise wide-ranging rabbinic leadership, influencing numerous individuals in a variety of ways. The Brickners entertained often and on a grand scale. On Rosh Hashanah, they hosted an open house attended by some 2,000 congregants. Rebecca trained recent brides in the congregation to serve as hostesses; she and Barnett stood at the door to greet each and every person. As they entered, Rebecca would acknowledge them individually, thus discreetly signaling their names to her husband. Similarly, she engaged in pastoral work, keeping track of those who would benefit from visits or notes and also reminding Barnett to follow up with specific people on his own. Brickner also worked with her husband to start a young people's congregation in the temple, an initiative designed to appeal to couples under the age of thirty-five. Barnett proposed the idea, but she then called all of the prospective participants and invited them to an initial gathering in their home. As spiritual leader of the Temple's Sisterhood, Brickner gave countless invocations, talks, lessons, and speeches to its members on a wide variety of topics in Jewish life. She promoted Jewish education in her temple and community, lectured frequently to a wide variety of Jewish organizations, and was one of the founders of the Cleveland College of Jewish Studies. A passionate Zionist, Brickner took her own sabbatical to Palestine to further her learning and experience life in the Holy Land. She hoped to draw inspiration and intellectual nourishment to better promote the Zionist cause upon her return to the United States. Unexpectedly widowed in 1958, Brickner remained in Cleveland and continued to function as a rebbetzin for the temple community and especially its Sisterhood. She also gradually resumed her involvement in national and international organizations, devoting special attention to the World Union for Progressive Judaism.

Brickner's career exemplifies that of many interwar, activist rebbetzins. Blessed with intensive Jewish upbringings, high levels of secular and Jewish education, and exposure to Zionism—especially through Henrietta Szold and Hadassah—they were determined to strengthen Jewish life both within their husbands' congregations and in the wider Jewish community. Each of these women came to realize that they could most effectively accomplish this goal by leveraging their status as rabbis' wives.

These accomplished rebbetzins then influenced the postwar rebbetzins. This younger generation shouldered with their husbands the burden of ensuring Jewish continuity in the post-Holocaust world. They were determined to work in partnership with their husbands to cultivate flourishing Jewish communities in the United States, the country that now was home to the largest Jewish community in the world. As congregations formed in new areas of settlement and young Jewish families during this baby boom era sought out synagogue affiliation, rebbetzins—like my mother—found numerous opportunities to serve. How fortunate they were to be able to build on precedents established by their predecessors.

Rabbis' wives ran the Sunday school, served as advisors to Sisterhood, led holiday and Jewish life-cycle workshops, taught courses in Hebrew, Bible, Jewish literature, and Jewish life, regularly attended congregants' life-cycle events, and paid condolence calls. Still others made homes kosher, gave book reviews and delivered invocations, started Judaica gift shops, counseled brides, and served often—hosting meetings, welcoming visiting dignitaries, and entertaining congregants for holiday dinners and open houses.

Some reached an even larger audience through leadership in national women's organizations, public speaking, and especially their publications. For example, Sadie Rose Weilerstein, whose husband Rubin Weilerstein served as rabbi of Beth Judah Congregation in Atlantic City, New Jersey, decided to write Jewish children's books to provide entertaining age-appropriate stories with Jewish content for parents to read to their children. Her stories evolved into the wildly popular *K'ton Ton* series, which nourished Jewish families for decades and garnered her literary awards from the Jewish Book Council and Sydney Taylor.[8] Similarly, rabbis' wives Althea Silverman and Betty Greenberg wrote the perennially popular *The Jewish Home Beautiful*, which illustrates how to set a beautiful table for each Jewish holiday. This slim volume made it possible for women to more easily and joyfully introduce Jewish observances into the home for their husbands and children, while at the same time cementing their status as refined middle-class Americans.[9]

Of course, rebbetzins in each generation recognized the challenges and difficulties of their role. They knew that they were in an enviable position, but they also knew how dependent they remained for their status and position not only on their husbands but also on the goodwill of the congregation. Rebbetzins in the postwar era may have felt particularly vulnerable because they were following in the footsteps of accomplished interwar rebbetzins, whose shoes felt impossible to fill. Feeling scrutinized for their every action, they experienced the sting of the congregations' judgment for failing to meet expectations, a critique that may have reinforced their own sense of inadequacy. On balance, however, most rebbetzins at the time concluded that the benefits of the role far outweighed the liabilities.

Though no woman had as yet been ordained in the United States and only a handful had even contemplated the idea, a few rebbetzins at the time did have the opportunity to serve as rabbis when their husbands were ill or traveling. Rebecca Brickner, for example, led services several times when Barnett was away. One rabbi's wife, Paula Herskovitz Ackerman, famously served as rabbi of her husband's congregation for almost two years after his death.[10] As discussed earlier, widowhood was the most common way for women to assume male leadership roles when they assumed their husbands' portfolios, and Ackerman's experience followed that prototype. Within two weeks of her husband's sudden death in 1950, the synagogue board requested that she take over her husband's position. In deciding to accede to this request, Ackerman drew on her traditional Jewish upbringing and synagogue involvement and especially on her decades-long experience as a rabbi's wife. Born in Pensacola, Florida, in 1893, she had married her congregation's rabbi, William Ackerman, in 1919. They moved to Natchez, Mississippi, where their only child, William Jr., was born; then from 1922 until his death in 1950, William served as the rabbi of Temple Beth Israel in Meridian, Mississippi. During these years, Ackerman taught the pre-confirmation class. Active in the temple's Sisterhood in an advisory capacity, she also served as secretary and program chairman. She got involved beyond the congregation through the National Federation of Temple Sisterhoods, where she chaired the National Committee on Religious Schools. A member of the speaker's bureau, she also chaired the Federation's House of Living Judaism fundraising campaign.

In explaining her decision to take on her late husband's role, Ackerman acknowledged that "the only training I've had is experience." She worried about the inadequacy of her Hebrew proficiency and her limitations as a preacher. As a widow living in a parsonage, Ackerman was also painfully aware of her pressing need to secure her living arrangements. Despite her vulnerability and humility, she understood that her rebbetzin role had uniquely prepared her to serve this congregation at this time and that what congregants needed most was her heartfelt sincerity. She also recognized the broader implications of her situation and the path-breaking nature of her decision. By assuming her husband's rabbinate, she demonstrated that women were fully capable of serving as rabbis, illustrating by example that if women could access the learning and training, they—all women, not just rabbis' widows—could effectively serve as rabbis. She believed that if her actions might "plant a seed for the Jewish woman's larger participation—if perhaps it will open a way for woman students to train for congregational leadership then my life would have some meaning." Asked during her tenure as rabbi whether she thought women should be allowed to study for the rabbinate, she replied with an unequivocal yes.

Like Hattie Caraway in the U.S. Senate earlier in the century, Ackerman successfully served her constituency. For almost two years, she led services, delivered sermons, performed pastoral duties, officiated at life-cycle events, and represented the congregation at regional rabbis' meetings. A decade later, Ackerman served as an interim rabbi for six months in her childhood congregation in Pensacola. Ackerman later recalled these experiences fondly but confessed that "it was never my secret wish to be a rabbi. My life was very rich and full and satisfying as a 'rebbetzin' and mother. Sabbath school and Sisterhood—local, state, and national—gave me an outlet for my intense devotion to Judaism." Even in 1986, she expressed skepticism about a woman rabbi unless "she is married to a rabbi. I can see them working in the rabbinate together, but otherwise, I don't know." Thankfully for future generations of aspiring rabbis, Ackerman's actions spoke louder than her words. Though she remained emotionally tied to the gender norms of her era, her achievements as a rabbi laid the groundwork for women's rabbinic leadership by expanding the realm of the possible in American Jewish life.

It took the feminist revolution of the 1960s and 1970s to bring the question of women's ordination to the fore. First, women were encouraged to imagine themselves as doctors, lawyers, politicians—and, yes, clergy—rather than marrying what they wanted to be. Second, second-wave feminism disparaged vicarious careers for women. Third, volunteerism lost its luster, and women were encouraged to expect a salary for their efforts. In this climate, rebbetzins began to doubt the significance of their role, and Jewishly educated and motivated women with a sense of religious calling (including some rabbis' wives) began clamoring for entry into rabbinical schools. Reform and Reconstructionist rabbinical seminaries moved quickly to ordain women, and the Conservative movement began a decade-long process deliberating the issue. In 1972, Ezrat Nashim, a newly formed group of Conservative Jewish activists, issued a call for change that endorsed women's equality in terms of education, participation in religious life, and leadership roles.[11] It stopped short of advocating women's ordination, but by demanding that women be permitted and encouraged to attend rabbinical and cantorial schools, ordination was the implied final goal of this initiative. The group decided to plead its case at the annual Rabbinical Assembly convention. Upon arrival, Ezrat Nashim learned that it had been excluded from the official program. On the spot, the group decided to approach the rebbetzins who had accompanied their husbands to the convention. Ezrat Nashim was smart to do so—rebbetzins knew better than anyone how important women's religious participation was to the flourishing of Jewish life—and the activists encountered a wellspring of support among them. Though not all rebbetzins supported the notion of women's ordination, rabbis' wives needed no convincing that women were capable of assuming religious roles reserved for men and that they could serve as first-rate leaders.[12]

In 1985, the Jewish Theological Seminary ordained its first woman, Amy Eilberg, and the focus of the ordination struggle shifted to the Orthodox world. Here, too, progress in this arena is directly attributable to the efforts of a rebbetzin. Noted author and lecturer and founding president of the Jewish Orthodox Feminist Alliance (1997), Blu Greenberg is often described as the "spiritual mother of Orthodox feminism." Daring the Orthodox establishment to respond to the feminist challenge, she asserted that "where there's been a rabbinic will, there's been a *halakhic* way."

Like Brickner and many other rebbetzins, Greenberg too had an intensive Jewish upbringing and education. Her husband Irving (Yitz) Greenberg became a prominent Orthodox rabbi, scholar, and founder of CLAL—The National Jewish Center for Learning and Leadership. When Yitz served as rabbi of the Riverdale Jewish Center (1965–1972), Blu functioned as a traditional rebbetzin, rearing five children, hosting guests constantly, going to every shiva house, paying many hospital visits, and attending synagogue, dinners, and bar mitzvah receptions.

Her evolution into Jewish feminist activism stemmed directly from her rebbetzin status. The leaders planning the 1973 First National Jewish Women's Conference visited the Greenberg home with the intention of persuading Yitz to deliver the keynote address. But they were so taken with Blu's articulate views that they decided to invite *her* to deliver the address. Being in the right place at the right time—a frequent benefit of the rebbetzin position—led to a long, fruitful, and enormously impactful career through writing, public speaking, advocacy, and organizational leadership.

Greenberg presciently predicted that there would be Orthodox women rabbis in her lifetime. A generation later, she witnessed the realization of her forecast when Rabbi Avi Weiss ordained Sara Hurwitz in 2009. Upon ordination, Rabba Sara Hurwitz then opened Yeshivat Maharat, the first yeshiva to ordain women as Orthodox Jewish clergy. Since that time, dozens of Orthodox women have earned ordination and assumed rabbinic positions throughout the world.

Interestingly, the question of what to call female Orthodox rabbis reinforces the direct link between rebbetzins and women rabbis. Early advocates for women's ordination proposed the term "rabbanit," the Hebrew equivalent of rebbetzin, as the appropriate term for a woman rabbi. Why wouldn't they? The term "rabbanit" was up to this point the only available Hebrew word that signaled female learning, piety, and honor. Indeed, in Israel, the first Orthodox synagogue to hire a female rabbi refers to her by this title.[13] "Rabbanit" was rejected in the United States in favor of such titles as "maharat" (a Hebrew acronym for a female leader of Jewish law, spirituality, and Torah) or "rabba" (a feminine form of the Hebrew word for rabbi), but in 2015, Lila Kagedan became the first Orthodox rabbi to take the title "rabbi," surely an acknowledgment that, in the United States at least, only this title would gain her recognition and status equal to that of a male rabbi.[14]

So what has become of the rebbetzin role in the contemporary era? Has this position simply served as a way station in the long arc of women's religious leadership advancement? Is the role approaching obsolescence in an era when women can become rabbis, many rabbis' wives are employed outside of the home, and many rebbetzins choose to limit their involvement in their husbands' synagogues? The uniqueness of the role is threatened in other ways as well. Rabbinic spouses today are now men as well as women, some rabbinic marriages are same-sex, and some rabbinic couples are two rabbis married to each other. While many male spouses report both congregational and self-imposed expectations to support and assist their rabbi spouses, none experience the same level of expectation historically experienced by rabbis' wives, and this may, in turn, subconsciously serve to lower the expectations for contemporary rebbetzins as well.[15] Congregations have adjusted their expectations accordingly. In the contemporary period, the vacuum left by rabbis' wives who have taken on other professional or volunteer roles has been filled by full-time professionals who perform numerous functions once filled by rebbetzins, including assistant rabbis, social workers, education directors, and executive directors. Some rabbis' wives may, in fact, fill these paid professional positions, but they do so because of their own earned credentials, not because of their rebbetzin positions, and they are compensated accordingly.

And yet, the rebbetzin role continues to resonate in different ways. Among ultra-Orthodox and Hasidic groups, rebbetzins continue to perform robust duties in the community. Lubavitcher women who feel called to serve the Jewish people often marry men who want to be emissaries. Then they, just like the pioneering rabbinic couples of the mid-twentieth century, serve together, bringing Judaism to college campuses and remote Jewish areas around the world. This model has a more recent iteration among the Orthodox in the Jewish Learning Initiative on Campus (JLIC), a collaborative effort of the Orthodox Union and Hillel, which places rabbinic couples on college campuses to serve as Torah educators. Like rabbinic couples of earlier generations, they work as a team to bring Jewish life and learning to their constituents, and like the rabbinic couples of prior generations, the man is the clergy and the wife an essential partner. But in a nod to contemporary realities and sensibilities, both the male rabbi and the female spouse must be highly educated Jewishly and both draw a salary.[16]

The traditional rebbetzin role has even been acknowledged of late in the American legal system. In 2015, Esther Fischer and Sarah Goldblatt, wives employed with their rabbi husbands by the Portland (Oregon) Community Kollel, were subpoenaed in a divorce trial. Asked to disclose personal and confidential information that they had acquired from the wife in the case, the women refused, citing clergy-client privilege. The opposing counsel objected, noting that the Kollel wives' rebbetzin titles were only honorific, and thus the rebbetzins were simply friends of the wife in question. The judge ruled in favor of the rebbetzins, de facto acknowledging their special status.[17]

Moreover, even when rebbetzins work outside the home, do not embrace the role as a career, and devote less time and energy to it, they nonetheless impact Jewish lives because of their position as rabbis' wives. I grew to appreciate that in a very personal way at the book party that my children hosted for me when *The Rabbi's Wife*, the book that marked the culmination of this research, was published in 2006. One of the attendees was a young mom whom I had known when she was young and with whom I had since reconnected. When we first met, she was the teenage daughter of congregants in my husband's congregation. Very smart, funny, warm, and energetic, she became a favorite babysitter of my children and a frequent presence in our home. One winter after she had left for college, I bumped into her in the produce section of the local supermarket. We began chatting about her experiences, and she eagerly shared that she had just attended a summer-long intensive Jewish program and had been especially enamored of the opportunity to study full-time and completely experience Shabbat. Excited for her, I also realized she was in need of Jewish mentorship and guidance to help her process what she had learned. It saddened me that her intellectual and religious growth as a Jew had not kept pace with her secular learning, leaving her without the tools to evaluate for herself what she was experiencing and how she might incorporate it into her life. I invited her to come over that evening to my home to continue the conversation with me and my husband. When she arrived, we began a wide-ranging discussion on Jewish life, learning, and identity. My husband felt frustrated knowing she would be returning to school and that there would be no opportunity in the short run for a face-to-face follow-up conversation. Unbeknownst to me, he decided to send her a package at school containing the three-volume set of *The Jewish Catalogue*, which he thought would appeal to her intellect and passion for Judaism, provide her with the tools for further learning, and encourage her to find her own path to Jewish adulthood.[18] Years later, when she and I reconnected as members of the same synagogue, she reflected that the books my late husband sent her had proved life-altering, for they signaled that he had understood, even before she did, that a path of egalitarian, participatory Judaism would likely be the truest path for her. But the story doesn't end here, for when we discussed the publication of my book on rabbis' wives, she emphatically reminded me that though the experience of reconnecting with my husband, her childhood rabbi, had been transformative, *I* had been the catalyst by initiating a conversation in the supermarket and insisting that she accept my invitation to come over to the house.

What I take away from this experience and that of many rabbis' wives today is manifold. First, there continues to be power in couplehood, for a rabbinic couple provides a sense of family—something important to Jews of all stripes, including empty nesters looking for a family connection now that their own children no longer live at home, young couples seeking to create Jewish families of their own, college students living away from their parents for the first time, older adults who miss the warm embrace of the family they once had, or disaffected twentysomethings looking for community. Many appreciate the opportunity to experience Jewish life not just with a rabbi—male or female—but within the embrace of a clergy couple. And in the contemporary world, Jews benefit from this whether the couple is heteronormative or not, whether the spouse is male or female. As our notions of what constitutes a family continue to evolve, I suspect that the impact of new kinds of rabbinic families will progress accordingly. At the same time, individuals attracted to nostalgic notions of traditional Judaism and family life will continue to be attracted to and gain comfort from a heteronormative model.

Second, the enduring power of the rebbetzin role lies in the intangible, hidden job description of rabbinic leadership. When a spouse hosts, teaches, models Jewish living, offers comfort and support, and joyously shares Jewish holidays and rituals, this person enhances the partner's rabbinate immeasurably. To the extent that prevailing gender norms continue to privilege such behavior in women, rabbis' wives will continue to have an outsized opportunity to play crucial roles in enriching their spouses' rabbinates. In this way, then, despite the presence of inspiring, effective, charismatic women rabbis, the rebbetzin will continue to exert influence in the Jewish world. Assuming such norms evolve, it seems likely that male spouses may come to similarly play an increasingly important role, though without the weight of historical expectations, I suspect that male spouses will never achieve parity in this realm.

Thus, in addition to their monumental contributions to the growth of Jewish religious life in America and the evolution of female religious leadership, rebbetzins presaged the future. They paved the way not only for women rabbis but also for contemporary rabbis' wives—and to a lesser extent male spouses—who continue, albeit it in different ways, to enrich the Jewish world immeasurably.

NOTES

1. Michael Barbaro, "Did Hillary Clinton Have to Be First?," *The Run-Up* (podcast), *New York Times*, September 9, 2016,
http://www.nytimes.com/2016/09/09/podcasts/did-hillary-clinton-have-to-be-first.html?_r=0.

2. So common was this phenomenon that it became known as the "widow's mandate." Caraway served in the Senate for fourteen years. "Caraway, Hattie Wyatt," History, Art, and Archives, United States House of Representatives, accessed December 25, 2016, http://history.house.gov/People/Listing/C/CARAWAY,-Hattie-Wyatt-(C000138)/.

3. Hana Papanek, "Men, Women, and Work: Reflections on the Two-Person Career," *American Journal of Sociology* 78 (January 1973): 852–72; Arlie Hochschild, "The Role of the Ambassador's Wife: An Exploratory Study," *Journal of Marriage and Family* 31 (February 1969): 73–74; and Janet Finch, *Married to the Job: Wives' Incorporation in Men's Work* (Boston: George Allen & Unwin, 1983), 7, 101.

4. For more on the Eastern European rebbetzin, see Shuly Rubin Schwartz, *The Rabbi's Wife: The Rebbetzin in American Jewish Life* (New York: New York University Press, 2016), 8–13.

5. For more on the history of the role of the American minister's wife, see Schwartz, *The Rabbi's Wife*, 13–16.

6. Rebekah Kohut, "The Wife of the Rabbi," in *Problems of the Jewish Ministry* (New York: New York Board of Jewish Ministers, 1927), 210–17; and Mrs. Moses Hyamson, "The Rabbi's Wife," *Jewish Forum* 8 (December 1925): 583–85.

7. For citations and more detailed information on Rebecca Brickner, see Shuly Rubin Schwartz, "Rebecca Aaronson Brickner: Preacher, Teacher and Rebbetzin in Israel," *American Jewish Archives* 54 (2002): 64–83; and Schwartz, *The Rabbi's Wife*, 101–13.

8. Weilerstein's books include *The Adventures of K'ton Ton, K'ton Ton in the Circus, K'ton Ton in Israel, K'ton Ton on an Island in the Sea,* and *K'ton Ton's Yom Kippur Kitten.*

9. Morris Silverman served as rabbi of Emanuel Synagogue in Hartford, Connecticut, from 1923 to 1961. Simon Greenberg served as rabbi of Har Zion Temple, Philadelphia, Pennsylvania, from 1925 to 1946, when he left to assume the position of provost at the Jewish Theological Seminary. Betty D. Greenberg and Althea O. Silverman, *The Jewish Home Beautiful* (New York: Harper & Row, 1967).

10. Information on Ackerman in this and the following paragraphs is drawn from Shuly Rubin Schwartz, "Paula Ackerman: From Rebbetzin to Rabbi," *American Jewish Archives* 59 (2007): 99–206; and Schwartz, *The Rabbi's Wife*, 160–64.

11. "Ezrat Nashim's 'Jewish Women Call for Change,' March 14, 1972," Jewish Women's Archive, accessed January 16, 2017, https://jwa.org/media/jewish-women-call-for-change .

12. Alan Silverstein, "The Evolution of Ezrat Nashim," *Conservative Judaism* 30 (Fall 1975): 41–51; and Pamela S. Nadell, *Women Who Would Be Rabbis: A History of Women's Ordination, 1889–1985* (Boston: Beacon Press, 1998), 170–71.

13. Julie Wiener, "Orthodox Synagogue Hires Female 'Rabbinit' in First for Israel," *Forward*, August 23, 2016, http://forward.com/sisterhood/348239/orthodox-synagogue-hires-female-rabbanit-in-first-for-israel/.

14. "Lila Kagedan," Jewish Women's Archive, accessed January 16, 2017, https://jwa.org/people/kagedan-lila .

15. For more on the role of the male spouse, see Schwartz, *The Rabbi's Wife*, 211–12; and Dan Pine, "Meet the Rebbetzers: Husbands of Female Rabbis Find the Role Challenging, Fun," *J. The Jewish News of Northern California*, November 24, 2011, http://www.jweekly.com/article/full/63591/meet-the-rebbetzers-husbands-of-female-rabbis-find-the-role-challenging-fun/.

16. OU-JLIC, accessed January 16, 2017, https://oujlic.org/category/about_jlic/ .

17. Debbie Maimon, "Oregon Court Scrutinizes Rebbetzin's Role in Trailblazing Case," *Yated Ne'eman*, September 24, 2015, https://yated.com/oregon-court-scrutinizes-rebbetzinaes-role-in-trailblazing-case/.

18. *The First Jewish Catalog: A Do-It-Yourself Kit*, ed. Richard Siegel, Michael Strassfeld, and Sharon Strassfeld (Philadelphia: Jewish Publication Society, 1973); *The Second Jewish Catalog: Sources and Resources*, ed. Sharon Strassfeld and Michael Strassfeld (Philadelphia: Jewish Publication Society, 1976); and *The Third Jewish Catalog: Creating Community*, ed. Sharon Strassfeld and Michael Strassfeld (Philadelphia: Jewish Publication Society, 1980).

BIBLIOGRAPHY

Barbaro, Michael, "Did Hillary Clinton Have to Be First?," *The Run-Up* (podcast), *New York Times*, September 9, 2016.

Finch, Janet, *Married to the Job: Wives' Incorporation in Men's Work* (Boston: George Allen & Unwin, 1983).

Greenberg, Betty D., and Silverman, Althea O., *The Jewish Home Beautiful* (New York: Harper & Row, 1967).

Hochschild, Arlie, "The Role of the Ambassador's Wife: An Exploratory Study," *Journal of Marriage and Family* 31 (February 1969): 73–74.

Hyamson, Moses, "The Rabbi's Wife," *Jewish Forum* 8 (December 1925): 583–85.

Kohut, Rebekah, "The Wife of the Rabbi," in *Problems of the Jewish Ministry* (New York: New York Board of Jewish Ministers, 1927), 210–17.

Maimon, Debbie, "Oregon Court Scrutinizes Rebbetzin's Role in Trailblazing Case," *Yated Ne'eman*, September 24, 2015, https://yated.com/oregon-court-scrutinizes-rebbetzinaes-role-in-trailblazing-case/ .

Nadell, Pamela S., *Women Who Would Be Rabbis: A History of Women's Ordination, 1889–1985* (Boston: Beacon Press, 1998).

Papanek, Hana, "Men, Women, and Work: Reflections on the Two-Person Career," *American Journal of Sociology* 78 (January 1973): 852–72.

Pine, Dan, "Meet the Rebbetzers: Husbands of Female Rabbis Find the Role Challenging, Fun," *J. The Jewish News of Northern California*, November 24, 2011, http://www.jweekly.com/article/full/63591/meet-the-rebbetzers-husbands-of-female-rabbis-find-the-role-challenging-fun/.

Schwartz, Shuly Rubin, *The Rabbi's Wife: The Rebbetzin in American Jewish Life* (New York: New York University Press, 2016).

Schwartz, Shuly Rubin, "Paula Ackerman: From Rebbetzin to Rabbi," *American Jewish Archives* 59 (2007): 99–206.

Schwartz, Shuly Rubin, "Rebecca Aaronson Brickner: Preacher, Teacher and Rebbetzin in Israel," *American Jewish Archives* 54 (2002): 64–83.

Siegel, Richard, et al. (eds.), *The First Jewish Catalog: A Do-It-Yourself Kit*, (Philadelphia: Jewish Publication Society, 1973).

Silverstein, Alan, "The Evolution of Ezrat Nashim," *Conservative Judaism* 30 (Fall 1975): 41–51.

Strassfeld, Sharon, and Strassfeld, Michael (eds.), *The Second Jewish Catalog: Sources and Resources*, (Philadelphia: Jewish Publication Society, 1976).

Strassfeld, Sharon, and Strassfeld, Michael (eds.), *The Third Jewish Catalog: Creating Community* (Philadelphia: Jewish Publication Society, 1980).

Weilerstein, Sadie Rose, *K'ton Ton's Yom Kippur Kitten* (Philadelphia: Jewish Publication Society of America, 1995).

Weilerstein, Sadie Rose, *K'ton Ton in Israel* (Baltimore: Judy Chernak Productions, 1984).

Weilerstein, Sadie Rose, *K'ton Ton in the Circus* (Philadelphia: Jewish Publication Society of America, 1981).

Weilerstein, Sadie Rose, *K'ton Ton on an Island in the Sea* (Philadelphia: Jewish Publication Society of America, 1976).

Weilerstein, Sadie Rose, *The Adventures of K'ton Ton* (New York: National Women's League of the United Synagoge, 1956).

Wiener, Julie, "Orthodox Synagogue Hires Female 'Rabbinit' in First for Israel," *Forward*, August 23, 2016, http://forward.com/sisterhood/348239/orthodox-synagogue-hires-female-rabbanit-in-first-for-israel/.

Chapter Eleven

Looking Back

Religion as Container for Memory and Tradition

Sandy Eisenberg Sasso

1. WHAT TO DO WITH TRADITION: ACCEPTANCE OF REJECTION

In the Bible, Serach bat Asher is mentioned twice over a span of centuries. She is said to be among those who went down to Egypt (Genesis 46:17) and to have come out of Egypt (Numbers 26:46). Some even suggest that she was still alive at the time of King David and that she never died, having entered the Garden of Eden alive. While many women characters in the Bible have stories without names, such as Lot's and Noah's wives, Pharaoh's and Jephtah's daughters, Serach is a unique example of a woman's name without a story. The rabbinic interpretive tradition offers a fascinating narrative of her as a woman who told Jacob that his son Joseph was still alive (Sefer ha-Yashar, Vayigash, chap. 14), who recognized Moses as the redeemer of Israel, who showed Moses where the bones of Joseph were buried (Genesis Rabbah 94:9), and who saved her city from destruction (Ecclesiastes Rabba 9:18:2).

An expositor of Torah (Pesikta de-Rav Kahana 11:13), Serach was the first keeper of memory whose wisdom enabled the redemption of the people of Israel. Yet for centuries, Jewish memory has been male memory. Even the word for memory in Hebrew is *zicharon*, the root of which is the same as the word for male—*zachar*. While the wide effort of women to confront the inadequacy of male memory has appeared as something altogether new in the late 1960s and early 1970s, the yearning to be able to tell her story was evident much earlier in both Eastern European and Sephardic folklore.

A Yiddish folktale tells of a time when women complained that everything in the world belonged to men, including Torah. They decided they would build a tower of women, one on top of the other, until one woman could pull herself into heaven to present their case. They choose Skotsl to be that woman. All went well until the woman at the bottom of the tower could no longer bear the weight of the others. The tower collapsed and Skotsl disappeared. There was no one to talk to God. According to custom, from that time on, whenever someone came into a house, women called out, "Skotsl Kumt, Here comes Skotsl," in the hope that someday she would really arrive and change things.[1]

A similar Turkish folktale tells of how women asked King Solomon why men were allowed to marry more than one woman and women could only marry one man. Solomon did not know the answer, so he wrote the question on a piece of parchment and tied it to the leg of a bird. He told the women that the bird was a messenger to God and would return with the answer. Unfortunately, the bird did not return and women are still waiting. Whenever a bird would stand at a window, it became customary for women to say, "Haberes Buenos–Good News" in hoping that they would finally have an answer.[2]

In other words, women recognized that the traditional Jewish containers of memory were ill-suited to hold their spiritual yearnings. Apologetics sought to simply polish the container without changing it. It was often argued that women had an equal but different role than men within Judaism. Ignoring the patriarchal textual container, apologists highlighted biblical women like Deborah, Ruth, and Esther as examples of women's power.

Some women sought to discard the container altogether, claiming that religion had been so damaged by patriarchy that it was an irredeemable vessel. Theology, liturgical language, ritual, scriptural text, and interpretation were intrinsically male. The secular world offered greater opportunity for change. Despairing of always being the "other," they rejected the container as a whole.

One of the premiere magazines of the 1970s feminist movement was *Ms*. Its editors and contributors were predominately Jewish women, but never once did they speak to the concerns of women within religious tradition. Thinking that the intrinsic nature of religion was conservative, slow to change, they decided to ignore it altogether.[3]

2. A COMPROMISE: RECONSTRUCTING MEMORY

There were women who were unwilling to completely reject Jewish religion and at the same time were loath to offer excuses for its evident masculine perspective. They began to claim Judaism for themselves and reconstruct it. In 1972, the author was a third-year rabbinical student at the Reconstructionist Rabbinical College. In her presentation to the American Jewish Committee in May 1972, she called on Jews to

> relinquish their rationalization and their blind apologetics to see clearly the status assigned to Jewish women through history. However, recognition is only the first step. The second needs to be constructive. It must not be a rash judgment of Jewish history [. . .] It must be directed towards creating within Jewish life a feminine counterpart to a heavily masculine based perspective. This creation must necessarily be founded on knowledge and commitment to Jewish life. . . . Judaism will not suffer from such growth; it will be enriched by it.[4]

As feminist author Rachel Adler indicated, the ultimate goal was not judgment but restoration. She imagined stories as "continuous performances unbounded by time."[5] Such imagination started a revolution.

Memory is never static; it shapes us and is shaped by us. What we choose to recall and what to forget forms our present and our future. Women who sought a bridge between their Judaism and their feminism began to take control of Jewish memory; assuming a power that had been reserved only for men. As their relationship to the past was transformed, they created meaningful memories.[6]

Alice Ostriker, in the introduction to her 1997 poetic revisioning of biblical texts, expressed both her deep sense of Jewish identity and her marginality as a Jewish woman. She insisted that we have "to enter the tents/texts, invade the sanctuary, uncover the father's nakedness. We have to do it, believe it or not, because we love him."[7] It is out of our love of Judaism that women refused to be eavesdroppers like the matriarch, Sarah, and chose to enter the "tent" and become part of the conversation.

In the beginning, there were few partners for this conversation. When the first women to become rabbis in the United States started rabbinical seminary in the late 1960s and early 1970s, the Jewish community was not addressing feminism and the feminist community was not engaging with Judaism. There were no models for what it meant to be a woman rabbi or a woman reading Torah. One way across that wide chasm was women's interpretation of biblical text.

Feminist theologian Judith Plaskow writes in her groundbreaking book, *Standing Again at Sinai*:

> I am not a Jew in the synagogue and a feminist in the world. I am a Jewish feminist and a feminist Jew in every moment of my life. I have increasingly come to realize that in setting up Judaism and feminism as conflicting ideologies and communities, I was handing over to a supposedly monolithic Jewish tradition the power and the right to define Judaism for the past and for the future. [. . .] Like the wicked child of the Passover Seder, I was handing over Judaism to *them*, denying my own power as a Jew to help shape what Judaism will become.[8]

Reading Torah through the eyes of women's experience, women began to raise questions of the text. It is not that those questions had never been answered before; it is that they had never been asked. Plaskow highlighted one of the most troublesome verses in the Torah. As Israel is about to receive the Ten Commandments, Moses warned, "Be ready for the third day; do not go near a woman." (Exodus 19:15) The Exodus report of revelation was a male account. We did not know what women saw, heard, or felt.

To accept our absence from Sinai would be to allow the male text to define us and our connection to Judaism. To stand on the ground of our experience, on the other hand, to start with the certainty of our membership in our own people is to be forced to re-member and recreate its history to reshape Torah.[9]

Shortly after the publication of Plaskow's book, Merle Feld captured that sense of exclusion in her poem, *We All Stood Together*. She remarked on how women at Sinai could not write down their experience because they were always holding a baby, their own or someone else's. Men had a record of what they heard. She wrote what would happen if women remembered what they heard:

> we could recreate holy time
> sparks flying.[10]

Aviva Zornberg noted the omission of women from the Exodus narrative, except in regard to birth. While women were essentially absent, she demonstrated that in many midrashic accounts there is an alternative women's history that offers a counter narrative.[11]

Zornberg's in-depth study of midrash about women opened up a rich resource of material which served as a means to recall the past in new ways. But re-membering is more than recalling. Re-membering required Jewish women to own the past by becoming the narrators of the story, members of the people who told sacred stories. Stories mirror the perspective of their tellers, not only reflecting what was, but also imagining what could be.

Story conveys the moral heft and heat that differentiates God as a living presence from the bodiless, passionless abstraction of the philosophers: A story is a body for God.[12]

3. THE DIFFERENCE BETWEEN RELIGION AND SPIRITUALITY

Story conveys the power of the spiritual encounter of being in the presence of the divine, the sacred. After story comes religion, which provides the ritual, celebration, and liturgy necessary to contain that life of the spirit. Religion is the gravity that anchors spirit to earth, translating the vision of the soul into the life of the community.

When Moses ascended Mt. Sinai, he had a spiritual experience. For forty days and forty nights he lived in the constant presence of the Divine. It was an encounter of indescribable magnitude. The Biblical text tells us that, when Moses descended from the mountain, his face glowed. The container for Moses' vision was the Ten Commandments, the covenantal relationship between a people and God. Moses's forty days and nights on Sinai was a spiritual encounter; the Decalogue was the embodiment of that spirit; in other words, religion.

In the best of all possible worlds, spirituality and religion are handmaidens. The soul's most profound experiences with a presence greater than the self are given form and articulation through liturgy, ritual, and moral law. Religious forms, in turn, remain constantly open to the renewal of sacred moments. Through new midrash, women sought to infuse religion with their spiritual experience, their own divine encounters. Those occurrences often happened in places other than mountains.

For women seekers, religion was facing the danger of being a container without a woman's soul. Women sought to ignite the kindling of religious tradition with the spark of feminism. They knew that spirit without a body was bound to evaporate. But they also knew that a spark without kindling dies. Sinai without the Ten Commandments is just another mountain.

If spirituality, at its best, lifted them up, religion, at its best, kept them rooted. If women's spirituality was what happened in consciousness-raising groups, religion was what happened with others in the broader Jewish community.

If religion were to be compelling to this new generation, it needed to be attuned to those spiritual seekers and their pilgrimage. If women's spirituality were to make a contribution to the next generation of travelers, it needed grounding, a structure to hold it gently and translate it into celebration and ritual. Women's spirituality sought to keep religion from absolutism, and to remember that the breath of God blows through each and every human soul.

4. WOMEN AS INTERPRETERS OF TORAH

Even before Plaskow's powerful articulation of the problem and Feld's poem, women were beginning to see themselves as both receivers of Torah and also narrators of it. They recognized themselves not only as descendants, but also the spiritual ancestors of the next generation. In accepting their role as forbearers of the future, they began to have a conversation with the sacred narrative, retelling old stories and creating new ones. They became interpreters of Torah—writing commentary, creating, like the ancient rabbis, new Midrash. Biblical women were given voices, names, and stories. Using the rabbinic interpretive process, Jewish women wove together classic midrash with their imaginations and experiences. They recovered rabbinic commentary and midrash about women that was largely unknown; they brought attention to what was missing, and they read the spaces between the lines.[13]

Using the image in the piyyut for Yom Kippur, based on verses from Jeremiah 18, women's midrash saw the sacred text like "clay in the hand of the potter."[14] Only now they, and the divine through them, were the potters who sought to expand, contract and thereby reshape the container. The process was not a rejection of the covenant but in keeping with the divine covenant that celebrated human interpretation. The creation of old/new stories allowed women re-member themselves into Torah by translating the silences. Such midrash making "is an act of prayer because it is a gift to the sacred: It is a way of offering back to the Torah the fruits of our encounter with it."[15]

5. THE LILITH LEGEND

One of the first formal expressions of this new way of understanding Torah came in 1972 when Plaskow wrote an article entitled "The Coming of Lilith: Toward a Feminist Theology."[16] The eleventh-century legend of Lilith contained in *The Alphabet of Ben Sira* attempted to reconcile the two accounts of creation in Genesis. In Genesis 1, woman was created equal to Adam from the same dust of the earth. In chapter 2, the first woman, Eve, was created from Adam's rib. Eve was viewed as Adam's subordinate. Medieval legend called the woman of Genesis 1, Lilith, who in wishing to be equal to Adam became the disobedient night demon who threatened grown men and male children. But in the hands of many a feminist midrashist, she became a symbol of independence and hope. The Jewish feminist magazine created in 1976 was named *Lilith*.

The popularity of Lilith among early Jewish feminists expressed itself in a proliferation of midrashim. The 1998 collection, *Which Lilith: Feminist Writers Re-create the World's First Woman*, included the poetry and writings of numerous women authors, as women sought to understand themselves in the light of this powerful, sexually alluring, and autonomous archetype.[17]

The complaint, sometimes angry, could be seen in Alice Ostriker's "The Lilith Poems:"

> ... I take in your laundry, suckle your young
> ... In this place you name paradise, while you
> Wear amulets and cast spells
> Against me in your weakness.[18]

Enid Dame's "Lilith" was protest against both Adam and the male god he imagined.

> [...]
> sometimes
> I cry in the bathroom
> remembering Eden
> and the man and the god
> I couldn't live with[19]

Rachel Adler understood the fear and reluctance that some in the Jewish community had in retelling sacred legends and narratives in ways that reflected changing understandings of sexuality and women.

Perhaps we fear that if we try to read them contextually, we will not be able to redeem them as sacred text. If so, we have forgotten that what makes

Torah sacred is not that it has one fixed eternal meaning, but that its meanings are inexhaustible. We have forgotten how to wander in the company of the sacred, without fearing that, because we do not know where we are heading, we will be lost.[20]

6. MIRIAM AS THE NEW ARCHETYPE

Artist and writer Rivka Walton noted that in time, Jewish feminism turned from the Lilith legend to Miriam. Lilith was the one who had been kicked out of Eden for wanting equality. Jewish women felt that they too were on the outside and experienced resistance to their inclusion. In 1972, I received a letter responding to an article in the *New York Times* that spoke of my studies for the rabbinate. The typed note concluded: "I usually sign my letters by wishing success, but in your case, I will refrain. I hope you don't make it [into the rabbinate] for your sake, my sake and Judaism's sake."[21]

But, as more and more women entered rabbinical seminaries and became interpreters of Torah, they began to see themselves not as outsiders clamoring for equal access but as Jewish citizens reconstructing tradition as equal participants and making it home. They turned to the character of Miriam. She was a more congenial figure than Lilith. Miriam was a powerful woman leader, intrinsic to the community, who both nurtured others and protested injustice.[22]

The recovering and creating of midrashim on Miriam taught Jewish women how to celebrate. Miriam's story was told in a song composed in 1988 by popular singer and songwriter Debbie Friedman. The music and lyrics became a feature of Passover seders as did a special cup set aside for Miriam. As the seder ritual required that a cup be set aside for Elijah, representing the promise of and hope for future redemption, Miriam's cup, filled with water, came to symbolize what sustains us as we work toward redemption. Ritual artists began to create Miriam's cups and also tambourines. Miriam was the woman who was invoked in prayers for healing. As Miriam's well was said to accompany the Israelites in the wilderness, so the image of her well became a source of strength for the contemporary Jewish community thirsting for full inclusion and participation in Jewish life.

As Rabbi Lynn Gottlieb in her book, *She Who Dwells Within: A Feminist Vision of a Renewed Judaism* (1995) sought to break free of the language that saw God as masculine and women as other by suggesting that we image the divine through the language of the *Shechina*, the One Who Dwells Within.

Listening to that presence, Gottlieb addressed the need for reshaping the container by telling new stories about our tribal matriarchs, Sarah, Rebekah, Rachel, and Leah and the mothers of the freedom generation, Yocheved, Shifra, and Puah and especially Miriam. In poetic verse she offered a recast container infused with a woman soul.

> When Miriam died,
> She bequeathed her power to find water
> to the women who sang with her at the sea. [23]

7. REENVISIONING GOD, ISRAEL, AND TORAH

Women's midrashim served as ways of reenvisioning what was meant by Israel, God, and Torah. The people of Israel were once understood as the sons of Jacob who formed the twelve tribes. In new midrash, women blessed Dinah, Jacob's daughter, and all the other women whose stories had not fully been told. Those midrashim also expanded the theological conversation, offering images of God that reflect partnership, intimacy, and mutuality. Women were viewed as the embodiment of Torah. Inspired by the verse in the Talmud which teaches that the fetus learns the entire Torah while still in the womb, artist Jacqueline Nicholl created a Torah scroll cover in the shape of a corset based on a pregnant women's body shape. In this striking piece of art, a woman's body becomes a place of revelation. [24]

It is this listening to voices that had long been silenced that the container of Torah began to change shape, to throb with a woman's pulse, move with a woman's rhythm, and inhale and exhale with a woman's breath. When Professor Lori Lefkovitz imagined these new voices she wrote:

> As for voices I think not of the articulate voice of patriarchal order and reason, but woman's more anarchic voices, metaphorically represented in Hebrew Scriptures but Miriam's singing, Hannah's unintelligible whispering that was confused for drunkenness, the ambiguous screams of childbirth and the laughter of Sarah. [25]

In engaging with biblical narrative, women wandered in the company of the sacred, gave texture to the text, and reimagined it in ways that addressed the emerging concerns of feminism. Adler writes about the question she, as a Jewish feminist, brought to Torah.

What is God telling us through the story? What are we telling God through the story? Having wrestled the story for a blessing, what meanings have we wrested from it? How does the story shape our collective memory as a people? What demands does it make upon us that we must integrate into the way we live our lives? How will we transmit the story?[26]

8. LOT'S WIFE

A powerful example of women struggling with the sacred story and how to transmit it is women's retelling of the story of Lot's wife. The Genesis account tells of Lot and his family escaping the impending destruction of Sodom and Gomorrah. They are told to flee in order to be saved. There is only one requirement: do not look back. As the story goes, Lot's wife does not follow God's commands and turns to see the destruction visited upon Sodom and Gomorrah. She is turned into a pillar of salt. Traveling in the Negev, one can still see her standing there, a clear and ever-present symbol of women's disobedience. It is even possible to buy a postcard with a pillar of salt on one side. The words on the back of the card read: "Lot's Wife."

Classical midrash explained that Lot's wife became a pillar of salt as punishment because she sinned with salt. In Genesis Rabbah, R. Isaac said:

> She sinned through salt. On the night that the angels visited Lot, Lot said to his wife, 'Give these guests a bit of salt.' But she replied, '[Besides entertaining guests], is it your wish to introduce into Sodom another vile custom [that of seasoning their food]?' What did she do? She went around among all her neighbors, saying to each one, 'Give me salt. We have guests,' intending thereby to have the townspeople become aware of the presence of guests in her home [and penalize Lot for it]. Hence, she herself became a pillar of salt. (Genesis Rabbah 51:5)

A woman without a name becomes an image of foolish woman's inability to follow directions and a symbol of disobedience. But one midrash turns the story on its head. It suggests that Lot's wife did not turn out of waywardness but rather out of compassion for her daughters (Tanhuma, Vayera 8, Nachmanides). An eighth-century midrash from Pirkei d'Rabbi Eliezer states: The angels said to Lot and his family, "Do not look behind you since the Divine Presence of the Holy One, blessed be He, has descended to rain brimstone and fire upon Sodom and Gomorrah." In this midrash, what Lot's wife sees is the *Shechina*, the presence of God.

Women's midrash imagined the thunder of the cataclysm loud in a mother's ears as she turned to ensure the safety of her own daughters who were behind her. Women, in retelling the narrative, went a step beyond the rabbinic imagination. In her poem, *Lot's Wife*, Tova Beck-Friedman, raised question why a woman must always obey and not be allowed to look back and into her own soul.27

Other women using the name given to her in rabbinic literature, Idit, spoke of her as unique witness (Tanhuma, Vayera 8; the Hebrew root of her name means witness). In one such retelling, Idit looked back and saw her daughters following her as well as those other children who remained in the cities. Realizing that Lot had refused to turn to check on the well-being of his children, Idit was no longer able to follow him without question. Her turning (*teshuvah*) was also a question, like Abraham's to God.28

What would it mean to retell this narrative in a way that spoke of Idit's turning to God, mirroring?

Abraham's questioning the divine decision to destroy Sodom and Gomorrah? Might the God of this midrash listen to Idit and respond, "I will not destroy the cities, but perchance they will destroy themselves." In such a midrash, disobedience, more accurately called "challenge," would be honored and deemed a worthy human act.

When Idit saw how humanity could destroy itself, she wept. The pillar of salt was her tears. A closer reading of the biblical text revealed that Lot's wife was never turned into a pillar of salt; she became one. No one saw with Idit's eyes the wrath of God poured upon Sodom. Only her daughters bore witness to the reflection in their mother's eyes. From the descendants of Idit's daughters came Ruth, the great-grandmother of David, and from hence the promise of the Messiah.

According to classical midrash, anyone who saw Lot's wife was required to recite two blessings. The first, "Blessed be the One who remembers the righteous," expressed thanksgiving and praise to God for having remembered Abraham, by the merit of whose righteousness Lot and his wife were saved from the upheaval. This blessing related to the miracle that was performed for Lot. The second blessing, "Blessed be the true Judge" (recited upon hearing of someone's death), was recited for the punishment visited on Lot's wife (BT *Berakhot* 54a–b). A late *aggadah* described Lot's wife as standing forever while oxen lick her feet daily. She is said to rise once again every morning as a pillar of salt (*Sefer ha-Yashar*, *Vayera* 39).

Through the lived experiences of women, this narrative takes on a life of its own. The blessing of thanksgiving becomes a blessing for the witness of Idit. The blessing recited upon hearing of death is not recited for her punishment but for her compassion. This retelling is grounded both in maternal compassion and in the reality of war, destruction, and witness. It remembers the old narrative container and reconstructs and reimagines it in ways that hold the experience of both women and men.

Upon hearing my midrash of Idit during a study session, one elderly gentleman from Prague commented, "I know. During the Holocaust, my parents and I arrived in Auschwitz. We got off the train. The Nazis divided us into two lines. My parents were sent one way and I the other. I turned around and I saw the smoke from the crematoria. I was a pillar of salt."[29]

In a painting by Anselm Kiefer, *Lot's Wife* (1982), this Czech gentleman's horror came alive in art. On canvas is an image of the Holocaust: railroad tracks crossing the landscape. The tracks diverge in the middle distance but appear to merge again near the horizon, at the vanishing point. The camps are a vanishing point of human understanding, as well as the literal vanishing point for millions of human beings. The artist suggests that we must look back; that we cannot afford historical amnesia.[30]

As the author of this midrash on Idit, I sought for ways to retell this story as a part of recurring ritual. Tradition recorded the day of Idit's death on the sixteenth of Nisan, the date when centuries later, Israel would be freed from Egyptian bondage. I suggested that her story be told when the seder participants dipped *karpas* into salt water. This reminder of slavery also could become a reminder by a woman of the importance of bearing witness, and the need to remember.

9. COLLECTIONS OF WOMEN'S COMMENTARY AND MIDRASHIM

Over the last decades, women have brought to awareness classical midrashim that told of women's power, righteousness, and compassion even as they imagined God in new ways. They looked back and saw and heard what others had neglected to see and hear. They look back in order to move forward.

In biblical commentary from Aviva Zornberg's books on Genesis (1995) and Exodus (2001), to Ellen Frankel's *The Five Books of Miriam* to *The Women's Torah Commentary* edited by Elyse Goldstein (2000), to *The Torah: A Woman's Commentary* edited by Tamara Eskenazi and Andrea Weiss (2007), women have both lifted up positive female images in little-noticed midrashim and remade them in ways that brought women's perspective to bear upon the text.[31] In addition, women's collections of midrash, such as *Miriam's Well* by Alice Bach and J. Cheryl Exum in 1991, *Biblical Women Unbound* by Norma Rosen in 1997, *Sisters at Sinai: New Tales of Biblical Women* by Jill Hammer (2001), the poetry of Alicia Ostriker in *The Nakedness of the Fathers: Biblical Visions and Revisions* (1994), and *For the Love of God, The Bible as an Open Book* (2007) added new voices to those of tradition.[32] Women's midrash also took the form of art.[33]

Jewish women authors began to introduce children to new midrashim about women.[34] If religious containers refashioned by writers, artists, and scholars were to become part of "tradition," they would have to be received by children, who in turn, would carry them and reshape them for future generations. It would not be enough for a select group of Jewish feminists to tell these stories among themselves. They had to be the narratives that students learned in religious school, that were transmitted as part of their sacred heritage and that helped to shape their Jewish identity.

10. MAKING WHAT IS NEW TRADITION

At one Jewish feminist conference in the United States in the early 1990s, a leading feminist remarked, "If tradition won't give us a seat at tradition's table, we will set our own table." As a respondent, I proposed, "We need to take a seat at tradition's table and help to reset it."[35] No longer are women's prayers, rituals, and midrash supplemental or alternative. They are finding their way into sacred collections of texts that are kissed when they fall, that are told to children. From covenantal birth ceremonies for girls, to Miriam's cup, to new midrashic tellings of biblical women, tradition is being created and renewed.

Those women, and now also men, who participated in this creative process to fashion new stories and transform old ones, recognized it as an awe-filled task and approached it with both humility and audacity. After all, they reasoned, who are we, tied as we are to our own time and place, to fashion the sacred words and create the holy drama to carry us through the passages of our years? After all, who are we, bearers of the image of God, not to pour our souls into the crucible of time, to affix our name to the holy narrative of our people?

11. A NEW KIND OF PILGRIMAGE

When Judith Kaplan Eisenstein, the first female to become bat mitzvah in 1922, marked the seventieth anniversary of her Bat Mitzvah, I wrote the following poem:

> Must we always go up to some mountain
> With Abraham, with Isaac to Moriah?
> The air is so thin up there,
> And it's hard to breathe.
> Must we always go up to some mountain
> With Moses to Sinai?
> It's so far from the earth,
> And what's below appears so small
> You can forget it's real.
> Must we always go up to some mountain
> With Moses to Nebo?
> Climbing- there's only one way
> And loneliness.
> Must we always go up to some mountain
> With Elijah to Carmel?
> The ascent is not hard.
> It's the descending
> Too easy to slip with no one to catch your fall.
> I'm weary of mountains
> Where we're always looking up
> Or looking down and sacrificing
> So our neck hurts
> And we need glasses.
> Our feet upon the mountains
> Are blistered
> And or shoes are always wrong-
> Not enough "sole".
> Can we sit with Sarah in a tent,
> Next to Deborah under a palm tree,
> Alongside Rebekkah by the well-
> With Judith in the synagogue reading Torah,
> to wash our feet,
> to catch our breath
> and our soul?[36]

Learning about Rabbi Regina Jonas and helping to dedicate a plaque in her memory at Terezin, I changed the last stanza and added more:

> Now at Terezin with Regina,
> A different pilgrimage
> On sanctified ground.
> No knife, no stone tablets, no altar;
> Another revelation
> In a woman's words:
> "To be blessed by God
> Means to bless . . . wherever one goes."
> God remembered Regina
> As God remembered Noah
> As God remembered Sarah and Abraham
> As God remembered Rachel
> As God remembered Hannah
> And each time made a new beginning.
> God remembered Regina
> Until we too remembered.
> She is our heritage; we are her legacy.
> We will make a new beginning
> As we catch our breath and our soul.[37]

When the people of Israel crossed the Sea of Reeds, Miriam took a timbrel and led the women in singing and rejoicing. With no map to guide her, Miriam stood at the front of a multitude of slaves and taught them to dance. Like Miriam, women often felt they had no map, no guide to provide the words and the story to make sense of their sacred journey. Like Miriam, they took a chance and danced. They altered the hierarchical metaphors of God and sacred pilgrimage. They understood revelation not as a top-down encounter but rather an ongoing process that happened within a community of men *and* women. By looking back, they re-membered women, so that they became subjects of the people's stories and full members in the community of Israel.

Since 1970, Jewish women have read traditional stories through the lens of their experience. They have poured their souls into the ancient text and affixed their names to the holy narrative of our people. The way Jews read texts, understand religion, God, the sacred and Scripture have been transformed. What happened was nothing short of a revolution. Like Jacob wrestling with the "angel," women wrestled with the text and did not let it go until it blessed them. Their struggle has strengthened and renewed Judaism.

NOTES

1. Beatrice Silverman Weinreich, ed., "Skotsl Kumt: Skotsl's Here" in *Yiddish Folktales,* trans. Leonard Wolf (New York: Pantheon Books, 1988), 246. The story was recorded in 1931. The story and the expression are likely several hundred years old.

2. Naftali Haleva, "Haberes Buenos," in *Chosen Tales: Stories Told by Jewish Storytellers,* ed. Peninnah Schram (Lanham: Jason Aronson, 1955), 142–44. (The tale was told to Naftali Haleva by his grandmother. The family is from Turkey.)

3. Later, many of these women embraced Jewish feminism.

4. Sandy Eisenberg Sasso, Speech to the American Jewish Committee in New York, May 1972, unpublished, original in the American Jewish Archives.

5. Rachel Adler, *Engendering Judaism: An Inclusive Theology and Ethics* (Boston: Beacon Press, 1998), 2.

6. A striking example of re-membering is the story of Rabbi Regina Jonas. The first woman ordained as a rabbi in Berlin in 1935, her life story was lost in the years after the holocaust. Men and male-led institutions chose not to tell her story, perhaps because of her gender. While her name appeared in the 1970s, it wasn't until the 1990s after the fall of the Berlin Wall, that archival materials were found. In 2004, Rabbi Elisa Klapheck published a book about her life: *Fraulein Rabbiner Jonas: The Story of the First Woman Rabbi,* trans. Toby Axelrod (San Francisco: Wiley, 2004).

7. Alice Ostriker, *The Nakedness of the Fathers: Biblical Visions and Revision* (New Brunswick: Rutgers University Press, 1994), 7–8.

8. Judith Plaskow, *Standing Again at Sinai: Judaism from a Feminist Perspective* (New York: Harper and Row, 1990), ix–x.

9. Plaskow, *Standing Again at Sinai,* 27–28.

10. Merle Feld, "We All Stood Together," in *Biblical Women in the Midrash,* ed. Naomi Mara Hyman (Lanham: Jason Aronson, 1997): xli–xlii.

11. Aviva Gottlieb Zornberg, *The Particulars of Rapture: Reflections on Exodus* (New York: Doubleday, 2001): 7–8.

12. Adler, *Engendering Judaism,* 96.

13. In 1983, Sandy Eisenberg Sasso and Sue Levi Elwell created a mini-course for Jewish youth that addressed the issues of Jewish women. Among the several responses to women's exclusion that were noted was women's midrash. Sandy Eisenberg Sasso and Sue Levi Elwell, *Jewish Women: Preserving Life Studying and Teaching Seeking God Building Community Making Connections* (Denver: Alternatives in Religion Education, 1983).

14. "Ki Hinei Kahomer," in *Mahzor for Rosh Hashanah and Yom Kippur,* ed. Jules Harlow (New York: The Rabbinical Assembly, 1972), 395.

15. Jill Hammer, *Sisters at Sinai: New Tales of Biblical Women* (Philadelphia: Jewish Publication Society, 2001): xiv–xv.

16. Judith Plaskow, "The Coming of Lilith: Toward a Feminist Theology," in *Womanspirit Rising: A Feminist Reader in Religion,* ed. Carol Christ and Judith Plaskow (San Francisco: Harper and Row, 1979).

17. *Which Lilith? Feminist Writers Re-create the World's First Woman,* ed. Enid Dame, Lilly Rivlin, and Henry Wenkart (Lanham: Jason Aronson, 1998).

18. Alice Ostriker, "The Lilith Poems," in *Which Lilith?,* 43–48.

19. Enid Dame, "Lilith," in *Which Lilith?,* 71–72.

20. Adler, *Engendering Judaism,* 126.

21. Original letter in the American Jewish Archives; the letter writer's identity is irrelevant in the given context.

22. Rivka Walton, "Lilith's Daughters, Miriam's Chorus: Two Decades of Feminist Midrash," *Religion and Literature* 43 (2011): 11–127.

23. Lynn Gottlieb, *She Who Dwells Within: A Feminist Vision of a Renewed Judaism* (San Francisco: Harper, 1995), 113.

24. Jacqueline Nicholls, "Torat Imecha, Maternal Torah," www.jacquelinenicholls.com/maternal-torah.

25. Lori Hope Lefkovitz, "Eavesdropping on Angels and Laughing at God: Theorizing a Subversive Matriarchy," in *Gender and Judaism: The Transformation of Tradition*, ed. T. M. Rudavsky (New York: New York University Press, 1995), 157.

26. Adler, *Engendering Judaism*, xxv.

27. Tova Beck-Friedman, "Lot's Wife" (2011). Beck-Friedman reads the poem in a video of the same title, available at http://tbfstudio.com/lot's_wife.html (accessed February 1, 2017).

28. Sandy Eisenberg Sasso, "Idit," *Reconstructionist: A Journal of Creative Jewish Thought* LVI (1990–1991): 20–22.

29. The study session that my husband, Dennis C. Sasso and I conducted took place after Friday evening services in Bejt Simcha, a liberal congregation in Prague.

30. Brian A Oard, "The Necessity of Looking Back," in *Beauty and Terror: Essays on the Power of Painting* (ebook, 1989).

31. Aviva Gottlieb Zornberg, *Genesis: The Beginning Of Desire* (Philadelphia: Jewish Publication Society, 1995); idem, *Particulars of Rapture;* Ellen Frankel, *The Five Books of Miriam* (New York, Putnam, 1996); Tamara Eskenazi and Andreas L. Weiss, eds., *The Torah: A Woman's Commentary* (New York: Women of Reform Judaism, 2008).

32. Alice Bach and J. Cheryl Exum, *Miriam's Well: Stories About Women in the Bible* (New York, Delacorte Press, 1991); Norma Rosen, *Biblical Women Unbound* (Philadelphia, Jewish Publication Society, 1996); Hammer, *Sisters at Sinai*; Ostriker, *Nakedness of the Fathers*; idem, *For the Love of God: The Bible as an Open Book.* (New Brunswick: Rutgers University Press, 2007).

33. Jo Milgrom, *Handmade Midrash: Workshops in Visual Theology* (Philadelphia: Jewish Publication Society 1992).

34. Sandy Eisenberg Sasso, *A Prayer for the Earth: The Story of Naamah, Noah's Wife* (Woodstock: Jewish Lights, 1996). The book was later reprinted under the title, *Noah's Wife: The Story of Naamah* (Jewish Lights, 2001); idem, *But God Remembered: Stories of Women from Creation to the Promised Land* (Woodstock: Jewish Lights, 1995).

35. Sandy Eisenberg Sasso, "[Response to Letty Cottin Pogrebin at Jewish Feminist Conference, Chicago, March 16, 1992]," unpublished.

36. Sandy Eisenberg Sasso, "Introduction, Unwrapping the Gift," in *Women and Religious Ritual*, ed. Lesley A. Northup (Washington: The Pastoral Press, 1993), ix–xvi. Judith Kaplan Eisenstein was the daughter of Mordecai Menahem Kaplan, intellectual founder of Reconstructionist Judaism.

37. This was delivered July 2014 when a plaque was dedicated in Regina Jonas's memory at Terezin by a delegation of women rabbis under the auspices of the American Jewish Archives and the Jewish Women's Archives.

BIBLIOGRAPHY

Adler, Rachel, *Engendering Judaism: An Inclusive Theology and Ethics* (Boston: Beacon Press, 1998).
Bach, Alice, and Exum, J. Cheryl, *Miriam's Well: Stories About Women in the Bible* (New York, Delacorte Press, 1991).
Dame, Enid, et al. (eds.), *Which Lilith? Feminist Writers Re-create the World's First Woman*, (Lanham: Jason Aronson, 1998).
Eisenberg Sasso, Sandy, "[Response to Letty Cottin Pogrebin at Jewish Feminist Conference, Chicago, March 16, 1992]," unpublished.
Eisenberg Sasso, Sandy, "Idit," *Reconstructionist: A Journal of Creative Jewish Thought* LVI (1990–1991): 20–22.
Eisenberg Sasso, Sandy, "Introduction, Unwrapping the Gift," in *Women and Religious Ritual*, ed. Lesley A. Northup (Washington: The Pastoral Press, 1993), ix–xvi.
Eisenberg Sasso, Sandy, *A Prayer for the Earth: The Story of Naamah, Noah's Wife* (Woodstock: Jewish Lights, 1996).
Eisenberg Sasso, Sandy, and Levi Elwell, Sue, *Jewish Women: Preserving Life Studying and Teaching Seeking God Building Community Making Connections* (Denver: Alternatives in Religion Education, 1983).
Eisenberg Sasso, Sandy, *But God Remembered: Stories of Women from Creation to the Promised Land* (Woodstock: Jewish Lights, 1995).
Eskenazi, Tamara, and Weiss, Andreas L., (eds.), *The Torah: A Woman's Commentary* (New York: Women of Reform Judaism, 2008).
Feld, Merle, "We All Stood Together," in *Biblical Women in the Midrash*, ed. Naomi Mara Hyman (Lanham: Jason Aronson, 1997): xli–xlii.
Gottlieb Zornberg, Aviva *The Particulars of Rapture: Reflections on Exodus* (New York: Doubleday, 2001).
Gottlieb Zornberg, Aviva, *Particulars of Rapture;* Ellen Frankel, *The Five Books of Miriam* (New York, Putnam, 1996).
Gottlieb Zornberg, Aviva, *Genesis: The Beginning Of Desire* (Philadelphia: Jewish Publication Society, 1995).
Gottlieb, Lynn, *She Who Dwells Within: A Feminist Vision of a Renewed Judaism* (San Francisco: Harper, 1995).
Haleva, Naftali, "Haberes Buenos," in *Chosen Tales: Stories Told by Jewish Storytellers*, ed. Peninnah Schram (Lanham: Jason Aronson, 1955), 142–44.
Hammer, Jill, *Sisters at Sinai: New Tales of Biblical Women* (Philadelphia: Jewish Publication Society, 2001).
Harlow, Jules, (ed.), *Mahzor for Rosh Hashanah and Yom Kippur*, (New York: The Rabbinical Assembly, 1972).
Klapheck, Elisa, *Fraulein Rabbiner Jonas: The Story of the First Woman Rabbi*, trans. Toby Axelrod (San Francisco: Wiley, 2004).
Lefkovitz, Lori Hope, "Eavesdropping on Angels and Laughing at God: Theorizing a Subversive Matriarchy," in *Gender and Judaism: The Transformation of Tradition*, ed. T. M. Rudavsky (New York: New York University Press, 1995).
Milgrom, Jo, *Handmade Midrash: Workshops in Visual Theology* (Philadelphia: Jewish Publication Society 1992).
Oard, Brian A., "The Necessity of Looking Back," in *Beauty and Terror: Essays on the Power of Painting* (ebook, 1989).

Ostriker, Alice, *The Nakedness of the Fathers: Biblical Visions and Revision* (New Brunswick: Rutgers University Press, 1994).

Plaskow, Judith, "The Coming of Lilith: Toward a Feminist Theology," in *Womanspirit Rising: A Feminist Reader in Religion*, ed. Carol Christ and Judith Plaskow (San Francisco: Harper and Row, 1979).

Plaskow, Judith, *Standing Again at Sinai: Judaism from a Feminist Perspective* (New York: Harper and Row, 1990).

Rosen, Norma, *Biblical Women Unbound* (Philadelphia, Jewish Publication Society, 1996).

Ostriker, Alicia, *For the Love of God: The Bible as an Open Book.* (New Brunswick: Rutgers University Press, 2007).

Silverman Weinreich, Beatrice, ed., "Skotsl Kumt: Skotsl's Here" in *Yiddish Folktales*, trans. Leonard Wolf (New York: Pantheon Books, 1988): 246.

Walton, Rivka, "Lilith's Daughters, Miriam's Chorus: Two Decades of Feminist Midrash," *Religion and Literature* 43 (2011): 11–127.

Part IV

Comparing Notes

Female Religious Leadership Today

Chapter Twelve

Women's Leadership in the Roman Catholic Church

A Survey of Half a Century's Development with Particular Reference to Germany

Marie-Theres Wacker

During an audience on May 12, 2016, where the pope of the Roman Catholic Church received the International Union of Superiors General, the organization of Institutes of Roman Catholic Women Religious worldwide and their female leaders, he was asked the following question:

> Pope Francis, you said that "the feminine genius is needed in all expressions in the life of society . . . and in the Church," and yet women are excluded from decision-making processes in the Church, especially at the highest levels, and from preaching at the Eucharist. An important obstacle to the Church's full embrace of "feminine genius" is the bond that decision-making processes and preaching both have with priestly ordination. Do you see a way of separating leadership roles and preaching at the Eucharist from ordination, so that our Church can be more open to receiving the genius of women in the very near future?[1]

The 870 women religious present at the audience put their finger on what they saw as a contradiction in the Roman Catholic Church: on the one hand, the pope affirms the church's need for women's specific gifts; on the other hand, women are structurally excluded from important functions within the church. The two functions or roles they mentioned relate to leadership: leadership as the power of decision making on many levels of the church, especially on the highest level of the Roman Curia, but also leadership as the power to preach in the Eucharist, that is, to authoritatively proclaim the Gospel within the context of a holy mass, after the readings from the Holy Scriptures, in the form of a homily. For the questioners, the topic of preaching the homily was crucial, as it concerned a central part of their spiritual life in their convents, but also the center of liturgical life for all Catholics. Moreover, although (or maybe even because) the women present at the audience held leading positions in their religious orders or congregations, they saw the need to point out a problem for the church as a whole.

The structural obstacle to the integration of women into leadership within the Roman Catholic church that the women superiors identified is the bond that the above-mentioned forms of leadership have with ordination as priest. According to the Catholic *Code of Canon Law* (CIC; revised version of 1983), "a baptized male alone receives sacred ordination validly" (can. 1024),[2] which means that women are excluded from ordination (as deacon, priest, and bishop)[3] because of their sex as a matter of principle. The solution proposed by the questioners does not touch upon that principle but suggests that the bond between ordained ministry and leadership roles might be reconsidered.

The women superiors' intervention can be seen as a mirror text for the complex issue of women's leadership in the Roman Catholic Church. Engaging this intervention, I will reflect first on the history of debates concerning the exclusion of women from priestly ordination since the Second Vatican Council (1962–1965) and on the actual status quo. In a further step, I will include the subject of ordained women deacons, a subject the religious sisters brought up during the same audience of May 12, 2016, in their second statement, as it evidently relates to their first question. Another topic linked with the ordination issue is the topic of women students, doctors, and academic teachers of theology, a specific field of preparing for or exercising leadership. My fourth point concerns the actual presence of women in decision-making positions within the Roman Catholic Church, with a focus on the highest levels and on paid work.[4]

As for my theoretical framework, the growing awareness of women as equal in rights with men is one fundamental concept of modernity with which the Roman Catholic Church is confronted. I will use this observation as a starting point rather than work with a theory of the "feminization" of religion occurring since the nineteenth century, a theory actually under critique as being historically, geographically, and socially too global to explain processes of modernization in religion.[5] Instead, I will use perspectives of gender, status, and power and their intersections to describe positive developments, but also structures of resistance, regarding women and leadership in the Roman Catholic Church.

1. WOMEN PRIESTS?

The first *Code of Canon Law* issued in 1917 already contained a canon, based on a long legal tradition in the Latin Church, specifying that a baptized male alone receives ordination validly (can. 968 § 1). After some initial discussions in the 1920s at a time when Protestant women studying theology in Germany raised the question of women as ordained ministers in their churches, an attempt was made at the Second Vatican Council to make Roman Catholic women's ordination for priesthood a topic of debate and decision.[6] In a climate of *aggiornamento*, a new awareness of reflecting on "the church in the modern world," there was hope that the church would be ready to include women into the priesthood.[7] However, the two petitions submitted by Swiss lawyer Gertrud Heinzelmann and two German Catholic theologians, Ida Raming and Iris Mueller, did not enter the agenda of the council fathers.[8] When some Anglican churches—in Hong Kong, Canada, and the United States—approved the ordination of women or even started to ordain women priests around 1975, the Sacred Congregation for the Doctrine of Faith, the highest Roman Curial institution concerning doctrinal issues, prepared and issued in 1976 *Declaration on the Question of Admission of Women to the Ministerial Priesthood*, usually quoted with its first Latin words, *Inter Insigniores*.[9] Already in the introduction, the document states, "The Sacred Congregation for the Doctrine of the Faith judges it necessary to recall that the Church, in fidelity to the example of the Lord, does not consider herself authorized to admit women to priestly ordination."[10] Three principal reasons are given. First, the church's long and unbroken tradition of not ordaining women is mentioned as a crucial argument for Roman Catholic hermeneutics. From the New Testament as a primary source for Catholic doctrines in matters of faith and ethics, the document derives the example of Christ not including women among the twelve disciples, as well as the attitude of the apostles. These arguments from tradition and scripture are reinforced by a reflection on the (male) priest acting as representative of Christ (*in persona Christi*) and the sacramental or symbolic presuppositions of this concept. Grounded on these considerations, the document explicitly refuses to recognize admission to ministerial priesthood as a human right. Indeed, women like Ida Raming had claimed priesthood for women as a question of human rights in the sense that women must not be excluded because of their sex.[11] They had insisted that the long and unbroken tradition is de facto a tradition of patriarchy not respecting the full equality of women and men. Moreover, they saw the formula in the letter of Saint Paul to the Galatian communities describing that "there is no longer Jew or Greek, there is no longer slave or free, there is no longer male and female; for all of you are one in Christ Jesus" (Galatians 3:28) as a manifesto for the equality of men and women in the community of Christ. Finally, they were convinced that the biblical doctrine of the likeness of all humans to the image of God (Genesis 1:26–28) contradicts the exclusion of women from one of the seven sacraments, each sacrament being a precious means of receiving divine grace in and for the life of a Christian.

In spite of the authoritative character of *Inter Insigniores*, an extensive debate arose in the late 1970s. The specific practice of using the New Testament to derive from it God's will for the church to have male priests only was called into question as hermeneutically oversimplified. Similarly, the fact that the symbolic equivalence between Christ and a human being acting as his representative focuses on Christ being a biological male was considered sexist and even heretical, contradicting the dogma of Christ being fully divine and fully human. Pope John Paul II (1978–2005) made it an important issue for him to deepen the arguments of *Inter Insigniores*. On many occasions, he praised the "genius of women" as needed in the world and in the church.[12] At the same time, he insisted on the symbolic correspondence of a male priest acting *in persona Christi* and Christ himself, underlining the complementary symbolism of Christ's female counterpart, the church, represented by Mary, as well as the analogous symbolism in the Hebrew scriptures, the first part of the Christian Bible, of God/male and Israel/female.[13] Furthermore, the pope emphasized the distinction between *dignity* and *rights*: there is no doubt that the church stands and stands up for women's dignity and women's equal dignity with men (and for women's rights in the world), but access to sacred ordination cannot be treated as a right, as it is part of God's plan for his church and therefore not subject to the church's discretion.

Finally, John Paul II wanted to put an end to the debate with his "Apostolic Letter to the Bishops of the Catholic Church on Reserving Priestly Ordination to Men Alone," quoted as *Ordinatio Sacerdotalis* (1994). After having repeated the arguments of *Inter Insigniores*, he concludes with a solemn and authoritative formula:

> In order that all doubt may be removed regarding a matter of great importance, a matter which pertains to the Church's divine constitution itself, in virtue of my ministry of confirming the brethren . . . I declare that the Church has no authority whatsoever to confer priestly ordination on women and that this judgment is to be definitively held by all the Church's faithful.[14]

With this declaration, it has become much more difficult for Catholics to continue the discussion. Such an insistence can be considered as insubordination against a definitive decision and might have negative consequences, for example, for teachers at Catholic schools, seminaries, or faculties.[15] This background sheds light on the way the women superiors put their question during the 2016 audience. They adopted the papal rhetoric of a female "genius" and did not request access for women to the priesthood, but rather asked to reconsider the link between priestly ordination and certain roles or functions within the church. Indeed, one could be reminded of the very powerful jurisdictional roles of some abbesses from medieval times until the nineteenth century, who not only installed parish priests in the territories belonging to their abbeys, but also heard confessions of the nuns under their jurisdiction. Their case reveals that there were women in the church's history who possessed authority usually bound to sacramental ordination.[16] Pope Francis's answer shows that he sees some leeway for decision making that does not touch ecclesiastical or pastoral jurisdiction proper, but also that he prefers to talk about including women into the reflection processes *preceding* a decision. To put it another way, he is willing to extend women's presence up to high levels of the Curia and certainly trust women in leadership positions. With the year 2017, art historian Barbara Jatta officially became director of the Vatican Museums, to which she was appointed by Pope Francis. She is the most recent example of the pope's policy of including women into leading positions within the Vatican administration.[17] But, when it comes to pastoral issues, he sees women as consultants rather than as responsible decision makers.

In 2002, a group of seven Roman Catholic women, among them Ida Raming and Iris Müller from Münster, celebrated their priestly ordination *contra legem*, against the Canon Law.[18] They were confident to have acted in anticipatory obedience to a church that will convert to the unrestricted equality of men and women before God. For these women, access to priestly ordination was and is a question not of modernity, but of justice. On a sociological-analytical level, it is exactly that bond between justice and equality of the sexes that is one of the very precious outcomes of modernity.

2. WOMEN DEACONS?

After Vatican II, the tripartite structure of ordained ministry (bishop, priest, deacon) was reformed so that the diaconate was (re-)established as a clerical order in itself instead of being only a transitional stage before priesthood. At the same time, the question of whether married men could be ordained permanent deacons was decided positively; only deacons who wanted to be priests had to vow celibacy. Traditionally, a deacon is seen as an auxiliary clergy, hence with no specific leadership functions. Nevertheless, there are some decision-making positions in the Roman Catholic Church that do not demand a priest but a clergy member in general, so that deacons can fulfill these tasks.[19] As well, deacons are allowed to preach in the Eucharist (CIC can. 767 § 1). Access for women to the permanent diaconate could be seen as a first step toward the inclusion of women in specific roles bound to the tripartite order. Therefore, it appears consistent that the women superiors, in their second question, addressed the question of a female diaconate:

> Consecrated women already do much work with the poor and the marginalized, they teach catechism, they accompany the sick and the dying, they distribute Communion; in many countries they lead the communal prayers in the absence of a priest and in those circumstances they give a homily. In the Church there is the office of the permanent diaconate, but it is open only to men, married or not. What prevents the Church from including women among permanent deacons, as was the case in the primitive Church? Why not constitute an official commission to study the matter?[20]

Here, the line of argumentation takes a different course compared to the first question. The women superiors proceed from what the religious sisters are doing in their everyday lives, knowing that what they describe are typical functions and tasks of a (permanent) deacon. Why not officially recognize the diaconal practice of women?

Again, the question is put in a rather cautious way, not as an unadorned request for sacramental ordination but as a suggestion to "include" women, although there can be little doubt that an equal footing with male permanent deacons is meant. Again, as in the first question, the superiors move from a consideration of their specific status as "consecrated women"—women who have received a specific blessing and who have pronounced specific vows, usually the vows of poverty, chastity, and obedience —to a broader inclusion of all women in the church, thus indicating that they do not want privileges as women religious. This is all the more remarkable, as there is a traditional line of self-conception in women religious to mark their distinction from women as wives and mothers. Further, members of the church's clergy are used to looking at women religious differently, not only because they hold a specific canonical status, but also because they might seem closer to what clergymen live, know, and experience. Usually, for example, women religious are much more easily coopted as members of papal councils or commissions than are lay women. Gender and status intersect here with significant practical implications.

The actual debate in the Roman Catholic Church on a female diaconate reveals a complex variety of arguments and perspectives. One initiative was started in Germany in 1999 as a joint venture between a woman's order, women's Catholic associations, and individual women to offer a three-year preparatory course to women, regardless of their status, who feel that they have a vocation to the deaconate. Their curriculum corresponds with that designed for permanent male deacons, which means that they are prepared to work in a specific field of social or pastoral care, to proclaim the Gospel in many contexts and circumstances, and to assist at liturgies. The women who went through this preparation course call themselves "deacons in waiting" for a sacramental ordination.[21] In a statement by German cardinal Walter Kasper held at the German bishops' conference meeting in 2013, he expressed reluctance with regard to a sacramental ordination of women deacons, as that would, according to him, be a significant break with tradition.[22] Instead, he explored the possibility of a special blessing for women deacons and suggested binding such a blessing to the vow of chastity, as consecrated women do. He explicitly referred to the above-mentioned abbesses as an important example—not so much for their power as for the type of specific blessing of women within the church's tradition. His model, then, tends toward the idea of a specific ministry for women, not simply the female form of the existing permanent diaconate, and seems not to include married women. Gender, status, and sexuality are used here as criteria to evaluate tradition, with the effect of narrowing considerably the inclusion of women in the diaconate.

The pope's answer to the women religious at the audience did not start from tradition but from practical "doing." Pope Francis admitted a similarity of practice between what these consecrated women do and what ordained male deacons do, and he even affirmed, "Some might say that the 'permanent deaconesses' in the life of the Church are the [religious] sisters."[23] But, he also turned the argument the other way around when he spoke of "maternal" works "where the maternity of the Church is expressed the most," and stated, "There are men who do the same."[24] In view of the harsh critics of gender perspectives in recent official documents issued by the Vatican, this reflection shows that a distinction between sex and gender including the possibilities of gender transgression nevertheless makes sense for him: "maternity"—or maybe a better term is "motherliness"—is seen as a quality obtainable not only for biological women-mothers, but also for women who are not biological mothers, and also for men. Moreover, if this could already have been said by his predecessors, Pope Francis goes one step further.[25] He seems to think that if "motherliness" is a quality essential for deacons, men and women alike can fulfill the roles and tasks of a deacon. His perspective of actual, common pastoral work as a form of making visible the maternal face of the church leads him to the conclusion that there could be reasons to admit women—even regardless of their status—to the order of deacon. I feel that this conclusion was one of the reasons he agreed that a commission to study the matter of a female deaconate should be established.[26] The commission thus established would then have to evaluate arguments from the Holy Scriptures and from tradition. As the letter of Saint Paul to the community in Rome testifies to the existence of a female deacon (cf. Romans 16:1), and as there are traces of female deacons throughout the history of the church, although somewhat scattered, it is a matter of assessment and of courage to open up the permanent diaconate to women.[27]

3. WOMEN IN CATHOLIC THEOLOGY AT UNIVERSITIES

In Germany, women's access to universities as regular students dates back only to the late nineteenth century; in Prussia, the last state of the German Empire, women were allowed to enroll as regular students only in 1908.[28] Catholic faculties, whose professors at the time were ordained priests without exception, as far as I can see, were reluctant to include women among their students. The dean of the Catholic Faculty in Münster, the place where I am teaching, reasoned that universities are "schools of manliness" and that it would be an "anomaly" to have women there. He suggested that women's colleges be established alongside the existing universities.[29] The dean envisioned a clear segregation of the sexes. Men governing public life are in need of a university education including not only male virtues but also male networks useless for women and from which women are to be excluded. However, this was not a typically Catholic perspective but was part of the ideology of the (German) universities during the empire.[30]

The first woman regularly enrolled as a student in a Catholic Faculty and admitted as an exception to pass an exam in theology (1929) was Franziska Werfer in Tübingen[31]—a contemporary of Regina Jonas, the first woman who became ordained as rabbi. Starting in 1930, Franziska Werfer was allowed to teach religion at girls' schools. During the Third Reich, some farsighted theologian professors at different places like Tübingen or Münster encouraged women to study theology in addition to other academic disciplines and to prepare themselves to teach religion, as they feared that, with an increasing governmental pressure on the church, there would soon be no priests anymore to do so. A similar pattern can be seen in the Protestant Church, where women who already had permission to attend a formal theological education, including a final exam at a university, became ordained as "emergency vicars" during World War II, when their male colleagues were recruited as soldiers—one could state with a slightly sarcastic tone that apparently situations of crisis help pave the way toward women's leadership in the church.

After World War II, Catholic faculties in Germany opened their doors to female students. Most of these women wanted to become teachers at schools and had no ambitions to obtain leadership positions in the church, probably not even considering it a possibility. Nevertheless, a few of them strove to engage in theological studies in an academic or scientific way. For them, no academic degrees were obtainable at the time, as the licentiate and doctorate in Catholic theology, the two academic degrees in existence, were bound to the sacred ordination as sub-deacon (a level of order preceding the diaconate, disestablished under Vatican II) and prepared for academic positions or functions in the church's hierarchy; a bishop, for example, had to be a doctor or licentiate in theology or canon law (CIC 1917; can. 331 § 1, 5°). One can see the circle closed: as women were not admitted to receive ordination, they could not obtain academic degrees bound to ordination, and without academic degrees they had no chance of entering the academy as teachers or professors of theology.

In the late 1940s, discussions began in the German faculties of Roman Catholic theology about opening that regulation to so-called lay students, men and women who were not priesthood candidates. At Münster, the dean started relevant negotiations with the bishop in 1952. One of the bishop's counselors, an expert in canon law, left a handwritten note on the back side of the dean's letter sent to the bishop recommending he not respond to the dean's demand. The reason he gave was the following: admitting women studying for a theological doctorate would require investing them, as was done for their ordained colleagues, with the insignia of a *doctor theologiae*, a ring with a gem or cameo, and a biretta, the classical headgear of Roman Catholic clergymen. For a male layperson that was tolerable, but to imagine the biretta on the head of a woman would expose that sign of clerical and academic honor to ridicule.[32] This high official at the bishop's curia feared—to put it that way—that the feminization of traditionally respected and respectful symbols would contribute to their devaluation or voiding. His thinking reveals a strong connection between gender, status, and honor. He probably never dreamed that just two years later the Catholic Faculty of Munich would bestow the degree of "Dr. theol." on two women, investing them not only with ring and biretta but also with soutane and cape! One of them, Elisabeth Gössmann, describes in her memoirs that she felt transformed, not into a man but into a clergyman, and that she did not feel honored by such disguising but rather driven into something spurious.[33] Both points are interesting. Indeed, the difference between female and male is not sufficient to describe the Roman Catholic hierarchical system in which the difference between ordained and non-ordained persons is considered essential in the twofold sense of being necessary and affecting the essence of a person, and in which men and women religious occupy a specific status different from either laypeople or clerics (ordained persons). And, indeed, the introduction into the new status of *doctor theologiae* by an "investiture" might reveal that the insignia and garments traditionally used and felt as "natural" are de facto gendered and not fitting for women—with the implication that they have to change or be completely removed, as was eventually done in German universities including theological faculties after the 1960s.

Both women, Elisabeth Gössmann and Uta Ranke-Heinemann, also tried, in the 1960s, to obtain what in Germany is called the "habilitation," the qualification to teach as a professor at a university. Elisabeth Gössmann did not succeed, as no German Catholic Faculty was ready to admit a layperson or, better, to tread the long path with her through the many bureaucracies needed to change existing state-church law. Uta Ranke-Heinemann succeeded in 1969, not in a Catholic Faculty but at a university educating elementary school teachers (Pädagogische Hochschule), and in 1970 she became a professor of theology at such an institution. It is obvious that women theologians were admitted at institutions where they corresponded to the image of women as educators of (younger) children, hence to the stereotype of "motherliness" by nature more closely connected with women.

It took until 1991 to see the first two female theologians, Anne Jensen at Tübingen and Teresa Berger at Münster, obtaining their *venia legendi*, the qualification to teach theology, from a Catholic Faculty.[34] Even today, habilitations of the non-ordained, that is, laypersons, are, from a legal perspective, regarded as exceptions to the rule.[35] Nevertheless, with the ongoing decrease in ordained qualified persons, lay professors now outnumber ordained ones, and numerous women theologians teach as professors at institutes of Catholic theology incorporated in faculties of philosophy or cultural sciences (curricula for future schoolteachers) and even at separate Catholic faculties in Germany. As academic interpreters of theology, they participate in the explication of the Christian faith, an important part of the church's mission and definitively a concrete form of leadership. Problems arise when a professor's teaching is considered (by a bishop or a Roman authority) to be not congruent with the doctrine of the church. At present, feminist theologians are still easily suspected of such incongruency, as they question traditions and develop new ways of thinking and acting. They question traditional symbols and metaphors for the divine reflecting power as male or males in power; traditional gender arrangements supported by the church where the description of "polarity" between man and woman veils the structures of "hierarchy" behind it and where homosexual orientations are regarded as part of God's creation but must not be lived out;[36] and traditional power distributions in the church's teaching and practice. They insist on thinking and acting from the margins and for the marginalized. An example is Elizabeth Johnson, professor of Catholic theology at Fordham University, New York, and religious sister, whose book *Quest for the Living God* (2007) was, four years later, declared by the U.S. Catholic Bishop Conference's Committee on Doctrine to "not accord with authentic Catholic teaching on essential points."[37] If, as the statement shows, the parameters of such authentic Catholic teaching include closeness to the language and thought forms of tradition, little space is left for an "authentic" meeting of tradition and modernity.

4. WOMEN IN LEADERSHIP FUNCTIONS NOT BOUND TO ORDINATION

The challenge for the Roman Catholic Church to include women in leadership functions and roles certainly became a strong one after Vatican II, with its emphatic theology of the people of God.[38] Already in 1964, during the council, the bishop of Mainz, Hermann Volk, appointed Dr. Irene Willig lecturer of biblical and dogmatic studies at his diocesan institute for the formation of female parish assistants (Seelsorgehelferinnen). Irene Willig is one of the very first women to obtain a theological doctorate at Münster University, where Volk was her professor of dogmatics before he became bishop. She impressed him with her intellectual brilliance, and he knew her sufficiently to know that she was able to execute a leadership role, so that she was entrusted by him, starting in 1972, with developing the institute into an academic college for students of social and pastoral work (Katholische Fachhochschule). In 1975, she became the first principal of that institution run by the diocese, an institution educating women and men who would apply for positions in dioceses and where bishops would typically prefer clerics as professors. It seems that her personality was such as to lead a bishop to not simply follow the traditional rules of recruitment at schools or academic institutions but to see the abilities of a woman and to give her a chance to apply and develop them. She even received a personal permit to preach.[39] Irene Willig, on the other hand, did not disguise her opinion that true equality of women and men was not yet present in the church. She followed the developments regarding women in theology and, in the late 1970s, invited as guest speaker to her institute Catharina Halkes, the famous Catholic theologian from the Netherlands and the first feminist theologian teaching at a theological faculty in Europe, though not as a regular professor.

In the years 1971 to 1975, the General Synod of the Dioceses in Germany was held to concretize and implement the resolutions from Vatican II. Authorized to vote, and hence part of decision making, were not only bishops and priests, but also laypersons, men and women, in particular representatives of the numerous and diverse associations of laypersons within the church. Among the four vice presidents was one woman (Hanna-Renate Laurien). It was an attempt to realize true synodal structures, although the resolution process and the resolutions proper reflect the manifold difficulties of such an attempt. Women's topics and perspectives were present but not yet focused specifically.[40] However, the innumerous men and, above all, women active in voluntary commitments in many forms—pastoral, education, social work, administration—and institutions, like parishes or associations, already came into the focus.

In 1981, the German bishops issued a programmatic paper on the "position of woman in Church and society."[41] They declared that "the Church should be a model for a cooperation of men and women based on equality and partnership," and they made a commitment to ensure "that in the entire church and within the jurisdiction of each of the German bishops, women are admitted to all offices theologically possible, pastorally meaningful, appropriate, and necessary."[42]

Recently, in a declaration issued in 2013 after their spring meeting devoted specifically to the interaction of women and men in the church, the German bishops even intensified their commitment.[43] They declared that they would "continue to clarify theologically what signifies leadership in the church. Where, from a theological point of view, is ordination mandatory? Which leadership functions can men or women fulfill on the basis of assignment by a bishop? We want to consider which new offices and ministries can be developed beyond the sacrament of ordination."[44]

In the run-up to that meeting, theologian Andrea Qualbrink, who at that time was preparing a doctoral thesis on women in leadership positions in the church, was entrusted with the task of collecting statistical data about women in leadership positions in the German dioceses.[45] She found out that at the highest level of a diocesan curia (immediately beyond the bishop and his general vicar), the first women started entering in 1989 as members of the church court, hence as specialists in canon law, and as directors of the charity institutions (Caritas association) in a diocese, an important area of presence of the Catholic Church in Germany. In January 2013, she identified, among others, five women directors of the diocesan Caritas association, three women responsible for the whole area of pastoral work and pastoral care, and two women acting as directors of the policy and/or strategic planning department of a diocesan administration. All in all, on the highest level 13 percent of all positions were held by (lay) women, 38 percent by men, and 49 percent by priests.[46]

Obviously, some bishops had decided to assign such leadership functions to these women. But, of course, these women now were confronted with the typical problems women in leadership positions encounter.[47] As they are alone among men/priests, they are often perceived primarily as women, not as competent colleagues. They have to anticipate that typical expectations regarding female behavior or abilities are placed on them, for example, that they bring "motherliness" into staff meetings. They are not included in the "old boys' networks" of their male colleagues, and so they might miss necessary or useful information. They have to learn about the dress codes in ecclesial contexts and professional behavior vis-à-vis church authorities. Often, they do not yet have role models and must develop on their own the ways in which they perform their office. Their own authority and power need to be clearly defined, and women sometimes need empowerment, for example, through mentoring. At the same time, however, the institution itself has to move toward more gender-inclusive structures and measures.

5. CONCLUSION

It seems that one can describe the development in the Roman Catholic Church as a successive extension of the fields for laypeople and especially for women in leadership positions. In order that this process not be seen as mere rearguard action, the church should move forward to act constructively and positively toward an inclusion of women in all tasks, offices, and ministries. The signs of the time indicate that the changes put into motion within the Roman Catholic Church toward more equality of the sexes are not reversible in the context of a judicial culture of equality of the sexes.[48] I want to conclude with the words of theologian and professor of canon law at the Faculty of Catholic theology at Regensburg, Sabine Demel:

> The question of women's issues in the Church must not remain a mere pragmatic one but must be, above all, a fundamental theological decision. It is time to express the fact that the Church needs women as equal partners—not because there is otherwise not enough staff to manage daily tasks and to realize the Church's mission, but because it is required by the fact that humans, men and women alike, are created in God's image.[49]

NOTES

1. See the first question in "Address of His Holiness Pope Francis to the International Union of Superiors General (UISG)," Paul VI Audience Hall, Vatican, May 12, 2016, https://w2.vatican.va/content/francesco/en/speeches/2016/may/documents/papa-francesco_20160512_uisg.html.

2. For the complete text of the CIC in English, see http://www.vatican.va/archive/ENG1104/__P3P.HTM.

3. CIC can. 1009 § 1 specifies: "The orders are the episcopate, the presbyterate, and the diaconate"; http://www.vatican.va/archive/ENG1104/__P3N.HTM. The women religious focus on the presbyterate here for reasons that will become clear in my later explanations.

4. There is no complete survey of women's leadership positions in the Roman Catholic Church, not even for individual countries like Germany, so inevitably my essay remains fragmentary and subjective.

5. See for both critical lines: Patrick Pasture, Jan Art, and Thomas Buermann, eds., *Beyond the Feminization Thesis: Gender and Christianity in Modern Europe* (Leuven: Leuven University Press, 2012), esp. 7–26; and Bernhard Schneider, "Feminisierung und (Re-)Maskulinisierung der Religion im 19. Jahrhundert. Tendenzen der Forschung aus der Perspektive des deutschen Katholizismus," in *Feminisierung oder (Re-)Maskulinisierung der Religion im 19. und 20. Jahrhundert? Forschungsbeiträge aus Christentum, Judentum und Islam*, ed. Michaela Sohn-Kronthaler (Wien: Böhlau, 2016), 11–41, as well as Gisela Muschiol, "Dienste, Ämter und das Geschlecht. Anfragen an die Feminisierungsthese aus katholischer Perspektive," in *Feminisierung oder (Re-) Maskulinisierung*, 42–51.

6. See Luise Schottroff, Silvia Schroer, and Marie-Theres Wacker, *Feminist Interpretation: The Bible in Women's Perspective* (Minneapolis: Fortress Press, 1998), 16–29.

7. See the heading of the important pastoral constitution *Gaudium et Spes* (December 7, 1965): "Pastoral Constitution on the Church in the Modern World," http://www.vatican.va/archive/hist_councils/ii_vatican_council/documents/vat-ii_const_19651207_gaudium-et-spes_en.html.

8. See, among many other publications, Ida Raming, "Women as Pioneers at Vatican II," *Concilium* 2012/5: 129–36.

9. For a timetable of events, see "The History of Women Clergy in the Anglican Communion," *Royal Gazette*, July 14, 2012, http://www.virtueonline.org/history-women-clergy-anglican-communion . See the official text in English: Sacred Congregation for the Doctrine of Faith, *Declaration on the Question of Admission of Women to the Ministerial Priesthood, Inter Insigniores*, Vatican, October 15, 1976, http://www.vatican.va/roman_curia/congregations/cfaith/documents/rc_con_cfaith_doc_19761015_inter-insigniores_en.html.

10. Sacred Congregation for the Doctrine of Faith, *Declaration on the Question of Admission of Women to the Ministerial Priesthood*.

11. See Ida Raming, *Der Ausschluss der Frau vom priesterlichen Amt: Gottgewollte Tradition oder Diskriminierung? Eine rechtshistorisch-dogmatische Untersuchung der Grundlagen von Kanon 968, § 1 d. Codex Iuris Canonici* (Köln: Böhlau, 1973). Her book is the printed version of her theological dissertation; she is one of the very first doctors of theology at the Catholic *Fakultät* of Münster University (see section 3 below). The term "Fakultät," while corresponding to the English "Faculty" (of Arts, etc.), implies the particular legal status of the institution as regulated in treaties between the Holy See and state institutions that give the church a say in crucial decisions.

12. See in particular the apostolic letter of John Paul II, "On the Dignity and Vocation of Women" (*Mulieris dignitatem*, 1988), end of § 26, https://w2.vatican.va/content/john-paul-ii/en/apost_letters/1988/documents/hf_jp-ii_apl_19880815_mulieris-dignitatem.html.

13. See *Mulieris dignitatem*, §§ 23–26.

14. John Paul II, "Apostolic Letter to the Bishops of the Catholic Church on Reserving Priestly Ordination to Men Alone," Vatican, May 22, 1994, https://w2.vatican.va/content/john-paul-ii/en/apost_letters/1994/documents/hf_jp-ii_apl_19940522_ordinatio-sacerdotalis.html.

15. The debate continued for some time on the meta-level, asking whether the letter had to be considered an infallible decision.

16. See the contribution of Sarah Roettger, "Abbesses as Model for Female Diaconate? Historical Considerations," *Concilium* 53/2 (2017).

17. For the history of women's inclusion in Vatican offices and statistics from 2015, see Gudrun Sailer, "Immer mehr Frauen im Vatikan," Vatican News, http://de.radiovaticana.va/news/2015/03/05/immer_mehr_frauen_im_vatikan/1127085 .

18. For initial details, see Wikipedia, s.v. "Danube Seven," last modified January 25, 2018, https://en.wikipedia.org/wiki/Danube_Seven. For more, see Roman Catholic Womenpriests, http://www.romancatholicwomenpriests.org/index.php. See also Ludmila Javorová, who fulfilled the ministry of a general vicar of a diocese during the time of the "underground church" in Czechia: Miriam Therese Winter, *Out of the Depths: The Story of Ludmila Javorová Ordained Roman Catholic Priest* (New York: Crossroads , 2001); Hildegard König, "Gender, Kirche, Gesellschaft—Strategien der Marginalisierung und Exklusion von Frauen in der Darstellung und Deutung kirchlicher Zeitgeschichte," in *Gender studieren: Lernprozess für Theologie und Kirche*, ed. Margit Eckhold (Ostfildern: Grünewald, 2017), 73–103.

19. See Phyllis Zagano, "Justice for the Life of the Parish: Restoring Women to the Ordained Diaconate," *Concilium* 53/2 (2017), 141–148.

20. See second question in "Address of His Holiness."

21. Netzwerk Diakonat der Frau, http://www.diakonat.de/.

22. Walter Kasper, *Das Zusammenleben von Frauen und Männern in Leben und Dienst der Kirche*, February 20, 2012, http://www.dbk.de/fileadmin/redaktion/diverse_downloads/presse_2012/2013-035-Studientag-FVV-Trier_Vortrag-K-Kasper.pdf.

23. His answer, originally in Italian, runs as "Qualcuno potrà dire che le 'diaconesse permanenti' nella vita della Chiesa sono le suocere," "suocere" signifying "mothers-in-law." One can be sure that the pope mixed up "suocere" and "suore," "suore" signifying "[religious] sisters." The translations keep "mothers-in-law" here; the German media reporting tacitly corrected.

24. See the answer to the second question in "Address of His Holiness."

25. See, e.g., the "Letter to the Bishops of the Catholic Church on the Collaboration of Men and Women in the Church and in the World" issued in 2004 by Joseph Ratzinger, prefect of the Congregation for the Doctrine of the Faith, then Pope Benedict XVI, a letter declaring women who adhere to feminism and gender theory as guilty of destroying the fundamental structures of the family, but also a letter proclaiming maternity as a virtue of women mothers or spiritual mothers and even men. See http://www.vatican.va/roman_curia/congregations/cfaith/documents/rc_con_cfaith_doc_20040731_collaboration_en.html.

26. The commission was established on August 2, 2016, and held its first meeting on November 25 and 26, 2016. See http://en.radiovaticana.va/news/2016/11/25/vatican_commission_on_female_diaconate_holds_first_meeting/1274887. In June 2018 a final report was transmitted to the Pope. In January 2019, two members of the commission made first public comments. Their statements show that the debate is still open. See https://www.ncronline.org/news/parish/members-papal-commission-womens-diaconate-make-first-public-comments.

27. See, e.g., Phyllis Zagano, ed., *Women Deacons? Essays with Answers* (Collegeville: Liturgical Press, 2016). I cannot discuss in more depth the problem that there can be doubts whether a deacon acts *in persona Christi* according to Canon Law CIC can 1009 § 3 and its modification by Pope Benedict XVI in his apostolic letter *Omnium in mentem* (2009). If not, access to the diaconate for women would only confirm or, at least, not question their non-capacity to represent Christ. See http://w2.vatican.va/content/benedict-xvi/en/apost_letters/documents/hf_ben-xvi_apl_20091026_codex-iuris-canonici.html.

28. "Lasst sie doch denken." *100 Jahre Studium für Frauen in Münster*, ed. Sabine Happ and Veronica Jüttemann (Münster: Aschendorff, 2008), 9, 19, and passim.

29. Marie-Theres Wacker, "Frauen in der (theologischen) Wissenschaft—die Anfänge in Münster 1892-1909," in *Feminist Theology in Europe: More Than Half a Life; A Reader in Honour of Hedwig Meyer-Wilmes,* ed. Elżbieta Adamiak and Marie-Theres Wacker (Münster: Lit, 2013), 158–73, esp. 159–63.

30. See Happ and Jüttemann, *"Lasst sie doch denken,"* 14–16, and passim.

31. Schottroff, Schroer, and Wacker, *Feminist Interpretation,* 25–26.

32. See Marie-Theres Wacker and Franziska Birke, *Grenzüberschreitung. Anfänge der Promotion von Frauen an der Katholisch-Theologischen Fakultät der Universität Münster* (Münster: Aschendorff, forthcoming).

33. Elisabeth Gössmann, *Geburtsfehler weiblich. Lebenserinnerungen einer katholischen Theologin* (München: Iudicium, 2003), 237–38.

34. See Anne Jensen's autobiographical reflections: Anne Jensen, "Auf dem Weg zur feministischen Theologie," http://static.uni-graz.at/fileadmin/projekte/genderforschung-theologie/Jensen_Auf_dem_Weg_zur_feministischen_Theologie.pdf. As early as 1972, however, the legal preconditions for the habilitation of a lay (=non-ordained) person in all disciplines of Catholic theology were established in Germany; see *Katholische Theologie und Kirchliches Hochschulrecht. Einführung und Dokumentation der kirchlichen Rechtsnormen,* ed. Deutsche Bischofskonferenz, Arbeitshilfen 100 (Bonn: Sekretariat der Deutschen Bischofskonferenz, 1972).

35. See, e.g., Eric W. Steinhauer, "Eine kurze Geschichte der Ausbildung katholischer Theologen in Deutschland," in *Ortskirche und Weltkirche in der Geschichte,* ed. Heinz Finger, Reimund Haas, and Hermann-Josef Scheidgen (Köln: Böhlau, 2011), 899–916, 907 n. 40.

36. See *Catechism of the Catholic Church,* §§ 2357–59, http://www.vatican.va/archive/ENG0015/__P85.HTM .

37. See Committee on Doctrine, United States Conference of Catholic Bishops, "Statement on *Quest for the Living God: Mapping Frontiers in the Theology of God,* by Sister Elizabeth A. Johnson," March 24, 2011, http://www.usccb.org/about/doctrine/publications/upload/statement-quest-for-the-living-god-2011-03-24.pdf, last sentence.

38. Many thanks go to Andrea Qualbrink, who in January 2017 submitted to the Catholic Faculty of Graz/Austria her doctoral thesis on leadership of women in the Catholic Church and helped me to describe and evaluate recent developments in Germany. See now: Andrea Qualbrink, *Frauen in kirchlichen Leitungspositionen. Möglichkeiten, Bedingungen und Folgen der Gestaltungsmacht von Frauen in der katholischen Kirche* (Praktische Theologie heute, 156; Stuttgart: Kohlhammer, 2018).

39. See Wacker and Birke, *Grenzüberschreitung,* paragraph on Irene Willig; *Wegbereiterin—Wegbegleiterin. Festschrift zum 75. Geburtstag von Prof. Dr. Irene Willig,* ed. Katholische Frauengemeinschaft Deutschlands, Diözesanverband Mainz (Mainz: kfd, 2001), esp. 12–18 (where *missio canonica* [permission to teach] has to be corrected to *missio homiletica* [permission to preach]) and 30–32.

40. In her doctoral thesis, Melanie Kolm focused on women in synodal processes in four German dioceses who initiated further processes of common (synodal) reflection. See Melanie Kolm, *Frauen in der katholischen Kirche—betroffen und beteiligt. Ekklesiologische Reflexionen über nachkonziliare synodale Prozesse,* Theologische Frauenforschung in Europa 27 (Münster: Lit, 2015).

41. *Zu Fragen der Stellung der Frau in Kirche und Gesellschaft,* ed. Deutsche Bischofskonferenz (Bonn: DBK, 2981), http://www.dbk.de/fileadmin/redaktion/diverse_downloads/presse/DBK_1130.pdf.

42. *Zu Fragen der Stellung der Frau,* 19.

43. Erklärung der deutschen Bischöfe vom 21. Februar 2013: "Das Zusammenwirken von Frauen und Männern im Dienst und Leben der Kirche," http://www.dbk.de/fileadmin/redaktion/diverse_downloads/presse_2012/2013-038-Anlage-1-Pressebericht-FVV-Trier.pdf. It seems probable that the title of that resolution was coined as a conscious, positive counterpart to the "Letter to the Bishops of the Catholic Church on the Collaboration of Men and Women in the Church and in the World" issued in 2004 by Joseph Ratzinger, prefect of the Congregation for the Doctrine of the Faith, a letter declaring persons who adhere to feminism and gender theory guilty of destroying the fundamental structures of the family. See http://www.vatican.va/roman_curia/congregations/cfaith/documents/rc_con_cfaith_doc_20040731_collaboration_en.html.

44. "Das Zusammenwirken von Frauen und Männern," seventh paragraph.

45. See the report given by Gabriele Rüttiger, "Frauen in kirchlichen Leitungspositionen—Erfahrungen und Perspektiven," in *Als Frau und Mann schuf er sie. Über das Zusammenwirken von Frauen und Männern in der Kirche*, ed. Franz-Josef Bode (Paderborn: Bonifatius, 2013), 29–36.

46. See Daniela Engelhard and Andrea Qualbrink, "Frauen in Führungspositionen—Perspektiven für Pastoral, Bildung, Caritas und Verwaltung," in Bode, *Als Frau und Mann schuf er sie*, 75–82, 78.

47. See Andrea Qualbrink, "Leadership revisited. Esther trifft auf Führungsfrauen," in *Esthers unbekannte Seiten. Theologische Perspektiven auf ein vergessenes biblisches Buch*, ed. Stephanie Feder and Aurica Nutt (Ostfildern: Grünewald, 2012), 123–38. See also Andrea Qualbrink, "Geschlechtergerechtigkeit auch in kirchlichen Führungspositionen?," in *Geschlechtersensible Pastoral und Bildung. Studientag 14. April 2016 Freising, Dokumentation*, ed. Wiltrud Huml and Anna Sedlmaier (Erzdiözese München und Freising, 2016), 48–57; see http://www.frauenseelsorge-bayern.de/fileadmin/Redaktion/Aktuelles/Dokumentation_Studientagung_geschlechtersensible_Pastoral_und_Bildung_14_04_2016-pdf.pdf.

48. "Wird die Kirche in einer Rechtskultur der Gleichstellung der Geschlechter eine Struktur der Ungleichstellung der Geschlechter aufrechterhalten können? Die Zeichen der Zeit sprechen dafür, dass die begonnene Veränderung nicht umkehrbar ist." Adrian Loretan, "Frauen in kirchlichen Ämtern. Eine rechtliche Standortbesimmung," in *Gleichstellung der Geschlechter und die Kirchen. Ein Beitrag zur menschenrechtlichen und ökumenischen Diskussion*, ed. Denise Buser and Adrian Loretan (Freiburg: Universitätsverlag, 1999), 64.

49. "Die kirchliche Frauenfrage darf *keine nur pragmatische*, sondern muss vor allem eine *theologische* Grundentscheidung sein. Es muss endlich zum Ausdruck gebracht werden, dass die Kirche die Frauen braucht, und zwar als gleichberechtigte Partnerinnen braucht—nicht weil sie sonst zu wenig Personal für die tägliche Arbeit und Umsetzung ihrer Sendung hätte, sondern weil dies die Gottebenbildlichkeit des Menschen als Mann und Frau verlangt." Sabine Demel: "Nur weil wir Frauen sind? Die Frage nach der Gleichstellung in der katholischen Kirche," in *Nur weil wir Frauen sind? 30 Jahre Wort der Deutschen Bischöfe "Zu Fragen der Stellung der Frau in Kirche und Gesellschaft" 1981–2011. Studientag mit Prof. Dr. Sabine Demel am 7. Juli 2011 im CPH Nürnberg, Dokumentation*, ed. Arbeitsgemeinschaft Frauenseelsorge Bayern et al.; see http://frauenseelsorge-muenchen.de/fileadmin/Redaktion/Bilder/Buchempfehlungen/Dokumentation7-2011-1.pdf, 18.

BIBLIOGRAPHY

Demel, Sabine: "Nur weil wir Frauen sind? Die Frage nach der Gleichstellung in der katholischen Kirche," in *Nur weil wir Frauen sind? 30 Jahre Wort der Deutschen Bischöfe "Zu*

Fragen der Stellung der Frau in Kirche und Gesellschaft" 1981–2011. Studientag mit Prof. Dr. Sabine Demel am 7. Juli 2011 im CPH Nürnberg, Dokumentation, ed. Arbeitsgemeinschaft Frauenseelsorge Bayern et al.; seehttp://frauenseelsorge-muenchen.de/fileadmin/Redaktion/Bilder/Buchempfehlungen/Dokumentation7-2011-1.pdf.

Engelhard, Daniela, and Qualbrink, Andrea, "Frauen in Führungspositionen—Perspektiven für Pastoral, Bildung, Caritas und Verwaltung," in ed. Franz-Josef Bode, *Als Frau und Mann schuf er sie* (Paderborn: Bonifatius, 2013), 75–82.

Gössmann, Elisabeth, *Geburtsfehler weiblich. Lebenserinnerungen einer katholischen Theologin* (München: Iudicium, 2003).

Happ, Sabine, and Jüttemann, Veronica (eds.), *"Lasst sie doch denken." 100 Jahre Studium für Frauen in Münster* (Münster: Aschendorff, 2008).

Jensen, Anne, "Auf dem Weg zur feministischen Theologie," http://static.uni-graz.at/fileadmin/projekte/genderforschung-theologie/Jensen_Auf_dem_Weg_zur_feministischen_Theologie.pdf.

Kasper, Walter, *Das Zusammenleben von Frauen und Männern in Leben und Dienst der Kirche*, February 20, 2012,http://www.dbk.de/fileadmin/redaktion/diverse_downloads/presse_2012/2013-035-Studientag-FVV-Trier_Vortrag-K-Kasper.pdf.

Katholische Frauengemeinschaft Deutschlands, Diözesanverband Mainz (ed.), *Wegbereiterin—Wegbegleiterin. Festschrift zum 75. Geburtstag von Prof. Dr. Irene Willig*, (Mainz: kfd, 2001).

Kolm, Melanie, *Frauen in der katholischen Kirche—betroffen und beteiligt. Ekklesiologische Reflexionen über nachkonziliare synodale Prozesse*, Theologische Frauenforschung in Europa 27 (Münster: Lit, 2015).

König, Hildegard, "Gender, Kirche, Gesellschaft—Strategien der Marginalisierung und Exklusion von Frauen in der Darstellung und Deutung kirchlicher Zeitgeschichte," in *Gender studieren: Lernprozess für Theologie und Kirche*, ed. Margit Eckhold (Ostfildern: Grünewald, 2017), 73–103.

Loretan, Adrian, "Frauen in kirchlichen Ämtern. Eine rechtliche Standortbestimmung," in *Gleichstellung der Geschlechter und die Kirchen. Ein Beitrag zur menschenrechtlichen und ökumenischen Diskussion*, ed. Denise Buser and Adrian Loretan (Freiburg: Universitätsverlag, 1999), 64.

Muschiol, Gisela, "Dienste, Ämter und das Geschlecht. Anfragen an die Feminisierungsthese aus katholischer Perspektive," in *Feminisierung oder (Re-) Maskulinisierung*, 42–51.

Pasture, Patrick, et al. (eds.), *Beyond the Feminization Thesis: Gender and Christianity in Modern Europe* (Leuven: Leuven University Press, 2012).

Qualbrink, Andrea, "Geschlechtergerechtigkeit auch in kirchlichen Führungspositionen?," in *Geschlechtersensible Pastoral und Bildung. Studientag 14. April 2016 Freising, Dokumentation*, ed. Wiltrud Huml and Anna Sedlmaier (Erzdiözese München und Freising, 2016), 48–57.

Qualbrink, Andrea, "Leadership revisited. Esther trifft auf Führungsfrauen," in *Esthers unbekannte Seiten. Theologische Perspektiven auf ein vergessenes biblisches Buch*, ed. Stephanie Feder and Aurica Nutt (Ostfildern: Grünewald, 2012), 123–38.

Qualbrink, Andrea, *Frauen in kirchlichen Leitungspositionen. Möglichkeiten, Bedingungen und Folgen der Gestaltungsmacht von Frauen in der katholischen Kirche* (Praktische Theologie heute, 156; Stuttgart: Kohlhammer, 2018).

Raming, Ida, *Der Ausschluss der Frau vom priesterlichen Amt: Gottgewollte Tradition oder Diskriminierung? Eine rechtshistorisch-dogmatische Untersuchung der Grundlagen von Kanon 968, § 1 d. Codex Iuris Canonici* (Köln: Böhlau, 1973).

Roettger, Sarah, "Abbesses as Model for Female Diaconate? Historical Considerations," *Concilium* 53/2 (2017).
Rüttiger, Gabriele, "Frauen in kirchlichen Leitungspositionen—Erfahrungen und Perspektiven," in *Als Frau und Mann schuf er sie. Über das Zusammenwirken von Frauen und Männern in der Kirche*, ed. Franz-Josef Bode (Paderborn: Bonifatius, 2013), 29–36.
Sailer, Gudrun, "Immer mehr Frauen im Vatikan," Vatican News,http://de.radiovaticana.va/news/2015/03/05/immer_mehr_frauen_im_vatikan/1127085.
Schneider, Bernhard, "Feminisierung und (Re-)Maskulinisierung der Religion im 19. Jahrhundert. Tendenzen der Forschung aus der Perspektive des deutschen Katholizismus," in *Feminisierung oder (Re-) Maskulinisierung der Religion im 19. und 20. Jahrhundert? Forschungsbeiträge aus Christentum, Judentum und Islam*, ed. Michaela Sohn-Kronthaler (Wien: Böhlau, 2016), 11–41.
Schottroff, Luise, Schroer, Silvia, and Wacker, Marie-Theres, *Feminist Interpretation: The Bible in Women's Perspective* (Minneapolis: Fortress Press, 1998).
Steinhauer, Eric W., "Eine kurze Geschichte der Ausbildung katholischer Theologen in Deutschland," in *Ortskirche und Weltkirche in der Geschichte*, ed. Heinz Finger, Reimund Haas, and Hermann-Josef Scheidgen (Köln: Böhlau, 2011), 899–916.
Wacker, Marie-Theres, "Frauen in der (theologischen) Wissenschaft—die Anfänge in Münster 1892-1909," in *Feminist Theology in Europe: More Than Half a Life; A Reader in Honour of Hedwig Meyer-Wilmes,* ed. Elżbieta Adamiak and Marie-Theres Wacker (Münster: Lit, 2013), 158–73.
Wacker, Marie-Theres, and Birke, Franziska, *Grenzüberschreitung. Anfänge der Promotion von Frauen an der Katholisch-Theologischen Fakultät der Universität Münster* (Münster: Aschendorff, forthcoming).
Winter, Miriam Therese, *Out of the Depths: The Story of Ludmila Javorová Ordained Roman Catholic Priest* (New York: Crossroads, 2001).
Zagano, Phyllis (ed.), *Women Deacons? Essays with Answers* (Collegeville: Liturgical Press, 2016).
Zagano, Phyllis, "Justice for the Life of the Parish: Restoring Women to the Ordained Diaconate," *Concilium* 53/2 (2017): 141–48.

Chapter Thirteen

The Impact of Women in Protestant Christian Ministry Today

Renate Jost

The path to the ordination of women in Protestant churches in Germany has been a long and rocky one, but their presence in this role is now firmly established. However, the fact that women are active in their faith communities in this formal role does not indicate how and in what ways this presence has had a specific impact on the communities, on society, and on the self-understanding and shaping of this role by women. In this essay, I wish to follow the trajectories of some of these impacts in a historical review and then focus on some specific aspects of the theological relevance of women in the ministry.

1. WOMEN IN THE MINISTRY—PAST AND PRESENT

After long and sustained campaigning, the ordination of women to the ministry in the established Protestant churches of Germany was achieved in the late 1960s through the mid-1970s. Although initially still under some restrictions, namely that women were specifically qualified for the jobs of counseling, performing children's services, and parish work with families and children, but were not allowed to be married else they lose their jobs, women eventually gained full equality with men in this office. Today, women hold positions at all levels and roles in the Protestant church.[1] The first Protestant church in Germany that established equal rights for men and women in terms of access to and regulations concerning the ministry was the Evangelische

Kirche in Hessen und Nassau (EKHN). Feminist pastor and scholar Simone Mantei draws attention to the fact that "the ministry was for the first time legally constituted as *'gender-comprehensive'* by the EHKN in 1970: not at all, as the title of the law stated, as an *'equalization* of women's rights to the rights of ministers,' but as a *transformation* of the 'male' ministry which had up to then not been affected by the development."[2] Mantei here refers to the innovative option introduced in this specific Protestant church for women *and* men to apply for a leave of absence for family reasons.

As of 2019, over 50 percent of the students enrolled in Protestant theology departments in Germany are female. A 2008 statistic of the Evangelische Kirche in Deutschland (EKD) identified 33.3 percent of the ministers as female, but since almost half of them held only part-time positions (45.79 percent), actually 28.1 percent of the parish work was done by women. Mantei interprets these figures as an indication that the Protestant ministry is heading toward a gender-transcendent profession.[3]

Also, in terms of leadership positions, women are represented at the highest level in Protestant churches, with currently three of the twenty-two leadership positions being held by women: Ilse Junkermann, bishop of the Thuringian Church; Kirstin Fehrs, bishop of Lübeck and Hamburg; and Annette Kurschus, praeses of the Westphalian Church.[4] In the Methodist Church of Germany, Rosemarie Wenner holds the position of bishop. In the Bavarian Church, more than 50 percent of the regional bishops are female.[5] This seems to be exceptional, since generally at the middle level of church management, which in some churches are called superintendents, only 16 percent of positions are held by women.[6] Vice Bishop Susanne Breit-Keßler has enquired as to why so few women are willing to take over more responsibility in the churches, especially in the middle level of church management.[7] Further research on this issue is required.

This indicates that despite these achievements of the last fifty years, the Protestant churches are still a significant step away from having arrived at a genuine gender balance in the ministry, especially when it comes to the higher leadership positions. Moreover, there are further aspects indicating that gender equality has not yet been fully achieved. The majority of women in the ministry work part-time, while there are rather few men working part-time or sharing their jobs, for example, with their wives. There is only a gradual increase in the equal sharing of child-care duties in families and society in Germany.[8] Caring for children and elderly parents as well as performing household duties is still predominantly the domain of women.

A number of factors contribute to this situation. Some are shared with issues generally identified as hindering women from climbing the career ladder; others are more specific to the role of church ministers. Thus, concerning factors that affect women in Western societies more broadly, Andrea Abele-Brehm notes that many women are not willing to spend less time with their children, family, and friends, as would be required by full-time employment. Additionally, they also value time to care for themselves and maintain a healthy work-life balance. Among the women themselves, as well as those looking for women to take up leadership positions, a prevalent mindset can still be found that Abele-Brehm calls a "culture of discouragement."[9] Self-perception and expectations as well as the perception and expectations of others can combine to form hurdles for women that are difficult to overcome. Being the first in a position traditionally held by men, women have to prove that they are as capable as men of filling that position.

Specific aspects pertaining to women in the ministry can be attributed similarly to women's specific choices, in that many women prefer to work in hospitals, schools, and social institutions, which are traditionally connected to female role models. Such positions provide fewer opportunities for climbing the career ladder and moving into leadership roles.

In parish work, women perform the same duties as men, that is, preaching, pastoral care, teaching, and the organizational and representational duties of a traditional minister, but in addition they also often perform the role of a traditional wife. This means that parish ministry for women implies a double or even triple caring role, thus rendering the task often more demanding than it would be for men. As long as the current structures in churches do not change, the institutional discouragement of women working as ministers remains. To facilitate a thorough analysis of this situation, the individual (personal identity, psychological factors), structural (organization of society), and symbolic levels should be connected to each other in order to develop a model of thinking that appropriately reflects the permeation of sameness and difference.[10] "From a deconstructive perspective, every female pastor and every male pastor are different, and each person is different depending on the situation or the relationship concerned."[11]

On the other hand, recent qualitative research demonstrates that young male and female ministers increasingly tend to perform their ministries in a similar way.[12] It also needs to be noted that over the past decades, the gap between gender roles has narrowed in many areas of life in Germany. The gender-specific expectations that still exist do not prevent men, for instance, from opting for parental leave or part-time work, or women from taking on leadership roles.

The development is different in Finland, as has been noted in a recent survey. The rather surprising findings demonstrated the following:

> Liberal views are more common among the young female clergy, but among young male clergy the case was just the opposite. Conservative theological views were most common among young male clergy. Of male clergy under 35 years old, half regarded themselves as mostly or decidedly theologically conservative compared with only one in ten of the young female clergy. . . . Regression analysis shows that theological orientation is clearly a gender issue . . . and not an age issue.[13]

It should therefore not come as a surprise that the situation in the Protestant churches in Germany and in the Protestant theological departments are similar. Here, less than 20 percent of chair holders, that is, full professors, are female. There are very few exceptions, such as the Augustana-Hochschule, a church institution of higher education for the Lutheran Church of Bavaria, with currently 150 students and eight professorial chairs where now 40 percent of the faculty are women. This is, in part, the result of nearly two decades of feminist theology and gender issues being a major focus of this school of theology, the support of the Bavarian Lutheran Church, especially of women's groups and bishops, open-minded colleagues, and the small size of this institution.[14] It is striking that none of the female professors at this institution are married or have children.

In general, it is still more difficult for women, especially if they have a feminist theological interest, to actually be granted a chair at a university. The only exceptions are the Roman Catholic department of the University of Münster and the Protestant department of the University of Marburg—both with more than forty years of a critical theological tradition that facilitated the appointment of feminist theologians.[15] This situation correlates with the waning presence of women in higher leadership positions in the Protestant churches.

Nevertheless, despite still being a minority, women in the ministry have become commonplace and accepted as competent to fulfill all the tasks of the position. They no longer even have to prove themselves as more competent than men, but are accepted on equal par with their colleagues.

Thus, the situation of women in the ministry in Protestant churches is an ambivalent one. Their having achieved acceptance on equal par with their male colleagues and also being part of the leadership teams at the higher levels in the hierarchy, there are aspects that need to be critically reconsidered, in that it is not sufficient for women in the ministry to be accepted as equal to men (that was the struggle of second-wave feminism). The point is that by slipping into a role that over the centuries has been held and defined exclusively by men, women risk replicating this role without embracing it as women and thus transforming it.[16] The alternative risk is that women are assigned tasks and judged in their work as ministers through the lens of traditional female roles, that is, as the opposite of the roles and functions traditionally assigned to men. Here, critical reflection and gender-sensitive theological approaches taught at university intersect with the practical performance of women's roles in the ministry. There are numerous aspects that are involved in such critical reflection, and I can only highlight a few of these here.

2. FROM DIFFERENCE TO (DE-)CONSTRUCTION AND INTERSECTIONALITY

There are a number of perceptions and situations in parish work that illustrate the problems arising from centuries of a male-defined function of the ministry. Thus, the way in which women execute their roles in church leadership is considered more participatory, they being more attuned to the emotional aspects it involves and experimenting more freely and creatively. These characteristics of a so-called female leadership style can also be critically challenged, as it is seen as being weak and lacking in authority.[17] Such assessments point to the perception of a binary division of gender roles in which women (and men) are often still trapped. The fact that a majority of hospital chaplains and teachers of religious education are female, whereas in team ministries the senior minister in the majority of cases is male, has to do with the fact that part-time ministerial positions, predominantly held by women, can more easily be pursued in educational and medical institutions.[18] Such perceptions, also known as "doing gender," are reinforced when a female minister is seen as an intimate friend for female parishioners, one who is better able to listen and comfort than men, while the male minister is more adored as a fatherly charismatic figure by women in the church.[19] A process of "undoing gender" can be initiated if male and female colleagues working together in a parish are aware of the traditional expectations and their own habitus, and thereby challenge male and female stereotypes.

In such necessary processes in practice and in everyday situations, the critical reflection on third-wave deconstructionist feminism and more recent approaches informed by the U.S. intersectionality discourses can enter into creative interaction.[20] Third-wave feminism critically drew attention to the fact that equality should not be confused with sameness. The step to equal standing in the ministry was a struggle that was necessary, but achieving this, at least in the established Protestant churches in Germany, is not the end of the road but only a step along the way. It is evident that with women having achieved equal status in the ministry, the challenge of what this implies for the self-understanding of women in this role and what it implies for the role as such needs to be taken up. Here, critical reflection in the vein of most recent gender approaches intersects with practical experience. The main insight is that equality of, and difference between, women and men are not in opposition to but actually presuppose each other. The recognition of difference indicates that the category of gender is not a stand-alone one, but intersects with various other categories in a polyvalent interplay in the emergence of identities, values, and practices.

To demonstrate the interdependence of different categories, I use the image of a star as shown below:

For reasons I have discussed elsewhere, I am using the categories of race, ethnicity, gender, body, class, sexuality, desire, religion, and culture as intersecting in the multidimensional star, which is also in motion so that all categories can be related to each other.[21] I am aware that by using categories to describe kyriarchal structures, there is a risk that what is being challenged is actually being reinforced. This means that the categories used have to be critically considered in an ongoing process of deconstruction. Doing and undoing gender are in a permanent process of mutual interaction.

As mentioned above, in these categories we also have to be aware of the different levels of our analysis: the macrolevel involves the structure and organization of our society, the microlevel includes our personal identity and psychological constitution, and the symbolic level is where all these categories are constructed.

Third-wave feminism even goes so far as to challenge the general category of *women*; the question of what this implies when considering the practice of the ministry, not only of women, is wide open.[22] This means that all people working in religious institutions should be given the possibility to be accepted and work in and with, or independent from, their specific gender roles. In different contexts, times, spaces, and churches, the embodying and

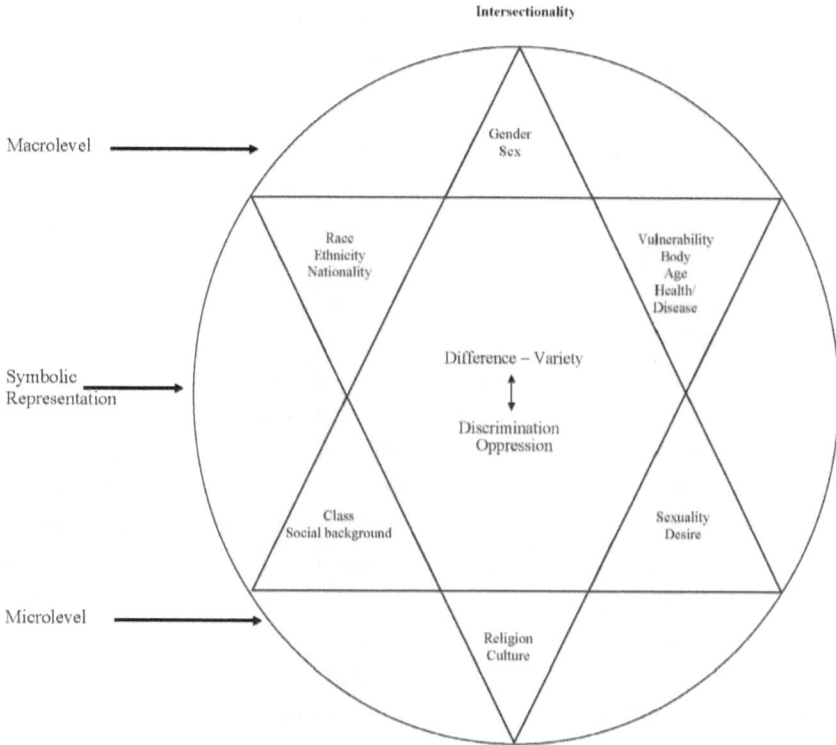

Figure 13.1. The Hermeneutic Star by Renate Jost

performance of male, female, or transgender ministerial roles may vary according to individuality and contingent on the situation. It certainly implies a shift in pastoral theology concerning gender theories in relation to the ministry from difference to (de-)construction.[23]

In the decades in which women now have had the opportunity to work on equal par with their male colleagues in the ministry, they have made a significant impact in many aspects of church life, which changed perceptions and fed back into the critical reflection in the academy.

3. THE IMPACT OF WOMEN IN THE MINISTRY

3.1 Women in the Ministry Change the Symbolic Order and Role Models

It cannot be overestimated that women as well as people with fluid gender identities in the Protestant ministry demonstrate, on a symbolic level, that all people have equal rights and that differences are not a matter of binary oppositions reduced to sex and gender, but fall along a spectrum of a variety of different personalities. The presence of women and people with fluid gender identities as such contributes to the undoing of gender stereotypes.

One important consequence of women in religious ministries is that men too are pressed to develop their role in a different way, since traditional masculinity is being questioned and is undergoing a process of deconstruction as well. With women and people with fluid gender identities appropriating the role of the minister in their own particular way, the critical reflection on and practical experimentation with the self-understanding of men in this role have become prevalent as well. Christoph Morgenthaler has critically reflected on this and identified "queer masculinities of straight men," referring to the male minister as "sissy boy," "social justice straight-queer," "elective straight queer," and as "male living in the shadow of masculinity."[24] Of course, these processes do not happen merely within the boundaries of Protestant churches, but rather the churches share in this regard as to the impact of the changing roles and self-perceptions of women and people with fluid gender identities on Western societies generally.

3.2 Women in the Ministry Change the Traditional Parsonage

Beginning with Martin Luther and Katharina von Bora through to the late 1960s, the traditional parsonage, one in which the wife kept the household and the husband was responsible for the public sphere, was a leading model for family life in Germany. It was so firmly established that women who were married to ministers were not allowed to get paid jobs from the church, and ordained female ministers were not allowed to get married until the mid 1970s. The church claimed that women who participated in the labor market were not able to care for their family properly, a status and perception never applied to men.[25]

Since women gained equal rights in the ministry, this has changed. Some female ministers live with men working as househusbands, some spouses share a job, or each holds separate jobs, all of these varieties occurring with or without children. The variations of family life are not restricted to heterosexual couples, but today in the parsonages ministers live as single, others as heterosexual, same-sex, or transsexual unmarried or married couples. Thus, women in the ministry were a vanguard in the struggle for the acceptance of different lifestyles in church and society. In many of the Protestant churches, blessings for gay and lesbian congregation members in different life situations have become part of the services offered.

Inasmuch as the traditional model of family life in the parsonage served as a role model for family life at large, these different and variable forms of family life and cohabitation present a variety of models for the wider society.

3.3 Women in the Ministry Introduce Specific Gender-Related Questions into the Church

In traditional gender perceptions since antiquity, women have been specifically associated with the body. Their being was ontologically defined through their bodily existence over and against men, who were ontologically defined via their intellectual capacity.[26] Rather than distancing themselves from this association with the body, women embrace this association and emphasize its significance not merely for themselves but for human existence as such.[27] The so-called body turn in cultural studies is reminiscent of this and in relation to the Protestant church has led to the raising of consciousness around aspects such as resilience, as well as vulnerability.[28] Relevant in relation to pastoral counseling and care is, for instance, the recognition of empowering religious traditions found in sacred texts as well as in rituals that can be supportive in trauma therapy in their potential to enhance resilience, that is, the power of inherent personal healing.

The issue of vulnerability has risen to prominence in the debates following recent terror attacks. The questions have circled around issues of human rights and security and to what extent it is necessary to secure oneself and one's community, and when and to what extent it is necessary to risk vulnerability for others. In these contexts, the Christian doctrine of incarnation is seen as a narrative of vulnerability from the birth in the manger to the message of God's justice and the violent death on the cross. The Nativity narrative in particular, then, was interpreted as a narrative symbolizing the vulnerability of human beings.

At a formal level, the issue of violence and sexual violence against women and children was discussed during a specific ecumenical decade

(1988–1998) proclaimed by the Ecumenical Council of Churches, and in the year 2000 the council of the Protestant churches in Germany published an official report on this issue.[29] The fact that violence against women was the focus of a specific program of churches worldwide indicates that the impact of women in official church roles as ministers, bishops, and church leaders has arrived at higher levels in church organizations. It includes social action and work against gender stereotyping, but also theological reflection, in that, for instance, a misunderstanding of Christology as supporting violent relationships and avoidable sufferings has to be radically revised. These are only two examples in which a focus on issues traditionally attributed to and affecting women can be traced to the impact of women in the ministry. This leads me to mention a final important aspect of the impact of women in the ministry, which is the recognition of feminist and gender studies in Protestant churches, as is particularly evident in biblical interpretation.

3.4 Women in the Ministry as Catalysts for the Acceptance of Feminist and Gender Studies' Insights in Religion and Theology

The[30] use of inclusive, or in Germany more prominent, fair language by ministers (male and female) in the church, especially the use of non-kyriarchal and gender-balanced metaphors for God is widely normative.[31] Thus, feminist theology had an impact on the recent reform of the official lectionaries for sermons in all churches of the EKD, which now include more gender-relevant texts.[32] This is a highly significant step when the decisive role of language and the images transported through language are considered. The language and passages imprint themselves in the minds of faith communities and influence perceptions and behavior.[33] This applies not only to the texts as such but also to their translations and interpretations. Thus, we will now take a brief look at the role of feminist biblical interpretation, which actually parallels the pathway of women in the ministry, both of which have mutually influenced one another.

4. REFORMATION AND FEMINIST INTERPRETATION OF THE BIBLE

The Reformation would have been unthinkable without the power of interpretation of scripture. One important element of biblical interpretation is the concept of the *priesthood of all believers* and how this doctrine was put into practice by Luther's translation of the Bible into German. This placed the power of textual interpretation into the hands of any literate individual. The freedom to interpret the Bible and the increasing literacy of girls and women led to points of conflict among the reformers. One example of this can be found when female followers of the Reformation claimed equal authority to preach. Such was the case of Argula von Grumbach, who was met with strong opposition from Luther.[34] In arguing their right to preach, women pointed to female prophets such as Deborah and Miriam, as well as the female disciples of Jesus, especially Mary Magdalene.

It was only after the women's movement during the nineteenth century, as a consequence of great struggle, that the possibility was opened for women to study in the German universities. Beginning in the 1900s, women in Protestant churches began to reassert their right to work in parish ministry. To achieve this right, some women, like Anna Paulsen (1893–1981), who in the 1950s was responsible for women's issues in Evangelische Kirche in Deutschland,[35] argued that women of spiritual authority were present in the biblical texts.[36] Again, we find evidence of this in biblical prophetesses, such as Miriam, Deborah, and Hulda, and the tradition of the *apostala apostolorum* Maria Magdalena and the missionary women working with Paul, as, for example, Junia.[37]

Thus, biblical interpretation presented a strong tool in the struggle of women for equal rights in the Protestant church, but it has to be admitted that the main arguments and eventual breakthroughs for women's equal rights as ministers in the Protestant German churches really arose in the aftermath of the equal rights granted to women in German society after 1945.

Even so, it took thirty years to establish the right for women to become ordained and another thirty years for female ministry to be accepted in this role more or less without question. Women had to work hard to convince parishioners and church leaders that they were able to fulfill this role as well as or even better than men.[38] As mentioned, feminist biblical interpretation played an important role in the arguments supporting and sustaining the struggle of women in the ministry.

In the 1970s in Germany, the publications of Mary Daly, Rosemary Radford Ruther, and Letty Russell were widely influential.[39] In the late 1970s and early 1980s, many groups both inside and outside the universities began to critically study the biblical texts from a feminist point of view.[40]

In 1974, the World Council of Churches Consultation on "Sexism in the 1970s" took place in Berlin. The discussion papers prepared for this consultation laid important groundwork arguing for complete equality for women pastors and subsequent processes of institutionalization of feminist theology in Protestant churches and seminaries.[41]

Important was the historical-critical and sociohistorical interpretation of biblical texts that seemingly argued for the subordination and silencing of women, thus providing the critical interpretive tool to challenge traditional male-stream interpretations.

Elisabeth Schüssler Fiorenza argued that the Jewish Jesus movement was relatively gender egalitarian and that those texts proclaiming the subordination of women were a later development to adjust the Christian communities to the "Kyriarchat" of the Roman Empire.[42]

Another good example is feminist work on 1 Corinthians 14:34–35, prohibiting women from speaking in public. Marlene Crüseman argues that this has no Jewish parallel but is to be found in Greco-Roman writings. A text from *Tosefta Megillah* 4:11 is frequently cited as rabbinic evidence, but most often the second half of the verse only: "One does not let a woman come forward to read (from the Torah) in public." "The sentence preceding this, stating the overall principle, declares: All are counted among the seven (that read the Torah on the Sabbath), even a boy under age, even a woman."[43] This highlights that the active participation of women in the synagogue worship cannot be categorically rejected and that their participation is subject, both in theory and in practice, to dispute.

Luke 13:13 is another example of a woman speaking in the synagogue. I agree with Luise Schottroff, who speaks of a "falsification" relating to 1 Corinthians 14:34–35 and argues:

> The text ties together the subordination of women . . . , the absolute prohibition to speak in public, the enthronement of the man (husband) as women's sole teacher, and the incarnation of women's activity in the home. In terms of content, it is to be seen as of equal substance with 1 Tim 2:9–15. Like the pastoral Epistles, it was inserted into the Pauline corpus most likely in the mid-second century C.E. Those additions wholly change Paul's hermeneutic of the politics of women. In the concrete case of 1 Corinthian 12–14, it means that all the Spirit's gifts to women associated with speaking are to be prohibited.[44]

In this context, Galatians 3:28 became prominent. Brigitte Kahl points out that this verse can be read as an interpretation of Genesis by Paul. She argues:

Through this, God's creative intervention, the one Messianic-Abrahamic "seed-Christ" (3:16), from now on "embodies" the uniqueness and unity of the people of God (= the children of Abraham; 3:29) and the unity and uniqueness of God (3:20) in a new, messianic way in becoming one with the "other" (3:28): "There is no longer Jew or Greek, there is no longer slave or free, there is no longer male and female; for all of you are one in Christ Jesus" (3:26–28). With this messianic "sperma(the)ology," Paul gives Jewish monotheism a radical, inclusive-universal and antihierarchical definition. Christ becomes the "nucleus" of a fellowship of Abraham's children that is plural in nature, which encroaches on the borders of the old national, religious, social, and gender-based identities.[45]

In 1987, the lectures and publications of American Jewish feminists such as Judith Plaskow and Susannah Heschel were important for prompting the debate concerning anti-Semitism in feminist theology and biblical interpretation. They pointed to the dangerous anti-Semitic cliché present in German biblical scholarship since the nineteenth century, which was perpetuated in the feminist thesis of an original matriarchy suppressed by the patriarchal Jewish YHWH and through the image of a women-friendly Jesus who distinguished himself from a Judaism that discriminated against women.[46] An understanding of the role in Judaism was deepened through the work on rabbinic scriptural exegesis from a feminist perspective by Jewish scholar Pnina Navè-Levinson, an initiator and professor until 1986 at the Hochschule für Jüdische Studien in Heidelberg.[47] These important critical debates with Jewish feminists informed my own research and influenced my dissertation, "Women, Men, and the Queen of Heaven in Jeremiah 7 and 44."[48] The book deals with questions of goddess religion in Israel. I took the issue up again later, in my habilitation, where I argued that egalitarian structures and ideas can be found throughout the Hebrew Bible. One prominent example for this is the Song of Deborah in Judges 5.[49]

Many of the results of feminist exegesis can be found in the Bible translation in inclusive language, that is, the *Bibel in gerechter Sprache*.[50] This translation used now in parishes and seminaries carries an important impact for an empowering understanding of the tradition.

The translation has been characterized as follows:

> Some of the trademarks of the *Bibel in gerechter Sprache* are as follows: the biblical name of God is continually highlighted and a range of reading options offered (Eternal [male/female] One, Adonaj, GOD, Living One [male/female etc.]); women are always explicitly mentioned wherever the intention of the

text, the context, or the research results of social history demonstrate that they are included in masculine terms. . . . The Reformation is identified with the biblical terms of justice sedaka (Hebrew), and dikaiosyne (Greek). God's justice is shown in fundamental acts of salvation and liberation such as the exodus, through which God virtually defines God's self as God (Ex 20:2). The praying women and men of the psalms of lamentation expect salvation through God's action, and even sinners hope for justice (Ps 51:16) that includes forgiveness. The coming messianic age is described as the coming of God's zedaka (Jer 56:19). God's justice is permanently attached to the Torah: God will speak impartially to those who live as directed by God.[51]

The *Bibel in gerechter Sprache* should and will do justice primarily to the particular source text. It has also been noted that "the *Bibel in gerechter Sprache* is a Christian translation that attempts to learn from Jewish-Christian dialogue. In recent decades it has been widely recognized how much the New Testament that emerged from a Jewish base has been read and translated in an anti-Semitic manner."[52] Liberation theology, feminist kyriarchal critique, postcolonial studies, and the discussion of empire have shown that biblical texts and their exegetical history are also determined by power structures. They allude to the close association of androcentrism, colonialism, racism, and militarism with other relationships of exploitation.[53] The Bible in just language is not used everywhere, but in many places. Specific life-cycle rituals are developed and accepted.[54]

The results of feminist exegesis have been made accessible to a wider public in numerous publications and are being spread in Bible study groups and through preaching by female and male pastors who have become familiar with gender-sensitive theology during their studies and in continuing education programs.[55] Some aspects have also been influential in the revision of the EKD lectionary.[56] These are significant achievements that will generate further impact. But, there is more that needs to be done. It is necessary to integrate theological gender studies broadly in the curricula of theological studies, as has been good practice already in higher education institutions of the EKD as well as some universities for more than twenty years. The initiatives for equal opportunities in the established churches have to be continued, not least as a contribution to the development of innovative models for the compatibility of family and work life for the benefit of society as a whole.

5. PERSPECTIVES

My own engagement in both the academy and the church is driven by my vision that all people be accepted in religious institutions as well as in the universities irrespective of their class, race, gender, and desire.

Since the acceptance of women in the rabbinate and ministry has been and still is a question of justice, it includes all discriminated groups, as well as animals and the whole of creation.

It follows naturally that issues of human rights and justice are getting more attention within religious institutions. This is seen through the action of groups working to abolish social injustice. Research and academic teaching centers for theology could be established where not only Christian theology is taught, but where also other religious traditions are part of the institutional setting on equal par with the Christian tradition. As the example of Harvard Divinity School demonstrates, it can be inspiring when Jews, Christians, Muslims, Buddhists, Hindus, and people from other backgrounds work and celebrate together without denying their differences. This could be a model for further work. The conference celebrating eighty years of the ordination of Regina Jonas was an important milestone in this direction. But, there is still a long way to go in the journey of undoing gender.

Informed by intersectionality approaches such as those mentioned in the beginning, and as Elisabeth Schüssler Fiorenza points out, the vision of a renewed creation includes not only a new heaven but also a qualified new earth—an earth liberated from all forms of kyriarchal exploitation and dehumanization. My vision is a community of people in religious institutions, as well as in society, with equal rights against the background of an alternative reality with justice and *shalom* for everybody.[57]

NOTES

1. For details and the history of women in ministry in the different Protestant churches, cf. *"Darum wagt es Schwestern . . ." Zur Geschichte Evangelischer Theologinnen in Deutschland, Neukirchen-Vluyn*, ed. Frauenforschungsprojekt zur Geschichte der Theologinnen (Neukirchen-Vluyn: Neukirchener Verlag, 1994); *Dem Himmel so nah—dem Pfarramt so fern. Erste Evangelische Theologinnen im Geistlichen Amt*, ed. Heike Köhler, Dagmar Henze, Dagmar Herbrecht, and Hannelore Erhart (Neukirchen-Vluyn: Neukirchener Verlag, 1996); Simone Mantei, "Pfarrberuf und Geschlecht," in *Schwellenkunde. Einsichten und Aussichten für den Pfarrberuf im 21. Jahrhundert. Ulrike Wagner-Rau zum 60 Geburtstag*, ed. Regina Sommer and Julia Koll (Stuttgart: Kohlhammer Verlag, 2012), 69–82; Auguste Zeiß-Horbach, *Evangelische Kirche und Frauenordination. Der Beitrag der Evangelisch-Lutherischen Kirche*

in Bayern zum deutschlandweiten Diskurs im 20. Jahrhundert (Leipzig: Evangelische Verlagsanstalt, 2017).

2. Mantei, "Pfarrberuf und Geschlecht," 72. ("Erstmals rechtlich '*geschlechterübergreifend*' wurde der Pfarrberuf in der EKHN 1970 verfasst und keineswegs wie der Gesetzestitel formulierte als '*Angleichung* des Rechtes der Frauen (sic!) an das Recht der Pfarrer,' sondern als *Transformation* des 'männlichen' Pfarramtes, das bis dahin von der Entwicklung unberührt war.'")

3. Cf. Mantei, "Pfarrberuf und Geschlecht," 74.

4. Cf. Transcript Podium, "Diversity: Die neue Gleichstellung—zur Zukunft der Gleichstellungsstelle in der Bayrischen Kirche," in Renate Jost and Sarah Jäger, *Vielfalt und Differenz. Intersektionale Perspektiven auf Feminismus und Religion* (Münster: LIT Verlag, 2017).

5. For further details, cf. Dr. Johanna Beyer with the support of stud. theol. Anja-Désirée Lipponer, *Geschlechterverteilung in Ausgewählten Leitungsbereichen, Frauengleichstellungsstelle der Evangelisch-Lutherischen Kirche in Bayern*, 2014.

6. Cf. *Atlas zur Gleichstellung von Frauen und Männern in der Evangelischen Kirche in Deutschland 2015.*

7. Unpublished speech by Breit-Keßler at the celebration of "80 Jahre Theologinnenkonvent in Bayern—40 Jahre Frauenordination " (Nürnberg, 2015).

8. Barbara Vinken, "Erkenne Dich selbst: Frauen–Mütter–Emanzipation," *Aus Politik und Zeitgeschichte (APuZ)* 2011: 37–38.

9. A. Abele-Brehm, "How Gender Influences Objective Career Success and Subjective Career Satisfaction: The Impact of Self-Concept and of Parenthood," in *Gender Differences in Aspirations and Attainment: A Life Course Perspective*, ed. Ingrid Schoon and Jacquelynne S. Eccles (Cambridge: Cambridge University Press, 2014).

10. Cf. the sketch in the section "From Difference to (De-)construction and Intersectionality."

11. "Jede Pfarrerin ist in dekonstruktiver Perspektive anders und auch jeder Pfarrer, und die gleiche Person ist von Situation zu Situation und von Beziehung zu Beziehung jeweils auch wieder anders." U. Pohl-Patalong, "Wie anders ist die Pfarrerin?," in *Deutsches Pfarrerblatt* 100 (2000): 298–302, 301. Cf. also U. Pohl-Patalong, "Vielfältige Kommunikation des Evangeliums: das 'Eigentliche' des Pfarrberufs in der Vielfalt der Handlungsfelder," in *Praktische Theologie* 44 (2009): 1, 25–31.

12. Cf. Mantei, "Pfarrberuf und Geschlecht"; also Anke Wiedekind, "'Frauen auf dem Sprung.' Dokumentation und Ergebnisse" (unpublished study).

13. Katie Niemelä, "Female Clergy as Agent of Religious Change?," *Religions* 2 (2001): 362–63; Mantei, "Pfarrberuf und Geschlecht," 81–82.

14. Cf. *Feministische Theologie: Initiativen, Kirchen, Universitäten—eine Erfolgsgeschichte*, ed. Gisela Matthiae, Renate Jost, Claudia Janssen, Annette Mehlhorn, and Antje Röckemann (Gütersloh: Gütersloher Verlagshaus 2008), 236–95. For the history of this professorship, cf. *Feministische Theologie: Initiativen*, 241–42.

15. For more details, cf. Renate Jost, *Erfolgsmodelle der Institutionalisierung Feministischer Theologie an Universitäten und Evangelischen Kirchlichen Hochschulen*, ed. Renate Jost and Claudia Janssen (Gütersloh: Gütersloher Verlagshaus, 2008), 241–47.

16. For further information, cf. also Ulrike Wagner-Rau, *Zwischen Vaterwelt und Feminismus. Eine Studie zur Pastoralen Identität von Frauen* (Gütersloh: Gütersloher Verlagshaus, 1992); Ulrike Wagner-Rau, *Auf der Schwelle. Das Pfarramt im Prozess kirchlichen Wandels* (Stuttgart: Kohlhammer Verlag, 2011). Cf. also Mantei, "Pfarrberuf und Geschlecht" and the literature mentioned there, especially 73.

17. For these and other gender-specific stereotypes, see, e.g., Manfred Josuttis, *Der Pfarrer ist anders. Aspekte einer zeitgenössischen Pastoraltheologie* (Munich: Chr. Kaiser Verlag, 1982).

18. For further details, cf. Beyer, *Geschlechterverteilung*; and also Studienzentrum der EKD für Gleichstellungsfragen/Konferenz der Frauenreferate und Gleichstellungsstellen in den Gliedkirchen der Evangelischen Kirche in Deutschland, ed., *Atlas zur Gleichstellung von Frauen und Männern in der Evangelischen Kirche in Deutschland. Eine Bestandsaufnahme* (Hannover: Evangelische Kirche in Deutschland, 2015), 50–51.

19. Cf. Ute E. Eisen, Christine Gerber, and Angela Standhartinger, eds., *Doing Gender—Doing Religion. Fallstudien zur Intersektionalität im frühen Judentum, Christentum und Islam*, WUNT 302 (Tübingen: Mohr Siebeck, 2013).

20. Gudrun-Axeli Knapp, "'Intersectionality'—Ein Neues Paradigma Feministischer Theorie? Zur Transatlantischen Reise von 'Race, Class, Gender,'" *Feministische Studien* 23 (2005): 1, 68–81. Cf. Renate Jost, "Intersektionalität als Herausforderung für Feministische Theologie, Gender Studies und Religion. Intersektionalität als Herausforderung. Einführende Überlegungen," in *Differenz und Vielfalt*, ed. Renate Jost and Sarah Jäger (Münster: LIT Verlag, 2017), 7–17.

21. Cf. Jost, "Intersektionalität als Herausforderung," 14.

22. Cf. Elisabeth Schüssler Fiorenza, "Between Movement and Academy: Feminist Biblical Scholarship in the Twentieth Century," in *Feminist Biblical Studies in the Twentieth Century. Scholarship and Movement*, ed. Elisabeth Schüssler Fiorenza (Atlanta: Society of Biblical Literature, 2014), 1–17, 6–9.

23. For details, cf. Mantei, "Pfarrberuf und Geschlecht," 75–78.

24. Cf. Christoph Morgenthaler, "Pfarrer sind Männer," in *Schwellenkunde. Einsichten und Aussichten für den Pfarrberuf im 21. Jahrhundert. Ulrike Wagner-Rau zum 60. Geburtstag*, ed. Regina Sommer and Julia Koll (Stuttgart: Kohlhammer Verlag, 2012), 83–93, 89. Cf. also Mantei, "Pfarrberuf und Geschlecht," 78–80.

25. For details on the history, cf. Auguste Zeiß Horbach, *Evangelische Kirche und Frauenordination. Der Beitrag der Evangelisch-Lutherischen Kirche in Bayern zum deutschlandweiten Diskurs im 20. Jahrhundert* (Leipzig: Evangelische Verlagsanstalt, 2017).

26. Cf., e.g., Rosemary Ruether, *New Woman, New Earth: Sexist Ideologies and Human Liberation* (New York: Seabury Press, 1975).

27. An early example of this is Elisabeth Moltmann-Wendel's *I am My Body: A Theology of Embodiment* (New York: Bloomsbury, 1995). Cf. also feminist theories in Elisabeth Grosz, *Volatile Bodies: Toward a Corporeal Feminism* (Bloomington: Indiana University Press, 1994).

28. Judith Butler, *Bodies That Matter: On the Discursive Limits of "Sex"* (London: Routledge, 1993); Roger Cooter, "The Turn of the Body: History and the Politics of the Corporeal," *Arbor: Ciencia, Pensamiento y Cultura* 186 (2010): 393–405.

29. Cf. EKD Studie "Gewalt gegen Frauen."

30. Cf. Renate Jost, "The Institutionalization of Feminist Biblical Studies in Its International and Ecumenical Contexts," in Schüssler Fiorenza, *Feminist Biblical Studies*, 365–94.

31. Renate Jost and Ulrike Schweiger, eds., *Feministische Impulse für den Gottesdienst* (Stuttgart: Kohlhammer Verlag, 2006); Renate Jost, "Feministische Impulse für eine neue Perikopenordnung," in *Auf dem Weg zur Perikopenrevision*, Kirchenamt der EKD, ed. Udo Hahn (Hannover: VELKD, 2010), 231–63; *Der Gottesdienst. Liturgische Texte in Gerechter Sprache, Band II: Das Abendmahl/Die Kasualien*, ed. Erhard Domay and Hanne Köhler (Gütersloh: Gütersloher Verlagshaus, 1998); *Der gottesdienst. Liturgische Texte in Gerechter Sprache, Band III: Die Psalmen*, ed. Erhard Domay and Hanne Köhler (Gütersloh, Gütersloher

Verlagshaus, 1998); Hanne Köhler and Arbeitsgruppe Abendmahl, *Brot des Lebens—Kelch des Heils*, Beratungsstelle für Gestaltung, Materialheft 85 (Frankfurt: Beratungsstelle für Gestaltung, 1999); *Raum Geben—Chancen für den Evangelischen Kirchenraum*, ed. Martin Benn and Hanne Köhler, Beratungsstelle für Gestaltung, Materialheft 12 (Frankfurt: Beratungsstelle für Gestaltung, 1999); *Der Gottesdienst. Liturgische Texte in Gerechter Sprache, Band IV: Die Lesungen*, ed. Erhard Domay and Hanne Köhler (Gütersloh: Gütersloher Verlagshaus, 2001); *Werkbuch gerechte Sprache. Praxisentwürfe für Gemeindearbeit und Gottesdienst*, ed. Erhard Domay and Hanne Köhler (Gütersloh: Gütersloher Verlagshaus, 2003); *Gottesdienstbuch in gerechter Sprache. Gebete, Lesungen, Fürbitten und Segenssprüche für die Sonn- und Feiertage des Kirchenjahres*, ed. Erhard Domay and Hanne Köhler (Gütersloh: Gütersloher Verlagshaus, 2003).

32. Jost, "Feministische Impulse," 231–63.

33. See, e.g., the classical article by Robin Lakoff, "Language and Woman's Place," *Language in Society* 2 (1973): 45–80.

34. Charlotte Methuen, "'And Your Daughters Shall Prophesy!' Luther, Reforming Women and the Construction of Authority," *Archiv für Reformationsgeschichte* 104 (1): 82–109.

35. Cf. Andrea Bieler, *Konstruktionen des Weiblichen. Die Theologin Anna Paulsen im Spannungsfeld bürgerlicher Frauenbewegung der Weimarer Republik und nationalsozialistischer Weiblichkeitsmythen* (Gütersloh: Gütersloher Verlagshaus, 1994).

36. Cf. Ruth Albrecht, "Das Weib Schweige? Protestantische Kontroversen über Predigerinnen und Evangelistinnen," in *Fromme Lektüre und Kritische Exegese im Langen 19. Jahrhundert*, ed. Michaela Sohn-Kronthaler and Ruth Albrecht (Stuttgart: Kohlhammer Verlag, 2014), 210–32.

37. Bernadette Brooten, "Junia . . . hervorragend unter den Aposteln (Röm. 16,7)," in *Frauenbefreiung. Biblische und Theologische Argumente*, ed. Elisabeth Moltmann-Wendel (München: Chr. Kaiser Verlag, 1982), 148–151. For the long history of women interpreting the Bible, cf. *Die Bibel und die Frauen*, vol. 5.1–9.1 (Stuttgart: Kohlhammer Verlag).

38. Cf. Auguste Zeiß-Horbach, "Nicht mit der Schürze Dienen, Sondern mit dem Wort. 80 Jahre Theologinnenkonvent in Bayern—40 Jahre Frauenordination," in *Deutsches Pfarrerblatt* 115 (2015): 345–48.

39. E.g., Mary Daly, *Beyond God the Father: Toward a Philosophy of Women's Liberation* (Boston: Beacon Press, 1973); Rosemary Radford Ruther, *New Woman, New Earth: Sexist Ideologies and Human Liberation* (New York: Seabury Press, 1975); Letty Russell, *Human Liberation in a Feminist Perspective: A Theology* (Philadelphia: Westminster John Knox Press, 1974); *The Liberating Word: A Guide to Nonsexist Interpretation of the Bible*, ed. Letty Russell (Philadelphia: Westminster John Knox Press, 1977).

40. Cf. Renate Jost, "The Institutionalization of Feminist Biblical Studies in 1st International and Ecumenical Contexts" (Dossier), 265–394, 368–69; Matthiae et al., *Feministische Theologie*.

41. Cf. Renate Jost, "The Institutionalization of Feminist Biblical Studies in Germany and Its International and Ecumenical Context," in *Feminist Biblical Studies*, 370.

42. Elisabeth Schüssler Fiorenza, *In Memory of Her: A Feminist Theological Reconstruction of Christian Origins* (New York: Crossroad, 1983).

43. Marlene Crüsemann, "Unrettbar frauenfeindlich: Der Kampf um das Wort von Frauen in 1 Kor 14(33b)34–35 im Spiegel antijudaistischer Elemente der Auslegung," in *Von der Wurzel Getragen. Christlich-Feministische Exegese in Auseinandersetzung mit Antijudaismus*, ed. Luise Schottroff and Marie-Theres Wacker (Leiden: Brill, 1996), 199–223, 211.

44. Luise Schottroff, "1 Corinthians: How Freedom Comes to Be," in *Feminist Biblical Interpretation: A Compendium of Critical Commentary on the Books of the Bible and Related*

Literature, ed. Luise Schottroff and Marie-Theres Wacker (Grand Rapids: Eerdmans, 2012), 718–42, 737.

45. Brigitte Kahl, "Galatians: On Discomfort about Gender and Other Problems of Otherness," in Schottroff and Wacker, *Feminist Biblical Interpretation*, 755–66, 760.

46. Cf. Susannah Heschel, *On Being a Jewish Feminist* (New York: Schocken Books, 1991); Judith Plaskow, *Standing again at Sinai: Judaism from a Feminist Perspective* (San Francisco: Harper, 1991); and the articles in Leonore Siegele-Wenschkewitz, *Verdrängte Vergangenheit, die uns bedrängt. Feministische Theologie in der Verantwortung für die Geschichte* (München: Chr. Kaiser, 1988); *Schlangenbrut* 1986; Schottroff and Wacker, *Von der Wurzel getragen*.

47. Jost, "The Institutionalization of Feminist Biblical Studies," 370.

48. Renate Jost, *Frauen, Männer und die Himmelskönigin. Exegetische Studien* (Gütersloh: Gütersloher Verlagshaus, 1995).

49. Renate Jost, *Gender, Sexualität und Macht in der Anthropologie des Richterbuches*, BWANT Bd. 164 (Stuttgart: Kohlhammer, 2006).

50. Ulrike Bail et al., *Bibel in Gerechter Sprache* (Gütersloh: Gütersloher Verlagshaus, 2006).

51. Claudia Janssen and Hanne Köhler, "A Long History of Sowing, from Which Miracles Occasionally Grow: Bible Translations in Language That Is Just," in Schüssler Fiorenza, *Feminist Biblical Studies*, 339–64.

52. Janssen and Köhler, "A Long History of Sowing."

53. Janssen and Köhler, "A Long History of Sowing."

54. Cf., e.g., Herta Leistner, *Laß Spüren Deine Kraft* (Gütersloh: Gütersloher Verlagshaus, 1997).

55. Cf. Jost, "The Institutionalization of Feminist Biblical Studies."

56. Cf. Jost, "Feministische Impulse für eine neue Perikopenordnung," 231–64.

57. Cf. Elisabeth Schüssler Fiorenza, "Intersektionalität, Kyriarchat und Christliche Religion," in *Vielfalt und Differenz. Intersektionale Perspektiven auf Feminismus und Religion*, ed. Renate Jost and Sarah Jäger (Münster: LIT, 2017), 19–36.

BIBLIOGRAPHY

Abele-Brehm, Andrea, "How Gender Influences Objective Career Success and Subjective Career Satisfaction: The Impact of Self-Concept and of Parenthood," in *Gender Differences in Aspirations and Attainment: A Life Course Perspective*, ed. Ingrid Schoon and Jacquelynne S. Eccles (Cambridge: Cambridge University Press, 2014).

Albrecht, Ruth, "Das Weib Schweige? Protestantische Kontroversen über Predigerinnen und Evangelistinnen," in *Fromme Lektüre und Kritische Exegese im Langen 19. Jahrhundert*, ed. Michaela Sohn-Kronthaler and Ruth Albrecht (Stuttgart: Kohlhammer Verlag, 2014), 210–32.

Bail, Ulrike, et al., *Bibel in Gerechter Sprache* (Gütersloh: Gütersloher Verlagshaus, 2006).

Benn, Martin, and Köhler, Hanne (eds.), *Raum Geben—Chancen für den Evangelischen Kirchenraum*, Beratungsstelle für Gestaltung, Materialheft 12 (Frankfurt: Beratungsstelle für Gestaltung, 1999).

Bieler, Andrea, *Konstruktionen des Weiblichen. Die Theologin Anna Paulsen im Spannungsfeld bürgerlicher Frauenbewegung der Weimarer Republik und Nationalsozialistischer Weiblichkeitsmythen* (Gütersloh: Gütersloher Verlagshaus, 1994).

Brooten, Bernadette, "Junia . . . Hervorragend Unter den Aposteln (Röm. 16,7)," in *Frauenbefreiung. Biblische und Theologische Argumente*, ed. Elisabeth Moltmann-Wendel (München: Chr. Kaiser Verlag, 1982), 148–51.

Butler, Judith, *Bodies That Matter: On the Discursive Limits of "Sex"* (London: Routledge, 1993).

Cooter, Roger, "The Turn of the Body: History and the Politics of the Corporeal," *Arbor: Ciencia, Pensamiento y Cultura* 186 (2010): 393–405.

Crüsemann, Marlene, "Unrettbar Frauenfeindlich: Der Kampf um das Wort von Frauen in 1 Kor 14(33b)34–35 im Spiegel Antijudaistischer Elemente der Auslegung," in *Von der Wurzel getragen. Christlich-Feministische Exegese in Auseinandersetzung mit Antijudaismus*, ed. Luise Schottroff and Marie-Theres Wacker (Leiden: Brill, 1996), 199–223.

Daly, Mary, *Beyond God the Father: Toward a Philosophy of Women's Liberation* (Boston: Beacon Press, 1973).

Domay, Erhard, and Köhler, Hanne (eds.), *Gottesdienstbuch in Gerechter Sprache. Gebete, Lesungen, Fürbitten und Segenssprüche für die Sonn-und Feiertage des Kirchenjahres* (Gütersloh: Gütersloher Verlagshaus, 2003).

Domay, Erhard, and Köhler, Hanne (eds.), *Werkbuch Gerechte Sprache. Praxisentwürfe für Gemeindearbeit und Gottesdienst* (Gütersloh: Gütersloher Verlagshaus, 2003).

Domay, Erhard, and Köhler, Hanne (eds.), *Der Gottesdienst. Liturgische Texte in Gerechter Sprache, Band IV: Die Lesungen* (Gütersloh: Gütersloher Verlagshaus, 2001).

Domay, Erhard, and Köhler, Hanne (eds.), *Der Gottesdienst. Liturgische Texte in Gerechter Sprache, Band II: Das Abendmahl/Die Kasualien*, (Gütersloh: Gütersloher Verlagshaus, 1998).

Domay, Erhard, and Köhler, Hanne (eds.), *Der Gottesdienst. Liturgische Texte in Gerechter Sprache, Band III: Die Psalmen* (Gütersloh, Gütersloher Verlagshaus, 1998).

Eisen, Ute E., Gerber, Christine, and Standhartinger, Angela (eds.), *Doing Gender—Doing Religion. Fallstudien zur Intersektionalität im Frühen Judentum, Christentum und Islam*, WUNT 302 (Tübingen: Mohr Siebeck, 2013).

Frauenforschungsprojekt zur Geschichte der Theologinnen (ed.), *"Darum wagt es Schwestern . . ." Zur Geschichte Evangelischer Theologinnen in Deutschland, Neukirchen-Vluyn* (Neukirchen-Vluyn: Neukirchener Verlag, 1994).

Gisela Matthiae, Renate Jost, et al. (eds.), *Feministische Theologie: Initiativen, Kirchen, Universitäten—Eine Erfolgsgeschichte*, (Gütersloh: Gütersloher Verlagshaus 2008).

Grosz, Elisabeth, *Volatile Bodies: Toward a Corporeal Feminism* (Bloomington: Indiana University Press, 1994).

Heschel, Susannah, *On Being a Jewish Feminist* (New York: Schocken Books, 1991).

Janssen, Claudia, and Köhler, Hanne, "A Long History of Sowing, from Which Miracles Occasionally Grow: Bible Translations in Language That Is Just," in Schüssler Fiorenza, *Feminist Biblical Studies*, 339–64.

Jost, Renate, and Jäger, Sarah, *Vielfalt und Differenz. Intersektionale Perspektiven auf Feminismus und Religion* (Münster: LIT Verlag, 2017).

Jost, Renate, "Intersektionalität als Herausforderung für Feministische Theologie, Gender Studies und Religion. Intersektionalität als Herausforderung. Einführende Überlegungen," in *Differenz und Vielfalt*, by Renate Jost and Sarah Jäger (Münster: LIT Verlag, 2017), 7–17.

Jost, Renate, "The Institutionalization of Feminist Biblical Studies in Its International and Ecumenical Contexts," in *Feminist Biblical Studies in the Twentieth Century. Scholarship and Movement*, ed. Elisabeth Schüssler Fiorenza (Atlanta: Society of Biblical Literature, 2014), 365–94.

Jost, Renate, "Feministische Impulse für eine neue Perikopenordnung," in *Auf dem Weg zur Perikopenrevision*, Kirchenamt der EKD, ed. Udo Hahn (Hannover: VELKD, 2010), 231–63.

Jost, Renate, *Erfolgsmodelle der Institutionalisierung Feministischer Theologie an Universitäten und Evangelischen Kirchlichen Hochschulen*, ed. Renate Jost and Claudia Janssen (Gütersloh: Gütersloher Verlagshaus, 2008), 241–47.

Jost, Renate, *Gender, Sexualität und Macht in der Anthropologie des Richterbuches*, BWANT Bd. 164 (Stuttgart: Kohlhammer, 2006).

Jost, Renate, and Schweiger, Ulrike (eds.), *Feministische Impulse für den Gottesdienst* (Stuttgart: Kohlhammer Verlag, 2006).

Jost, Renate, *Frauen, Männer und die Himmelskönigin. Exegetische Studien* (Gütersloh: Gütersloher Verlagshaus, 1995).

Jost, Renate, "The Institutionalization of Feminist Biblical Studies in 1st International and Ecumenical Contexts" (Dossier), 265–394.

Josuttis, Manfred, *Der Pfarrer ist Anders. Aspekte Einer Zeitgenössischen Pastoraltheologie* (Munich: Chr. Kaiser Verlag, 1982).

Kahl, Brigitte, "Galatians: On Discomfort about Gender and Other Problems of Otherness," in Schottroff and Wacker, *Feminist Biblical Interpretation*, 755–66.

Knapp, Gudrun-Axeli, "'Intersectionality'—Ein Neues Paradigma Feministischer Theorie? Zur Transatlantischen Reise von 'Race, Class, Gender,'" *Feministische Studien* 23 (2005): 1, 68–81.

Köhler, Hanne, and Arbeitsgruppe Abendmahl (eds.), *Brot des Lebens—Kelch des Heils*, Beratungsstelle für Gestaltung, Materialheft 85 (Frankfurt: Beratungsstelle für Gestaltung, 1999).

Köhler, Heike, et al. (eds.), *Dem Himmel so nah—Dem Pfarramt so Fern. Erste Evangelische Theologinnen im Geistlichen Amt*, (Neukirchen-Vluyn: Neukirchener Verlag, 1996).

Lakoff, Robin, "Language and Woman's Place," *Language in Society* 2 (1973): 45–80.

Leistner, Herta, *Laß Spüren deine Kraft* (Gütersloh: Gütersloher Verlagshaus, 1997).

Mantei, Simone, "Pfarrberuf und Geschlecht," in *Schwellenkunde. Einsichten und Aussichten für den Pfarrberuf im 21. Jahrhundert. Ulrike Wagner-Rau zum 60 Geburtstag*, ed. Regina Sommer and Julia Koll (Stuttgart: Kohlhammer Verlag, 2012), 69–82.

Methuen, Charlotte, "'And Your Daughters Shall Prophesy!' Luther, Reforming Women and the Construction of Authority," *Archiv für Reformationsgeschichte* 104 (1): 82–109.

Moltmann-Wendel, Elisabeth, *I am My Body: A Theology of Embodiment* (New York: Bloomsbury, 1995).

Morgenthaler, Christoph, "Pfarrer sind Männer," in *Schwellenkunde. Einsichten und Aussichten für den Pfarrberuf im 21. Jahrhundert. Ulrike Wagner-Rau zum 60. Geburtstag*, ed. Regina Sommer and Julia Koll (Stuttgart: Kohlhammer Verlag, 2012), 83–93.

Niemelä, Katie, "Female Clergy as Agent of Religious Change?," *Religions* 2 (2001): 362–363.

Plaskow, Judith, *Standing again at Sinai: Judaism from a Feminist Perspective* (San Francisco: Harper, 1991).

Pohl-Patalong, Uta, "Vielfältige Kommunikation des Evangeliums: das 'Eigentliche' des Pfarrberufs in der Vielfalt der Handlungsfelder," in *Praktische Theologie* 44 (2009): 1, 25–31.

Pohl-Patalong, Uta, "Wie Anders ist die Pfarrerin?," in *Deutsches Pfarrerblatt* 100 (2000): 298–302.

Radford Ruther, Rosemary, *New Woman, New Earth: Sexist Ideologies and Human Liberation* (New York: Seabury Press, 1975).

Ruether, Rosemary, *New Woman, New Earth: Sexist Ideologies and Human Liberation* (New York: Seabury Press, 1975).

Russell, Letty (ed.), *The Liberating Word: A Guide to Nonsexist Interpretation of the Bible* (Philadelphia: Westminster John Knox Press, 1977).

Russell, Letty, *Human Liberation in a Feminist Perspective: A Theology* (Philadelphia: Westminster John Knox Press, 1974).

Schottroff, Luise, "1 Corinthians: How Freedom Comes to Be," in *Feminist Biblical Interpretation: A Compendium of Critical Commentary on the Books of the Bible and Related Literature*, ed. Luise Schottroff and Marie-Theres Wacker (Grand Rapids: Eerdmans, 2012), 718–42.

Schüssler Fiorenza, Elisabeth, "Intersektionalität, Kyriarchat und Christliche Religion," in *Vielfalt und Differenz. Intersektionale Perspektiven auf Feminismus und Religion*, ed. Renate Jost and Sarah Jäger (Münster: LIT, 2017), 19–36.

Schüssler Fiorenza, Elisabeth, "Between Movement and Academy: Feminist Biblical Scholarship in the Twentieth Century," in *Feminist Biblical Studies in the Twentieth Century. Scholarship and Movement*, ed. Elisabeth Schüssler Fiorenza (Atlanta: Society of Biblical Literature, 2014), 1–17.

Schüssler Fiorenza, Elisabeth, *In Memory of Her: A Feminist Theological Reconstruction of Christian Origins* (New York: Crossroad, 1983).

Siegele-Wenschkewitz, Leonore, *Verdrängte Vergangenheit, die uns bedrängt. Feministische Theologie in der Verantwortung für die Geschichte* (München: Chr. Kaiser, 1988).

Studienzentrum der EKD für Gleichstellungsfragen/Konferenz der Frauenreferate und Gleichstellungsstellen in den Gliedkirchen der Evangelischen Kirche in Deutschland (ed.), *Atlas zur Gleichstellung von Frauen und Männern in der Evangelischen Kirche in Deutschland. Eine Bestandsaufnahme* (Hannover: Evangelische Kirche in Deutschland, 2015).

Vinken, Barbara, "Erkenne Dich selbst: Frauen–Mütter–Emanzipation," *Aus Politik und Zeitgeschichte (APuZ)* 2011: 37–38.

Wagner-Rau, Ulrike, *Auf der Schwelle. Das Pfarramt im Prozess Kirchlichen Wandels* (Stuttgart: Kohlhammer Verlag, 2011).

Wagner-Rau, Ulrike, *Zwischen Vaterwelt und Feminismus. Eine Studie zur Pastoralen Identität von Frauen* (Gütersloh: Gütersloher Verlagshaus, 1992).

Wiedekind, Anke, "'Frauen auf dem Sprung'. Dokumentation und Ergebnisse" (unpublished study).

Zeiß Horbach, Auguste, *Evangelische Kirche und Frauenordination. Der Beitrag der Evangelisch-Lutherischen Kirche in Bayern zum Deutschlandweiten Diskurs im 20. Jahrhundert* (Leipzig: Evangelische Verlagsanstalt, 2017).

Zeiß-Horbach, Auguste, "Nicht mit der Schürze Dienen, Sondern mit dem Wort. 80 Jahre Theologinnenkonvent in Bayern—40 Jahre Frauenordination," in *Deutsches Pfarrerblatt* 115 (2015): 345–48.

Chapter Fourteen

Rereading Male Chauvinism

Muslim Women's Own Approach to Their Holy Text

Katajun Amirpur

The struggle of Muslim women for leadership positions in their faith community is above all a struggle over the authority to interpret the Qur'an. For centuries, exegesis has been the privilege of men. This, women's rights advocates claim, has resulted in a patriarchal interpretation that disadvantages women legally and socially across Islamic societies. Muslim women today are challenging this male monopoly on Qur'anic interpretation, claiming an equal audience for women's voices.

This endeavor is part of a broader context; many Muslims today see the need for a comprehensive rethinking of many issues. Muslim intellectuals are well aware of the crisis in which Islamic thought finds itself, and this awareness has given rise to many proposals for reform, most of which go unrecognized in the West. Their ideas cover many aspects, including the relationship with the religious other, political pluralism, and, of course, gender equality. The question raised here is how to reconcile being both genuinely Muslim and genuinely modern, the latter understood as being part of a liberal democratic society. Muhammad Abduh, who died in 1905, already tried to answer this question by proposing a new reading of Qur'anic teachings and suggested treating them as separate from the eternally constant tenets of the faith. In his commentary on chapter ii, verse 243 of the Quran Abduh rejected the practice of *taqlid*. "How far those who believe in [*taqlid*] are from the guidance of the [*Quran*]! It propounds its laws in a way that prepares us to use reason, and makes us people of insight. . . . It forbids us to submit to [*taqlid*]."[1]

His method (*manhaj*) of procedure is to investigate "that which is in the Book (i.e., the *Quran*) and a small part of the Sunnah (Usage of the Prophet) relating to the matters of practice."[2] He also formulated the aim "to understand the religion (of Islam) as the early generation understood it, before the appearance of divisions among them, and to return to the original sources of the branches of the sciences (of Islam) in order to attain a proper knowledge of them."[3]

His approach remains substantially valid today, though there is no general agreement over what should and should not be considered unchanging. Reformist endeavors are thus nothing new to Islam, and the discourse on them continues to be lively. Its key protagonists refer back to forebears like Muhammad Abduh, as well as later predecessors of their respective traditions. One name frequently mentioned is that of Fazlur Rahman,[4] one of the most influential Islamic thinkers in the second half of the twentieth century, who emigrated from Pakistan to the United States, where he died in 1988. Not only do the two women presented in this essay, Amina Wadud and Asma Barlas, refer to him frequently, but also Ebrahim Moosa, a vocal critic of both Wadud and Barlas, whose accusation of hermeneutical acrobatics is quoted here, was a student of Rahman as well. Like many others, Ebrahim Moosa is a long-time participant in the reform debate[5] who has been continuously engaged in reinventing himself and developing his stance. What we find is that new ideas are formulated by adopting, criticizing, and refining earlier thoughts and that free criticism serves to make them more systematic and precise.

Barlas and Wadud belong to a generation that laid the groundwork for today's debates. They were considered radical innovators in their time but are now being overtaken by a younger generation of scholars. Nonetheless, the effort to challenge male authority has been defined internationally above all by the writings and efforts of these two women. This is why their activities will be the main focus of this study, though it will also be necessary to look at their biographies, which are inseparable from their theological approaches. In both cases, their conceptions of God and thus their theological stance were centrally shaped by the context of their lives.

1. INSIDE THE GENDER JIHAD

This is obviously true for Amina Wadud, perhaps the best-known Muslim women's rights activist of our time. Born Mary Teasley in 1952 in Bethesda, Maryland, she was the daughter of a Methodist pastor. Her childhood in a familiar, rural environment growing up with five brothers and one sister imparted an acute sensitivity to injustice. She states that the idea of seeing God connected in any way with oppression was alien to her: "My father, as a minister, introduced me, by his example, to the idea of an interconnection between faith and freedom, between God and justice."[6] As an African American, she experienced the receiving end of segregation very consciously. As a black student attending a mostly white Boston high school, she learned what it meant to be black in America. In reaction, she joined the civil rights movement and became a Black Power activist, attending Martin Luther King's famous March to Jackson together with her father.

Wadud was a Buddhist before encountering Islam almost by coincidence at the age of twenty. Acquaintances took her to the mosque in her neighborhood and tried to talk her into reciting the *shahada*, the Islamic profession of faith. Wadud wrote much later in her book *Inside the Gender Jihad*, a strong criticism of conservative Islam, that they were very likely trying to increase the number of women in their community. She suggests that her conversion to Islam was a spur-of-the-moment decision with no great level of consideration behind it at that point. On the other hand, Islam, with its radical premise of equality for all races, was an attractive option for African Americans since the rise of the Nation of Islam and of Malcolm X at the latest. The convert who called herself Wadud—one of the ninety-nine most beautiful names of God, meaning "the Loving One Desiring Justice"—also hoped for greater freedom in her new religion. Today, she describes as naive her hope that her life would change positively as a result of her conversion to Islam. She had expected it to be easier to join the Islamic community, where she was instead treated very poorly at times. Public reactions to her activism were often harsh, with opponents dismissing her as a "devil in a headscarf" and a "feminist fundamentalist."

The decisive impulse prompting her to truly turn to Islam was provided by her engagement with the Qur'an. As a convert, Wadud brought not only a specific consciousness shaped by her experiences, but also a spirit of critical inquiry. Since 1972, Wadud has studied the meanings of the Self laid out in the Qur'an and their possible interpretations, especially pertaining to the female self. She argues that the Qur'an supports equality for women even though this is contrary to practice in Muslim countries. Her scholarly efforts in her most important book, *Qur'an and Women*,[7] concentrate above all on the Qur'an as the authoritative reference for all Muslims and less on the Sunna, the collection of words and acts of the Prophet that other Islamic feminists, such as the Moroccan Fatima Mernissi and the Egyptian Nawal el-Saadawi, both scholars of another, older generation, prefer to focus on. Amina Wadud argues that Muhammad's sayings are no longer valid today if they disagree with the Qur'an. Her goal is to create a Qur'anic basis for gender justice in Islam.

Thus, for the first time, Amina Wadud put the idea and concept of woman in the Qur'an at the heart of academic work on women in Islam. She refused to accept the many strictures imposed on women in the name of Islam, as she experienced them herself while living in Libya. In response, she began questioning whether this was, in fact, what Islam really said about women. In her inquiry, she asked: Can the situation of women in Muslim countries be thought of as Islamic, that is, as in keeping with God's wishes? Wadud aimed to trace the idea of equality through the Qur'an and use it for what she calls "gender jihad."[8] Qur'anic legitimacy is a means to challenge and reform the views many Muslims have of women. She began reading primary sources and pursued this inquiry as part of her doctoral research at Cairo University, where she attended lectures both at al-Azhar, the spiritual center of Sunni Islam, and at the American University.

In the course of her exegetic instruction, her frustration with the methods used by her teachers grew. She did not just want to know what a certain term or a specific surah meant, but rather to examine the exegetic literature herself. She wanted to analyze, debate, and read the Qur'an together with her teacher, not merely hear and absorb his interpretation of it. To convince one instructor to read together with her, she demonstrated that in the Qur'an, women were not, in fact, forbidden from studying it. Wadud thus showed that critical inquiry was not a Western approach, but an integral part of Qur'anic scholarship. Submission to the will of God (*Islam*) as required in the Qur'an does not mean blind obedience, but rather the free choice of humans who are, by their nature, "an agent, not a puppet."[9] She describes the attitude demanded by the Qur'an as "engaged surrender."[10]

Having moved to Malaysia for an academic position, Wadud was instrumental in founding the organization Sisters in Islam. This group—today an influential nongovernmental organization—aimed to move the issue of women and gender justice out into the center of public attention and combat discrimination. Arguing for equality based on the Qur'an was the only way these women could escape charges that their demands were contrary to Islam. Together with other women from the organization, Wadud published works proving that gender equality was supported in the Qur'an. One of these publications dating from 1991 bore the provocative title *Are Muslim Men Allowed to Beat Their Wives?*[11] In it, Wadud writes that Qur'anic exegesis is not enough to effect change in gender relations. To do this would require a social movement akin to that which led to the abolition of slavery in the United States, a genuine civil rights movement.

In her second famous book, *Inside the Gender Jihad*, Wadud describes her positive and negative experiences both within the Muslim community and the academic world. For many years, she was the only female Islamic scholar in the United States who taught wearing a headscarf. Even among her fellow teachers of religious studies, she noticed negative attitudes toward Islam. She accused Western Islamic studies of rejecting the idea that Muslims were capable of academically engaging with Islam. They were considered less than objective in a way that Christian or Jewish experts in Islamic studies were not. It was as though the Orientalism debate had never occurred: "Western postmodern mastery over religious and theological discourse," Wadud writes, "is just another form of cultural imperialism."[12] Wadud also criticizes her purported allies in the struggle against religious conservativism. Even in progressive discourses, women are marginalized or excluded. She fights one more battle in addition: African-American Muslims often perceive condescending attitudes toward them from immigrants from majority Muslim countries, because Muslims from Islamic countries believe that they are the more authentic Muslims.

Her advocacy for gender equality on the basis of Qur'anic exegesis is frequently misunderstood by other Muslims as a criticism of their shared religion. Yet, her criticism is directed squarely at those who speak for Islam or in the name of Islam. The hardest lesson she had to learn in her life was that the mainstream Muslim communities had no place for her. For some, Amina Wadud became a courageous reformist and freedom fighter; for others, a heretic, or at least a theologian who need not be taken seriously. In academia, she is accused of being too personal in her statements on Islam and her interpretation of it. She retorts, however, that the personal is political.[13]

It was as a leader of Friday prayers that Amina Wadud became globally famous. In March 2005, she headed the prayers of a New York congregation of about one hundred men and women. Women had led mixed prayers before: the Prophet had asked one of his wives to do so, and Wadud had done so on a previous occasion in South Africa several years before, but the New York Friday prayer was still an innovation. Normally, women only led women in prayer. In this case, the call to prayer was also raised by a woman, another break with tradition. The historic event had been advertised widely in the media, and men and women from Kentucky and Michigan, even Turkey and Egypt, traveled there to participate. It was sponsored by several progressive Muslim and Muslim feminist groups. Three New York mosques originally intended as the venue refused to host prayers led by a female imam, which forced the event to be held in an Anglican church, Synod House.[14]

Though protests in front of the building itself were limited to a handful of individuals, the outcry the event produced throughout the Islamic world was considerable. While American Muslims—a term that commonly refers to African-American Muslims as opposed to Middle Eastern ones—were concerned "only" about a split between the more conservative religious views of immigrants and the more liberal forms of "U.S. Islam" practiced by their families, conservatives in Egypt and Saudi Arabia saw a grand conspiracy to discredit Islam. The Riyadh great mufti Abdul-Aziz ash-Sheikh proclaimed that everyone who defended Wadud's actions was in violation of God's law.[15] Mohammed Sayyed at-Tantawi, grand sheikh of Egypt's al-Azhar University and thus the highest authority of Sunni Islam, declared that women were permitted only to lead the prayer in the presence of other women, but never of men.[16] Television preacher Yusuf al-Qaradawi adopted a similar stance on al-Jazeera, rejecting the event as heretical and un-Islamic. The Egyptian paper *Al-Massa* (*The Evening*) accused Wadud in large print across page one, "You Besmirch Islam!"[17]

Wadud's defenders also joined the debate with vigor. The *Progressive Muslim Union* pointed out that neither the Qur'an nor the Sunna prohibited women from leading mixed prayers. The Prophet even expressly supported the practice. The influential Egyptian mufti Sheikh 'Ali Gomaa was quoted on the TV station Al-'Arabiya as saying that mixed Friday prayers led by a woman were to be tolerated if the congregation agreed. He quoted the exegete Tabari and the mystic Ibn 'Arabi in support of his opinion. Reformist scholar Gamal al-Banna, the brother of Hasan al-Banna, founder of the Muslim Brotherhood, agreed.[18]

When Amina Wadud is asked what her gesture accomplished, she points out that more people now accept women leading mixed prayers than before, though agreement remains a minority position. The Muhammadiyah, Indonesia's second largest Muslim organization, with thirty million members, has just decided to involve women in leading prayer, though only under specific circumstances. Other mosque communities in different countries now routinely have women leading Friday prayers.[19] These small steps are becoming more frequent.

In the long run, however, it is likely that Wadud's writings will have a greater impact on the situation of women than publicity-seeking events like the New York Friday prayer. Feminist researcher Margot Badran believes that Wadud started a revolution with her book *Qur'an and Women*.[20] She considers the breakthrough in Islamic thought at the beginning of the twenty-first century comparable to that caused by Muhammad Abduh, who is considered by some to be the godfather of modern rationalistic Qur'an exegesis, a century earlier. The female legal scholar Madhavi Sunder sees her as a revolutionary philosopher, not so much for interpreting the Qur'an from a feminist perspective as for teaching simple women elsewhere to do the same.[21]

Wadud's numerous studies all center around one topic: the conceptualization of gender and gender relations in the Qur'an. She argues that before new ideas are accepted in the Islamic world, they have to be shown to be legitimate within the context of Islamic thought. This is only possible through the Qur'an. That is why she interprets the Qur'an as an Islamic scholar—a surprisingly rare endeavor for a woman. Alongside Wadud and Asma Barlas, the Egyptian Aisha Abd ar-Rahman remains the only woman to have undertaken extensive exegesis in her *tafsir al-bayani li-l'qur'an* (Explanatory Comment on the Qur'an).[22] Other Islamic feminists such as Riffat Hassan (b. 1943), who taught religious studies at the University of Louisville until her retirement in 2009, agree with Wadud's position on the Qur'an on many points but have not published exegetic literature of their own. This absence of women in modern exegesis is all the more remarkable because many women were active in classical Islamic scholarship.[23]

The goal of Wadud's study *Qur'an and Women* is to find out how to best read the text and, above all, how to recognize the female voice in it. She readily admits that her reading is invariably subjective. She sees reading as an interpretative act and intends to show the relationship between the Qur'anic exegesis and the person of the exegete. Her focus is on what the Qur'an says, how it says this, what is said about the Qur'an, and who says these things.

Wadud believes that the traditional method of exegesis is atomistic, proceeding from the beginning of the Qur'an to the end, verse by verse.[24] Hardly anyone has tried to develop overarching themes or draw connections between disparate verses and surahs. Methods that link similar ideas, syntactic structures, principles, or themes are practically nonexistent. By viewing the Qur'an as a quarry, traditional exegetes have failed to open up the fundamental thoughts underlying its message. This leads them to generalize specific statements. Many of the restrictions on women, she contends, are rooted in the application of solutions intended originally for specific situations more broadly as general principles.

One example Wadud mentions is dress code restrictions. Regarding female dress, the Qur'an provides only general instruction: modest clothing is best. Islamic law, though, raises the specific concept of what was considered modest female attire at the time of the seventh century to a general principle, requiring a headscarf to be worn under all circumstances. The Qur'an, Wadud claims, is descriptive, not normative, on this matter. Making headscarves a requirement universalizes attitudes and habits of a specific cultural and economic situation that defined ideas of modesty in the Arab peninsula of the seventh century. Passing this cultural specificity off as a Qur'anic requirement limits the reach of its message in different cultures that do not share the same standards of decency. To Wadud, it is central to understand that though the Qur'an teaches the principle of modesty, it does not define it in detail.[25]

Thus, Wadud's scholarly analysis emphasizes the context within which the teachings of the Qur'an were revealed. She believes that the message must be at the heart of Qur'anic study, that it must be explored and placed at the heart of faith, and not the detailed strictures of traditional law. To that end, she proposes a hermeneutics of *tawhid*. *Tawhid* is the principle of the oneness of God in Islam. The Fatiha, the opening surah of the Qur'an, proclaims that God is one. To Wadud, this affirms the universal message of the Qur'an: the principle of justice and equality. She wants to demonstrate how this idea of unity pervades every part of the text.

To this end, for example, she investigates the language of the Qur'an in detail with regard to the surah in which an account of creation occurs.

Arabic original:

Ya ayuha an-nas ittaqu rabakum allathi khalaqa-kum min nafsin wahidatin wa khalqa min-ha zaujaha wa baththa minhuma rijalan kathiran wa nisa'an.

English translation with Wadud's explanatory notes:

> And *min* His *ayat* (is this:) that He created You (humankind) *min* a single *nafs*, and created *min* (that *nafs*) its *zawj*, and from these two He spread (through the earth) countless men and women.²⁶

The verse contains the basic elements of the Qur'anic version of the origin of humanity, the creation of Adam and Eve. Wadud considers the four core words *ayat*, *min*, *nafs*, and *zawj*, but in particular the words *min*, *nafs*, and *zawj*. If, like the exegete Abu al-Qasim al-Zamakhshari (1074–1144), one relies on the biblical version of the account to understand the Arabic *min* (the second *min* in the verse) in the sense of an extraction, then the superiority of the man is assumed. This *min* in effect conveys the idea that the first created being was perfect and complete. Consequently, the second created being, a woman, is not perfect since she was extracted out of a whole.

But, if conversely *min* is translated as "in" or "in the same way," the verse takes on a completely different meaning: "and in the same way He created." In fact, *min* can be understood in this way, as a comparison with other verses (e.g., 42:11 and 30:21) shows. Unfortunately, exegesis has followed Zamakhshari's interpretation, who enjoys great esteem because of his meticulous linguistic commentary; however, in this instance, according to Wadud, he was clearly influenced by the Bible. Wadud believes that according to the Qur'an, God never proposed to begin creation with the male. There is not even one reference to Adam as the beginning of mankind. In her opinion, the Qur'anic version of the account of creation does not acknowledge gender at all.

This brings Wadud to the following gender-neutral translation of verse 4:1:

> O Mankind! Be careful of your duty to your Lord Who created you from a single *nafs* and from it created its *zawj*, and from that pair spread abroad [over the earth] a multitude of men and women.²⁷

Along with this kind of re-reading, Wadud sees the key challenge for each new generation of Muslims in internalizing the underlying principles of the Qur'an and applying them to their respective social situations. This concrete analysis and application of principle will vary over time according to the social and cultural realities of the era. She explains the dearth of such re-evaluation and application in history through the fact that exegetes did not view the content and context of the Qur'an as a unity. Emphasizing that the Qu'ran introduced practices that changed those extant in seventh-century society, she writes, "In the area of gender, conservative thinkers read explicit Qur'anic reforms of existing historical and cultural practices as the literal and definitive statement on these practices for all times and places. What I am calling for is a reading that regards those reforms as establishing precedent for continual development toward a just social order."[28]

That is to say that when the Qur'an states that the testimony of a woman counts as half that of a man, it does not follow that it still only carries half as much weight. Rather, it indicates that the Qur'an improved the standing of women, whose testimony had counted for nothing prior to this. Other examples of such improvements are the recognition of women as human beings having individual rights and the ban on female infanticide. Women, who had been viewed as the property of their fathers or husbands before, gained the right to own property, inherit, receive an education, and file for divorce. Thus, the Qur'an marks the beginning of a reform that is in the interest of women. It is this reformist intent that Wadud believes must be further pursued. The point is not to insist that a woman's testimony be given half the value of a man's in the Qur'anic text. The important point is to follow the spirit of the Qur'an, not the letter, which often reflects the context of its time. Here, Wadud is entirely in keeping with an approach going back to traditional exegesis that is relatively common today. Traditionalist scholars already looked for what they called the aims of Revelation, the *maqasid ash-sharia*. Even during the classical age, Islamic jurisprudence moved away from a strict adherence to literal interpretation, trying to establish the ultimate goal to which the Revelation referred.

A key point of criticism for Wadud is that for most of history, interpreting the Qur'an was a purely male pursuit. Women and their experiences were systematically excluded. This way, no holistic understanding of what it means to be Muslim could be developed. Wadud holds that men and women are equal in Islam, but they are not the same. It follows that their experiences differ. This is nowhere accounted for in traditional *tafsir* (Qur'anic exegesis), where men had made it their business to tell women what it meant to be women. "Men not only determine what it means to be a Muslim, but what it means to be a Muslim woman."[29] This not only violates their human dignity, it is also contrary to the Qur'anic mission of both men and women to be *khalifa*, God's successors and trustees on earth. Wadud contends that the purpose of creation is expressed in Surah 2:30: "I am setting in the earth a viceroy."

This term and its attendant concept form a further key fulcrum in her approach to interpreting the Qur'an. Wadud believes that both men and women are equally bound to the duty of *khalifa*, successorship, or trusteeship. In the Qur'anic view, the fulfillment of this divine trusteeship is the raison d'être of human existence. Denying women full personhood also denies them the ability to be *khalifa*. It robs them of the opportunity to fulfill the responsibility God placed on all human beings. Wadud argues that since the Qur'an does not stipulate any essential difference in the value of men and women, there is no reason women should be subjected to greater limitations than men. The Qur'anic view of creation can thus serve as the basis of an Islamic intellectual ethos, but such an ethos cannot exist without giving a voice to women both as part of the text and in response to it.

Wadud's intent is not just to point out the errors of the patriarchal exegetic tradition. She wants to show Muslims what they are missing. If women were listened to, they could develop a more authentic Muslim identity, which would in turn allow them to participate more fully in religious life.

2. A POLITICAL SCIENTIST PERSPECTIVE

The idea that oppressing women is fundamentally antithetical to the Qur'an is also embraced by Asma Barlas.[30] Like Amina Wadud, she reads the Qur'an as a liberating text that shows women a path out of oppression—under certain circumstances. Barlas's work is far less academic than Wadud's, and she has no formal background in Islamic studies.

Born in Pakistan in 1950, Barlas now lives in the United States, where her book *Believing Women in Islam* has made her moderately famous. Barlas states that her book was written in constant dialogue with Amina Wadud. *Believing Women in Islam* also heavily criticizes the traditional male monopoly on Qur'anic exegesis, pointing to specifically male views on the Qur'an and offering an alternative anti-patriarchal reading. Unlike others, such as the Egyptian scholar Nasr Hamid Abu Zayd or Amina Wadud, Barlas does not believe that misconceptions arise because exegetes have failed to view the Qur'an as a product of its specific culture. She argues that the problem is not the way the Qur'anic text emerged in dialogue with its environment and thus reacted specifically to it, but the manner in which interpreters engage with the text in the first place.

Barlas's motivation for studying the Qur'an was less academic curiosity than personal suffering. While still living in Pakistan, she painfully experienced the lack of rights she had as a woman during her divorce proceedings. In response, she began to engage with the Qur'anic text. Many women suffer, but few question the restrictions that are presented to them as Qur'anic commandments. Many do not believe they are able to read the Qur'an themselves. Barlas professes surprise at this reticence and timidity. Feminists had long called on women to break the male monopoly. As early as 1980, she writes, Fatima Mernissi had encouraged women to become Qur'anic scholars in order to face down men who were trying to pass their view of Islam off as the only one.[31]

Barlas believes that Muslim women need to develop greater confidence in the unavoidable struggle to secure their rights. To her, it is a matter of common sense that oppressive practices legitimized with reference to Islam are contrary to the spirit of the Qur'an. Barlas argues based on the nature of God: If you assume that God is not unjust to his creation, then his word cannot be used to preach injustice (*zulm*) toward any being created by God. Why should he be unjust toward women, but not men? Refusing to recognize women as fully human cannot be the divine will, Barlas concludes. Logically, the error must be in the interpretation, since all Muslims believe that justice is the most important attribute of God.[32]

There is, then, a connection between divine ontology and Qur'anic discourse. Muslims would not even need to agree on the definition of *zulm* to understand how incoherent the assumption must be that God could teach *zulm*—that a just God would preach injustice. Nonetheless, Muslims who call upon God just read injustice into his word.

Barlas argues that the emergence of this interpretation has its roots in history. The foundational texts for exegesis and law were produced in the early centuries of Islam, a period that was characterized by strong misogyny. Since the holy text is often conflated with its commentary, the Qu'ran itself could be perceived as misogynistic.

Along with many reformists, Barlas is especially critical of Imam ash-Shafi'i, a highly influential legal scholar in the eighth and ninth centuries, whom she accuses of preferring the hadith—the tradition of the Prophet's life—to the Qur'an. Since the body of religious knowledge and the consensus of exegetes was codified around the time of ash-Shafi'i, his views remain centrally important. In this formative period, exegesis and the hadith were placed above the Qur'an itself, and the consensus of scholars above *ijtihad*, the pursuit of independent judgment. Interpretations of Qur'anic texts regarding women were framed in accordance with the norms and values of the age.

Further negative views entered the discourse through the hadith, where misogynistic traditions were favored over positive ones.

Barlas doubts the accuracy of those hadith; she regards them less as recording history than as inventing it. Criticism of the hadith is key to her view of Qur'anic scholarship, and she sees much work that needs to be done to address the root of this great evil. One hadith claims that obedience to a husband is equal to obedience to God. This, she claims, is clearly nonsensical, since we know the Prophet did not treat his wives in this manner. They are known to have debated with him, and he asked for their opinions and valued their counsel. Muhammad was no misogynist, and these traditions must therefore be the invention of men keen to secure their dominance over women. Yet, generations of women had lived believing that these words attributed to the Prophet truly were his.

Since it is difficult to ultimately decide which traditions genuinely go back to Muhammad, Barlas argues against the exegetic custom of interpreting the Qur'an through the hadith in general.[33] This might work in some cases; we know, Barlas argues, that the Prophet never beat his wives, and it is recorded that he also counseled other men not to beat theirs. Taking the Prophet as the first interpreter of the Qur'an—in this case, Surah 4:34—and thus as the most important exegetic reference could be a gain for women at first glance. However, some problematic ideas (beside polygamy as a potentially misogynist practice), such as the creation of Eve from the rib of Adam or the punishment of stoning, are solely based on the hadith. This is why, in Barlas's opinion, it creates more problems than it solves when interpreters go back to the hadith and the Sunna.[34]

Of course, Barlas is aware that a new Qur'anic hermeneutic will not end patriarchy. Nonetheless, she considers it important. There is a link between the things we read and believe about the holy texts and our beliefs about and treatment of women. Thus, the act of reading the holy texts is linked to liberation. A liberating reading must be accorded legitimacy. "Even if such readings do not succeed in effecting a radical change in Muslim societies, it is safe to say that no meaningful change can occur in these societies that does not derive its legitimacy from the Qur'ān's teachings, a lesson secular Muslims everywhere are having to learn to their own detriment."[35]

Like other women who place the Qur'an at the center of their struggle for equality, Barlas questions the motif of male supremacy that traditional exegesis has historically read into the text. However, alluding to Amina Wadud, she identifies a tendency among other scholars to say no to the text itself, citing a need to go beyond it. Her own stance is an unequivocal yes to putting the text at the core of her work, though it includes a reading that goes contrary to traditional exegesis. In her estimation, an anti-patriarchal interpretation is sounder both in methodology and theology than the dominant patriarchal reading. She has described her endeavor as interpreting patriarchy out of the Qur'an:

> When I ask whether we can read the Qur'ān for liberation, I am asking whether its teachings about God as well as about human creation, ontology, sexuality, and marital relationships challenge sexual inequality and patriarchy. Alternatively, do the teachings of the Qur'ān allow us to theorize the equality, sameness, similarity, or equivalence, as the context demands, of women and men?[36]

Patriarchy here refers to two distinct things. It means, on the one hand, the manner in which a patriarch governs, a concept that is related to the conception of God as a patriarchal figure (traditional patriarchy) and, on the other hand, a policy of distinction between the genders that privileges men and excludes women (modern/secular patriarchy). Barlas identifies two reasons why she believes the Qur'an does not support either traditional or modern patriarchy. First, God is not identified as a father in the Qur'an; the concept is explicitly repudiated. The Islamic view of God differs significantly from the Christian one, where the idea of God as a father is common. Unlike Christianity, she sees Islam as undermining patriarchy, rejecting the traditional rights and sanctification of fathers and fatherhood. Instead, the Qur'an specifically warns against following the path of the fathers, which is in error and leads away from that of God. Barlas reads this as a repudiation of traditional patriarchy. She concedes that the Qur'an acknowledges the existence of patriarchy and male power, not least in frequently addressing men specifically, but argues that acknowledging the existence of patriarchy and addressing men does not amount to a defense of traditional male supremacy.

Moreover, the Qur'an does not address God as either a father or as male. Indeed, it bans any form of image; God is described as not having been created and thus not capable of being depicted. Though human language uses a male pronoun to describe God, Barlas states that God is beyond gender.[37]

Her most important argument against patriarchy relies on the way in which God is represented in the Qur'an. A God that rejects the imposition of patriarchy cannot serve as a model for it. The Qur'an further postulates the ontological equality of men and women in teaching that both were created from the same *nafs* (self, soul), are fully responsible for their moral conduct, and will be judged according to the same criteria.

Barlas finds it illogical to assume that human beings who are morally equal should not also be legal equals. Further, she points out that the Qur'an never links biological sex to privileging men or excluding women the way modern, secular patriarchies do. Sex is not even connected with gender in the Qur'an: Biological (sex) differences are acknowledged, but not tied into specific gender symbolism. Not a single verse assigns specific spheres to men and women nor states that biological differences mean men and women are unequal, incompatible, beyond comparison, or opposed to one another. Nor does the Qu'ran stigmatize sex or give a basis for patriarchal constructions of sexuality, both extraneous imports from Jewish and Christian traditions.[38]

All of this shows that Barlas's hermeneutics is rooted in her theology. The word of God must relate to God directly. Accordingly, she focuses on three primary divine characteristics. The first is unity, *tawhid*, symbolizing the indivisible nature of God and divine sovereignty. God's sovereignty is absolute and nobody can share in it. Thus, there can be no rule of men over women; the very idea would be heresy.

The second principle is divine justice, which allows for no injustice toward any being created by God. The third principle is the incomparable nature of God, which above all forbids any anthropomorphic depiction. God must not be imagined as a man or a father. This is mandated by the central and absolute prohibition of idols in Islam.

Thus, Barlas views the failure of traditional Islam to produce a contextually legitimized method of reading the Qur'an not just as a hermeneutical shortcoming, but as a theological error. Traditional exegetes' understanding of the text remained unconnected to their image of God. A coherent idea of God, however, is key to the emancipation of women, as it teaches that obedience is owed solely to God and no one else.

Reform, to Barlas, depends not on the reinterpretation of the so-called misogynistic verses that refer to purported male supremacy, the "beating" of wives, polygyny, witness statements, inheritance, and so on. She considers a criticism of the theology underlying their traditional interpretation more important. Introducing a new conception of God into theological thought would automatically resolve the problem of misogynistic verses in the Qur'an.

On closer inspection, for example, we find that the Qur'anic text only uses the word for degree (*darajah*), which many pious Muslims interpret as referring to the degree of superiority men have been endowed with by God in the context of divorce, where men enjoy certain privileges. The nature of the privilege referred to is not entirely clear. Some scholars believe that it is the right to unilaterally initiate a divorce, while others argue the reference is to the ability to revoke it. In no possible interpretation, Barlas argues, can this be read as referring to aspects of male ontology or biology. Ontologically, men cannot be superior to women because the Qur'an states clearly that both originate from the same nature (*nafs*).

Similarly, the word *qawwamun* may refer to the financial function of husbands as providers for the family, rather than their legal guardianship over women. The Qur'an designates men and women as *awliya*, friends or examples to one another, and charges both with prescribing what is right and prohibiting what is wrong. This, Barlas points out, would not be possible if men had such absolute power over women.[39]

The well-known verse referring to the "beating" of wives, too, disappears on realizing that the word traditionally translated as "to beat" has numerous possible meanings, including "to separate." To Barlas, this raises the question of why Muslims preferred one interpretation—and the one most deleterious to women's rights—above all others. After all, the Qur'an also teaches that love is the foundation of marriage and calls on spouses to show mercy and generosity to each other even in divorce. Careful analysis also undermines the traditional reading that gives the man's testimony generally greater weight than the woman's.

Barlas deploys these examples to show that Qur'anic interpretation always depends on who interprets, by what method, and in what context. If the interpretation is done solely by men—as has historically been the case—as well as being fragmentary and taking place in a patriarchal context, the results can hardly be surprising.

It is possible, Barlas concedes, to read the Qur'an as a patriarchal text, but only by selecting specific parts while excluding its core message. She shares this conviction with Wadud and Rahman, who have also insisted on the importance of seeing the overall meaning instead of focusing on detailed strictures. Contextualization is key to understanding this. We must understand who said what when and, above all, why. "In other words, a restrictive and oppressive exegesis results both from the failure to historicize the Qur'ān's teachings and to read the text as 'a whole, a totality.'"[40]

Her answer to the question of whether her ideas would result in the liberation of women and democratization is in the negative. Barlas says that reading the Qur'an the anti-patriarchial way is not enough to produce a functioning democracy. However, she does see that democratization processes in Islamic countries depend on a far-reaching change in the way believers approach their holy texts and interpret their religion. That, at least, is how she put it in an interview with the author. Barlas is not optimistic about the prospects of success for her nonpatriarchal interpretation. Seeing even women, who suffer most from the conservative mainstream mentality, defend patriarchy, she doubts she will live to see a significant change in Muslim thinking. Today's battles for cultural authority are all fought on the backs of women. The issue of headscarves is just one of those conflicts. Nonetheless, Barlas is resolved to continue fighting for what she thinks is right as a matter of ethical duty toward herself and her religion.

In the United States, these ideas are received well beyond the realm of academia. Barlas is often invited to speak by influential Muslim organizations. Audiences are often disturbed by arguments such as that against assigning God a male persona. Barlas finds this argument entirely in keeping with the Qur'an and says she finds it hard to understand how it could be controversial. The fact remains, though, that men define religious knowledge in many contemporary Muslim communities. Her call for every Muslim to have the right to read and interpret the Qur'an is worrying to many simple believers who consider this the preserve of specialists trained in the various branches of Islamic scholarship. Against this, Asma Barlas argues that the Qur'an originally spoke to uneducated Bedouins. A text like this could not rightly be monopolized by legal scholars and academics, especially not in Sunni Islam, where no priestly caste exists.

Barlas regards her positions as common sense. And she knows that the reason for the ongoing attacks on her is that they pose a threat to structures of male authority in Muslim communities. Many view her personally as a mole in the service of Western cultural imperialism. Equality, after all, is widely seen as a Western value, which makes it difficult to argue for it from inside an Islamic reference system. Others yet regard her as an apologist. She finds encouragement in the stories of young Muslims and especially Muslim women who tell her that they are happy to have found these ideas in her work and that they opened up new horizons for them. Asma Barlas is an important figure especially for many women in the younger generation, daughters of immigrants who no longer identify with the conservative Islam of their parents. She addresses a question that is centrally important to them: How can I believe in the religion of my fathers and mothers in which I am invested when the conservative interpretation with which I am confronted clashes with the values I have internalized?

Barlas is often challenged with the argument that as a woman and one not speaking Arabic, she has no authority to discuss the Qur'an. She counters this by saying that all the faithful have the right to discuss their faith. The Qur'an is addressed neither solely to men nor to Arabs, but to all who wish to hear it. Especially as a woman, she feels duty-bound to speak up: "However, as a Muslim woman, I have a great deal at stake."[41] She realizes that her chances of recognition as an authority are slim and that states that benefit from patriarchal interpretations will not simply relinquish them.

Her critics are found not only among conservatives. Reformist scholar Ebrahim Moosa stated that we will have to come to terms with the Qur'an speaking in a patriarchal voice. Generations of scholars were right to conclude that it propagates the norms of patriarchy. Barlas counters this by pointing out that this could hardly have been consensus for generations, given that Muslim women and feminists have only been applying the concept of patriarchy to Qur'anic interpretation for roughly two decades. Further, she dismisses the idea that the Qur'an speaks with a patriarchal voice as textual fundamentalism. When Moosa charges that feminists cling to a few verses that vindicate their views to claim that the Qur'an teaches equality, she argues that this is hardly questionable and that his own interpretation of the Qur'an as a patriarchal document is based on a similarly selective reading. Or, are we to assume that the interpretation by women is prejudiced, while that of men is authentically objective?

Barlas does not. Neither does Amina Wadud, and neither do a growing number of young women who turn against a patriarchal reading of Islam to develop their own interpretation. Through this re-reading, they gain a new perspective on their existence within religious institutions, formulate a claim for participation, and enforce it by questioning truths that used to be considered God-given.

We can read the fact that women are challenging male authority and demanding participation in religious leadership as evidence of modernization in a religious community. However, in the case of Islam, it needs to be said that women in leading roles were far more common in the early period than they were in the years following the death of the Prophet in 632. His wife Aisha not only commanded a battle, she is also central to the study of the hadith, since many of the most important traditions go back to her as the first source. She has become a reference point especially for young Muslim women looking for role models, because she was ready to challenge male authority, even that of the Prophet. He himself, too, serves as a positive example, because he often did not insist on this authority, but readily accepted the advice and support of his wife, in this case Khadija. Many women find the knowledge that she was the first convert to Islam, that the Prophet turned to her when he felt overburdened by his first Revelation, and that it was she who convinced him of the rightness of his calling, invaluable in the current reform discourse. The current struggle for the right to participate, contribute, and be heard is often argued by returning to the earliest age of Islam. Amina Wadud, too, declared that she assumed the right to lead others in prayer because the Prophet had allowed his wives to lead mixed congregations. What Muslim would dare claim he was not obligated to follow the example of the Prophet?

NOTES

1. See *Al-Manar*, viii. 892. Translated in *Islam and Modernism in Egypt: A Study of the Modern Reform Movement Inaugurated by Muhammad 'Abduh*, trans. Charles C. Adams (London: Oxford University Press 1933), 130.

2. See *Risala al-tawhid*, 224. Translated in *Islam and Modernism in Egypt: A Study of the Modern Reform Movement Inaugurated by Muhammad 'Abduh*, trans. Charles C. Adams (London: Oxford University Press 1933), 174.

3. Ibid.

4. Fazlur Rahman, *Islamic Methodology in History* (Karachi: Central Institute of Islamic Research, 1965); Fazlur Rahman, "The Concept of Hadd in Islamic Law," in *Islamic Studies* 4.3 (1965): 237–51; Fazlur Rahman, "The Impact of Modernity on Islam," in: *Islamic Studies* 5.2 (1966): 113–28; Fazlur Rahman, *Islam* (Chicago: The University of Chicago Press, 1966).

5. For example: Ebrahim Moosa, "The Debts and Burdens of Critical Islam," in *Progressive Muslims. On Justice, Gender and Pluralism*, ed. Omid Safi (Oxford: Oneworld Publications, 2003), 111–27; *Revival and Reform: A Study in Islamic Fundamentalism*, ed. Ebrahim Moosa (Oxford: Oneworld Publications, 1999); Ebrahim Moosa (Interview, 2016): "The Reinvention of Islam." https://en.qantara.de/content/interview-with-the-islamic-scholar-ebrahim-moosa-the-reinvention-of-islam ; Ebrahim Moosa, "Islamic Reform or Designer Fundamentalism?," in: *Georgetown Journal of International Affairs*, Winter/Spring 2006: 139–44.

6. Amina Wadud, interview with the author, September 25, 2012.

7. Amina Wadud, *Qur'an and Woman: Rereading the Sacred Text from a Woman's Perspective* (New York: Oxford University Press, 1999).

8. Amina Wadud, *Inside the Gender Jihad: Women's Reform in Islam* (Oxford: Oneworld Publications, 2008).

9. Ibid., 23.

10. Wadud, *Inside the Gender Jihad*, 23.

11. Sisters in Islam and Yasmin Masidi, *Are Muslim Men Allowed to Beat Their Wives?* (Malaysia: SIS Forum, 1991), ht tp://www.sistersinislam.org.my/files/downloads/are_muslim_men_allow_to_beat_their_wives_v12-1.pdf.

12. Wadud, *Inside the Gender Jihad*, 64–65.
13. The phrase "the personal is political" was coined by Carol Hanisch (1970). It was the title of the paper, "The Personal Is Political," originally published in Notes from the Second Year: Women's Liberation in 1970. See: Carol Hanisch, "The Personal is Political," posted on her website: http://www.carolhanisch.org/CHwritings/PIP.html (accessed: 14.03.2019).
14. See: Andrea Elliot, "Woman Leads Muslim Prayer Service in New York," *New York Times* March 19, 2005, posted on: https://www.nytimes.com/2005/03/19/nyregion/woman-leads-muslim-prayer-service-in-new-york.html (accessed: 15.03.2019); "Woman Leads Controversial US Prayer," *Aljazeera* (online ed.), https://www.aljazeera.com/archive/2005/03/200849145527855944.html (accessed: 15.03.2019).
15. See: "Reformversuch in New York Weltweite Empörung über muslimische Vorbeterin," *Spiegel* (online edition) March 19, 2005, http://www.spiegel.de/politik/ausland/reformversuch-in-new-york-weltweite-empoerung-ueber-muslimische-vorbeterin-a-347395.html (accessed: 15.03.2019).
16. Ibid.
17. Ibid.
18. See: Khaled Abou El Fadl, Forword," in *Inside the Gender Jihad: Women's Reform in Islam*, ed. Amina Wadud (Oxford: Oneworld Publications, 2008), vii–viii.
19. For Canada, see Jen Gerson, "Woman Leads Islamic Prayers in Mosque, a First for Canada—Country Could Become the Conscience of the Religion, She Says in Friday Sermon," *Globe & Mail* , July 2, 2005; for the UK, Jerome Taylor, "First Woman to Lead Friday Prayers in UK," *Independent*, June 10, 2010, http://www.independent.co.uk/news/uk/home-news/first-woman-to-lead-friday-prayers-in-uk-1996228.html; for China, see "Muslim Women Do It Their Way in Ningxia," *Taipei Times*, December 20, 2006, http://www.taipeitimes.com/News/editorials/archives/2006/12/20/2003341218; for Denmark, see "Women-Led Mosque Opens in Denmark," *Guardian*, February 12, 2016, https://www.theguardian.com/world/2016/feb/12/women-led-mosque-opens-in-denmark.
20. Margot Badran, "Seismic Shift from Patriarchy to Equality: Amina Wadud on Reading the Quran." *A Jihad for Justice. Honoring the Work and Life of Amina Wadud*, ed. Kecia Ali, Juliane Hammer, Laury Silvers (Internet resrouce, 2012), http://www.bu.edu/religion/files/2010/03/A-Jihad-for-Justice-for-Amina-Wadud-2012-1.pdf (accessed on 15.03.2019).
21. Sunder Madhavi, "Democratizing Islam" in *A Jihad for Justice: Honoring the Work and Life of Amina Wadud*, ed. Kecia Ali, Juliane Hammer, and Laury Silvers (Internet resource, 2012), 179, https://www.bu.edu/religion/files/2010/03/A-Jihad-for-Justice-for-Amina-Wadud-2012-1.pdf.
22. 'Ā'ishah 'Abd al-Rahmān, and Bint al-Šāṭi', *At-Tafsir al-Bayani li-l-Qur'an al-Karim* (Kairo: Dar al-Ma'arif, 1977).
23. See *Muslima Theology: The Voices of Muslim Women Theologians*, ed. Ednan Aslan, Marcia K. Hermansen, Elif Medeni (Wien: Peter Lang Edition, 2013); Mohammad Akram Nadwi, *Al-Muhaddithat: The Women Scholars in Islam*, 2nd rev. ed. (Oxford: Interface Publications, 2013); Asma Sayeed, *Women and the Transmission of Religious Knowledge in Islam* (Cambridge: Cambridge University Press, 2013).
24. Wadud, *Qur'an and Woman*, 1–2.
25. Ibid., 37.
26. Ibid., 17.
27. Ibid., 22.
28. Ibid., xiii.
29. Wadud, *Inside the Gender Jihad*, 96.

30. Asma Barlas: DW=http://www.dw.de/dw/article/0191936200.html; Asma Barlas: *Believing Women in Islam. Unreading Patriarchal Interpretations of the Qur'an* (Austin: University of Texas, 2002); Asma Barlas, "Morality: For Women and Girls Only," in *The Daily Times*, Pakistan, January 14, 2003; Asma Barlas, "Muslims in the US (I)," in: *The Daily Times*, Pakistan, June 17, 2003; Asma Barlas, "Muslims in the US (II)," in *The Daily Times*, Pakistan, July 1, 2003; Asma Barlas, "Un-reading Patriarchal Interpretations of the Qur'an: Beyond the Binaries of Tradition and Modernity." Vortrag vor der Association of Muslim Social Scientists: Conference on Islam: Tradition and Modernity, Toronto, Canada, November 4, 2006; Asma Barlas, "Re-understanding Islam: A Double Critique." Spinoza Lectures (Van Gorcum: Amsterdam 2008).

31. Asma Barlas, *Believing Women in Islam: Unreading Patriarchal Interpretations of the Qur'an* (Austin: University of Texas Press, 2002), 4.

32. Asma Barlas, *Re-understanding Islam: A Double Critique* (Amsterdam: Van Gorcum, 2008), 21.

33. Barlas, *Re-understanding Islam*, 14.

34. Ibid., 14.

35. Ibid., 3.

36. Ibid., 1.

37. Ibid., 100.

38. Ibid., 49, 130.

39. Ibid., 186.

40. Ibid., 169.

41. Ibid., 209.

BIBLIOGRAPHY

'Abd al-Rahmān, 'Ā'ishah, and al-Šāṭi,' Bint, *At-Tafsir al-Bayani li-l-Qur'an al-Karim* (Kairo: Dar al-Ma'arif, 1977).

Abou El Fadl, Khaled, "Foreword," in *Inside the Gender Jihad: Women's Reform in Islam*, ed. Amina Wadud (Oxford: Oneworld Publications, 2008), vii–viii.

Adams, Charles C. (trans.), *Islam and Modernism in Egypt: A Study of the Modern Reform Movement Inaugurated by Muhammad 'Abduh* (London: Oxford University Press 1933).

Akram Nadwi, Mohammad, *Al-Muhaddithat: The Women Scholars in Islam*, 2nd rev. ed. (Oxford: Interface Publications, 2013).

Aslan, Ednan, et al. (eds.), *Muslima Theology: The Voices of Muslim Women Theologians*, (Wien: Peter Lang Edition, 2013).

Badran, Margot, "Seismic Shift from Patriarchy to Equality: Amina Wadud on Reading the Quran." *A Jihad for Justice. Honoring the Work and Life of Amina Wadud*, ed. Kecia Ali, Juliane Hammer, Laury Silvers (Internet resrouce, 2012), accessed on 15 March 2019, http://www.bu.edu/religion/files/2010/03/A-Jihad-for-Justice-for-Amina-Wadud-2012-1.pdf.

Barlas, Asma, "Re-understanding Islam: A Double Critique." *Spinoza Lectures* (Van Gorcum: Amsterdam 2008).

Barlas, Asma, *Re-understanding Islam: A Double Critique* (Amsterdam: Van Gorcum, 2008).

Barlas, Asma, "Un-reading Patriarchal Interpretations of the Qur'an: Beyond the Binaries of Tradition and Modernity." Vortrag vor der Association of Muslim Social Scientists: Conference on Islam: Tradition and Modernity, Toronto, Canada, November 4, 2006.

Barlas, Asma, "Morality: For Women and Girls Only," in *The Daily Times*, Pakistan, January 14, 2003.

Barlas, Asma, "Muslims in the US (II) ," in *The Daily Times*, Pakistan, July 1, 2003.
Barlas, Asma, "Muslims in the US (I) ," in: *The Daily Times*, Pakistan, June 17, 2003.
Barlas, Asma, *Believing Women in Islam. Unreading Patriarchal Interpretations of the Qur'an* (Austin: University of Texas, 2002).
Elliot, Andrea, "Woman Leads Muslim Prayer Service in New York," *New York Times* March 19, 2005, accessed on 15 March 2019, https://www.nytimes.com/2005/03/19/nyregion/woman-leads-muslim-prayer-service-in-new-york.html.
Gerson, Jen, "Woman Leads Islamic Prayers in Mosque, a First for Canada—Country Could Become the Conscience of the Religion, She Says in Friday Sermon," *Globe & Mail*, July 2, 2005.
Madhavi, Sunder, "Democratizing Islam" in *A Jihad for Justice: Honoring the Work and Life of Amina Wadud*, ed. Kecia Ali, Juliane Hammer, and Laury Silvers (Internet resource, 2012), 179, https://www.bu.edu/religion/files/2010/03/A-Jihad-for-Justice-for-Amina-Wadud-2012-1.pdf.
Moosa, Ebrahim, "Islamic Reform or Designer Fundamentalism?," in: *Georgetown Journal of International Affairs*, Winter/Spring 2006: 139–44.
Moosa, Ebrahim, "The Debts and Burdens of Critical Islam," in *Progressive Muslims. On Justice, Gender and Pluralism*, ed. Omid Safi (Oxford: Oneworld Publications, 2003), 111–27.
Moosa, Ebrahim (ed.), *Revival and Reform: A Study in Islamic Fundamentalism*, (Oxford: Oneworld Publications, 1999).
Rahman, Fazlur, "The Impact of Modernity on Islam," in: *Islamic Studies* 5.2 (1966): 113–28.
Rahman, Fazlur, *Islam* (Chicago: The University of Chicago Press, 1966).
Rahman, Fazlur, *Islamic Methodology in History* (Karachi: Central Institute of Islamic Research, 1965).
Rahman, Fazlur, "The Concept of Hadd in Islamic Law," in *Islamic Studies* 4.3 (1965): 237–51.
Sayeed, Asma, *Women and the Transmission of Religious Knowledge in Islam* (Cambridge: Cambridge University Press, 2013).
Taylor, Jerome, "First Woman to Lead Friday Prayers in UK," *Independent*, June 10, 2010, http://www.independent.co.uk/news/uk/home-news/first-woman-to-lead-friday-prayers-in-uk-1996228.html .
Wadud, Amina, *Inside the Gender Jihad: Women's Reform in Islam* (Oxford: Oneworld Publications, 2008).
Wadud, Amina, *Qur'an and Woman: Rereading the Sacred Text from a Woman's Perspective* (New York: Oxford University Press, 1999).

Chapter Fifteen

The Ordination of Women and the Question of Religious Authority

Judith Frishman

1. INTRODUCTION

In February 2017, a newly issued statement by the Union of Orthodox Jewish Congregations of America (commonly known as the Orthodox Union, or the OU), perceived as a resolution against ordaining and hiring women rabbis, made Jewish, national, and international headlines. The statement, in the form of a letter, was based on the simultaneously published responses of a rabbinic panel appointed by the OU to address two questions regarding "professional synagogue roles":

1. Is it halachically acceptable for a synagogue to employ a woman in clergy function?
2. What is the broadest spectrum of professional roles within a synagogue that women can perform within the bounds of halacha?[1]

Despite stormy reactions, the OU's statement was not without precedence. The Rabbinical Council of America (RCA), an institution whose thousand members are graduates of the Rabbi Isaac Elchanan Theological Seminary of Yeshiva University and a myriad of yeshivot in Israel, America, and elsewhere, had already issued a resolution in 2015, "The RCA Policy Concerning Women Rabbis." This resolution, based on both an earlier resolution of April 2010 and an announcement made in May 2013, prohibited the following:

1. The ordination of women, regardless of the title used
2. Hiring or ratifying the hiring of a woman into a rabbinic position at an Orthodox institution
3. The use of a title implying rabbinic ordination by a teacher of Limudei Kodesh in an Orthodox institution[2]

Positions such as *yoatzot halakhah* (female halakhic advisors), community scholars, nonrabbinic school teachers, and the Graduate Program in Advanced Talmudic Studies at Yeshiva University were ostensibly not addressed by the resolution.

The resolutions and statement of the RCA were prompted by several groundbreaking events in the American and Israeli Orthodox Jewish community, that is, the ordination of women as rabbis (Sara Hurwitz, June 2009), the conferring of the title "rabba" (feminine form of "rabbi") or "maharat" (an acronym for *manhiga hilkhatit rukhanit Toranit*, or "leader of halakhah, spirituality, and Torah")[3] on women including graduates of Yeshivat Maharat (founded by Rabbi Avi Weiss in 2009), the use of the title "rabbi" (Lila Kagedan in 2016), and the hiring of women rabbis in leadership positions.[4] The hiring of Ruth Balinsky Friedman in 2013 as maharat of Ohev Shalom synagogue in Washington, D.C., made it clear that Sara Hurwitz would remain no exception: a steady stream of women was now studying for the rabbinate and even desired to occupy rabbinic positions in Orthodox congregations. This appointment and the subsequent decision of three other synagogues to hire women rabbis violated the RCA's prohibition.

The OU resolution is an apparent move on the part of some of its more conservative constituents to staunch the autonomous decision-making process of member congregations involving the hiring of ordained women. Whether OU members will conform to the resolution and what sanctions will or can be taken against its violators remains to be seen. In what follows, guided by Professor Mark Chaves's studies on women's ordination, I will discuss the relationship between the resolution's rules regarding women's ordination and actual everyday practice as far as women's participation in leadership roles in the Orthodox Jewish community is concerned. This will include some reflections on the symbolic significance of women's ordination within this same branch of Judaism.[5]

2. GENDER ROLES

The OU statement opens with the observation that (1) more than ever before, Orthodox Jewish women are learning Torah and have reached "unprecedented levels of scholarship and professional achievement"; and (2) women have taken on leadership roles "often closed to them in the past."[6] Commencing with the de facto situation, the OU's statement is the result of a quest for a de jure answer regarding the halakhic acceptability of and limits to these new roles. However, the fact that these roles already exist indicates that at least some rabbis and congregations already consider these new developments halakhically valid.

While the compilers of the OU statement do assume that women are motivated by "*yirat shamayim* and *ahavat Hashem*" (awe of heaven and love of God),[7] they nevertheless introduce the section "Some Observations on the Response of the Rabbinic Panel" by noting that "the American culture of personal autonomy and the egalitarian ethos inexorably clashes [*sic*] with the Torah values of placing normative halachic conduct above individual choice and halachic dictates above individual freedom."[8] The wording of the rabbinic response differs from the statement, indicating from the start that the issue of female clergy "touches upon not only the dictates of *halakhah*, but also upon fundamental issues in our *hashkafat olam* [worldview] . . . Some perceive limitations on women's roles and titles as barriers to full involvement in the Orthodox community, while others view the lifting of traditional gender distinctions in ritual as representing a rejection of the *mesorah* [tradition].[9] The tension pits egalitarianism, a central value of modernity, against a time-honored tradition that clearly speaks of equally valued, yet different, roles for men and women."[10] The good or proper intentions of women (and/or men) calling for the opening of the clergy to women are described more obliquely in the response—without the use of traditional terminology—as a desire for "full involvement." However, the egalitarianism that is implied by "full involvement" is understood to be part and parcel of modernism that, as a matter of course, is in conflict with tradition and the roles it designates for men and women.

In a section entitled "The Halakhic Ethos of Gender Roles," the rabbinic response makes clear that, in service to God, the *mesorah* has determined distinct gender roles, and allowing women to serve as clergy contradicts this ethos. Nevertheless, women should be encouraged to play communal roles such as "(a) teaching ongoing classes and *shiurim*, and delivering lectures;

(b) serving as visiting scholar-in residence; (c) serving in senior managerial and administrative positions" and take on new roles "(a) serving as a synagogue staff member . . . to supplement synagogue rabbis in educational opportunities; (b) serving as a staff member in the role of professional counselor; (c) serving as a teacher and mentor to guide females through the conversion process."[11] The position of *yoetzet halakhah* (halakhic advisor) is more questionable, balancing between a mere advisory role and that of a halakhic expert and thus impinging on the role consigned to rabbis or "the clergy." The parallel section in the OU statement is again more positively formulated: women's increased role in Orthodox communal life is described as "positive developments [that] have transformed the face of synagogues and the Orthodox community."[12] Moreover, "the failure to fully embrace the talents of women and encourage women to assume greater lay and professional roles is a tragic forfeiture of communal talent. We should focus on creating and institutionalizing roles for women that address the needs of Orthodox Jews today, by removing barriers that impede women."[13]

The OU statement suggests creating new titles for women of significant accomplishment, ensuring their religious engagement in shul. Surprisingly, the OU, in "The Way Forward," declares its preparedness to enhance maternal/parental leave, grant equal remuneration to men and women in comparable positions, and stimulate women's engagement in all segments of the Orthodox community including Torah study and leadership, a declaration that is tantamount to acknowledging the inequality and disengagement women have suffered in the recent past. The question is whether in the long run women occupying these old and newly created positions will be satisfied with the legal boundaries set by the responses of the rabbinic panel.

The reactions in Orthodox circles to the OU statement and the rabbinic response have been mixed. In general, the positive side of the OU statement has been stressed and the prohibition of employing women in a clergy function rather downplayed by those who had hoped for a different outcome.[14] Laura Shaw Frank, director of Recruitment, Placement and Alumnae at Yeshivat Maharat, notes astutely in a column in *Lehrhaus* that whereas the Modern Orthodox world has refused the title of "clergy" for women, the ultra-Orthodox community—while declaring women's ordination "a radical and dangerous departure from Jewish tradition and the *mesoras haTorah*"— has already adopted the term "clergy" for their own women spiritual figures.[15] Referring to a recent study by Ferziger on the American Orthodox community,[16] Shaw Frank points out that "Chabad shluchos [female emissaries or missionaries] and Yeshivish outreach kollel rebbetzins [Haredi rabbis' wives who play active outreach roles]" are taking on clergy roles and view themselves as religious leaders "subject to the authority of the Rebbe and Halakhah, just as any male Chabad leader would be—but notably not subject to any other male authority simply because they are female." They address themselves to other women, consciously making concessions to the values of the modern world in order to reach unaffiliated Jews. While the use of the term "clergy" does offer financial privileges within the U.S. tax system, the community's approved use of this title by ultra-Orthodox women is not only about tax benefits but also reflects the latter's status within the community. Ironically, Shaw Frank concludes, the fact that these women minister almost solely to other women has granted them "much greater latitude in terms of pastoral leadership and religious functions than the OU statement seems to allow."[17] This evolving change can, in the end, result in social transformation.

3. THE DISJUNCTION BETWEEN FORMAL RULES AND EVERYDAY PRACTICE AND ITS SIGNIFICANCE

In an article from 1996 on the ordination of women, sociologist Chaves studies what he calls the loose coupling of formal rules with everyday practice. Chaves points to three aspects of this loose coupling within religious organizations with regard to ordination. First, there is disjunction between the institution of policy change and the number of women seeking clergy status. The year 1970 was a watershed: prior to 1970, few women wanted to join the clergy, even in denominations where this was possible; after 1970, the numbers swelled even in denominations where ordination was not yet possible. This was partially due to women's enrollment in seminaries and other religious institutions of higher learning. Second, even when denied formal leadership positions, women have occupied these positions and increasingly continue to do so. Finally, allowing ordination often does not lead to equal opportunity.[18] Chaves explains that universal loose coupling in religious organizations indicates that the rules are more a response to external institutional pressures rather than to what is happening within the organization. He identifies several external sources of pressure for women's ordination including the two feminist waves and the adoption of formal gender equality in other professions, such as medicine and law. This pressure can lead to both acceptance as well as resistance.

In addition, religious denominations, like other organizations, are generally most influenced by the practices of other denominations, particularly by those to whom they are closest. According to Chaves, perceptions of similarity lead to the spread of a practice, while contrarily, perceptions of dissimilarity can lead to its rejection.[19]

I would add that the fear of being perceived as dissimilar by those on the right could lead to resistance. To the outside world, the Conservative movement's decision to ordain women indicated that it was closer to the Reform and Reconstructionist movements than to Modern Orthodoxy. This, then, substantiated a claim made by the more right-wing Orthodox since the appointment of Solomon Schechter as president of the Jewish Theological Seminary of America and led to a break with more conservative members who then founded their own institution.[20] Similarly, if Modern Orthodoxy subscribed to the ordination of women, it would be alienated from the Orthodox camp, whether or not halakhic arguments in favor of ordination could be procured, as indeed they have been for quite some time.

Among other factors, Chaves identifies two cultural similarities among denominations that influence the spread of women's ordination: the degree to which a denomination is sacramental and considers the Bible inerrant.[21] Although in the first instance these similarities do not seem relevant for Jewish denominations, there are certain parallels when it comes to the degree to which revelation is understood as a divine, one-time event (*Torah mi-Sinai*) and halakhic decisions are to be based on precedence and normative practice with little or no consideration for extra-legal (e.g., historical or teleological) arguments.[22] In this sense, Orthodox Jewish organizations such as the OU and RCA occupy positions similar to those of Roman Catholics, Episcopalians, the Eastern Orthodox, and Lutherans, as opposed to Reform Judaism, which has been open to societal developments from its inception.

4. THE SYMBOLIC SIGNIFICANCE OF WOMEN'S ORDINATION

The disjunction between ruling and practice regarding gender equality, as in the case of Modern Orthodoxy discussed above, has led Chaves to deduce that "formal denominational policy regarding women's ordination . . . has a symbolic significance that is not reducible to the pragmatic internal operations of the organization."[23] In other words, "acceptance or rejection of women's ordination is not the same as acceptance or rejection of actual women functioning as religious leaders."[24] Women's formal positions within religious denominations seem to be *a*, if not *the*, key symbolic marker of membership in these denominations. Chaves notes that ecumenical issues, that is, denominational alliances, are often of influence on the official policies, although these need not reflect practice. But the perception of similarity without official connectedness would suffice as an influence on the decision-making process and the social construction of identity.[25] As mentioned above, sacramental and biblically/halakhically inerrant denominations tend to link the proper performance of sacraments and the proper roles assigned to men and women by the Bible/*mesorah* to the question of the proper gender of clergy. Resisting women's ordination becomes synonymous "with resisting 'modernism' and the gender equality perceived to come with it: on the other hand, they signal a positive orientation to an alternative institutional environment."[26] In this connection, the term "Modern Orthodoxy"—a term introduced in the United States in the 1960s to refer to the movement that arose in nineteenth-century Germany, inspired by Samson Raphael Hirsch and intended as an alternative to Reform Judaism—already indicates that a balancing act, if not a contradiction in terms, is involved here. For this movement in Judaism, which has and will of necessity always be searching, testing, and guarding its boundaries, the ordination of women is presented as a conundrum or one of the "societal trends which run counter to the ethos of the Torah."[27] When it comes to the ordination of women, Modern Orthodox Jews, like their Southern Baptist counterparts in 1984,[28] are encouraged to "embrace timeless principles—even when counter-cultural and incompatible with prevailing societal values. . . . 'There is no need for apology; we should have pride in our *mesorah*, in our heritage.'"[29] While the connection between women's ordination and modernism is explicit, the former stands not only for the modern in general, but at present also for the threat some experience from a new movement labeled "Open Orthodoxy," which attempts to come to terms with a broader "liberal" agenda and in which Rabbi Avi Weiss and others in favor of women's ordination are involved.[30] This new agenda is perceived as leading to the further marginalization of Modern Orthodoxy within the Orthodox Jewish community at large and its increasingly fundamentalist leanings.

5. WOMEN RABBIS AND THE QUESTION OF AUTHORITY

5.1 The Modern Orthodox Community

The response of the OU Rabbinic Panel states that women should not serve in functions expected from a synagogue rabbi, including "the ongoing practice of ruling on a full-range of halakhic matters, officiating at religiously significant life-cycle events . . . , the regular practice of delivering sermons from the pulpit during services, presiding over or 'leading services' at a *minyan* [prayer quorum, traditionally composed of ten males above the age of thirteen] and formally serving as the synagogue's primary religious mentor, teacher, and spiritual guide."[31] The objection to delivering sermons during services or presiding over the latter is a question of *tzeniut*, or modesty, whereby women are expected to occupy positions behind a *mechitzah* (partition separating men and women during public prayer). Moreover, women are not counted for a minyan. The objections to women serving as the primary spiritual guide in a synagogue or presiding over life-cycle events is less straightforward, in view of the fact that they—and certainly the OU statement—encourage women to exercise this type of function. The crux seems to lie in the designation "primary," whereby the panel members have recourse to religiously determined gender roles to justify their exclusion of women from primary positions in the synagogue. So too, denying women the authority to make halakhic decisions is derived from Maimonides's extension of the prohibition for women to be appointed kings to any position of *serarah*, or formal communal authority (*Mishneh Torah, Hilkhot Melakhim* 1:5), which would include rabbinic positions. One may, however, wonder how much authority present-day rabbis exercise. Accordingly, Chaim Twerski, rosh yeshiva and head of the *semikhah* program at Hebrew Theological College in Skokie, Illinois, writes: "It is not at all uncommon in a Modern Orthodox setting for congregants to take the ruling of the rabbi as a suggestion and his rulings are often routinely ignored. If so, it could be argued that that type of position could be taken by a woman who has the requisite halakhic knowledge to issue halakhic suggestions."[32]

The implication of Twerski's statement—that is, that the rabbinic loss of authority makes the acceptance of women clergy easier or unproblematic—is that if male rabbis still maintained authority, it would still be inappropriate for women to act as synagogue rabbis. Neither the Rambam nor the Rishonim or their present-day adherents find it necessary to explain why women shouldn't exercise authority; the obvious needs no explanation. Here, clearly, cultural developments of the past have been granted lasting legal hegemony so that only a position's loss of authority would make equal opportunity for women acceptable rather than granting women authority or acknowledging the fact that they have earned it or even exercise it.

5.2 The Non-Orthodox Jewish Community

The history of the ordination of women in the Reform (Sally Priesand in 1972) Reconstructionist (Sandy Eisenberg Sasso in 1974), and Conservative (Amy Eilberg in 1985) movements is well documented. The initial arguments of the Reform movement against women clergy were mainly social; those of the Rabbinical Assembly of the Conservative movement were mainly halakhic, as opposed to the congregants and lay leaders whose objections were cultural. The position and authority of women once ordained requires further research. Initial studies indicate that women rabbis were often not granted equal pay or offered positions in large congregations. In a comparative study of women rabbis and ministers published in 1993, the rabbis indicated that status and power—as opposed to the spiritual reasons proffered by the ministers—motivated their career choices.[33] Moreover, once ordained, they hoped to improve the world by engaging among others in social justice.[34] All concurred that they performed their duties in a fashion that deviated from that of their male contemporaries. "The women described themselves as: 'less formal,' 'more engaging,' 'more approachable,' 'more likely to reach out to touch and hug,' 'less likely to seek center stage,' 'more people-oriented,' 'more into pastoral care,' 'more personal,' and 'less concerned about power struggles.'"[35] Adjectives such as "warmer," "less hierarchical," and "spontaneous" were shared perceptions. Sermons were described as more relational, as opposed to the male rabbis' style of "pontificating." Daily activities were "people oriented," and the questioners noted a general reluctance to assume supervisory and administrative roles. When asked about the future of the rabbinate, the women rabbis foresaw a role for their female successors that would differ from that of male rabbis, particularly when it came to rabbi-congregant relations.[36]

A study carried out two years later compared the women's gendered description of their jobs with their male colleagues' perceptions of the differences and/or similarities between the male and female implementation of the rabbinic vocation.[37] All agreed that their roles were the same. However, most men, as opposed to the women, felt that male and female rabbis share and address the same concerns and that there was little or no difference in the way they and the women performed their duties.[38] The question remains as to whether women's understanding of the fulfillment of their roles has become and will increasingly become less gendered the longer women serve in the rabbinate and the greater their proportion among the graduates of the rabbinical seminaries. Noteworthy is that newly ordained Orthodox women and their congregants often emphasize different aspects of their roles when compared to their male counterparts. The women rabbis are said to be or characterize themselves as "spiritual" leaders and their presence particularly but not solely described as important for women, who feel free to consult the rabbi on sensitive questions, especially family purity.[39] Most of the newspaper interviews report that the women will deal with all matters of concern for their communities. However, none of the ordained women specifically mention making halakhic decisions as part of their job description or intended focus, although this will undoubtedly be the case. The question is whether they, as members of a vanguard, will initially envision the performance of their roles in gendered terms, as did their non-Orthodox colleagues twenty-five years ago or longer.

6. SECULARIZATION AND DECLINING RELIGIOUS AUTHORITY

Chaim Twerski is not the only scholar to ascertain that the authority of male rabbis in the (Modern) Orthodox community is on the wane.[40] And what is true of the Orthodox community certainly holds true for the non-Orthodox Jewish movements, where, according to the 2013 Pew survey on American Jews, commitment to the umbrella organizations is waning, synagogue attendance is low, and intermarriage on the rise.[41] However, despite secularization theories claiming that modernity and religion are incompatible, religion persists among individuals and is not disappearing, while the scope of religious authority is on the decline.[42] Religious authority, Chavez claims, is no longer demarcated by the ends or means it may use for compliance. It is a "social structure that attempts to enforce its order and reach its end by controlling the access of individuals to some desired goods, where the legitimation of that control includes some supernatural component, however weak."[43] These goods might include deliverance from negative experiences such as sickness, meaninglessness, or poverty or access to more positive elements such as eternal life, utopian community, perfect health, or wealth. They can be gained by membership, profession of certain beliefs, or following a set of dietary laws or ritual obligations. "No good is inherently religious but becomes so by being embedded in a specific social structure that legitimates its control of those goods by reference to the supernatural."[44]

Chaves discerns three dimensions of secularization and religious authority: (1) a societal process by which the ability of religious authority to gain control over institutions such as education, science, and the state is diminished; religion thereby loses its primacy and becomes just one institution among many to be reckoned with; (2) organizational transformation in which internal developments toward conformity with the secular world take place; and (3) individual disengagement characterized by a decline of religious beliefs and practices. Secularization on a societal level is evidenced in most Western societies, where the church and the synagogue have been losing influence on institutions such as education, science, or the state in general. They may express their opinions on matters such as abortion or euthanasia, but their voices are, at best, just one among many competing voices. On the organizational level, competition takes place among professional groups to the disadvantage of the clergy for jurisdiction over the church and synagogue and the larger institutions of which they are part. The Union of Reform Judaism, whose membership is shrinking, is illustrative; congregational boards are refusing to pay dues to the URJ and retracting support for the Hebrew Union College–Jewish Institute of Religion. Shifts in the measure of appreciation of the professional's academic knowledge (theology, halakhah) in favor of his or her practical knowledge (preaching, running a synagogue, counseling) have been visible for more than one-and-a-half centuries in more liberal denominations. Rabbis and cantors of established institutions are being replaced by graduates of other institutions or even lay leaders and professional singers because they are cheaper and priorities lie elsewhere. Within the Conservative movement, the members are decreasingly interested in the decisions of the Committee on Law and Standards, as the focus of the movement's own publications attest.[45] Yet even in more fundamentalist or orthodox denominations such as the Modern Orthodox movement in Judaism, the rabbis' dwindling authority has been noted, at least where halakhic matters are at stake, and greater emphasis is being placed on spiritual and pastoral leadership. However, not only the position of the clergy is being challenged. Surveys conducted in the late 1990s by Arnold Eisen and Steven Cohen among Jews in their thirties indicated that Jewish identity is no longer shaped by communal loyalties and norms but by personal motivation.[46] As the subtitle of their book—*The Jew Within: Self, Family, and Community in Ameri-*

ca—indicates, for the majority of those interviewed the autonomy of the individual takes precedence over the rabbi, the congregation, and the greater organization. This trend also extends to other than religious organizations, as in the case of philanthropy, where Jewish charities are no longer prioritized.

As far as individuals are concerned, Chaves departs from the conventional manner of measuring secularization—that is, whether one believes in God or is affiliated with an institution—examining instead the extent to which individuals' actions are regulated by religious authority.[47] Relevant data are intermarriage rates, attempted control over reproductive behavior (e.g., for the Catholic Church, artificial contraception; in Judaism, adherence to the laws of *taharat hamishpacha*, or family purity), diet (kashrut), and voting. Higher rates of religious intermarriage correlate to weaker religious authority; that is the increasing irrelevance of religious difference for marriage decisions indicates that religious authority's scope is narrowing. Turning once more to the Pew survey, it is clear that the majority of those interviewed considered being Jewish a matter of ancestry and culture rather than religion. Moreover, the percentage of intermarriage among those married between 2005 and 2012 rose to 58 percent, as opposed to 17 percent for those married prior to 1970.[48]

7. WOMEN'S ORDINATION, EQUALITY, AND THE FUTURE OF THE RABBINATE

Returning to the question of the ordination of women, the refusal of the Modern Orthodox community to grant women the title of "rabbi" clearly has to do with the RCA's and OU's sense of loss of authority, a loss that they consciously and purposefully associate with accommodation to the secular world. At the same time, the OU acknowledges the need to strive for greater equality between men and women occupying nonrabbinic leadership positions and substantial attention to women's needs and agendas. Within the non-Orthodox movements, the road to equality has been long but has progressed steadily, with the ever-increasing number of female graduates. Moreover, studies indicate that a gender transformation has taken place in these movements whereby Jewish American women surpass Jewish American men when it comes to the importance of Judaism in their lives, the performance of ritual practice, attending synagogue and adult education, and participation in Jewish cultural expressions.[49] Ironically, women's greater commitment to Judaism and participation in the clergy is concomitant with a rise in secularization, that is, a period in which the authority of the non-Orthodox institutions and their rabbis (the societal and organizational levels) is on the wane. For those concerned about the future of Jewish religious institutions, it might be salutary to compare the stability of membership as well as institutional loyalty of congregations led by women versus those led by men. Additionally, questions regarding the clergy roles valued by male and female congregants respectively and the degree and type of authority these congregants grant their rabbis, male and female, would be of interest for rabbinical seminaries and the future of the rabbinate. Recent surveys, for example, indicate that factors such as personal charisma are often more important for attracting members than the rabbi's learnedness, as are openness to interfaith, LGBT, and innovative programming.[50] Will Jews continue to identify with and commit themselves to the institutional forms of the past one-and-a-half centuries, and is their commitment gender-based? Are rabbinical school graduates equipped to deal with these changes? And are women clergy more open to the challenges of the twenty-first century and more capable of successfully dealing with these challenges than their male colleagues? These are just some of the questions that need to be posed in a time when, with the exception of the ultra-Orthodox, institutional Judaism is rapidly losing ground, the growing number of ordained women notwithstanding.

NOTES

1. Moishe Bane, Howard Tzvi Friedman, Allen I. Fagin, *Orthodox Union Statement*, retrieved July 30, 2017, https://www.ou.org/assets/OU-Statement.pdf, 1 (hereafter cited as "OU Statement"); and Daniel Feldman, Yaakov Neuberger, et al., *Response*, http://www.rabbis.org/pdfs/Responses-of-OU-Rabbinic-Panel.pdf, 1 (hereafter cited as "Rabbinic Response").

2. Rabbinical Council of America, "2015 Resolution: The RCA Policy Concerning Women Rabbis," October 31, 2015, https://rabbis.org/2015-resolution-rca-policy-concerning-women-rabbis/.

3. Sara Hurwitz was ordained by Rabbi Avi Weiss, who first conferred the title "maharat" on her, changing it to "rabba" in February 2010.

4. Kagedan, who bears the title "rabbi" rather than "rabba," served first as a member of the rabbinic staff of the Open Orthodox Mount Freedom Jewish Center in Randolph, New Jersey, and since the fall of 2016 at the Walnut Street Synagogue Agudath Shalom in Chelsea, Massachusetts.

5. My discussion will entail a comparison between the Modern Orthodox standpoints on women in the clergy and the findings of Professor Mark Chaves (Duke University) as reported in "Ordaining Women: The Diffusion of an Organizational Innovation," *American Journal of Sociology* 101, no. 4 (1996): 840–73; "The Symbolic Significance of Women's Ordination," *Journal of Religion* 77, no. 1 (1997): 87–114; and *Ordaining Women: Culture and Conflict in Religious Organizations* (Cambridge: Harvard University Press, 1997).

6. "OU Statement," 1.
7. Ibid., 1.
8. Ibid., 5.
9. The rabbinic response defines *mesorah* as "the appreciation for, and application of, tradition as the guide by which new ideas, challenges and circumstances are navigated"; "Rabbinic Response ," 6.
10. " Rabbinic Response ," 1.
11. Ibid., 13–14.
12. "OU Statement," 1.
13. Ibid., 10.
14. See, for example, the reactions of the seventeen participants in the symposium convened by *The Lehrhaus*, an online forum for discourse in the Orthodox community: http://www.thelehrhaus.com.
15. Laura Shaw Frank, "Yeshivish Women Clergy: The Secular State and Changing Roles for Women in Ultra-Orthodoxy," *Lehrhaus*, February 21, 2017, http://www.thelehrhaus.com/timely-thoughts/2017/2/20/yeshivish-women-clergy-the-secular-state-and-changing-roles-for-women-in-ultra-orthodoxy.
16. Adam Ferziger, *Beyond Sectarianism: The Realignment of American Orthodox Judaism* (Detroit: Wayne State University Press, 2015), 195–210.
17. Shaw Frank, "Yeshivish Women Clergy."
18. Chaves, "Ordaining Women: The Diffusion of an Organizational Innovation," 843.
19. Ibid., 850–51.
20. In 1985, the Union for Traditional Conservative Judaism (the word "Conservative" was dropped a few years later), under the leadership of Rabbi David Weiss Halivni, declared that it would make its own halakhic decisions in the future, as the decision to ordain women was not made by halakhic experts. This split-off from the Conservative movement no longer exists.
21. Chaves uses the term "sacramental" to refer to those for whom rituals such as the Eucharist are understood literally rather than symbolically.
22. Historical arguments pointing to the culturally determined position of women in Judaism whereby ordination was nearly impossible are not acceptable. On the contrary: the absence of women rabbis in the past serves to support arguments against women's ordination in the present.
23. Chaves, "Symbolic Significance of Women's Ordination," 89.
24. Ibid., 89.
25. So Chaves, "Symbolic Significance of Women's Ordination," 106, quoting David Strang and John W. Meyer, "Institutional Conditions for Diffusion," in *Institutional Environments and Organizations: Structural Complexity and Individualism*, ed. W. Richard Scott, John W. Meyer, and associates (Thousand Oaks: Sage, 1994), 103.
26. Chaves, "Symbolic Significance of Women's Ordination," 108.
27. "Rabbinic Response," 6.
28. The 1984 Resolution of the Southern Baptists declared: "Therefore, be it *Resolved*, That we not decide concerns of Christian doctrine and practice by modern cultural, sociological and ecclesiastical trends or by emotional factors; that we remind ourselves of the dearly bought Baptist principle of the final authority of Scripture in matters of faith and conduct; and that we encourage the service of women in all aspects of church life and work other than pastoral functions and leadership roles entailing ordination." Reproduced in *The Churches Speak On: Women's Ordination*, ed. J. Gordon Melton (Detroit: Gale Research, 1991), 236; and cited by Chaves, "The Symbolic Significance of Women's Ordination," 110.

29. " Rabbinic Response," 7, quoting Rabbi Joseph B. Soloveitchik, *The Rav Speaks: Five Addresses on Israel, History and the Jewish People* (New York: Judaica Press, 2002), 70–80.

30. For Open Orthodoxy, see Avraham Weiss, "Open Orthodoxy! A Modern Orthodox Rabbi's Creed," *Judaism* 46, no. 4 (Fall 1997): 409–421, http://library.yctorah.org/files/2016/07/aw-open-orthodoxy.pdf.

31. "Rabbinic Response," 12–13.

32. Chaim Twerski, "On the Lomdus of the OU Responsum," *Lehrhaus*, February 22, 2017, http://www.thelehrhaus.com/timely-thoughts/2017/2/21/on-the-lomdus-of-the-ou-responsum?rq=serarah .

33. Rita J. Simon, Angela J. Scanlan, and Pamela S. Nadell, "Rabbis and Ministers: Women of the Book and the Cloth," *Sociology of Religion* 54, no. 1 (1993): 115–22.

34. Simon, Scanlan, and Nadell, "Rabbis and Ministers," 121.

35. Ibid., 120.

36. Ibid., 121.

37. Rita J. Simon and Pamela S. Nadell, "In the Same Voice or Is It Different? Gender and the Clergy," *Sociology of Religion* 56, no. 1 (1995): 63–70.

38. Simon and Nadell, "In the Same Voice or Is It Different?," 67–69.

39. See, for example, the interview in the *Washington Post* with Rabbi Shmuel Herzfeld and Maharat Ruth Balinsky Friedman of Washington's Ohev Sholom synagogue following the OU statement: Julie Zauzmer, "Orthodox Union, Opposed to Female Clergy, Puts Pressure on Washington's Ohev Shalom," May 19, 2017, https://www.washingtonpost.com/news/acts-of-faith/wp/2017/05/19/orthodox-union-opposed-to-female-clergy-puts-pressure-on-washingtons-ohev-sholom/?utm_term=.1ad03057e9e3 .

40. Twerski, "On the Lomdus of the OU Responsum."

41. According to the Pew Research Center's 2013 survey, *A Portrait of Jewish Americans*, only 19 percent of American Jews consider observing Jewish law as essential to being Jewish, and 94 percent agree that working on the Sabbath is compatible with being Jewish. Pew Research Center's Religion and Public Life Project, *A Portrait of Jewish Americans* (Washington, DC: Pew Research Center, October 1, 2013), http://www.pewforum.org/2013/10/01/jewish-american-beliefs-attitudes-culture-survey/.

42. Mark Chaves, "Secularization as Declining Religious Authority," *Social Forces* 72, no. 3 (1994): 750.

43. Chaves, "Secularization as Declining Religious Authority," 756.

44. Ibid., 756.

45. A comparison of the contents and approach of Martin S. Cohen, ed., *The Observant Life: The Wisdom of Conservative Judaism for Contemporary Jews* (New York: Rabbinical Assembly, 2012) with Isaac Klein, *Guide to Jewish Religious Practice* (New York: Jewish Theological Seminary of America, 1979) clearly indicates that the halakhic approach has lost its primary position and been replaced by decisions made by rabbis locally. Moreover, the focus of the concerns has shifted to encompass contemporary matters such as singles and same-sex marriage.

46. Steven M. Cohen and Arnold J. Eisen, *The Jew Within: Self, Family, and Community in America* (Bloomington: Indiana University Press, 2000).

47. Chaves, "Secularization as Declining Religious Authority," 768.

48. Pew Research Center, A Portrait of Jewish Americans.

49. Sylvia Barack Fishman, "Gender in American Jewish Life," in *American Jewish Yearbook 2014: The Annual Record of the North American Communities*, vol. 114, ed. Arnold Dashefsky and Ira M. Sheshkin (Switzerland: Springer International, 2015), 91–131.

50. See, for example, articles in the *Jewish Advocate* and the *Forward* on keys to synagogue success: Alexandra Lapkin, "Several Local Synagogues Succeeding While Others Contending with Challenges," *Jewish Advocate*, November 6, 2015, http://www.tisrael.org/wp-content/uploads/2015/04/Several-local-synagogues-succeeding-while-others-contending-with-challenges-Jewish-Advocate-Nov-6-2015.pdf; and Lenore Skenazy, "7 Secrets of Highly Successful Synagogues—and Churches," *Forward*, February 11, 2014, http://forward.com/opinion/192545/7-secrets-of-highly-successful-synagogues-and-ch/ .

BIBLIOGRAPHY

Chaves, Marc, "The Symbolic Significance of Women's Ordination," *Journal of Religion* 77, no. 1 (1997): 87–114.
Chaves, Marc, *Ordaining Women: Culture and Conflict in Religious Organizations* (Cambridge: Harvard University Press, 1997).
Chaves, Marc, "Ordaining Women: The Diffusion of an Organizational Innovation," *American Journal of Sociology* 101, no. 4 (1996): 840–73.
Chaves, Mark, "Secularization as Declining Religious Authority," *Social Forces* 72, no. 3 (1994): 750.
Cohen, Martin S. (ed.), *The Observant Life: The Wisdom of Conservative Judaism for Contemporary Jews* (New York: Rabbinical Assembly, 2012).
Cohen, Steven M., and Eisen, Arnold J., *The Jew Within: Self, Family, and Community in America* (Bloomington: Indiana University Press, 2000).
Ferziger, Adam, *Beyond Sectarianism: The Realignment of American Orthodox Judaism* (Detroit: Wayne State University Press, 2015).
Fishman, Sylvia Barack, "Gender in American Jewish Life," in *American Jewish Yearbook 2014: The Annual Record of the North American Communities*, vol. 114, ed. Arnold Dashefsky and Ira M. Sheshkin (Switzerland: Springer International, 2015), 91–131.
Klein, Isaac, *Guide to Jewish Religious Practice* (New York: Jewish Theological Seminary of America, 1979).
Lapkin, Alexandra, "Several Local Synagogues Succeeding While Others Contending with Challenges," *Jewish Advocate*, November 6, 2015, http://www.tisrael.org/wp-content/uploads/2015/04/Several-local-synagogues-succeeding-while-others-contending-with-challenges-Jewish-Advocate-Nov-6-2015.pdf.
Melton, J. Gordon (ed.), *The Churches Speak On: Women's Ordination*, (Detroit: Gale Research, 1991).
Meyer, John W., "Institutional Conditions for Diffusion," in *Institutional Environments and Organizations: Structural Complexity and Individualism*, ed. W. Richard Scott, John W. Meyer, and associates (Thousand Oaks: Sage, 1994), 100–12.
Shaw Frank, Laura, "Yeshivish Women Clergy: The Secular State and Changing Roles for Women in Ultra-Orthodoxy," *Lehrhaus*, February 21, 2017, http://www.thelehrhaus.com/timely-thoughts/2017/2/20/yeshivish-women-clergy-the-secular-state-and-changing-roles-for-women-in-ultra-orthodoxy.
Simon, Rita J., and Nadell, Pamela S., "In the Same Voice or Is It Different? Gender and the Clergy," *Sociology of Religion* 56, no. 1 (1995): 63–70.
Simon, Rita J., Scanlan, Angela J., and Nadell, Pamela S., "Rabbis and Ministers: Women of the Book and the Cloth," *Sociology of Religion* 54, no. 1 (1993): 115–22.

Skenazy, Lenore, "7 Secrets of Highly Successful Synagogues—and Churches," *Forward*, February 11, 2014, http://forward.com/opinion/192545/7-secrets-of-highly-successful-synagogues-and-ch/.

Soloveitchik, Joseph B., *The Rav Speaks: Five Addresses on Israel, History and the Jewish People* (New York: Judaica Press, 2002), 70–80.

Twerski, Chaim, "On the Lomdus of the OU Responsum," *Lehrhaus*, February 22, 2017, http://www.thelehrhaus.com/timely-thoughts/2017/2/21/on-the-lomdus-of-the-ou-responsum?rq=serarah.

Weiss, Avraham, "Open Orthodoxy! A Modern Orthodox Rabbi's Creed," *Judaism* 46, no. 4 (Fall 1997): 409–421, http://library.yctorah.org/files/2016/07/aw-open-orthodoxy.pdf.

Zauzmer, Julie, "Orthodox Union, Opposed to Female Clergy, Puts Pressure on Washington's Ohev Shalom," May 19, 2017, https://www.washingtonpost.com/news/acts-of-faith/wp/2017/05/19/orthodox-union-opposed-to-female-clergy-puts-pressure-on-washingtons-ohev-sholom/?utm_term=.1ad03057e9e3.

Index

'Abd al-Rahmān, 'Ā'ishah, 273, 284, 286n22
Abduh, Muhammad, 267–268, 273
Abele-Brehm, Andrea, 247, 260n9
Abou El Fadl, Khaled, 286n18
Abrams, Judith, 174n2
Abu Zayd, Nasr Hamid, 277
Ackerman Herskovitz, Paula, 95–96, 193–194
Adler, Cyrus, 92, 122
Adler, Rachel, 205, 209, 218n5, 218n12, 218n20, 219n26
Aharon, Rachel, 66n29
Ajayi, Akin, 66n33
Akram Nadwi, Mohammad, 286n23
Albeck, Hanoch, xii
Albrecht, Ruth, 262n36
Alfers, Sandra, 84n28
Allen, Ann Taylor, 84n9
Amirpur, Katajun, 5, 267–288, 322
Antler, Joyce, 124n25
Art, Jan, 239n5
Askowitz, Dora, 93, 94, 106n23
Awad, Bushra, xvi

Baader, Benjamin, 25n2, 26n19, 27n26, 29n71, 38, 39, 42, 43, 49n10, 49n18, 49n20–49n23, 49n25, 50n29, 50n30
Bach, Alice, 214, 219n32
Bader Ginsburg, Ruth, 113
Badran, Margot, 273, 286n20

Badt-Strauss, Bertha, 84n20
Baeck, Leo, 58, 59, 66n23, 82, 85n49, 168, 176n28
Bail, Ulrike, 263n50
Baker, Leonard S., 58, 66n19–66n22, 66n24
Balinsky Friedman, Ruth, 290
Ball, Howard, 158n24
Bane, Moishe, 301n1, 302n6–302n8, 302n12–302n13
Barack Fishman, Sylvia, 303n49
Barbaro, Michael, 200n1
Barkai, Avraham, 48n2
Barlas, Asma, 268, 273, 277–284, 287n30
Beck-Friedman, Tova, 212, 219n27
Beer, Peter, 14, 23, 27n27
Berger, Teresa, 235
Berkowitz, Henry, 91, 105n11
Beyer, Johanna, 260n5, 261n18
Biale, Rachel, 27n36
Bieler, Andrea, 262n35
Birke, Franziska, 241n32, 241n39
Blaschke, Olaf, 29n70
Bloch, Ernst, 130
Blum, Edward J., 50n33
Bodemann, Michal Y., 176n29
Bomhoff, Harmut, 1–8, 71–87, 315
Bordin, Ruth, 49n24, 50n33
Boulouque, Clémence, 157n5, 171, 176n45
Boyarin, Daniel, 16, 27n41
Brämer, Andreas, 28n54

Braude, Ann, 48n6
Braun-Vogelstein, Julie, 56
Brechenmacher, Thomas, 177n62
Breit-Keßler, Susanne, 246
Brenner, Michael, 175n9
Brickner, Rebecca, 191–192, 193
Brooten, Bernadette, 262n37
Brumlik, Micha, 25n6, 139n6
Buerman, Thomas, 239n5
Burke, Kelsy C., 8n4, 8n8
Butler, Judith, 261n28

Carlebach, Julius, 29n79, 153, 156, 159n32
Celan, Paul, 137, 142n53
Chafe, William H., 105n6
Chaves, Mark, 290, 293–294, 294, 300, 301n5, 302n18–302n19, 302n21, 302n23–302n26, 303n42–303n44, 303n47
Clar, Reva, 105n13
Coblenz née Jacobsohn, Martha, 79, 85n38, 85n39
Cohen, Martin S., 303n45
Cohen, Mary M., 90, 99, 105n8
Cohen, Steve, 299, 303n46
Collin, Margaret, 149
Connelly, John, 159n43
Cooter, Roger, 261n28
Cott, Nancy, 105n6
Courty, Isabelle, 176n46
Crüsemann, Marlene, 256, 262n43
Cunow, Dietlinde, 159n38

Daly, Mary, 255, 262n39
Dame, Enid, 209, 218n19
Damelin, Robi, xvi
Dash, Joan, 123n2
Dayan, Aryeh, 157n5, 158n26
De Beauvoir, Simone, 12, 25n10
De Sola Pool, David, 49n7
De Sola Pool, Tamar, 49n7
De Sola, Katherine, 120
Deeg, Alexander, 28n44, 28n54
Dekel, Ayelet, 176n48, 176n50–176n51
Demel, Sabine, 238, 242n49
Derovan, David, 60, 67n40
Deutsch, Hayuta, 60
DeWolf, Rebecca, 105n5
Dienemann, Max, xii, 1, 145, 164

Diner, Dan, 158n23
Diner, Hasia, 48n2
Domay, Erhard, 261n31
Dormitzer, Else, 77
Durkheim, Émile, 74, 84n16
Dworkin, Susan, 124n5

Eger, Denise L., xi–xix, 1–8, 315–316
Ehrensperger, Kathy, 1–8, 316
Ehrlich, Martha, 82, 85n52
Eilberg, Amy, 101, 104, 196, 297
Einhorn, David, 38, 49n13, 49n14–49n17
Einstein Schorr, Rebecca, 176n35
Eisen, Arnold, 299, 303n46
Eisen, Ute E., 261n19
El-Saadawi, Nawal, 269
Elbogen Ronen, Susi (Shoshana), 62, 63, 64, 67n51
Elbogen, Ismar, 60, 62
Eleff, Zev, 48n2
Eliav, Mordechai, 27n30
Elliot, Andrea, 286n14
Engelhard, Daniela, 242n46
Erhart, Hannelore, 84n17
Ernst, Wolfgang, 177n67
Eskenazi, Tamara, 214, 219n31
Exum, J. Cheryl, 214, 219n32

Fagin, Allen I., 301n1, 302n6–302n8, 302n12–302n13
Falk, Gerhard, 105n7
Falkenberg, Bertha, 73
Fatal-Kna'ani, Tikva, 61, 67n41
Feifelson, Mimi, 102, 107n40
Feld, Merle, 206, 218n10
Feldman, Daniel, 301n1, 302n9–302n11, 302n27
Fermaglich, Kirsten Lise, 106n29
Ferziger, Adam, 302n16
Feustel, Adriane, 73, 84n11
Finch, Janet, 200n3
Fineman, Irvin, 123n2, 124n7, 124n9
Finkelstein, Louis, 99
Firor Scott, Anne, 49n24
Fonrobert, Charlotte Elisheva, 25n8
Frankel, Ellen, 214, 219n31
Frankl, Viktor, xviii, 149
Freidenreich Pass, Harriet, 56, 65n12
Freimark, Joseph, 85n38

Frevert, Ute, 26n12, 26n15, 26n22
Frie, Roger, 175n10
Friedan, Betty, 97
Friedman, Debbie, 210
Friedman, Howard Tzvi, 301n1, 302n6–302n8, 302n12–302n13
Frishman, Judith, 5, 289–305, 323
Füllenbach, Elias H., 159n43

Geiger, Abraham, 1, 8n1, 37, 49n11, 54, 72, 83n4
Geller, Laura, xixn11
Gerber, Christine, 261n19
Gerson, Jen, 286n19
Gillerman, Sharon, 20, 26n17, 27n38, 28n67, 29n86, 30n88, 76, 84n25
Gilligan, Carol, xiv, xviiin4–xviiin6
Gilman, Sander, 28n49
Glenn, Susan, 50n37
Goitein, Rahel, 56
Goldberg, Lea, 59–60, 66n31, 66n35
Goldman, Karla, 3, 33–52, 105n12, 319
Goldstein, Elyse, 214
Gössmann, Elisabeth, 234, 241n33
Gottlieb, Lynn, 210–211, 219n23
Gotzmann, Andreas, 29n73
Grab, Walter, 29n70
Greenberg, Betty, 193, 200n9
Greenberg, Blu, 102, 107n37, 196
Greenberg, Simon, 106n35
Greenebaum Solomon, Hannah, 75, 91, 105n14
Groó, Diana, 170, 171–172, 176n48, 176n52, 177n54–177n57
Grossmann, Atina, 158n12
Grosz, Elisabeth, 261n27
Gurock, Jeffrey S., 107n38–107n39
Guttmann, Alexander, 147, 151, 157n8–157n9, 159n29

Haarman, Julia, 28n58
Habermas, Jürgen, 166
Hahn, Barbara, 128, 139n4, 142n58
Haleva, Naftali, 218n2
Hamburger, Bianka, 79
Hammer, Jill, 214, 218n15, 219n32
Hanisch, Carol, 286n13
Happ, Sabine, 241n30
Harel, Ma'ayan, 66n34

Harris, Ben, 107n44
Härtler, Ilse, 159n39
Haskel, Perle, 58
Hassan, Riffat, 273
Hayuta Deutsch, Nehama, 67n39
Heller, Birgit, 25n6
Herselle Krinsky, Carol, 49n10
Hertz, Deborah, 25n1
Heschel, Susannah, 25n3, 154, 257, 263n46
Hill, Patricia R., 49n24
Hintze née Guggenheimer, Hedwig, 56
Hirsch, Emil G., 120, 125n34–125n35
Hirsch, Rahel, 56
Hochschild, Arlie, 200n3
Homolka, Walter, 1–8, 57, 65n14, 315, 316
Horch, Hans Otto, 28n46
Hübinger, Gangolf, 28n43
Huerkamp, Claudia, 65n13
Hume, Jack, 106n28
Hurwitz, Sara, 103, 104, 107n43, 196, 290, 301n3
Hyamson, Sara, 190
Hyman, Paula, 29n82, 39, 49n19

Ivry, Benjamin, 84n10

Jacobson, Jacob, 158n16
Jansen, Katrin Nele, 157n2
Janssen, Claudia, 263n51–263n53
Jatta, Barbara, 229
Jensen, Anne, 235, 241n34
Jensen, Uffa, 27n31
Jick, Leon, 48n2
Johnson, Elizabeth, 235
Jonas, Regina, xi, xiii, xvi, xvii, xvii–xviii, 1, 57–58, 59, 75, 81, 94–95, 98, 102, 125n33, 145–156, 163–174, 175n21, 175n24, 218n6, 259
Jost, Renate, 5, 245–266, 322
Josuttius, Manfred, 261n17
Jüttemann, Veronika, 241n30

Kagedan, Lila, 196, 290
Kahl, Brigitte, 256–257, 263n45
Kallman, Inge, 75, 84n22
Kalsky, Manuela, 8n7
Kaplan Eisenstein, Judith, 216

Kaplan, Marion, 22, 25n3–25n5, 26n11, 26n20, 27n34, 29n72, 29n75, 29n83–29n84, 39, 49n19, 50n31, 65n7, 65n13, 86n55, 152, 153, 158n12, 159n33
Kaplan, Mordecai M., 99
Kasper, Walter, 231, 240n22
Katz, Birgit, xviiin9
Katz, Jacob, 28n60
Katz, Joanna, 146
Kaufmann, Irene, 66n18
Kayserling, Meyer, 18, 28n48, 73
Kircher, Erwin, 130, 141n19
Klapheck, Elisa, 4, 66n16, 85n52, 106n23, 125n33, 127–144, 156, 157n1, 159n46, 164, 168, 170, 175n6, 175n7, 175n26–176n27, 176n29–176n30, 176n40–176n42, 176n44, 218n6, 320
Klapper, Melissa R., 50n37
Klein, Isaac, 303n45
Kley, Eduard Israel, 15, 27n28, 27n29
Knapp, Gudrun-Alexi, 261n20
Köhler, Hanne,13n31 13n51-13n53
Kohut, Alexander, 190
Kohut, Rebekah, 190, 200n6
Kolm, Melanie, 241n40
König, Hildegard, 240n18
Kraemer, Ross, 157n10
Kramer, William M., 105n13
Kratz-Ritter, Bettina, 85n32–85n33
Külper, Laura, 177n59–177n61
Kupferberg, Yael, 3, 11–32, 319
Kyte, Richard, xviiin5

Ladwig-Winters, Simone, 85n31
Lagiewski, Maciej, 85n42
Lakoff, Robin, 262n33
Lapidus Lerner, Anne, 124n5
Lapkin, Alexandra, 304n50
Lässig, Simone, 15–16, 17, 20, 22, 27n24–27n25, 27n33, 27n35, 27n37, 28n42–28n45, 28n51–28n53, 28n55–28n57, 28n62–28n64, 28n66, 29n76–29n78, 29n80–29n81, 29n85, 29n87
Lazarus, Paul, 55
Lee Levin, Alexandra, 123n2, 124n29
Lefkovitz, Lori Hope, 211, 219n25
Lehman, Israel O., 65n2

Lehman, Israel Otto, 148, 153
Leibowitz, Nechama, 60, 67n38
Leibowitz, Yeshayahu, 60
Leistner, Herta, 263n54
Lenzen, Verena, 26n11
Lerner, Gerda, 174n1
Levi Elwell, Sue, 218n13
Levinthal (Lyons), Helen, 75, 84n23, 93–94, 94
Lewkowitz, Julius, 84n19
Liberles, Robert, 48n3, 49n12
Liebrecht, Ruth, 62, 63, 64
Lindheim, Irma Levy, 92–93, 93, 94–106n18
Lipman, Jennifer, 177n58
Litman, Simon, 105n13
Littmann, Ellen, 59, 66n26
Loretan, Adrian, 242n48
Lowenthal, Marvin, 123n2
Ludwig, Hartmut, 159n42

Magnus, Shulamit, 145–146, 157n4
Magonet, Jonathan, 59, 66n28
Maimon, Debbie, 201n17
Mantei, Simone, 245–246, 259n1–260n3, 260n12, 260n16, 261n23
Marcus, Jacob R., 166, 175n15
May née Lövinson, Henriette, 78
Maybaum, Ignaz, 85n53
McDannell, Colleen, 49n24
Meitner, Lise, 56
Mendelson Graf, Alysa, 176n35
Mernissi, Fatima, 269, 277
Methuen, Charlotte, 262n34
Meyer, Michael A., 25n1, 28n68, 29n70, 66n23, 71, 73, 82, 83n3, 83n7, 84n13, 84n23, 84n30, 85n48, 85n50, 106n17, 148, 158n13, 176n28
Milgrom, Jo, 219n33
Miller, Elhanan, 107n45
Moltmann-Wendel, Elisabeth, 261n27
Montagu, Lilia (Lily) Helen, 71, 75, 83n1, 84n18
Montagu, Rachel, 175n12
Moore, Deborah Dash, xii, xviiin2
Moose, Ebrahim, 268, 284, 285n5
Morgenthaler, Christoph, 252, 261n24
Morris, Leslie, 158n23
Moses, Adolph, 91, 105n9

Index

Mueller, Iris, 227, 229
Muschiol, Gisela, 239n5
Muuss, Rolf E., xviiin4

Nadell, Pamela S., 4, 89–109, 119, 124n5–124n6, 125n31–125n32, 125n36, 201n12, 303n33–303n38, 320
Nashim, Ezrat, 195
Navè-Levinson, Pnina, 257
Ner-David, Haviva, 103, 107n41–107n42
Neuberger, Yaakov, 301n1, 302n9–302n11, 302n27
Neumark (Montor), Martha, 75, 92, 94, 98
Nicholls, Jacqueline, 219n24
Niemelä, Katie, 260n13
Nigg, Walter, 140n15
Nordmann, Ingeborg, 128, 138, 139n4, 142n57
Nussbaum Cohen, Debra, 107n44

Oard, Brian A., 219n30
Ollendorf, Paula, 80–81, 81
Orleck, Annelise, 50n37
Ostriker, Alice, 205, 209, 214, 218n7, 218n18

Papanek, Hanna, 188, 200n3
Pappenheim, Bertha, 73, 73–74, 84n14–84n15
Pascoe, Peggy, 49n24
Pasture, Patrick, 239n5
Paulsen, Anna, 255
Petuchowski, Jakob J., 48n2
Philippson, David, 83n4
Pickus, Keith H., 65n4
Plaskow, Judith, 206, 209, 218n8–218n9, 218n16, 257, 263n46
Pohl-Patalong, Uta, 8n6, 260n11
Pope Benedict XVI, 240n27
Pope Francis, 232
Pope John Paul II, 228–239n14
Prell, Riv-Ellen, 8n9
Priesand, Sally, 89, 97, 97–99, 99, 100, 104, 105n2, 106n30–106n31, 147, 154, 155, 157n7, 163, 166, 169, 170, 174, 175n16, 177n64, 177n65, 297

Qualbrink, Andrea, 237, 241n38, 242n46–242n47

Rabbi Eliezer, 12
Radford Ruther, Rosemary, 255, 262n39
Rahman, Fazlur, 268, 285n4
Raming, Ida, 227, 229, 239n8, 239n11
Ranke-Heinemann, Uta, 234
Ratzinger, Joseph, 240n25
Reimer, Gail Twersky, 4, 113–126, 169, 176n32–176n34, 176n36, 320
Reuther, Rosemary, 261n26
Richarz, Monika, 12, 16, 20, 25n9, 27n25, 27n39, 27n40, 28n58–28n60, 28n65, 65n10
Richter, Elise, 56
Riess, Hedwig, 78
Roettger, Sarah, 240n16
Rosen, Norma, 214, 219n32
Rosenzweig, Franz, 55, 127, 128, 129–130, 140n17
Roth, Joel, 107n36
Rothschild, Sylvia, 175n20
Rudin, James, 157n5
Ruskay, Esther, 120
Russell, Cannon Susan, xv–xvi, xviiin7
Russell, Letty, 255, 262n39
Rüttiger, Gabriele, 242n45

Sailer, Gudrun, 240n17
Salomon, Alice, 56
Salomon, Gotthold, 18, 22, 24, 28n47
Sarah, Elizabeth Tikvah, 84n22, 167, 175n23, 175n24
Sarna, Jonathan D., 48n4, 49n9, 85n51, 124n29
Sasso Eisenberg, Sandy, 5, 100, 104, 106n33, 203–221, 297, 321
Sayeed, Asma, 286n23
Scanlan, Angela J., 303n33–303n36
Schaeffler, Richard, 53
Schaffler, Richard, 65n1
Schechter, Solomon, 121–122, 294
Schneider, Bernhard, 239n5
Schoeps, Julius H., 152, 159n31
Scholem, Gershom, 127, 138, 139n2
Schottroff, Luise, 239n6, 241n31, 256, 262n44, 263n46
Schroer, Silvia, 239n6, 241n31
Schüssler Fiorenza, Elisabeth, 256, 259, 261n22, 262n42, 263n57

Schwartz, Shuly Rubin, 5, 106n25, 183–202, 321
Schwarz, Minna, 78, 79
Seelig, Rachel, 67n36
Seidel, Esther, 3, 53–69, 83, 86n54, 319
Shanahan, Eileen, 105n3
Shargel, Baila, 125n40
Shaw Frank, Laura, 292, 302n15, 302n17
Sheridan, Sybil, 165, 167, 175n12–175n14, 175n21, 175n24–175n25
Siegele-Wenschkewitz, Leonore, 263n46
Silverman Weinreich, Beatrice, 218n1
Silverman, Althea, 193, 200n9
Silverstein, Alan, 48n2, 201n12
Simmel, Georg, 130, 140n14
Simon, Heinrich, 130
Simon, Hermann, 159n44, 165, 170, 174n3, 176n43
Simon, Rita J., 303n33–303n38
Simons, Jake Wallis, 171
Sinclair, Stefanie, 4, 163–179, 321
Skenazy, Leonore, 304n50
Skrzycki, Cindy, 159n41
Sneeringer, Julia, 85n46
Solomon, Barbara Miller, 105n6
Soloveitchik, Joseph B., 303n29
Sorkin, David, 25n2
Standhartinger, Angela, 261n19
Stein Landau, Hannah, 62
Steinhauer, Eric W., 241n35
Stöltzner née Ziegelroth, Helene, 56
Stone, Amy, 176n49, 177n53
Strassfeld, Michael, 201n18
Strassfeld, Sharon, 201n18
Strauss, Herbert A., 65n5–65n6, 66n18, 148, 158n14
Strikovsky,, 103
Sunder, Madhavi, 273, 286n21
Susman, Margarete, 127–139
Szold, Benjamin, 114, 117, 122
Szold, Henrietta, 113–123, 124n8, 124n10–124n24, 124n26–124n27, 125n37–125n38, 125n41–125n44, 192

Tabick, Jackie, 166
Taitz, Emily, 157n3
Taylor, Jerome, 286n19
Traverso, Enzo, 158n23

Treiger, Alina, 6
Tucker, Eva, 171, 176n47
Twerski, Chaim, 296, 298–299, 303n32, 303n40

Untermann, Matthias, 65n8

Vance, Laura, 8n3
Vinken, Barbara, 260n8
Vogelstein, Hermann, 76–77, 81, 84n26, 85n45
Volk, Hermann, 236
Volkov, Shulamit, 22, 26n13, 27n32, 28n50, 29n69, 29n74
von Bendemann, Erwin, 142n56
von Kellenbach, Katharina, 4, 8n7, 66n16, 106n22, 106n23, 145–161, 157n6–158n17, 158n25, 159n36, 159n40, 159n42, 164, 166, 170, 175n5, 175n18, 175n19, 176n38, 320

Wacker, Marie-Theres, 5, 225–244, 263n46, 321
Wadud, Amina, 268, 269–277, 282, 284, 285n6–285n10, 286n12, 286n24–286n29
Wagner-Rau, Ulrike, 260n16
Wallach-Faller, Marianne, 26n16, 26n18
Wallach, Kerry, 84n29
Walton, Rivka, 210, 219n22
Weilerstein, Rubin, 193, 200n8
Weiss, Andrea L., 214, 219n31
Weiss, Avi, 103, 196, 290, 294, 301n3, 303n30
Weiss, Yfaat, 66n30
Weisz, George, 172–173, 177n59
Weltsch, Robert, 141n21
Westphal, Helene (Leni), 61
White, Thomas, xviiin6
Wiener, Julie, 201n13
Wiener, Max, 48n3, 54, 65n3
Wilhelm, Cornelia, 50n35
Willig, Irene, 236
Wilson, Nancy, xiii–xiv, xvi, xviiin3
Winter, Miriam Therese, 240n18
Wolff, Eberhard, 25n1
Wolff, Kerstin, 65n9
Woolf, Virginia, 147, 158n11
Wunderlich, Frieda, 56

Wyatt Caraway, Hattie, 183, 194

Yerushalmi, Yosef Hayim, 165, 167, 174, 175n8, 175n22, 177n63

Zagano, Phyllis, 240n19, 240n27
Zeiß-Horbach, Auguste, 261n25, 262n38
Zipes, Jack, 158n23
Zornberg, Aviva, 206–207, 214, 218n11, 219n31

About the Editors

Hartmut Bomhoff is senior research fellow at the Abraham Geiger College, University of Potsdam (Germany); he has been teaching at the School of Jewish Theology, University of Potsdam since 2013. His MA thesis *Ernst Ludwig Ehrlich—Prägende Jahre. Eine Biographie* [*Ernst Ludwig Ehrlich—The Formative Years: A Biography*] was published in 2014. Among his other publications are *Abraham Geiger. Durch Wissen zum Glauben/ Through Reason to Faith: Reform and the Science of Judaism*, 2006, *Israel Jacobson—Wegbereiter Jüdischer Emanzipation*, 2010, and—together with Walter Homolka and Andreas Nachama—*Basiswissen Judentum*, 2015, a comprehensive introduction to Judaism. Since 2012, he has served as chief editor of the *Jewish Voice from Germany*.

Rabbi Denise L. Eger is an international Jewish leader and social justice activist. She is the founding rabbi of Congregation Kol Ami, in West Hollywood, CA for the last twenty-seven years. She is past president of the Central Conference of American Rabbis, the international organization of over 2,300 Reform Rabbis. She served as the first openly gay or lesbian person in that position. She also was the first woman ever elected as president of the Southern California Board of Rabbis which includes Reform, Conservative, Reconstructionist, and Orthodox Rabbis.

Eger was named as one of the 50 most influential Jews by the *Jewish Daily Forward* in 2008 and one of the 50 most influential women rabbis in 2010. In October 2011, Rabbi Eger was one of the Gay Icons of Equality Forum's LGBT History Month. Huffington Post named her as the #1 LGBT

Clergy Person in America. She has won numerous awards for her leadership from the Human Rights Campaign, the City of Los Angeles, the California State Senate and Assembly. She recently has been named as one of 25 Jewish women trailblazers of the City of Los Angeles.

She is a noted author and speaker and has contributed to the *Women's Torah Commentary*, *Seven Days Many Voices: Insights into the Biblical Creation Story*, *The Sacred Calling: Four Decades of Women in the Rabbinate*, *Lights in the Forest*, *The Sacred Encounter*, and numerous articles in newspapers and magazines and appeared on radio and television.

Eger officiated at the first legal wedding for a lesbian couple in California. She has been a leading voice for LGBTQ equality and human rights.

Raised in Memphis, TN, Rabbi Eger graduated with honors from the University of Southern California with a Bachelor's Degree in Religion in 1982. She received her Master's Degree from Hebrew Union College—Jewish Institute of Religion in 1985 and was ordained as rabbi in 1988 at the New York campus of HUC. She received her Doctor of Divinity in 2013 from HUC-JIR. Eger is a Sr. Rabbinic Fellow of the Shalom Hartman Institute in Jerusalem.

Rabbi Eger is married to Rabbi Eleanor Steinman. She has an adult son, Benjamin.

You can follow her on Twitter @deniseeger or her blog "Walking Humbly. Seeking Justice. Living with Hope."

Kathy Ehrensperger is research professor of New Testament in Jewish Perspective at the Abraham Geiger Kolleg, University of Potsdam, Germany; she previously was a reader in New Testament Studies at the School of Theology, Religious Studies and Islamic Studies, University of Wales, Trinity Saint David, UK, and served as a pastor of the Swiss Reformed Church in Basel, Switzerland. Among her publications are *That We May Be Mutually Encouraged: Feminism and the New Perspective on Paul,* 2004; *Paul and the Dynamics of Power: Communication and Interaction in the Early Christ Movement,* 2008; *Paul at the Crossroads of Cultures: Theologizing in the Space-Between,* 2013. She is the executive editor of the *Encyclopedia of Jewish-Christian Relations.*

Rabbi Walter Homolka (PhD, King's College London, PhD, Trinity St. David Wales, DHL, Hebrew Union College—Jewish Institute of Religion New York) is full professor of Jewish Theology at the University of Potsdam

(Germany) and a coeditor of the *Encyclopedia of Jewish-Christian Relations*. Among his most recent publications are: *Jewish Jesus Research and its Challenge to Christology Today*, 2017; *Jesus Reclaimed. Jewish Perspectives on the Nazarene*, 2015;—with Shimon Shetreet, *Jewish and Israeli Law—An Introduction,* 2017;—with Hans Küng, *How to Do Good & Avoid Evil: A Global Ethic from the Sources of Judaism*, 2009.

About the Contributors

Yael Kupferberg is a literary scholar and guest professor at the Center for Research on Antisemitism (since October 2018). She held a postdoctoral position at the School of Jewish Theology at the University of Potsdam (2014–18). Dr. Kupferberg holds a Ph.D. from the Free University of Berlin. Her PhD dissertation focused on "Henrich Heine's Dimensions of the Joke and the Secularization of Poetic Language," and was funded partly by the German Academic Scholarship Foundation.

Karla Goldman is the Sol Drachler Professor of Social Work and professor of Judaic Studies at the University of Michigan, where she directs the Jewish Communal Leadership Program. Her research focuses on the history of the American Jewish experience with special attention to American Jewish communities and the evolving roles and contributions of American Jewish women. She previously served as historian in residence at the Jewish Women's Archive (JWA) in Brookline, Massachusetts and served as co-chair of the JWA Board of Directors from 2015–2019. She is the author of *Beyond the Synagogue Gallery: Finding a Place for Women in American Judaism*.

Esther I. Seidel lectured at Düsseldorf University, Germany, before training liberal rabbis in philosophy at the Leo Baeck College in London for about twenty years. She has been teaching courses on Wissenschaft des Judentums and Maimonides, both at the Abraham Geiger Kolleg, Potsdam, and the Shandong University (Jinan, China), where she was twice invited to lecture as a visiting professor. Her main areas of research are on Maimonides, Spinoza, Jews from Portugal and, in particular, Wissenschaft des Judentums, including the history of the two pre-war rabbinical colleges in Germany with regard to their roots in German philosophical thought.

Pamela S. Nadell holds the Patrick Clendenen Chair in Women's and Gender History at American University. Her books include *Women Who Would Be Rabbis: A History of Women's Ordination, 1889–1985* and *America's Jewish Women: A History from Colonial Times to Today*.

Gail Twersky Reimer served as the director of the Jewish Women's Archive for nearly twenty years, from 1995 to 2014. She was one of the founders of this organization, which uncovers, chronicles, and transmits the voices and stories of Jewish women. The coeditor of two anthologies of Jewish women's writings—*Reading Ruth: Women Reclaim a Sacred Story* and *Beginning Anew: A Woman's Companion to the High Holy Days*, Reimer has also produced two films, *Making Trouble*, a full-length documentary on Jewish women comedians, and *In the Footsteps of Regina Jonas*, a short documentary that follows America's pioneering rabbis on their pilgrimage to Berlin and Prague to honor their forgotten foremother, Regina Jonas.

Elisa Klapheck is a liberal rabbi based in Frankfurt and professor of Jewish studies in Paderborn. In 1999, she published "Fräulein Rabbiner Jonas—The Story of the First Woman Rabbi" (1999, English translation 2004). An important topic of Klapheck's rabbinic and academic work is the relationship between political ideas and Judaism. This culminated in her dissertation on the Jewish religious philosopher Margarete Susman in 2013.

Katharina von Kellenbach is professor of Religious Studies and former chair of the Department of Philosophy and Religious Studies at St. Mary's College of Maryland, the National Honors College of the State of Maryland. She is the Corcoran Visiting Chair in Christian-Jewish-Relations at Boston College 2019–2020 and convener of the ZIF Research Group "Felix Culpa: Guilt as Culturally Productive Force" at the Center for Interdisciplinary Research (ZIF) in Bielefeld in 2018–2019. Her areas of expertise include Holocaust Studies, Jewish-Christian relations, feminist theology, and interreligious dialogue. Her publications include: *Anti-Judaism in Feminist Religious Writings* (1994), *The Mark of Cain: Guilt and Denial in the Lives of Nazi*

Perpetrators (2013), and forthcoming *Composting Guilt: The Purification of Memory after Atrocity* (2020).

Stefanie Sinclair, PhD, is senior lecturer in Religious Studies and the director of the Centre for Scholarship and Innovation at the Faculty of Arts and Social Sciences at The Open University in the UK. She has a special research interest in the study of contemporary religion in historical perspective, with a particular focus on gender and national identities. Prior publications include her article on "Regina Jonas: Forgetting and Remembering the First Female Rabbi," published in the journal *Religion*.

Shuly Rubin Schwartz, PhD, is the provost of the Jewish Theological Seminary. She also serves as dean of the Gershon Kekst Graduate School and is the Irving Lehrman Research Associate Professor of American Jewish History. She is the author of the award-winning *The Rabbi's Wife: The Rebbetzin in American Jewish Life, The Emergence of Jewish Scholarship in America: The Publication of the Jewish Encyclopedia*, and numerous articles on American Jewish history and culture.

Sandy Eisenberg Sasso served as senior rabbi of Congregation Beth-El Zedeck, Indianapolis, Indiana from 1977–2013. She is currently the director of the Religion, Spirituality and the Arts Initiative at IUPUI Arts and Humanities Institute. She was the first women ordained from the Reconstructionist Rabbinical College in 1974 and received her Doctor of Ministry from CTS in 1996. Sasso is the author of two books for adults and many nationally acclaimed children's books, including *But God Remembered: Stories of Women from Creation to the Promised Land and Regina Persisted: An Untold Story*. She is a contributor to many publications on children's spirituality and is a coeditor of *Nurturing Children and Adolescent Spirituality: Perspectives from the World's Religions, 2006*. She was coeditor with Michael Shire of the *CCAR Journal on Spiritual Teaching and Transformation*, 2014. Active in the civic life of her community, she is the recipient of the highest civilian award in the State of Indiana (Sagamore of the Wabash) and in 2014, she was honored with the Heritage Keeper's Award from the Indiana State Museum.

Marie-Theres Wacker, 1998–2018 professor of Old Testament and Women's/Gender Research at Katholisch-Theologische Fakultät, University of Münster, Germany. Her research areas include: biblical monotheism, Jewish literature of the Hellenistic period, biblical hermeneutics, gender perspectives on holy scriptures in Judaism, Christianity, and Islam, and modern Jewish history and Anti-Semitism. Among her recent publications are: *Baruch and the Letter of Jeremiah*, 2016; *Early Jewish Writings*, 2017 (coedited with Eileen Schuller); "The Violence of Power and the Power of Violence: Hybrid, Contextual Perspectives on the Book of Esther," in: Carolyn J. Sharp and L. Juliana Claassens (eds.), *Feminist Frameworks and the Bible. Power, Ambiguity, and Intersectionality*, 2017, 99–115; *Ecclesia und Synagoga im Späten 19. und Frühen 20. Jahrhundert. Historische Sondierungen in Theologischem Interesse*. Franz-Delitzsch-Vorlesung 2017, 2018. Along with a team of collaborators she launched, in spring 2015, the website www.juedischer-friedhof-muenster.de.

Renate Jost, is professor of Feminist Theology and Gender Studies at the Augustana Hochschule at Neuendettelsau; she studied Protestant theology in Bethel, Göttingen, Marburg and at Union Theological Seminary, New York. From 1984–1988, she was in parish ministry in Frankfurt; research associate in Old Testament at the university in that city from 1989–1993; director of studies at the Frauenstudien-und-Bildungszentrum of the Evangelische Kirche Deutschlands; PhD in 1994 (dissertation on "The Queen of Heaven" in Jeremiah), habilitation in 2003. She is the translator of the book of Ruth in "Bibel in gerechter Sprache." Among her recent publications: *Das göttliche Mädchen. Jesus als das Weiblich-Göttliche in Vergangenheit und Gegenwart*, (2019); *Feministsiche Bibelauslegungen, Grundlagen. Forschungsgeschichtliches. Geschlechterstudien*, (2014); *Gender, Sexualität und Macht in Anthropologie des Richterbuches*, (2006); *Frauenmacht und Männerliebe, Egalitäre Utopien aus der Frühzeit Israels*, (2006); with Sarah Jäger eds., *Vielfalt und Differenz. Intersektionale Perspektiven auf Feminismus und Religion*, (2017).

Katajun Amirpur is professor of Iranian Studies at the University of Cologne. Her doctoral thesis and postdoctoral habilitation were on Iranian reformist thinkers. From 2011–2018, she served as a deputy director of the Academy of World Religions at Hamburg University. One of her most recognized publications is *New Thinking in Islam*, (2016). Her main research focus is Shi'i Islam.

Judith Frishman holds the chair for Jewish Studies at the Centre for the Study of Religion at Leiden University since her appointment in 2008. Her research deals with the history of the Jews in Western Europe in the nineteenth and early twentieth centuries with a focus on questions of citizenship, assimilation, historiography and religious reform. Prior to Leiden, she was full professor of Rabbinics at Tilburg University's School of Catholic Theology. She serves on the advisory boards of the Jewish Museum of Vienna and the research program "Dynamics of Jewish Ritual Practices in Pluralistic Contexts from Antiquity to the Present" at the Max Weber Kolleg, Universität Erfurt.